Priest Vol. 15
Created by Min-Woo Hyung

Translation - Ellen Choi
English Adaption - Jake Forbes
Retouch and Lettering - Lucas Rivera
Cover Design - Tomas Montalvo Lagos

Editor - Tim Beedle
Digital Imaging Manager - Chris Buford
Pre-Production Supervisor - Erika Terriquez
Art Director - Anne Marie Horne
Managing Editor - Vy Nguyen
Production Manager - Elisabeth Brizzi
VP of Production - Ron Klamert
Editor in Chief - Rob Tokar
Publisher - Mike Kiley
President and C.O.O. - John Parker
C.E.O. and Chief Creative Officer - Stuart Levy

A **TOKYOPOP** Maga

TOKYOPOP Inc.
5900 Wilshire Blvd. Suite 200
Los Angeles, CA 90036

E-mail: info@TOKYOPOP.com
Come visit us online at www.TOKYOOP.com

ISBN: 1-59182-516-4

First TOKYOPOP printing: November 2006
10 9 8 7 6 5 4 3 2
Printed in the USA

PRIEST

VOLUME 15

BY
MIN-WOO HYUNG

HAMBURG // LONDON // LOS ANGELES // TOKYO

THE CAST OF CHARACTERS

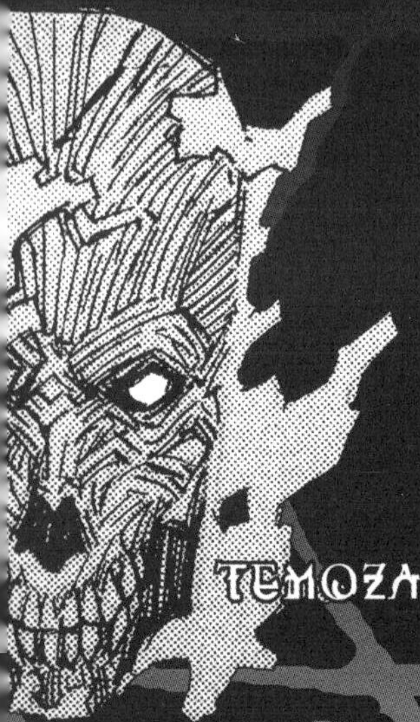

During the war against Lucifer, the archangel Temozarela led the agents of light. In the years that followed, Temozarela watched as God's attention shifted from his seraphim to his new creation—man. Jealousy caused Temozarela and his disciples to abandon their heavenly post and attempt to corrupt humanity to prove the superiority of the seraphim to God. During the Crusades he attempted to begin his plan, but Belial sealed him in the Domas Porada for 500 years. Now, released by Ivan Isaacs, Temozarela is free again, but too weak to carry out his dark designs. His disciples have begun sanctifying the ground in the American West, spreading plague and death in preparation for the Unholy Sabbath.

TEMOZARELA

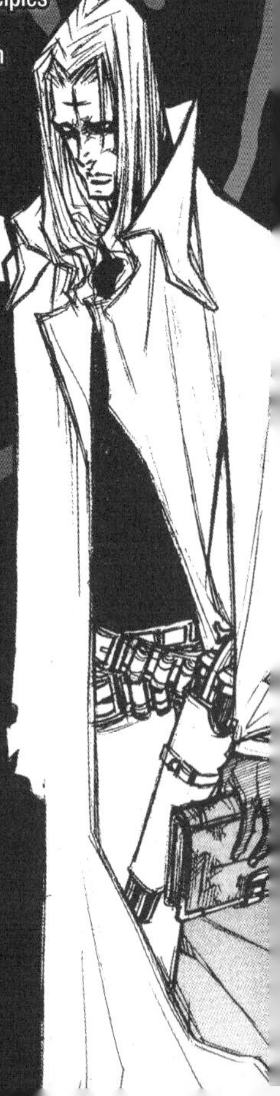

FATHER IVAN ISSACS

Ivan Isaacs was a young priest with a passion for ancient cultures when he was recruited to study the Domas Porada. Little did he know that this mission would be his last—at least his last in life. After helping revive an ancient battle for Heaven and Earth, Ivan and his beloved Gena were slain. In order to get revenge and atone for endangering the world, Ivan made a pact with the devil Belial: his soul in exchange for a second chance at life ... and superhuman strength. Now Ivan wanders the Old West, hunting down Temozarela's disciples and keeping a journal of his tragic tale.

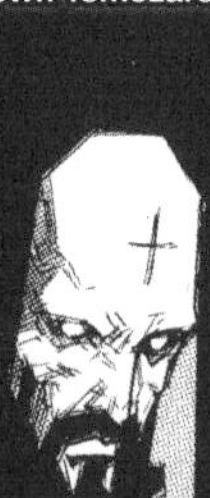

The devil Belial makes Ivan his agent in the mortal world so that he may battle the agents of the fallen archangel Temozarela, who is planning an upheaval of Heaven and Hell. Belial used to be Betheal, a Catholic priest in the Middle Ages where he was a prosecutor in trials of heresy. After Temozarela shattered his faith, Betheal turned himself into the demon Belial in order to get his revenge.

BELIAL

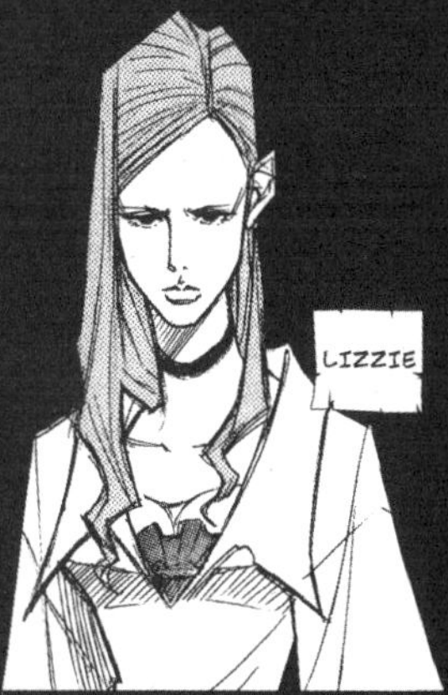
LIZZIE

Coburn is the only federal marshal investigating possible links between an outbreak of plague and other mysterious events happening around the Old West. Once he discovered the extent of the crisis, he sent to Washington for military mobilization orders. He's never much cared for religion, but ever since his friend and partner, Cairo the Indian tracker, was killed by agents of the Vatican, he's had a major beef with the righteous.

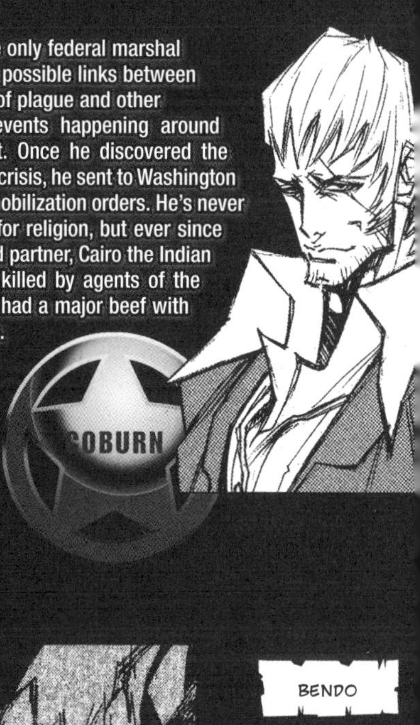
COBURN

A gang leader whose life was saved by Ivan Isaacs, but not before she became infected with Temozarela's zombie curse. She was taken into custody by Coburn, and for a while she helped the lawman in his search for Ivan. Lizzie escaped, and has since joined up with another band of outlaws. Her current whereabouts are unknown.

MR. EVAN DUDLEY

The de facto mayor of the remote town of Windtale, Mr. Dudley prides himself on keeping his town safe from what he sees as unsavory outside influences. He has the local officials in his pocket, the town in his debt...and Nera's troupe in his way.

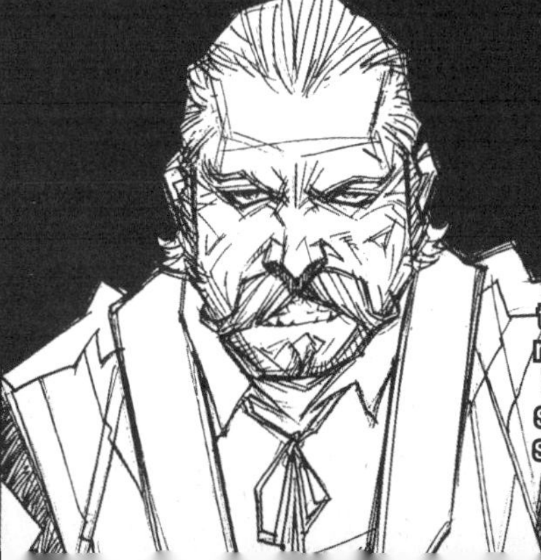

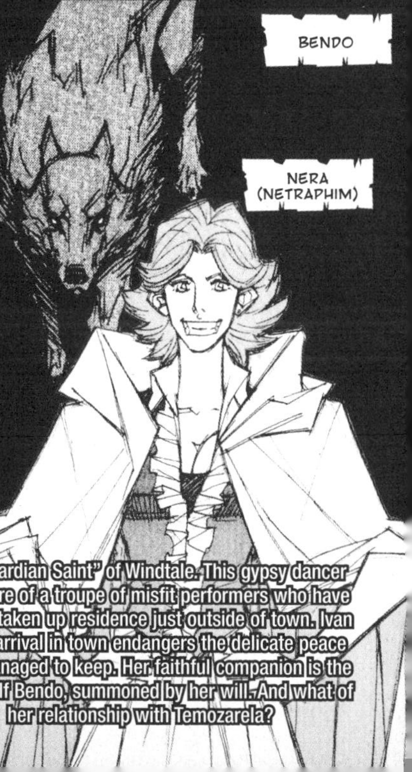
BENDO
NERA (NETRAPHIM)

The "Guardian Saint" of Windtale. This gypsy dancer takes care of a troupe of misfit performers who have recently taken up residence just outside of town. Ivan Isaac's arrival in town endangers the delicate peace she's managed to keep. Her faithful companion is the spirit-wolf Bendo, summoned by her will. And what of her relationship with Temozarela?

THE STORY SO FAR...

Call me simple if you will, but I live my life by two simple rules. The first, I learned from my mother, God rest her soul. Ma was a God-fearing woman and she taught me to do His will in all things. The second, I picked up from my father, a man of science. He introduced me to the world of unseen germs and infectious diseases—microscopic critters that can kill a man quick, and the only defense against them is keepin' yourself clean and pure.

Folks in Windtale have survived by remaining true to their traditions and their beliefs. Mr. Dudley understands this, and while his methods ain't always perfect, I believe he means well. And like my parents, Mr. Dudley also understands the importance of God and staying pure. Recently, folks have been talkin' in hushed tones, like there's a storm brewin' in the hills, the mere mention of which will bring it down on us, and at the center of this storm is none other than them folks on the outskirts of town—Miss Nera and the rest. Well, enough of the whisperin'. I say it's time to stand up for what we believe and what we know by God to be true, and we should do it together as a town.

Them folks hidin' out in the woods have no place in Windtale. I know they keep to themselves and are largely unseen, but that doesn't solve the problem. It's the fact that they hide themselves that CREATES the problem. God only knows what they get up to there in those woods, and as my Pa always told me, the unseen threats are the worst.

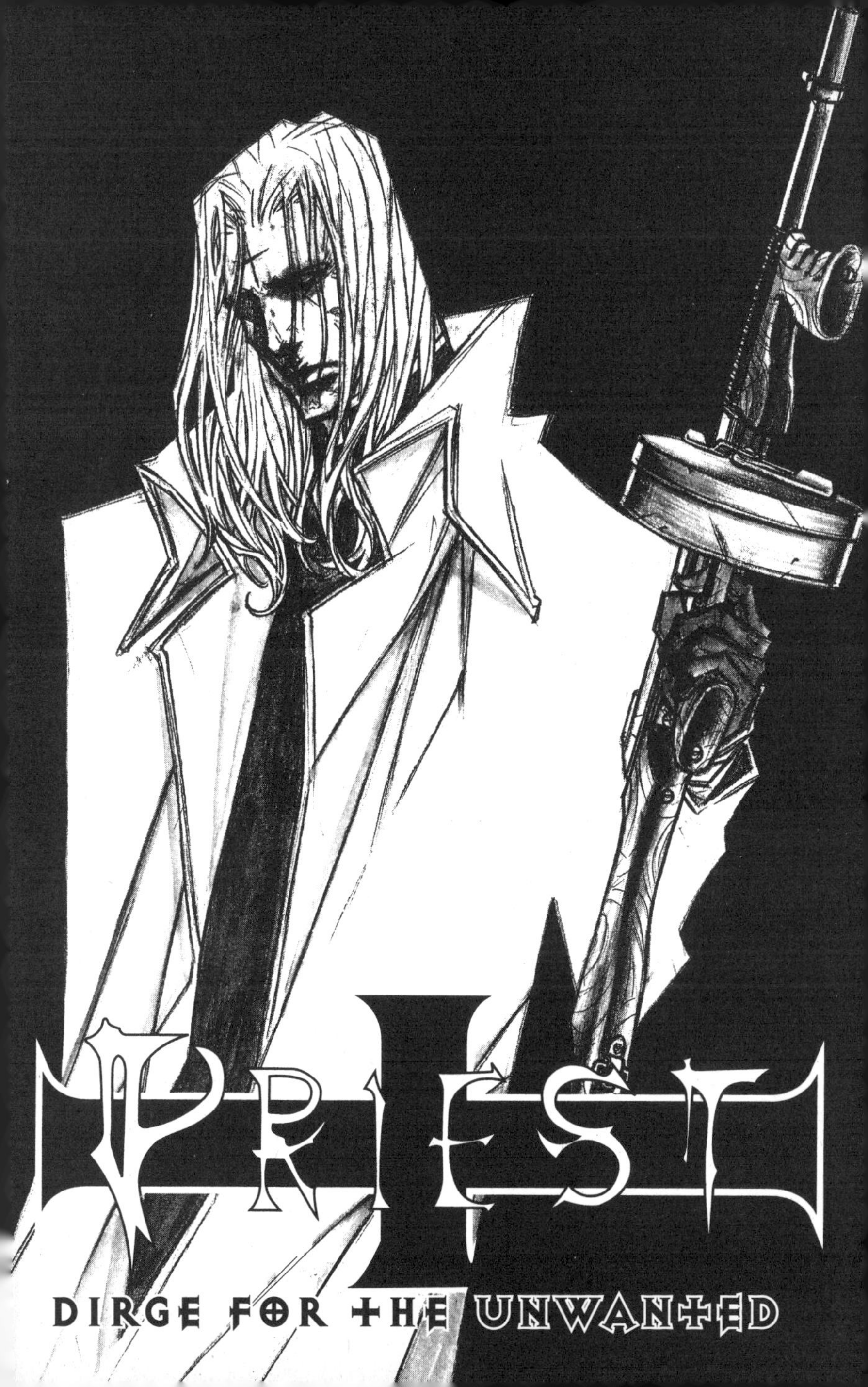
PRIEST
DIRGE FOR THE UNWANTED

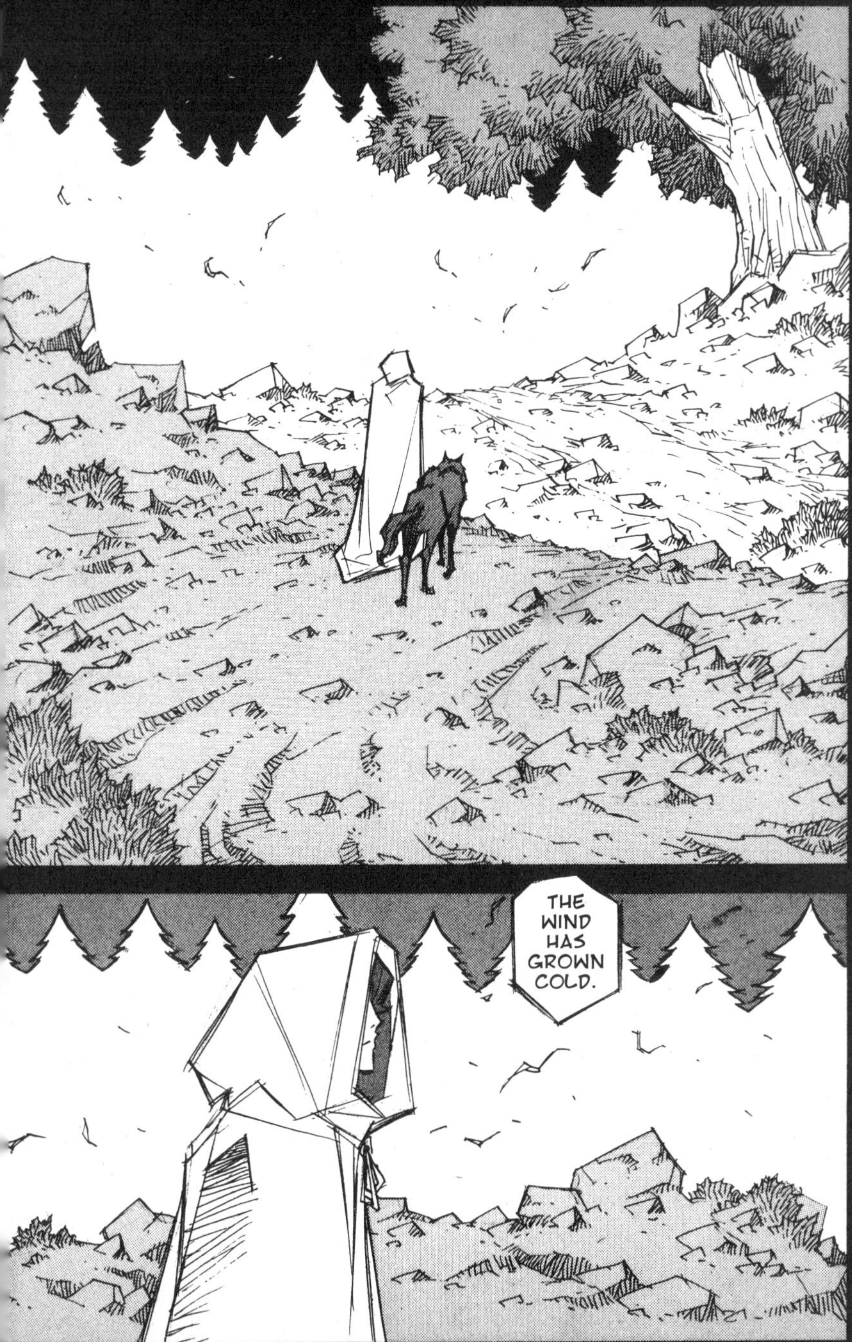
THE WIND HAS GROWN COLD.

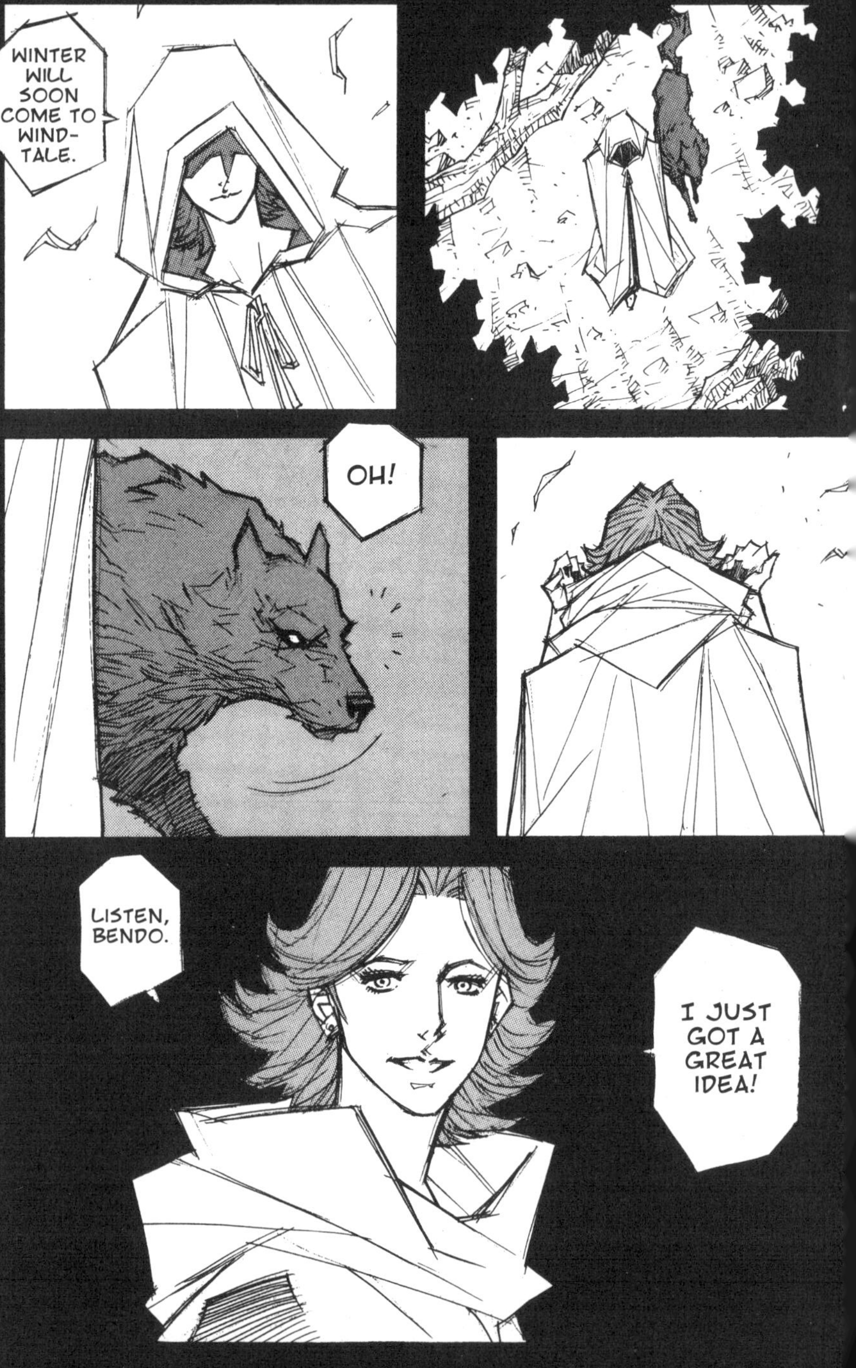
WINTER WILL SOON COME TO WIND-TALE.
OH!
LISTEN, BENDO.
I JUST GOT A GREAT IDEA!

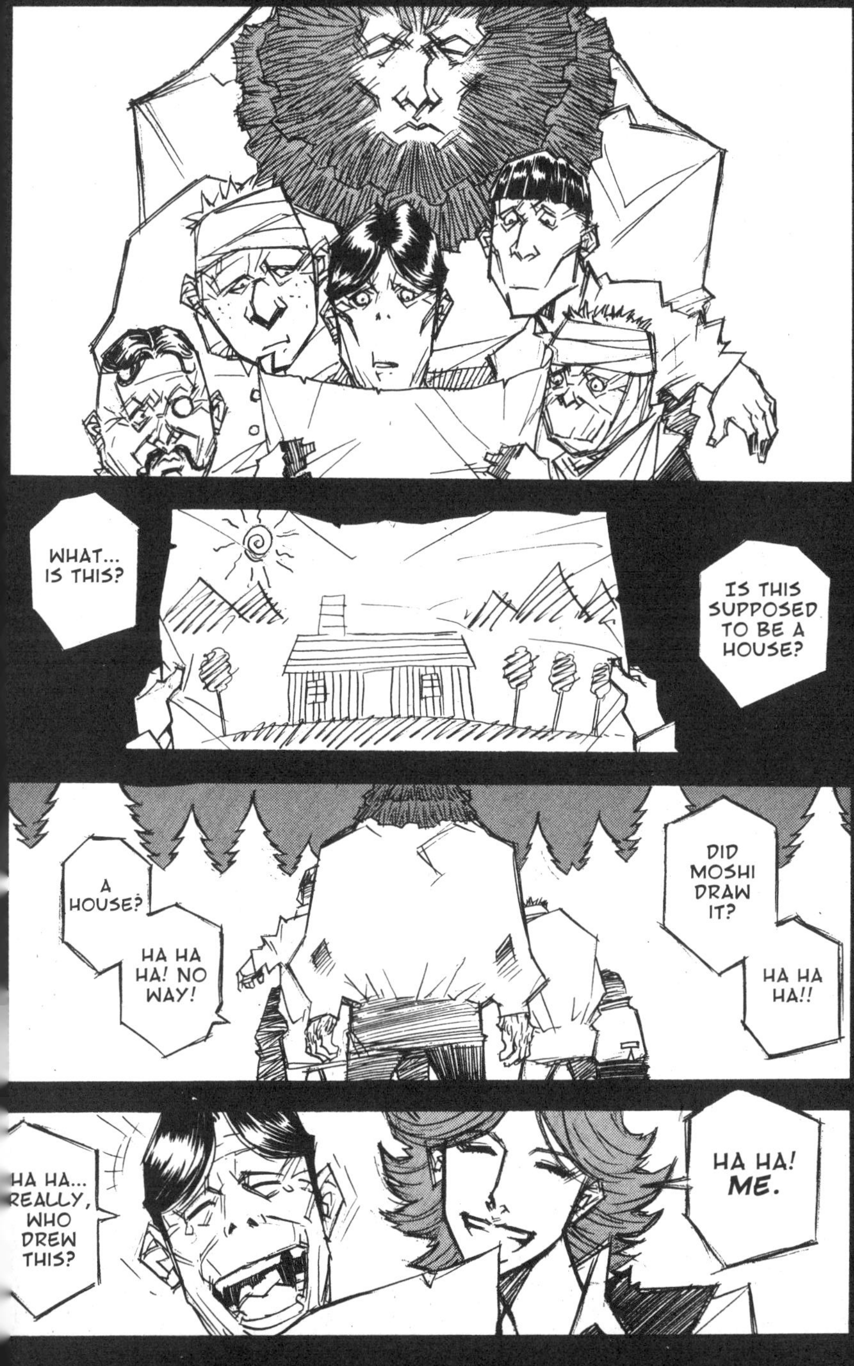
WHAT... IS THIS?
IS THIS SUPPOSED TO BE A HOUSE?
A HOUSE?
HA HA HA! NO WAY!
DID MOSHI DRAW IT?
HA HA HA!!
HA HA... REALLY, WHO DREW THIS?
HA HA! **ME.**

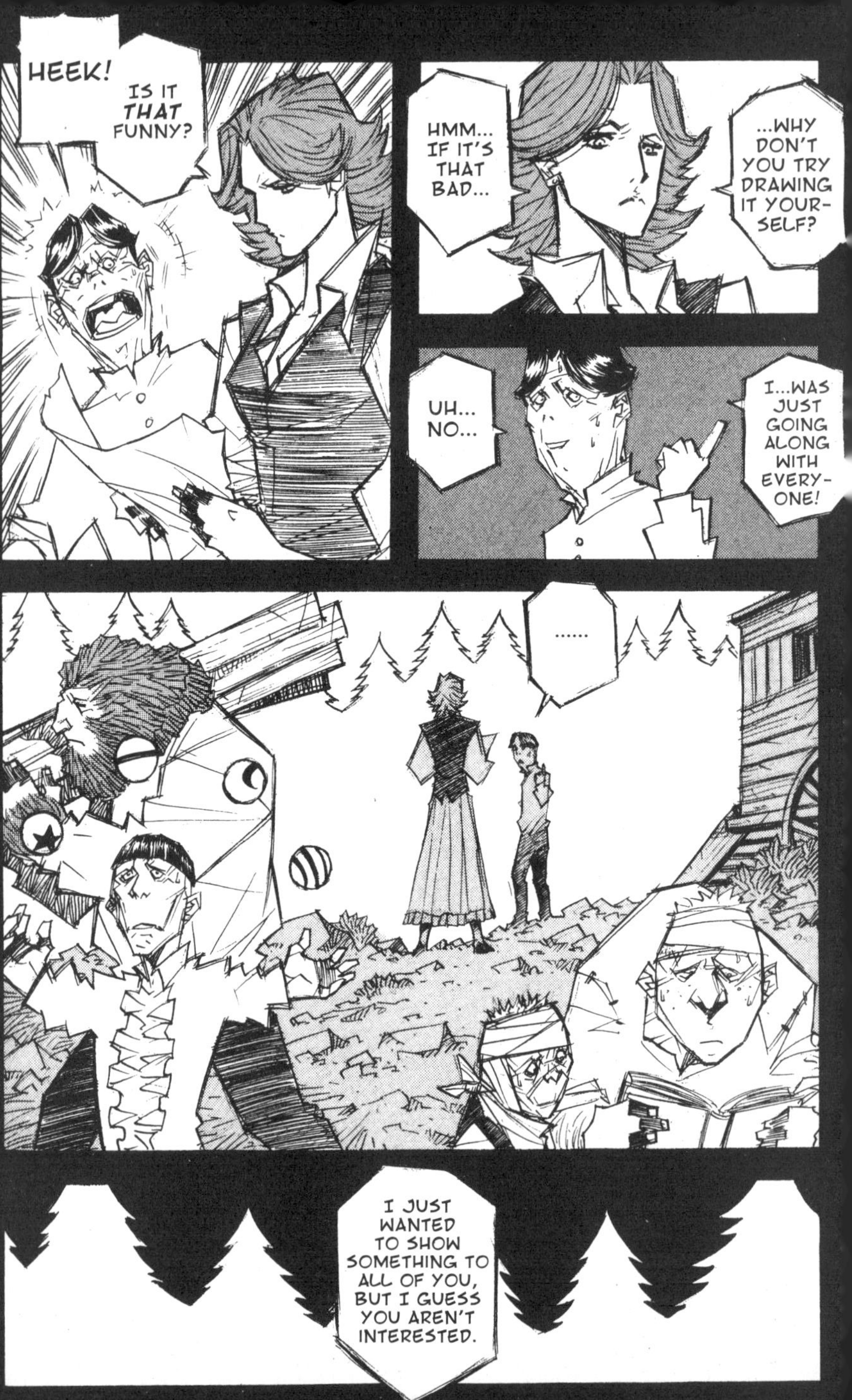
HEEK!
IS IT *THAT* FUNNY?
HMM... IF IT'S THAT BAD...
...WHY DON'T YOU TRY DRAWING IT YOURSELF?
UH... NO...
I...WAS JUST GOING ALONG WITH EVERYONE!
......
I JUST WANTED TO SHOW SOMETHING TO ALL OF YOU, BUT I GUESS YOU AREN'T INTERESTED.

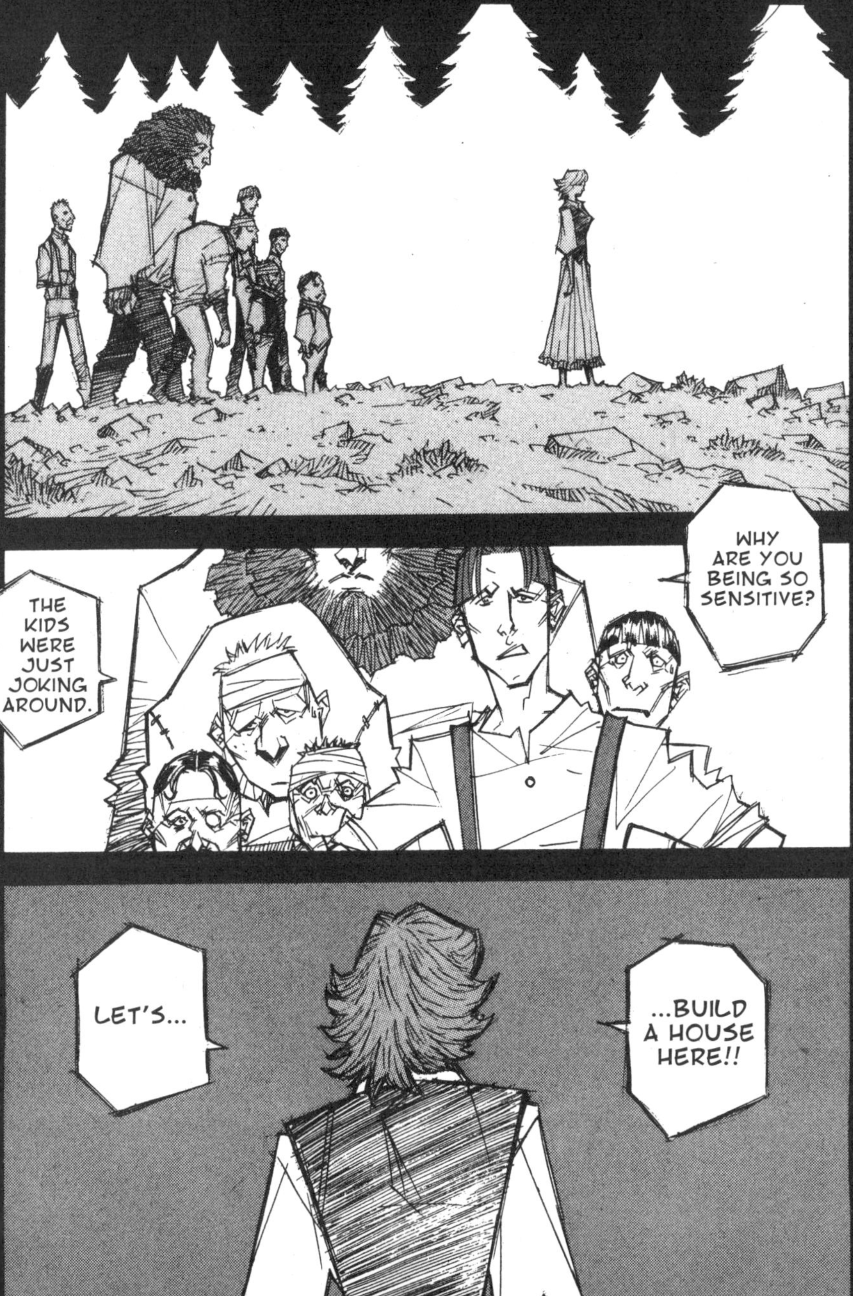
THE KIDS WERE JUST JOKING AROUND.
WHY ARE YOU BEING SO SENSITIVE?
LET'S...
...BUILD A HOUSE HERE!!

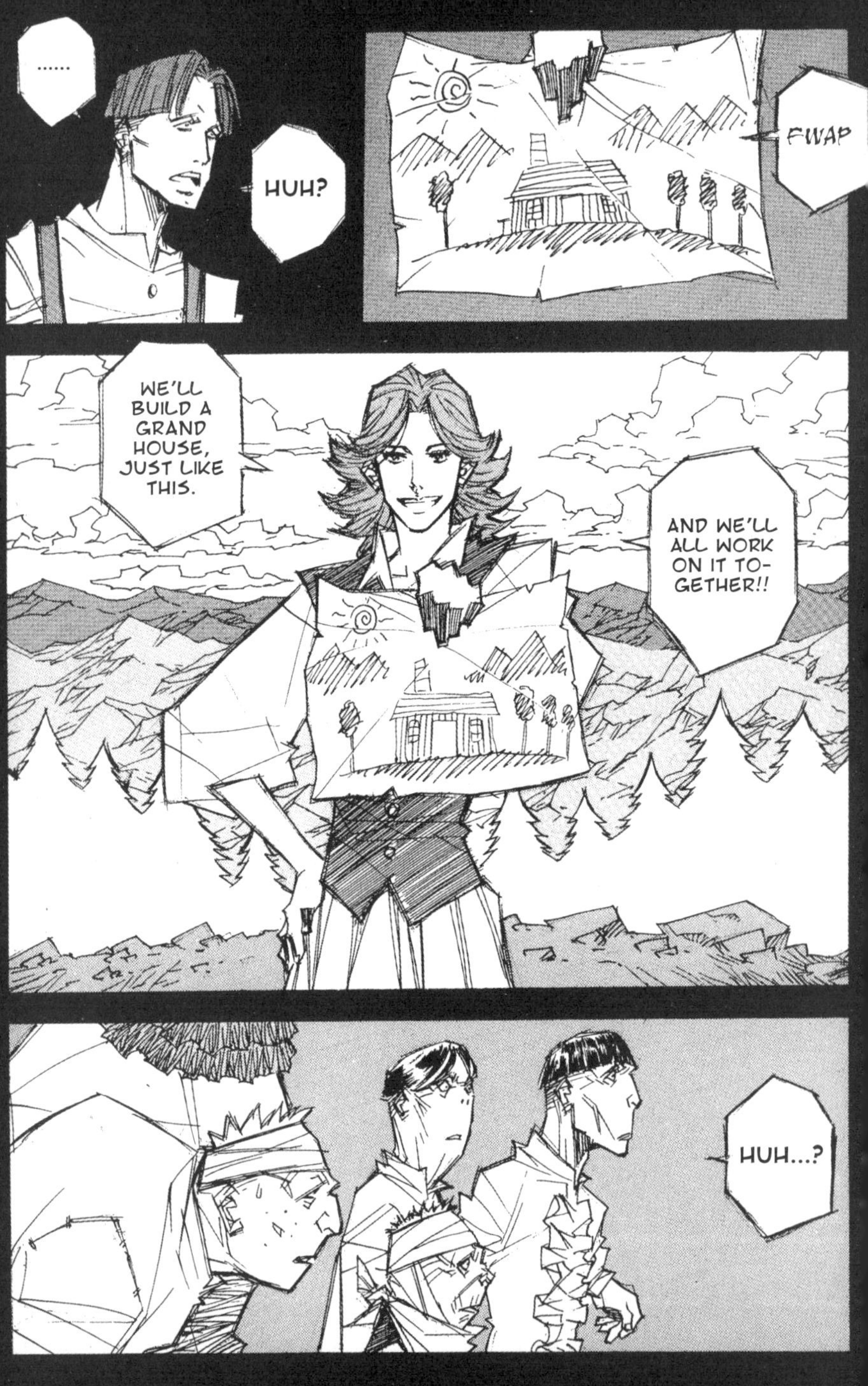
......
HUH?
FWAP
WE'LL BUILD A GRAND HOUSE, JUST LIKE THIS.
AND WE'LL ALL WORK ON IT TO-GETHER!!
HUH...?

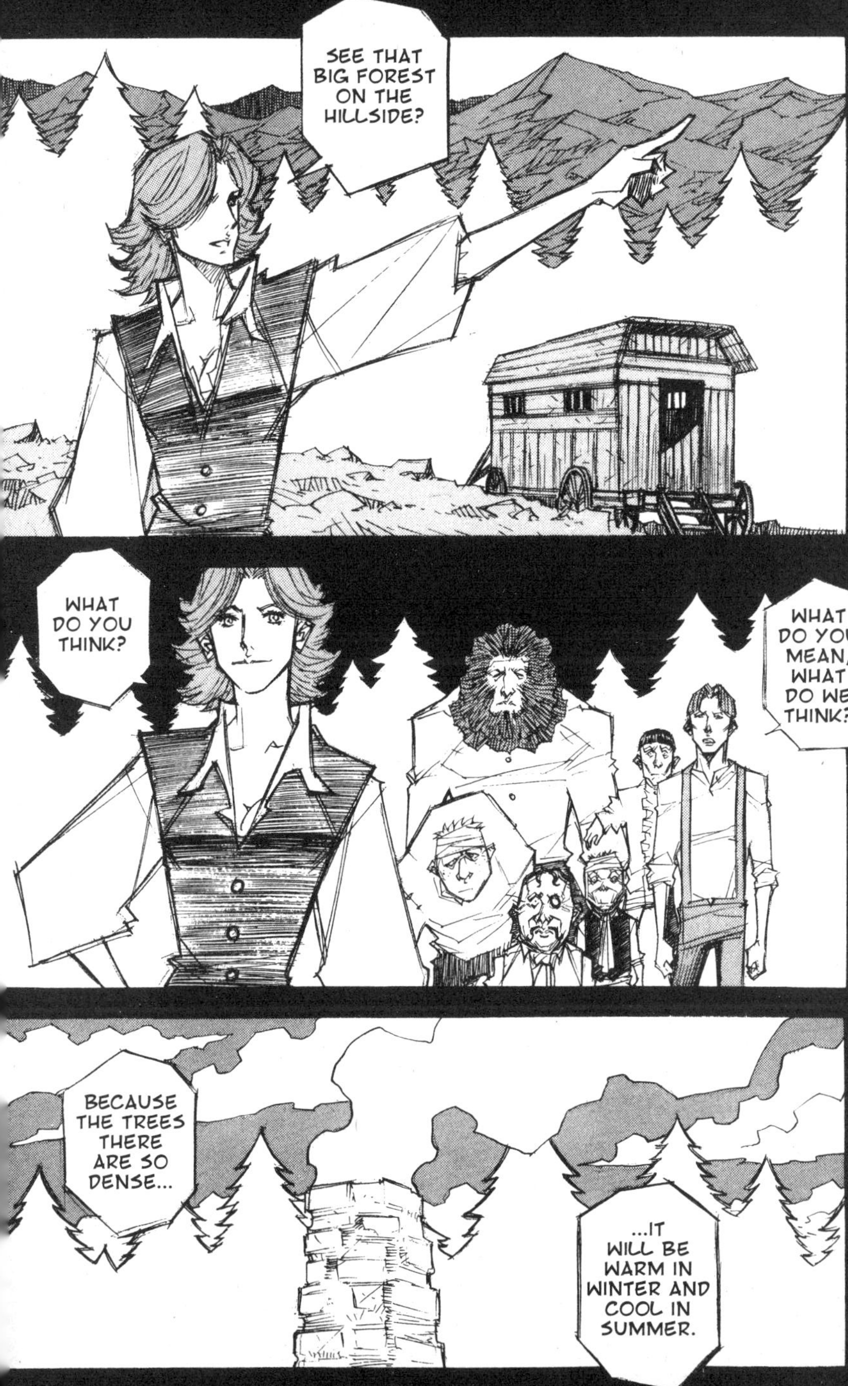
SEE THAT BIG FOREST ON THE HILLSIDE?
WHAT DO YOU THINK?
WHAT DO YOU MEAN, WHAT DO WE THINK?
BECAUSE THE TREES THERE ARE SO DENSE...
...IT WILL BE WARM IN WINTER AND COOL IN SUMMER.

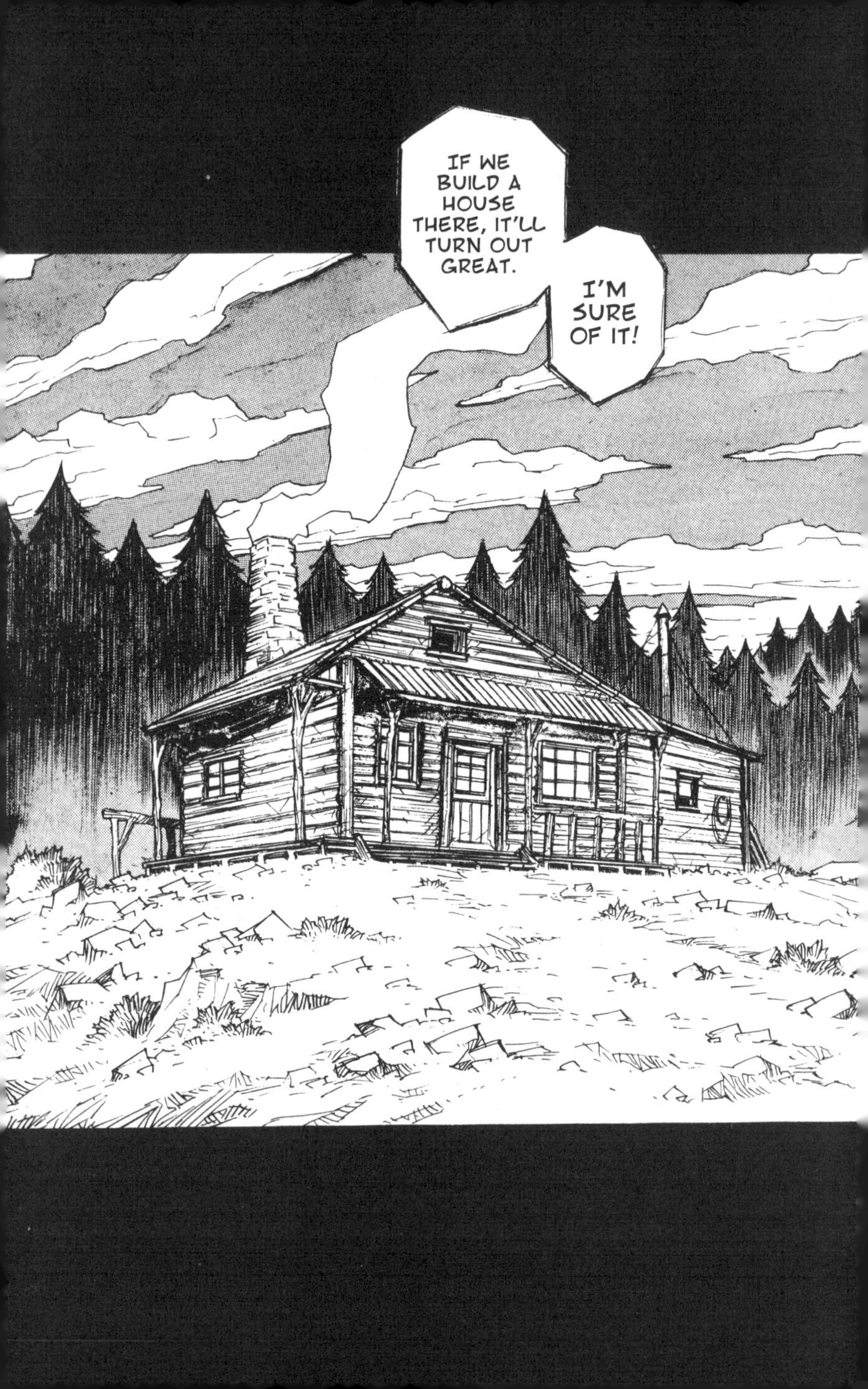
IF WE BUILD A HOUSE THERE, IT'LL TURN OUT GREAT.
I'M SURE OF IT!

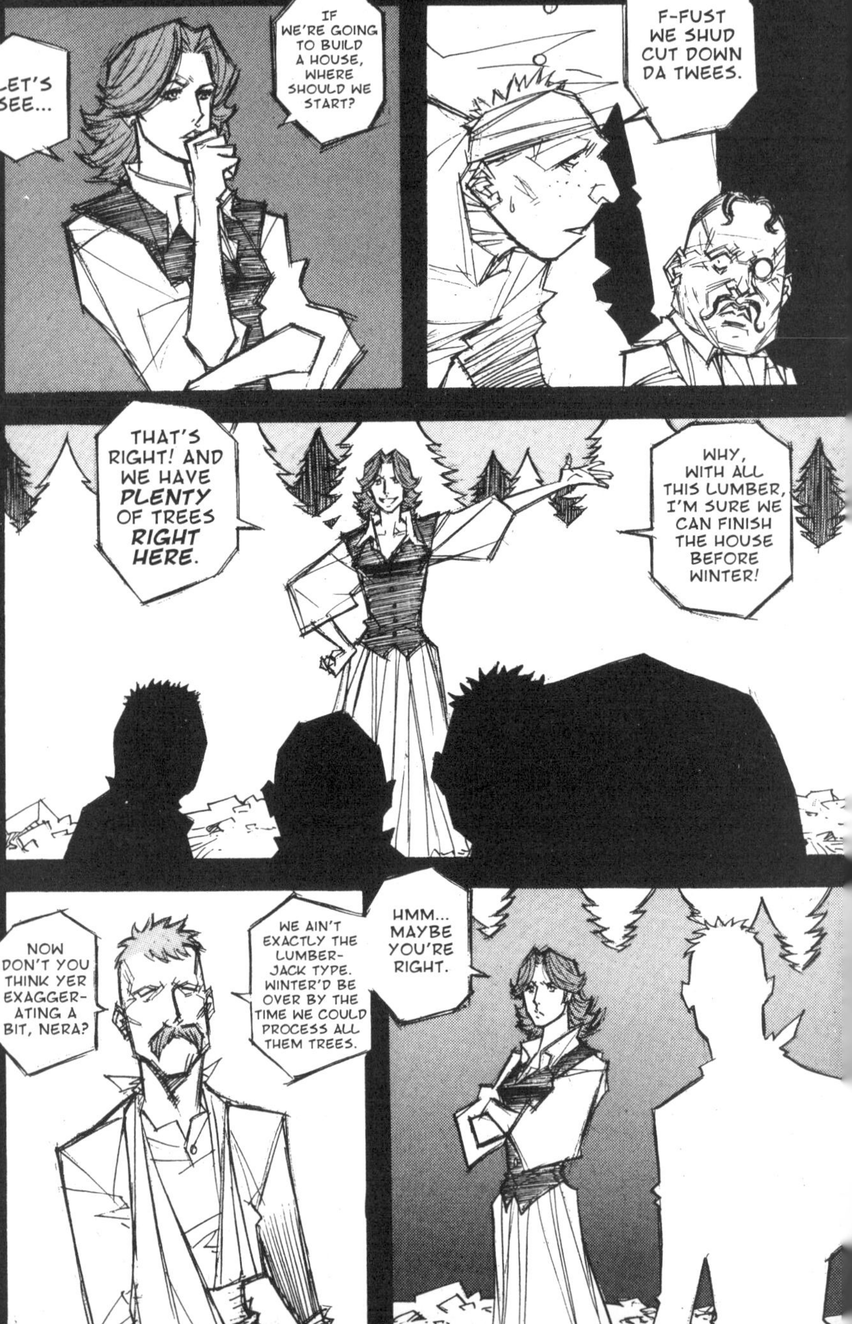
LET'S SEE...
IF WE'RE GOING TO BUILD A HOUSE, WHERE SHOULD WE START?
F-FUST WE SHUD CUT DOWN DA TWEES.
THAT'S RIGHT! AND WE HAVE PLENTY OF TREES RIGHT HERE.
WHY, WITH ALL THIS LUMBER, I'M SURE WE CAN FINISH THE HOUSE BEFORE WINTER!
NOW DON'T YOU THINK YER EXAGGER-ATING A BIT, NERA?
WE AIN'T EXACTLY THE LUMBER-JACK TYPE. WINTER'D BE OVER BY THE TIME WE COULD PROCESS ALL THEM TREES.
HMM... MAYBE YOU'RE RIGHT.

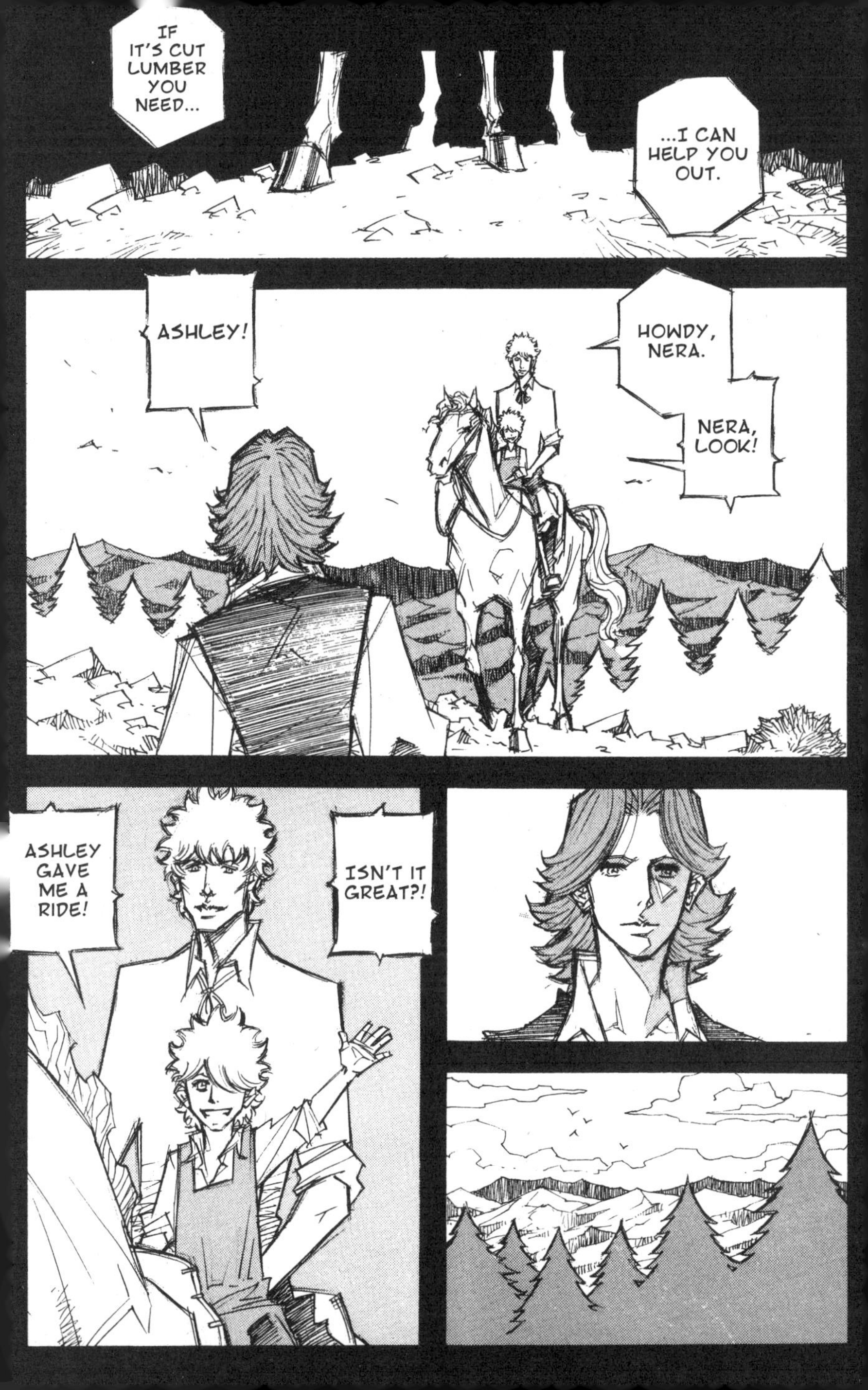
IF IT'S CUT LUMBER YOU NEED...
...I CAN HELP YOU OUT.
ASHLEY!
HOWDY, NERA.
NERA, LOOK!
ASHLEY GAVE ME A RIDE!
ISN'T IT GREAT?!

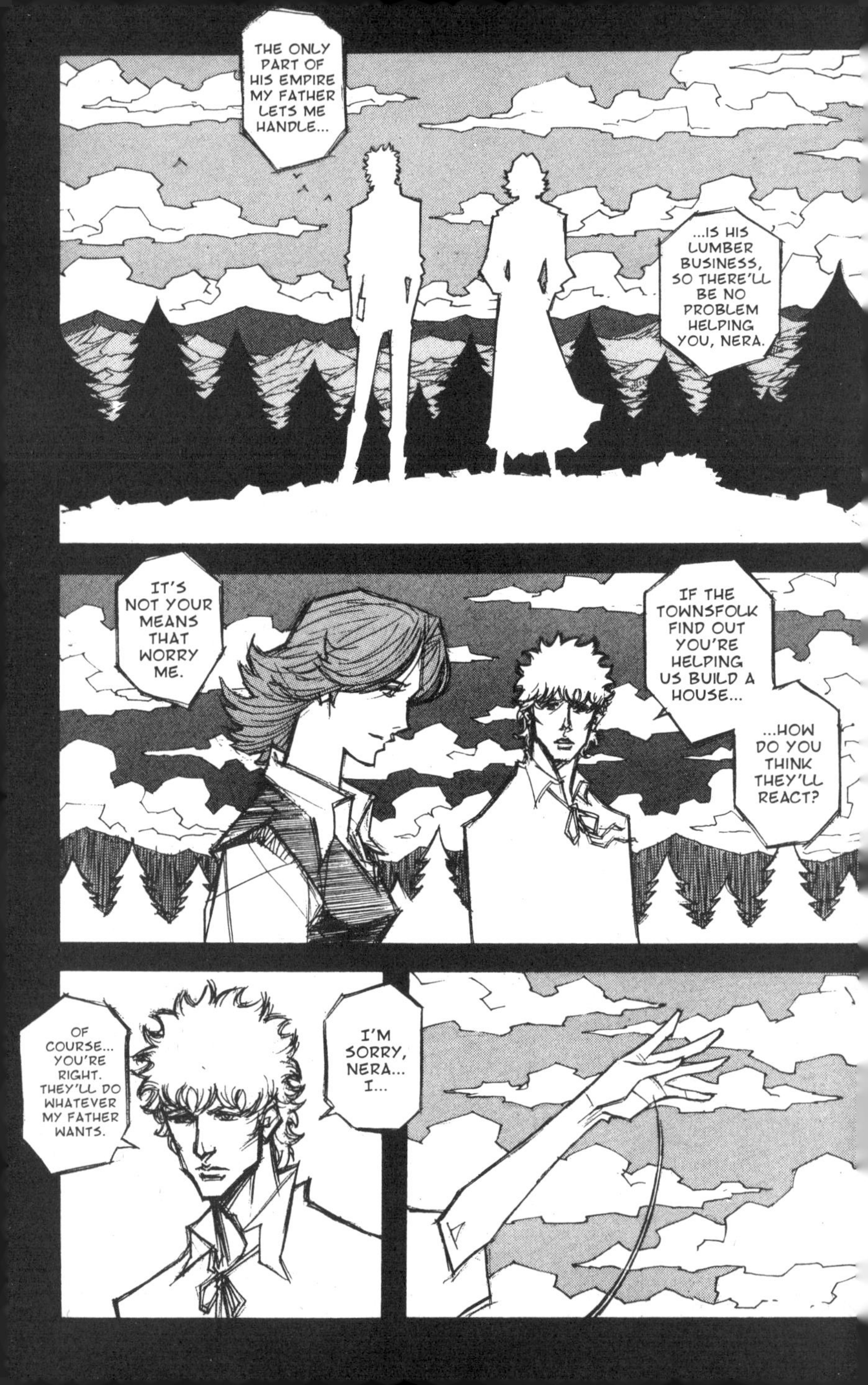
THE ONLY PART OF HIS EMPIRE MY FATHER LETS ME HANDLE...
...IS HIS LUMBER BUSINESS, SO THERE'LL BE NO PROBLEM HELPING YOU, NERA.
IT'S NOT YOUR MEANS THAT WORRY ME.
IF THE TOWNSFOLK FIND OUT YOU'RE HELPING US BUILD A HOUSE...
...HOW DO YOU THINK THEY'LL REACT?
OF COURSE... YOU'RE RIGHT. THEY'LL DO WHATEVER MY FATHER WANTS.
I'M SORRY, NERA... I...

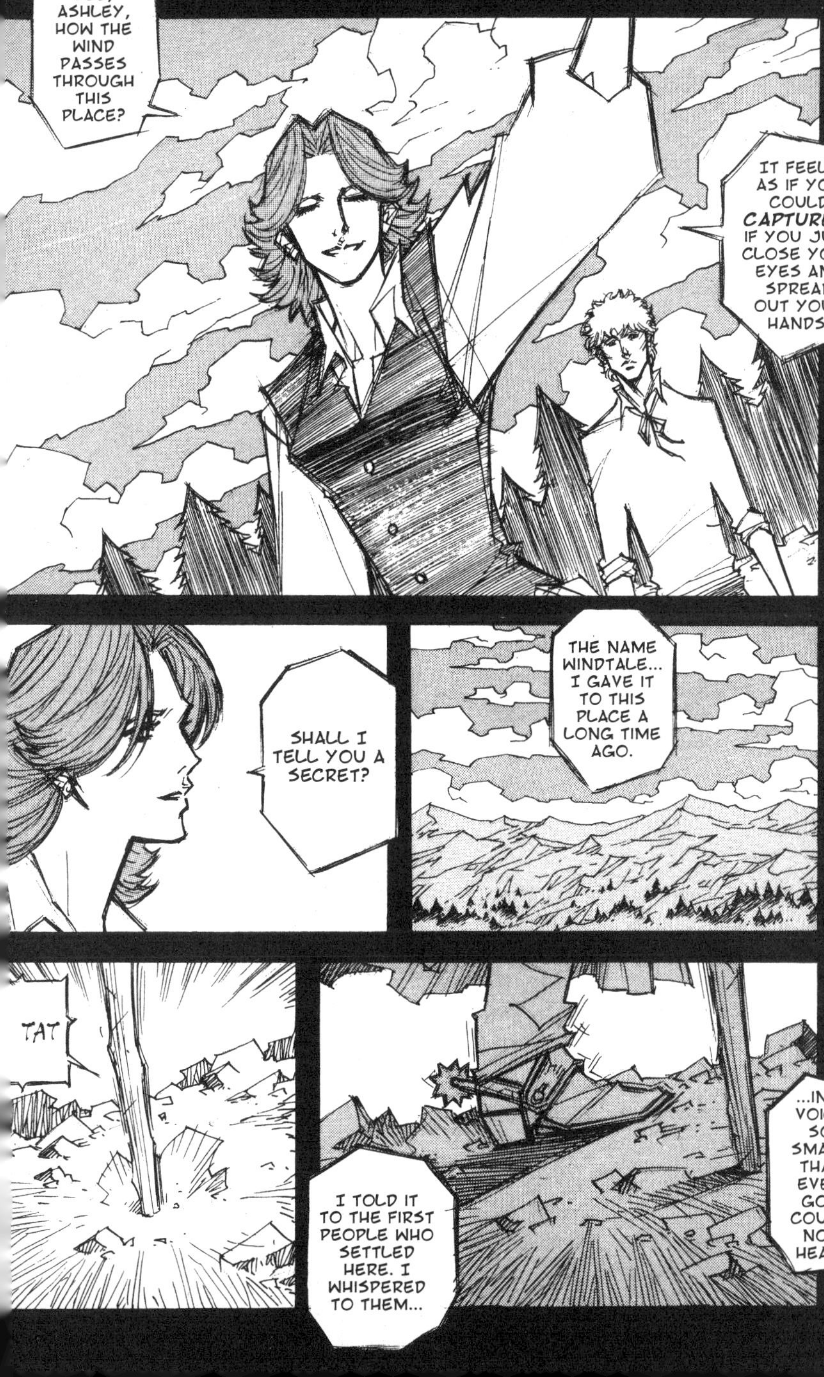
SEE, ASHLEY, HOW THE WIND PASSES THROUGH THIS PLACE?
IT FEELS AS IF YOU COULD **CAPTURE** IT IF YOU JUST CLOSE YOUR EYES AND SPREAD OUT YOUR HANDS.
SHALL I TELL YOU A SECRET?
THE NAME WINDTALE... I GAVE IT TO THIS PLACE A LONG TIME AGO.
TAT
I TOLD IT TO THE FIRST PEOPLE WHO SETTLED HERE. I WHISPERED TO THEM...
...IN A VOICE SO SMALL THAT EVEN GOD COULD NOT HEAR.

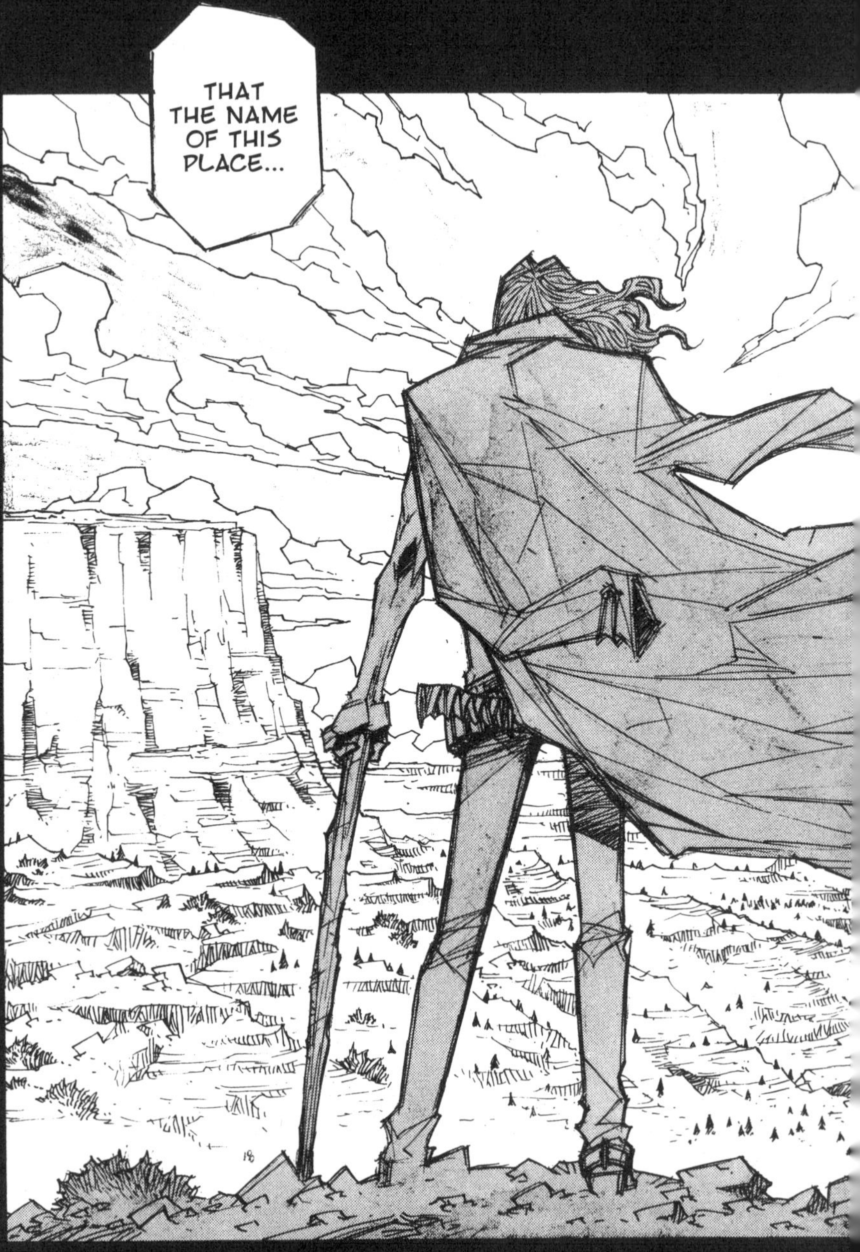
THAT THE NAME OF THIS PLACE...

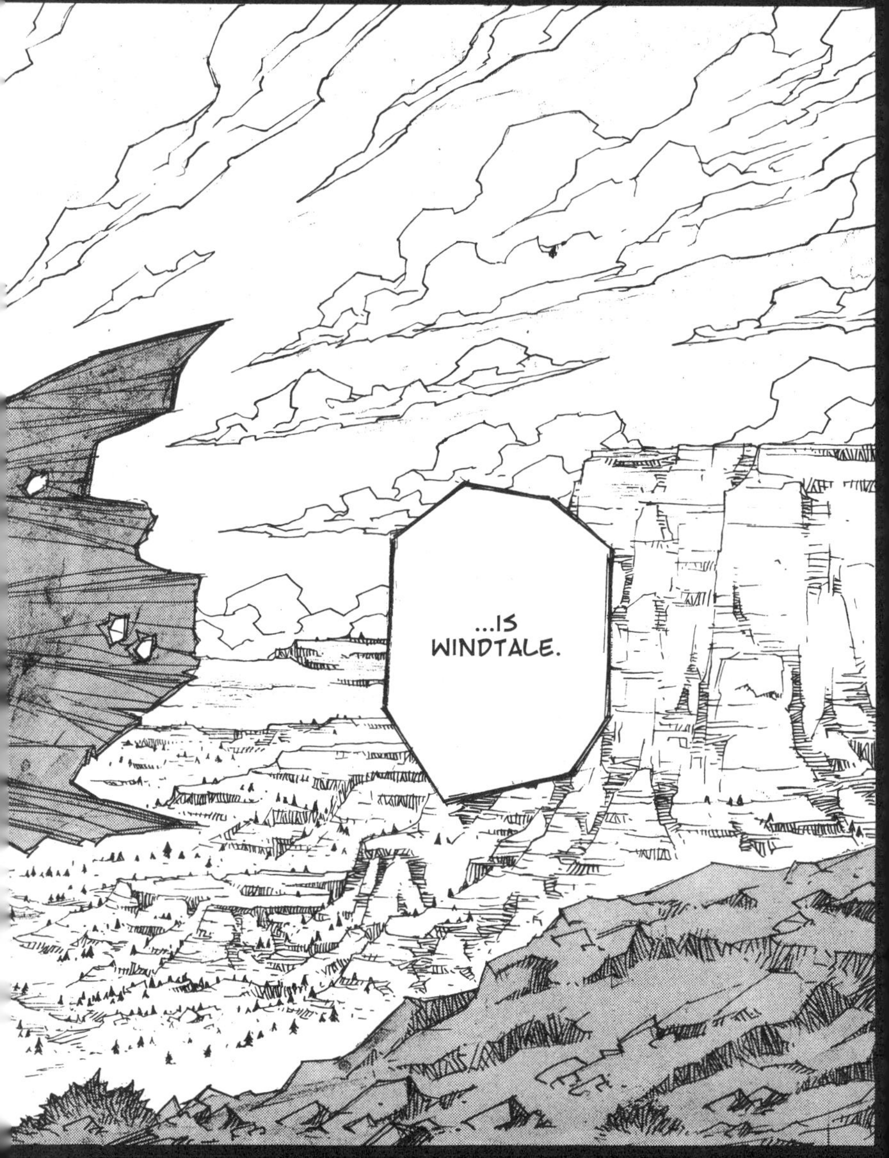
...IS WINDTALE.

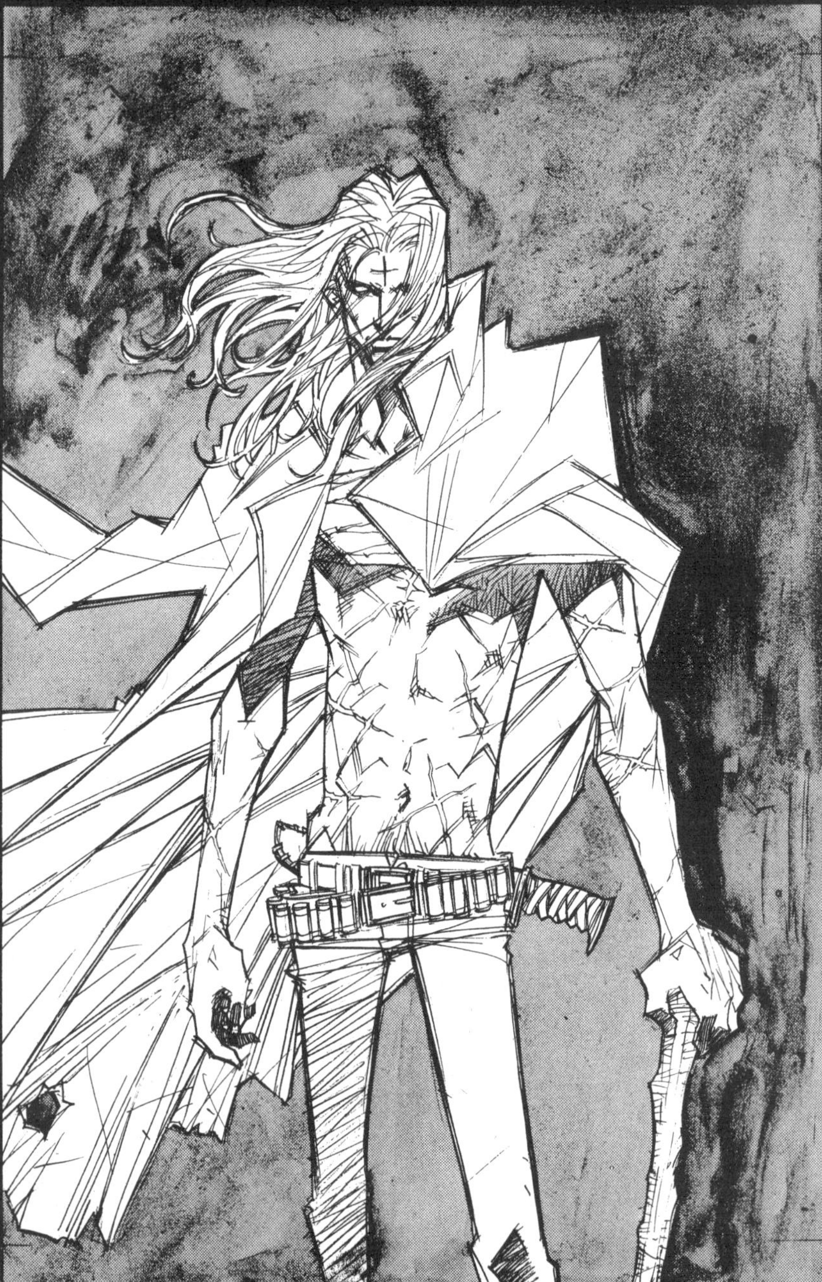

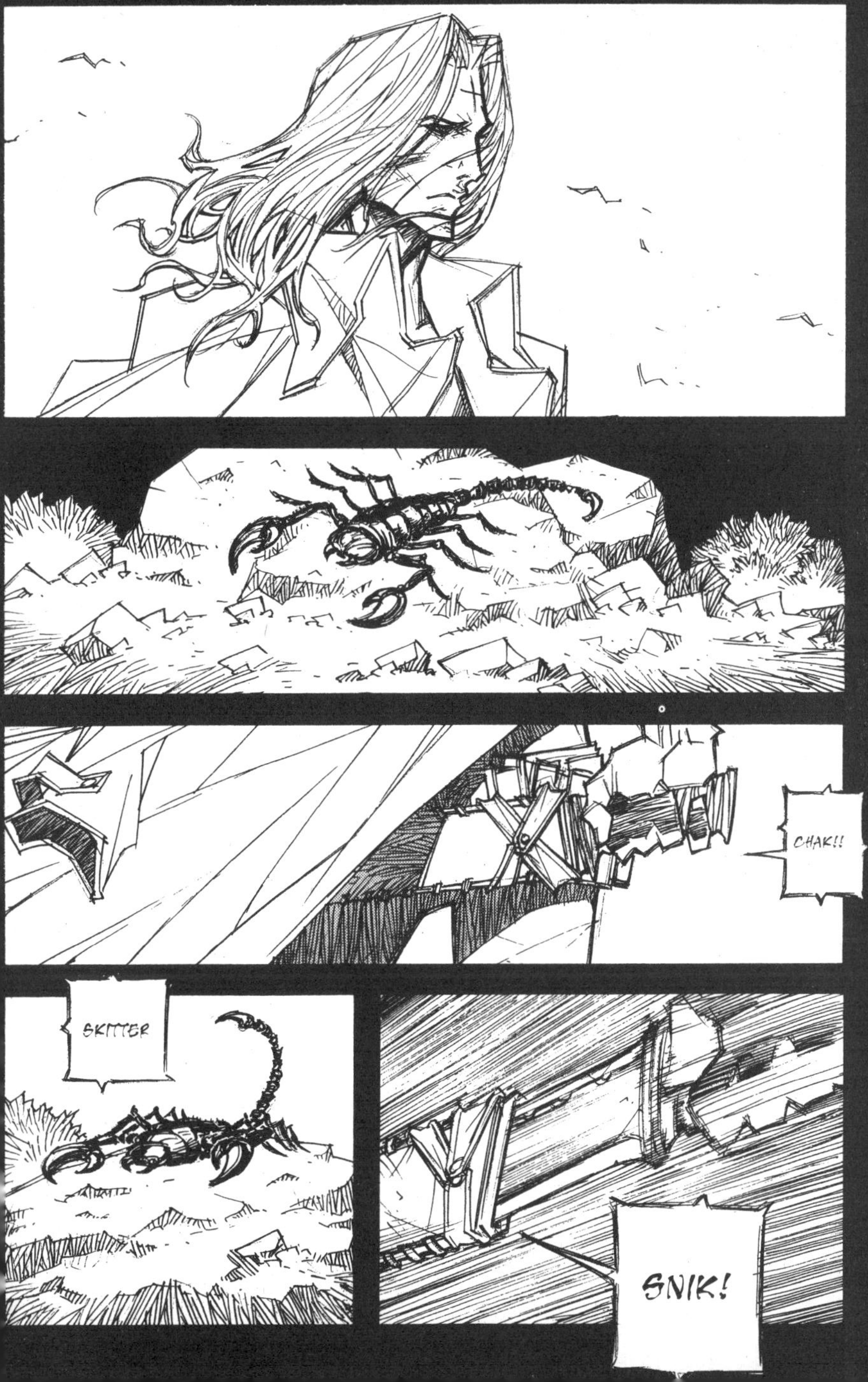
CHAK!!
SKITTER
SNIK!

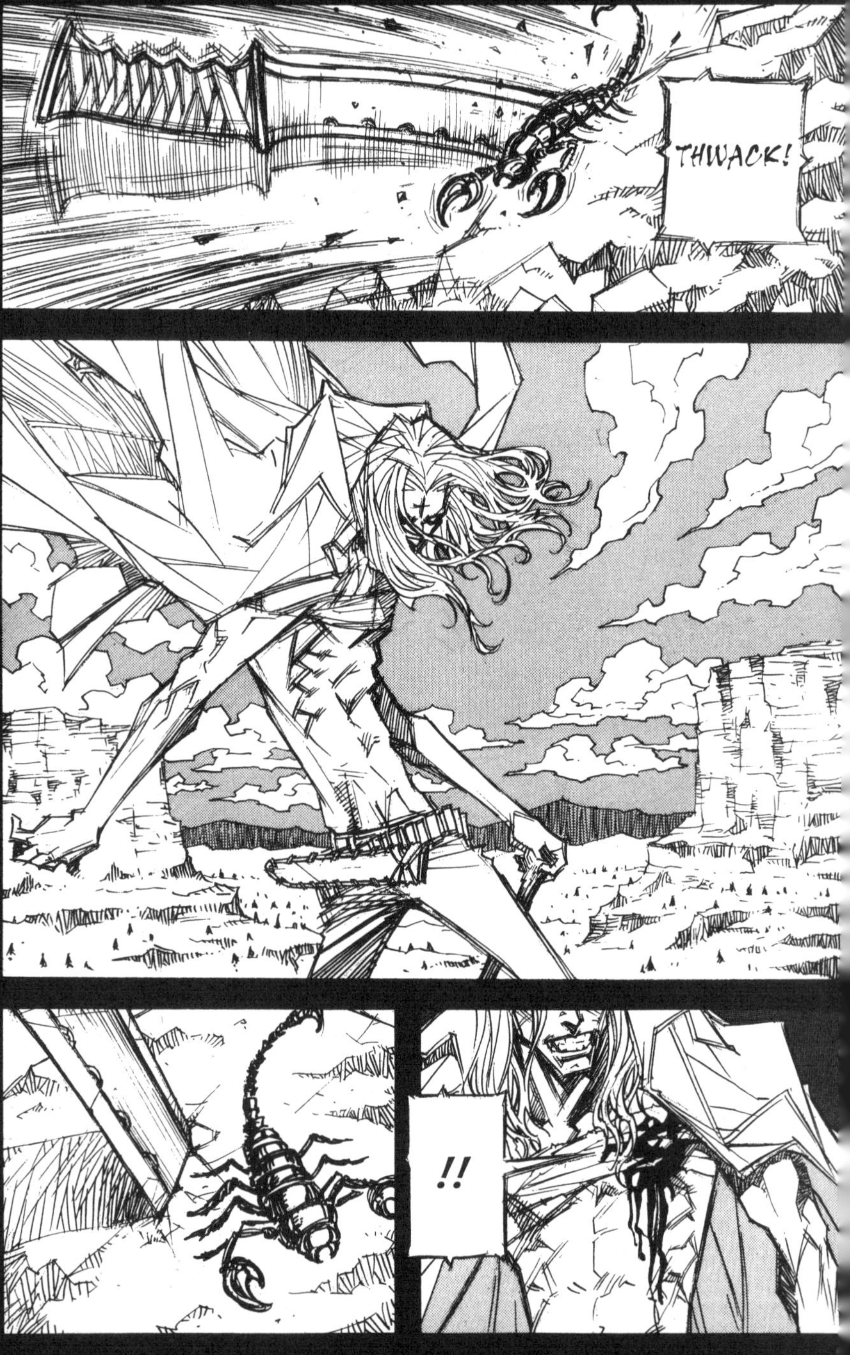
THWACK!
!!

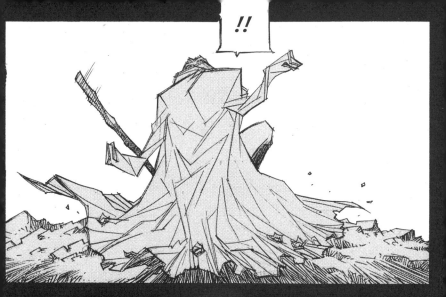

WAI+, IVAN!

YOU WILL KNOW I+ IS +IME +O AC+ WHEN YOUR BODY IS HEALED.

HEH HEH HEH...

THAT'S EASY FOR YOU TO SAY, BELIAL

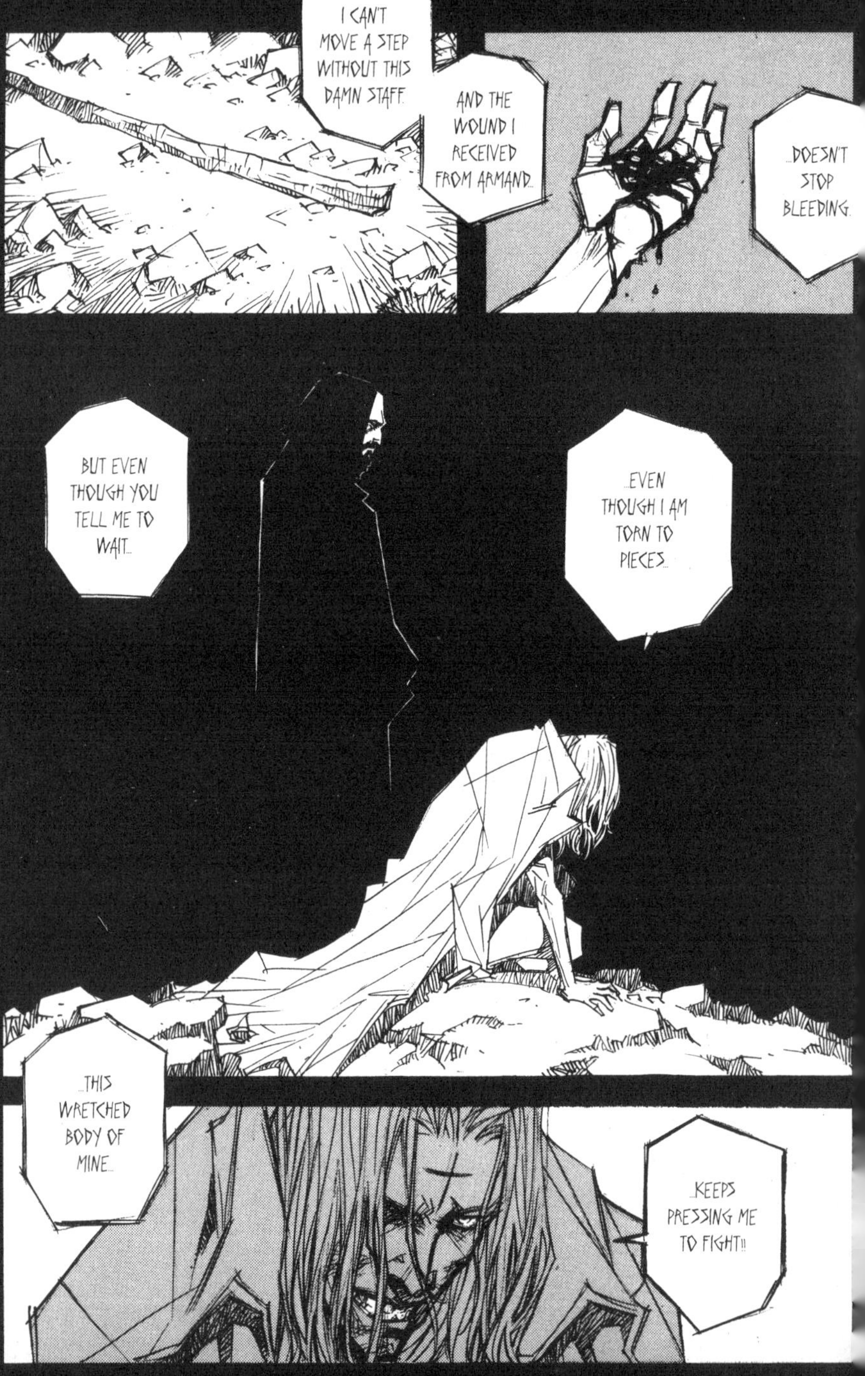
I CAN'T MOVE A STEP WITHOUT THIS DAMN STAFF.
AND THE WOUND I RECEIVED FROM ARMAND...
...DOESN'T STOP BLEEDING.
BUT EVEN THOUGH YOU TELL ME TO WAIT...
...EVEN THOUGH I AM TORN TO PIECES...
...THIS WRETCHED BODY OF MINE...
...KEEPS PRESSING ME TO FIGHT!!

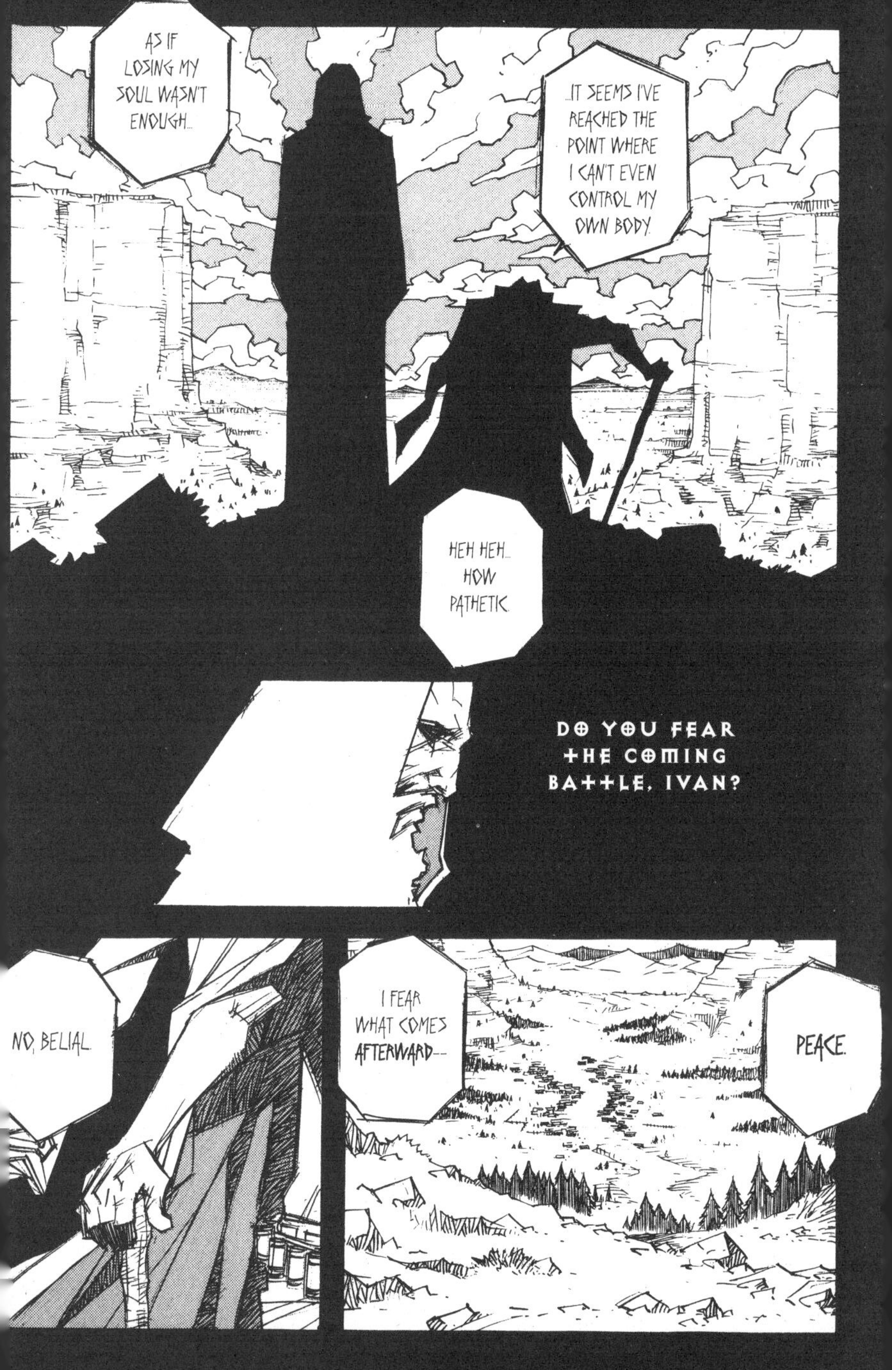
AS IF LOSING MY SOUL WASN'T ENOUGH...
...IT SEEMS I'VE REACHED THE POINT WHERE I CAN'T EVEN CONTROL MY OWN BODY.
HEH HEH... HOW PATHETIC.
DO YOU FEAR THE COMING BATTLE, IVAN?
NO, BELIAL.
I FEAR WHAT COMES AFTERWARD--
PEACE.

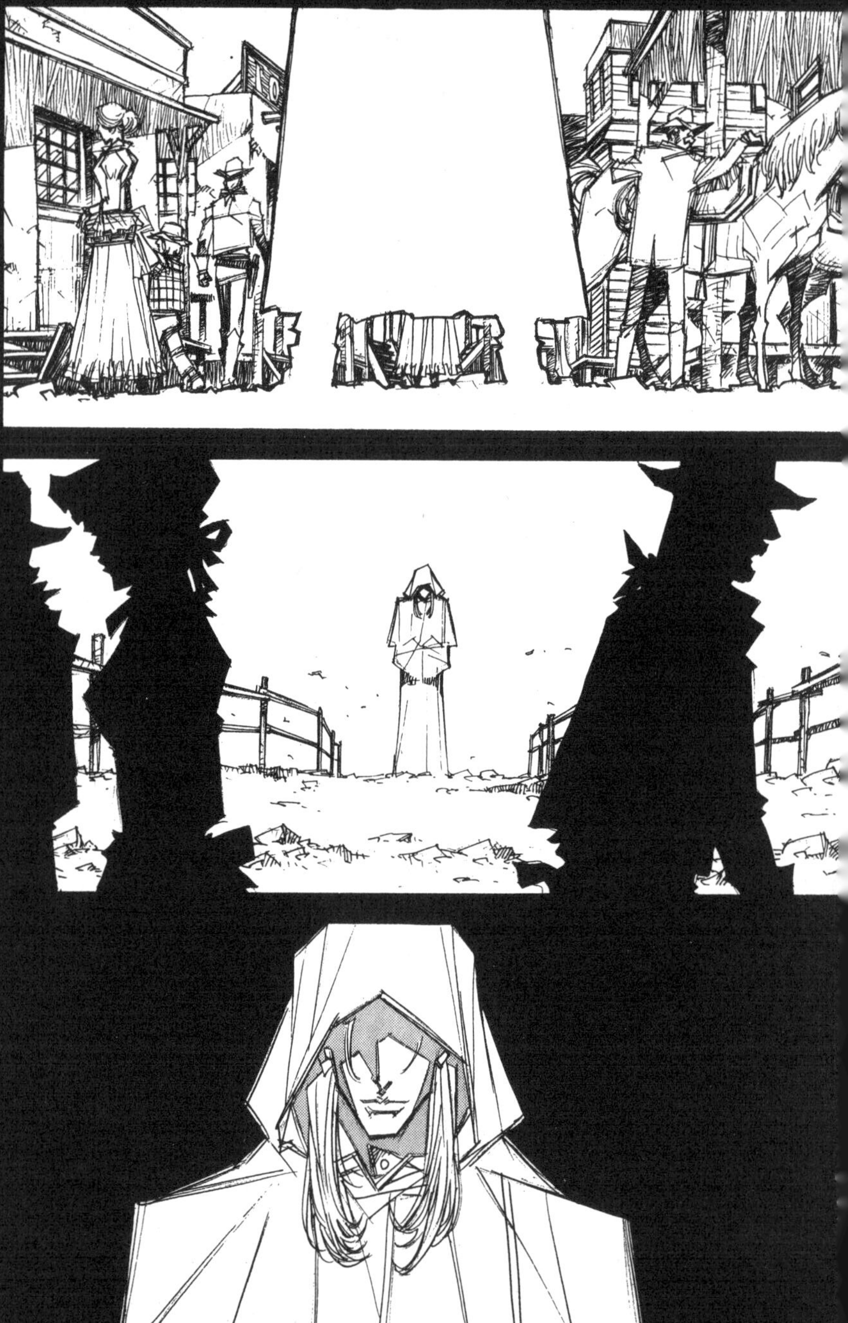

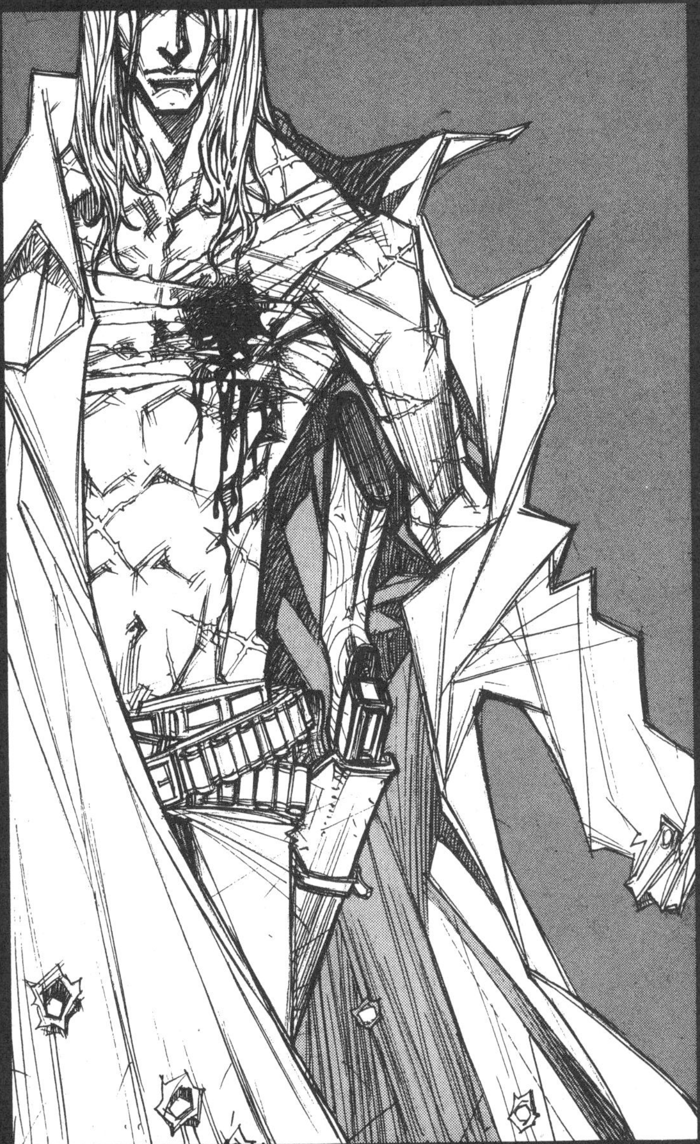

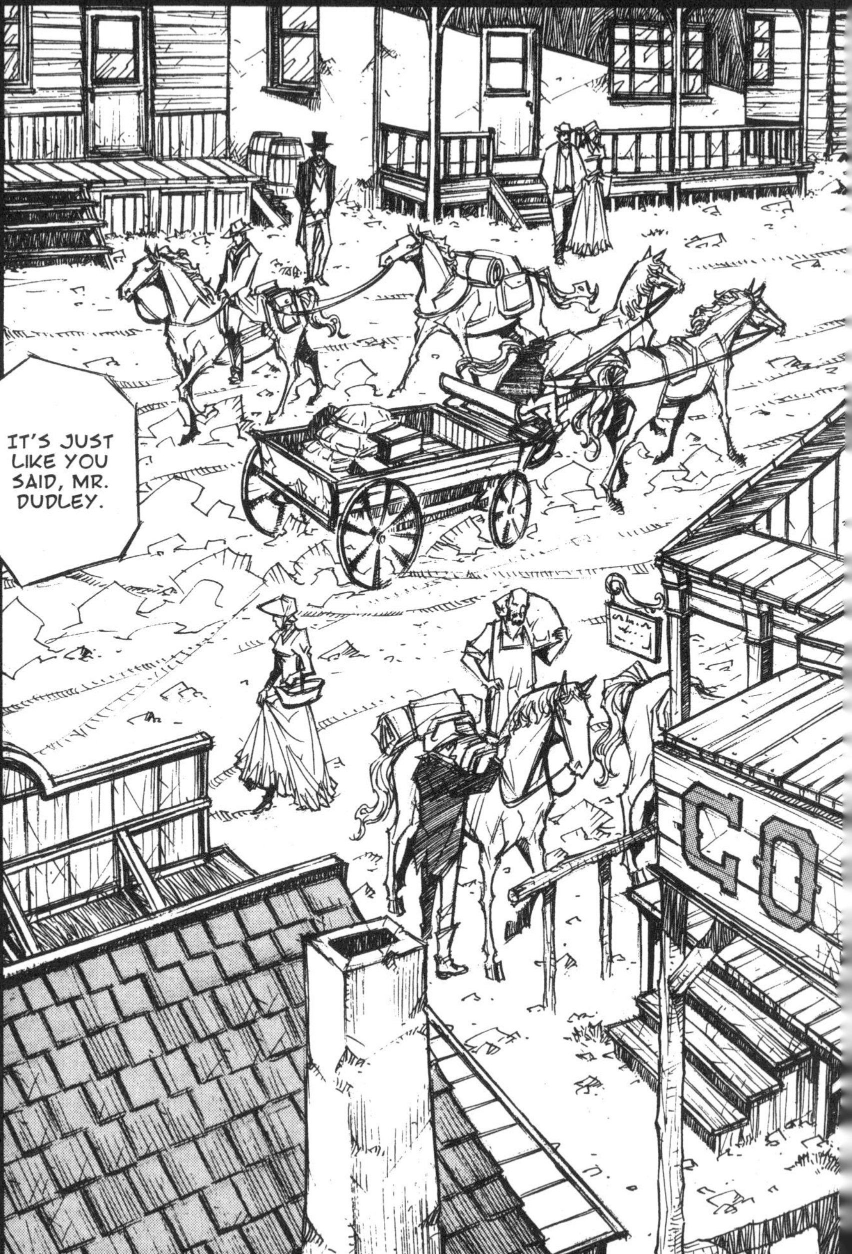
IT'S JUST LIKE YOU SAID, MR. DUDLEY.
GO

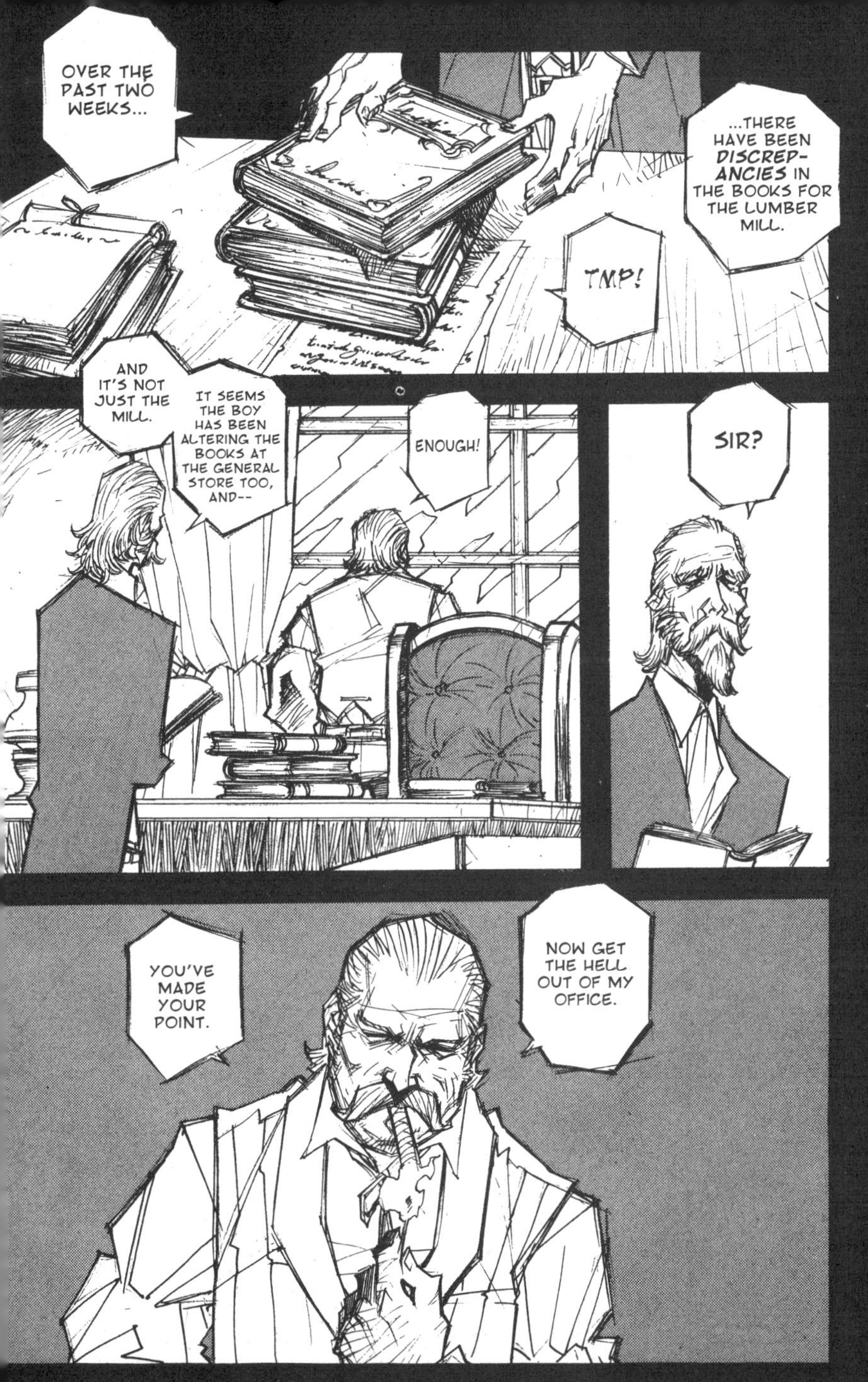
OVER THE PAST TWO WEEKS...
...THERE HAVE BEEN DISCREPANCIES IN THE BOOKS FOR THE LUMBER MILL.
TMP!
AND IT'S NOT JUST THE MILL.
IT SEEMS THE BOY HAS BEEN ALTERING THE BOOKS AT THE GENERAL STORE TOO, AND--
ENOUGH!
SIR?
YOU'VE MADE YOUR POINT.
NOW GET THE HELL OUT OF MY OFFICE.

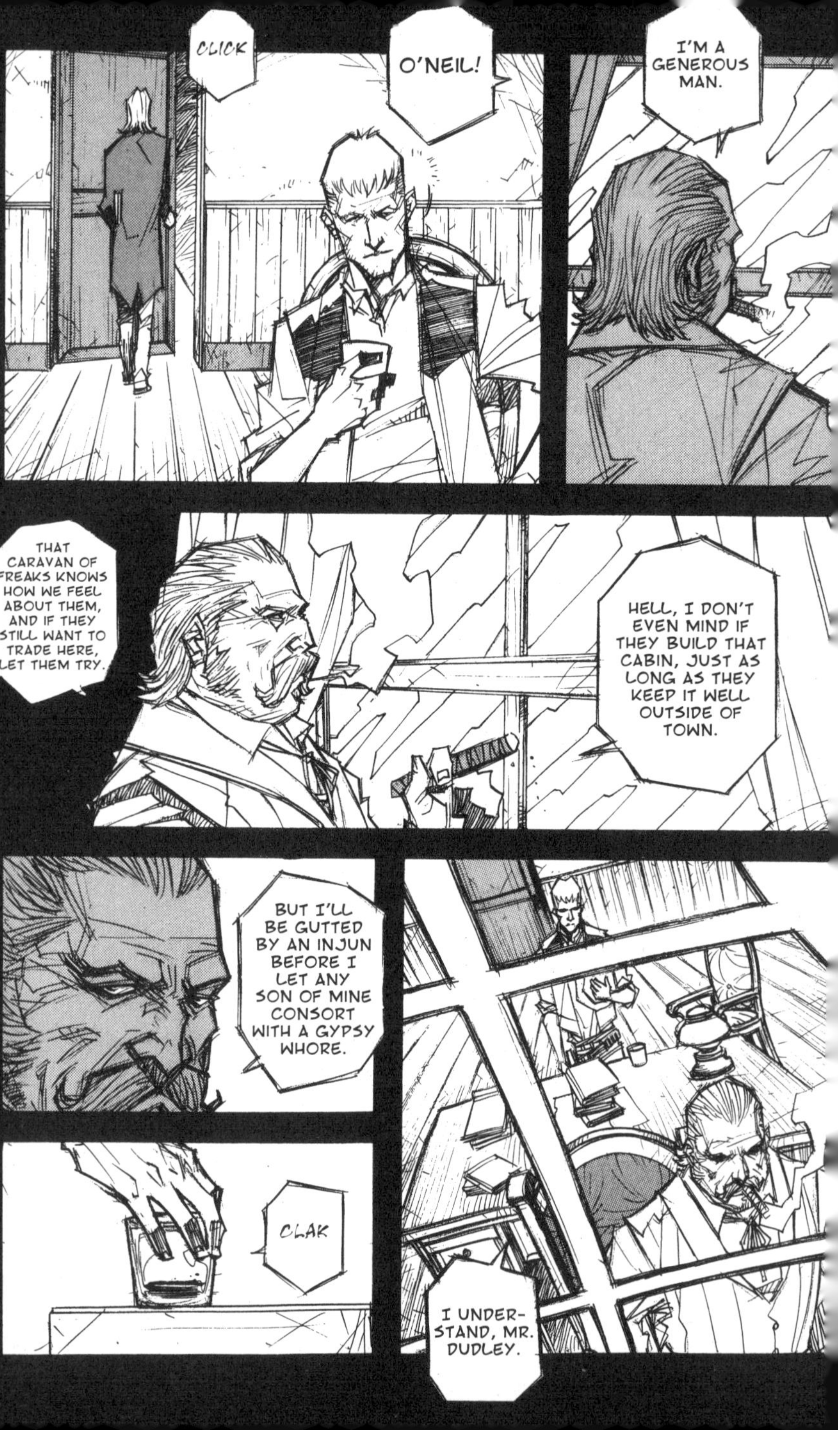

CLICK
O'NEIL!
I'M A GENEROUS MAN.
THAT CARAVAN OF FREAKS KNOWS HOW WE FEEL ABOUT THEM, AND IF THEY STILL WANT TO TRADE HERE, LET THEM TRY.
HELL, I DON'T EVEN MIND IF THEY BUILD THAT CABIN, JUST AS LONG AS THEY KEEP IT WELL OUTSIDE OF TOWN.
BUT I'LL BE GUTTED BY AN INJUN BEFORE I LET ANY SON OF MINE CONSORT WITH A GYPSY WHORE.
CLAK
I UNDER-STAND, MR. DUDLEY.

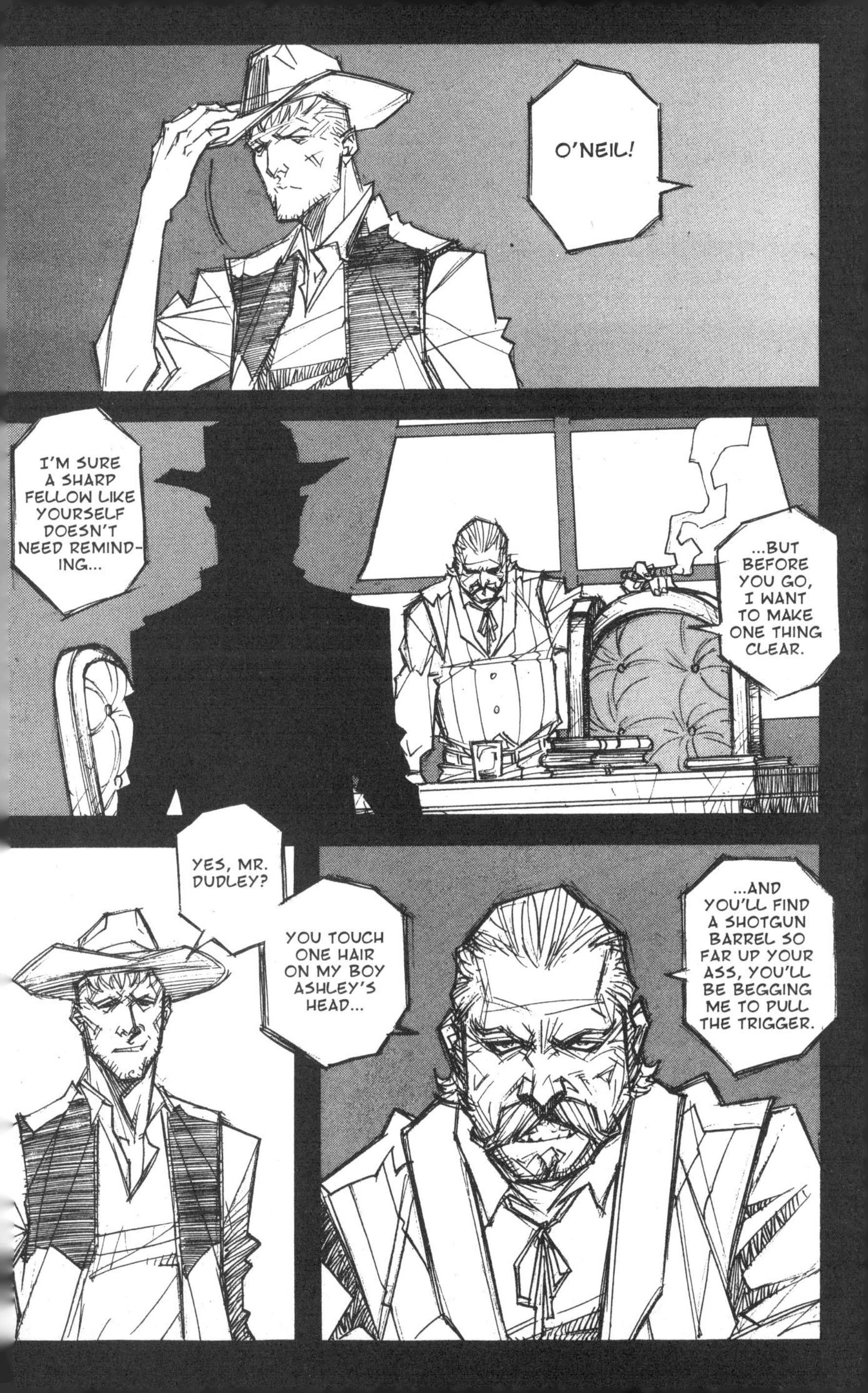
O'NEIL!
I'M SURE A SHARP FELLOW LIKE YOURSELF DOESN'T NEED REMIND-ING...
...BUT BEFORE YOU GO, I WANT TO MAKE ONE THING CLEAR.
YES, MR. DUDLEY?
YOU TOUCH ONE HAIR ON MY BOY ASHLEY'S HEAD...
...AND YOU'LL FIND A SHOTGUN BARREL SO FAR UP YOUR ASS, YOU'LL BE BEGGING ME TO PULL THE TRIGGER.

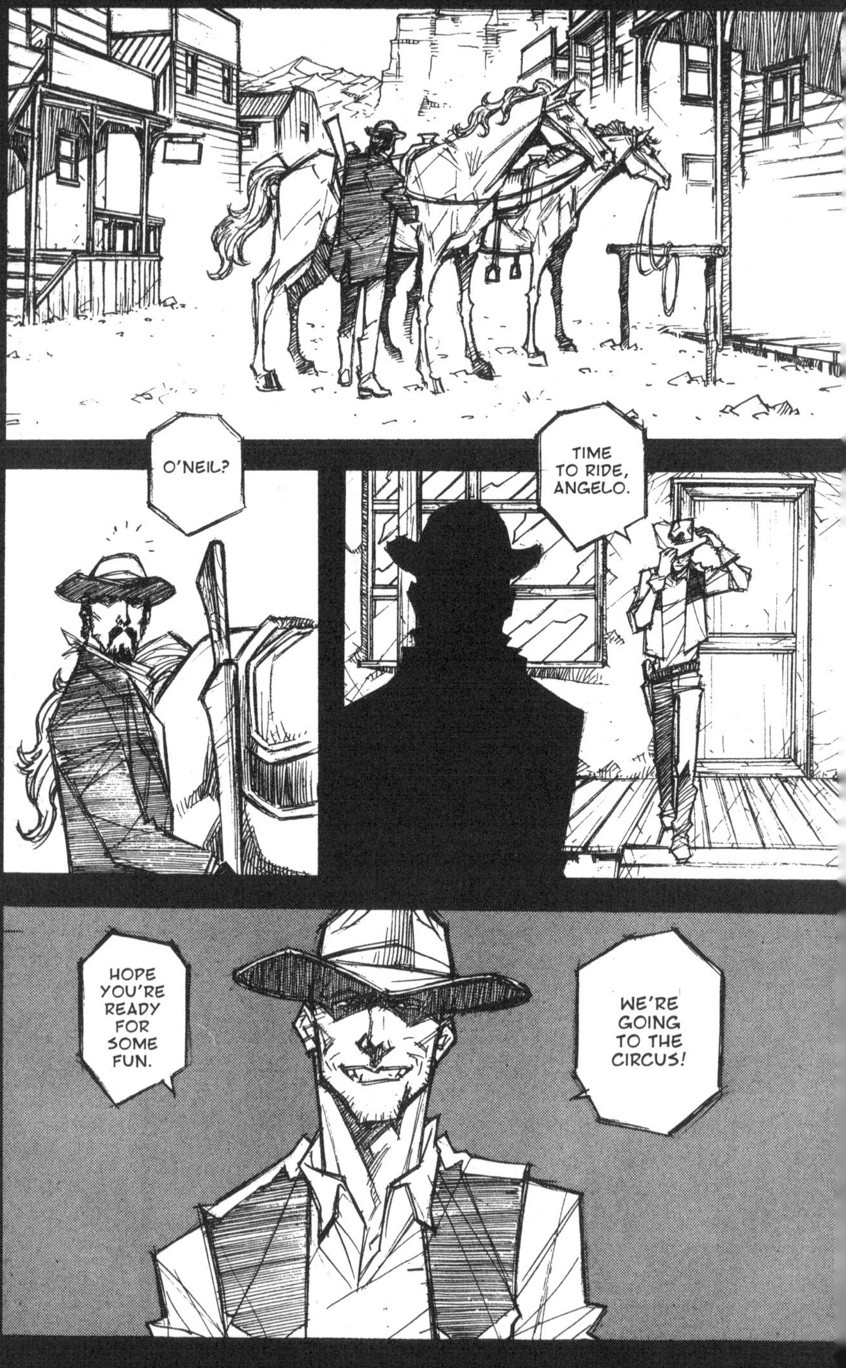
O'NEIL?
TIME TO RIDE, ANGELO.
HOPE YOU'RE READY FOR SOME FUN.
WE'RE GOING TO THE CIRCUS!

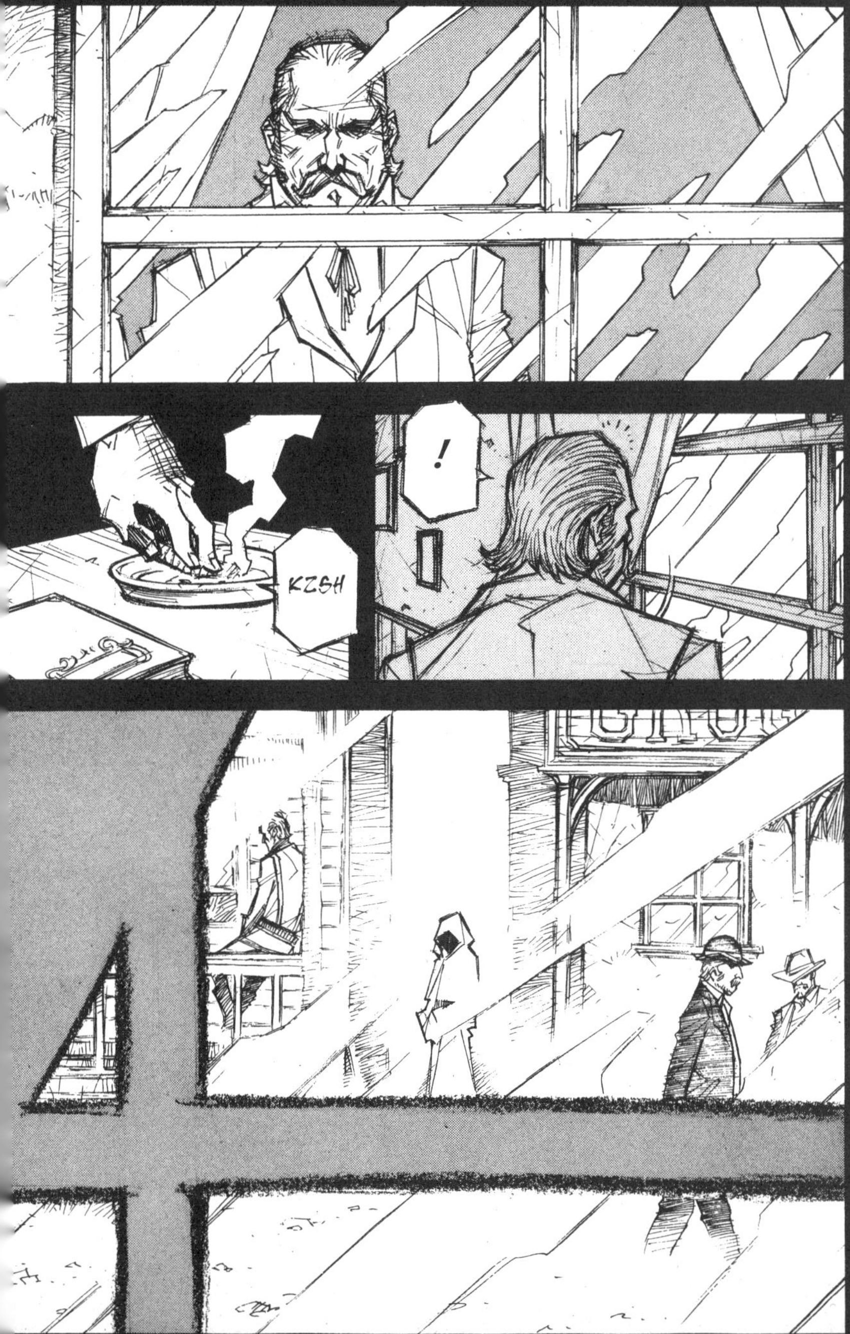
KZSH
!

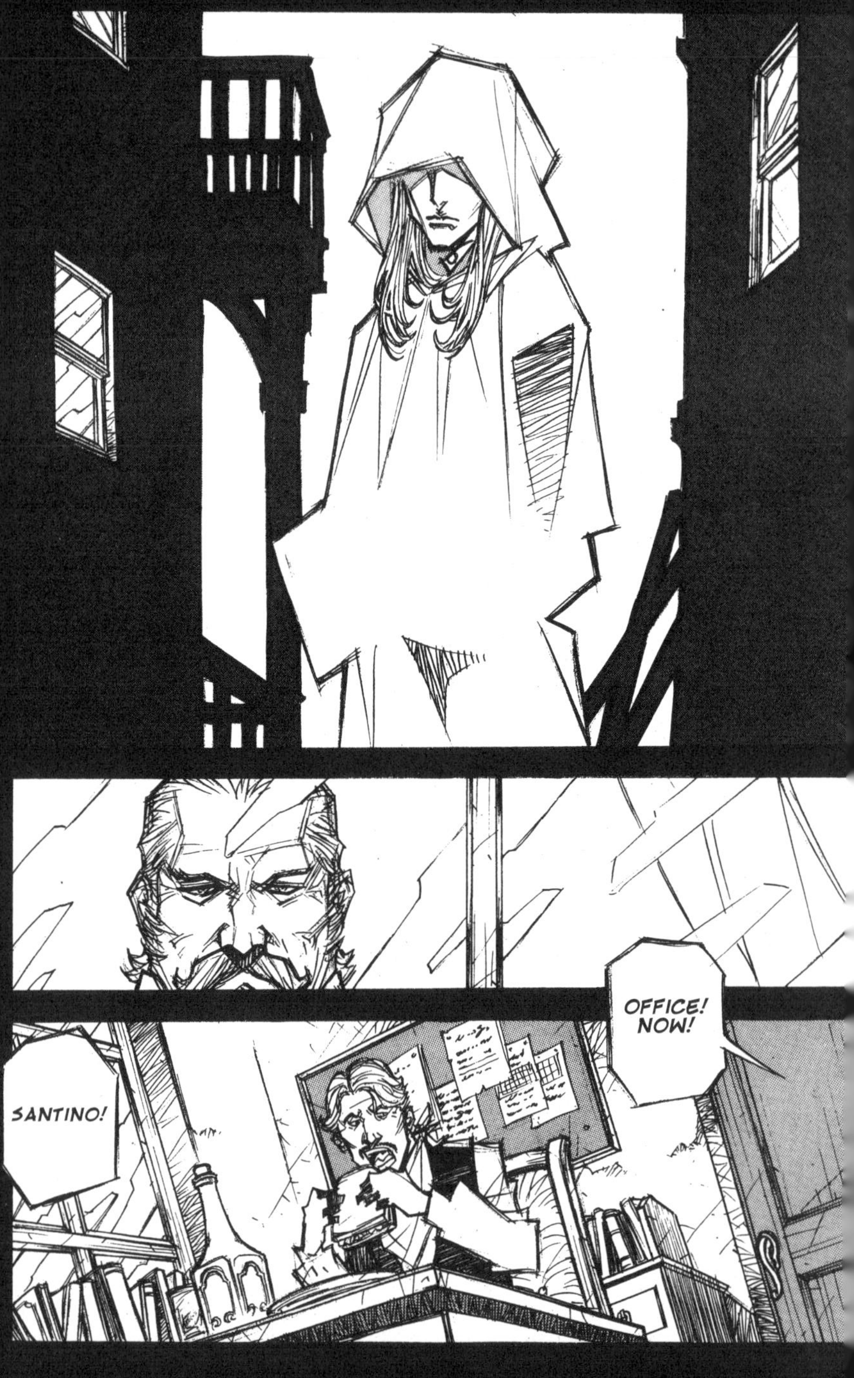
SANTINO!
OFFICE! NOW!

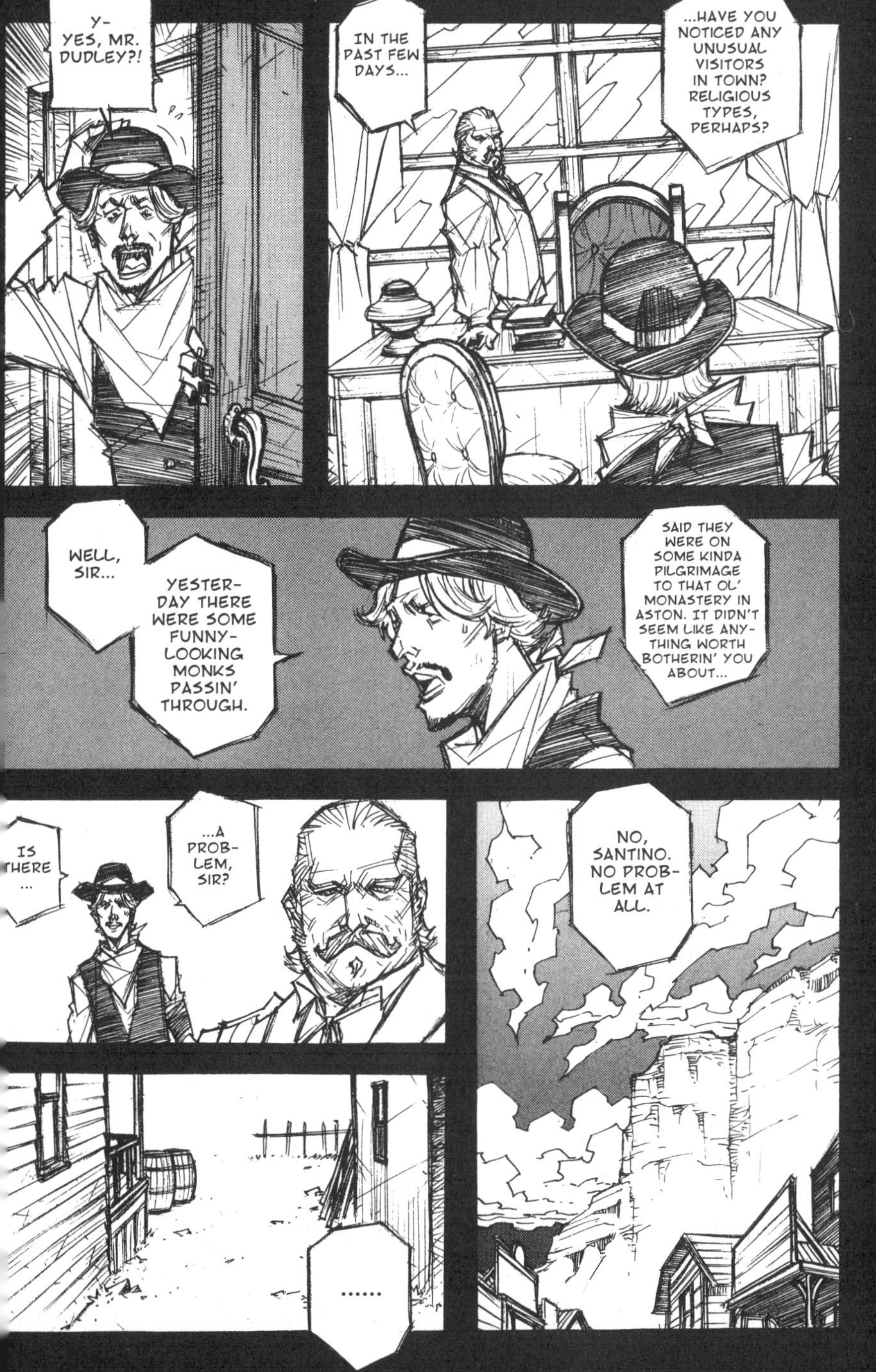
Y-YES, MR. DUDLEY?!
IN THE PAST FEW DAYS...
...HAVE YOU NOTICED ANY UNUSUAL VISITORS IN TOWN? RELIGIOUS TYPES, PERHAPS?
WELL, SIR...
YESTER-DAY THERE WERE SOME FUNNY-LOOKING MONKS PASSIN' THROUGH.
SAID THEY WERE ON SOME KINDA PILGRIMAGE TO THAT OL' MONASTERY IN ASTON. IT DIDN'T SEEM LIKE ANY-THING WORTH BOTHERIN' YOU ABOUT...
IS THERE ...
...A PROB-LEM, SIR?
NO, SANTINO. NO PROB-LEM AT ALL.
......

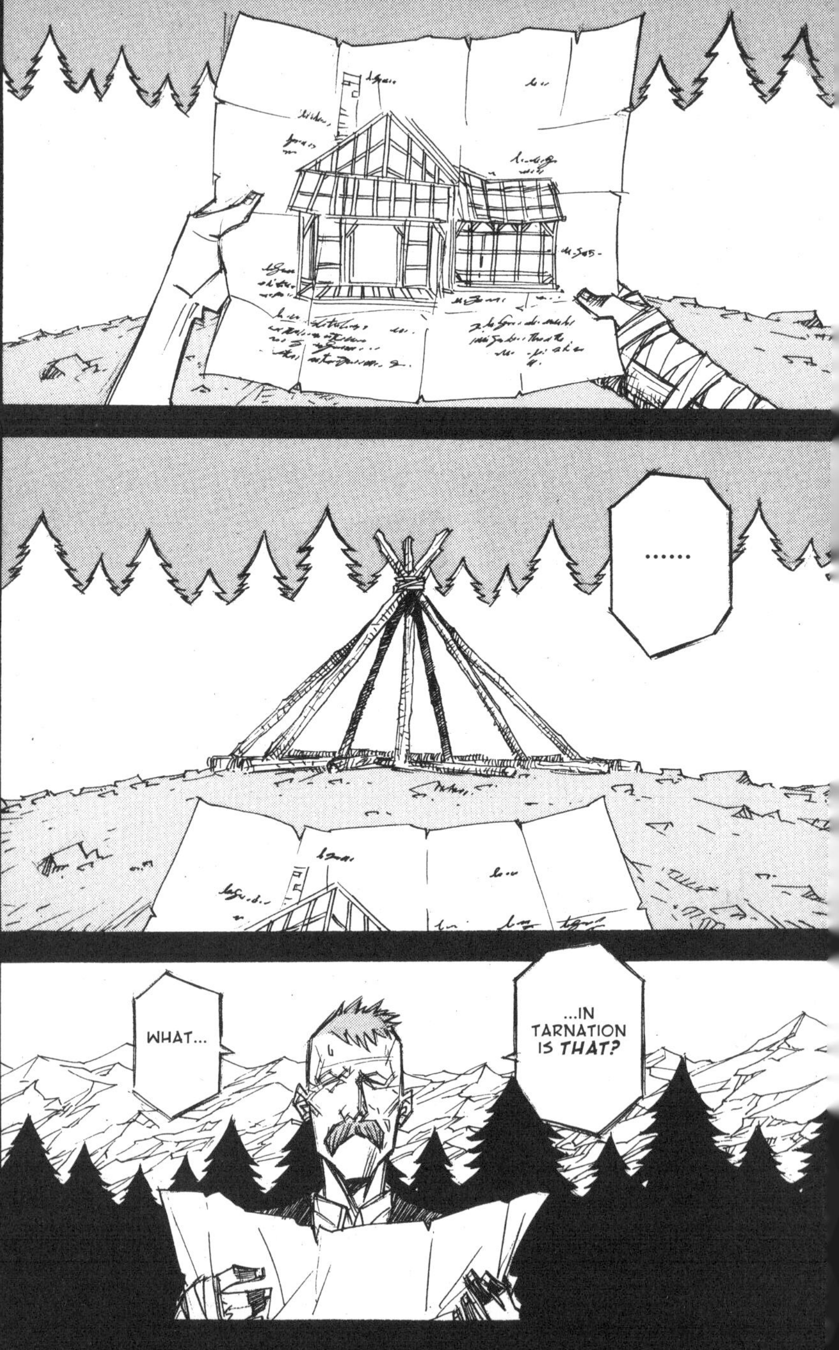

......
WHAT...
...IN TARNATION IS THAT?

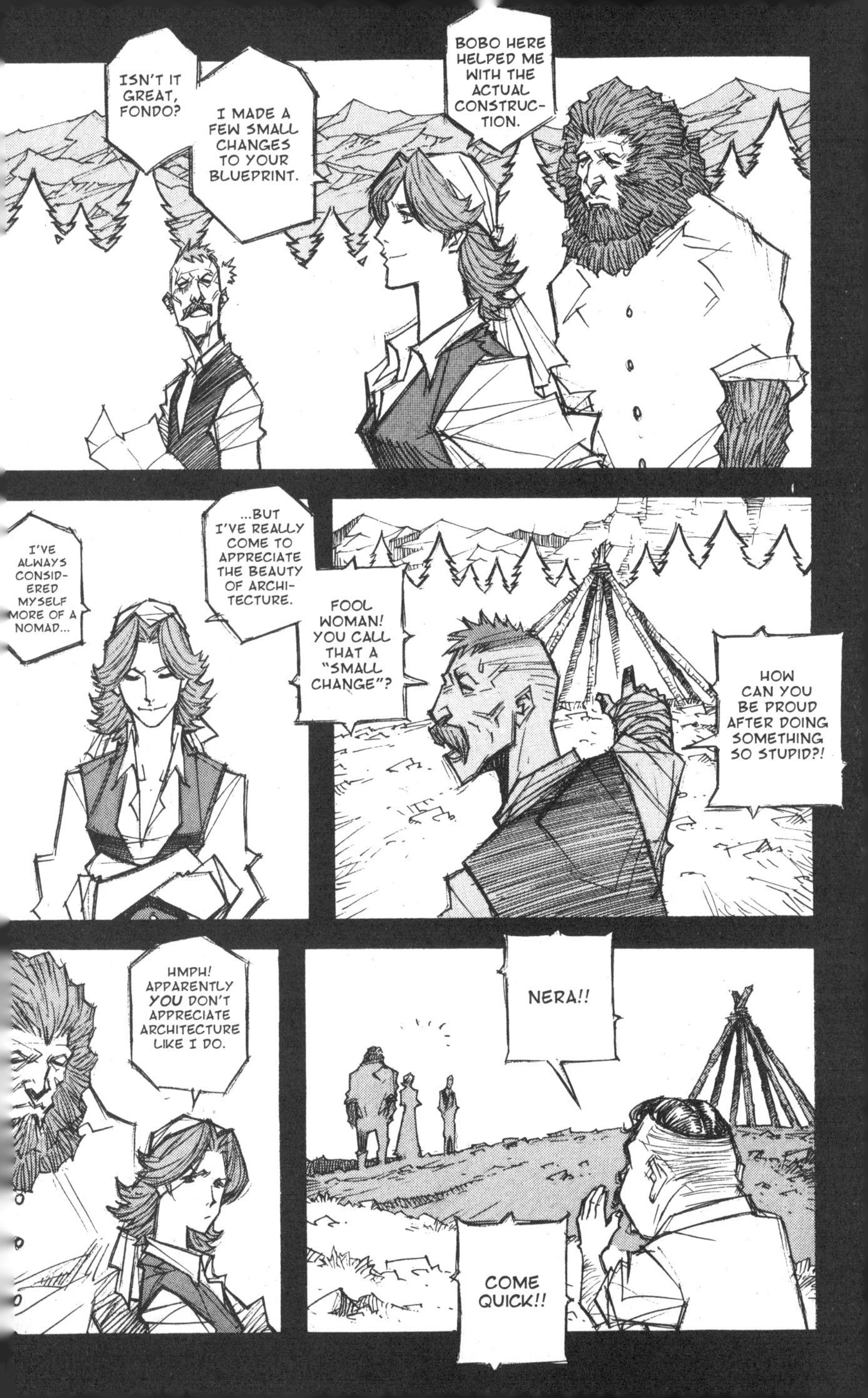
ISN'T IT GREAT, FONDO?
I MADE A FEW SMALL CHANGES TO YOUR BLUEPRINT.
BOBO HERE HELPED ME WITH THE ACTUAL CONSTRUC- TION.
I'VE ALWAYS CONSID- ERED MYSELF MORE OF A NOMAD...
...BUT I'VE REALLY COME TO APPRECIATE THE BEAUTY OF ARCHI- TECTURE.
FOOL WOMAN! YOU CALL THAT A "SMALL CHANGE"?
HOW CAN YOU BE PROUD AFTER DOING SOMETHING SO STUPID?!
HMPH! APPARENTLY YOU DON'T APPRECIATE ARCHITECTURE LIKE I DO.
NERA!!
COME QUICK!!

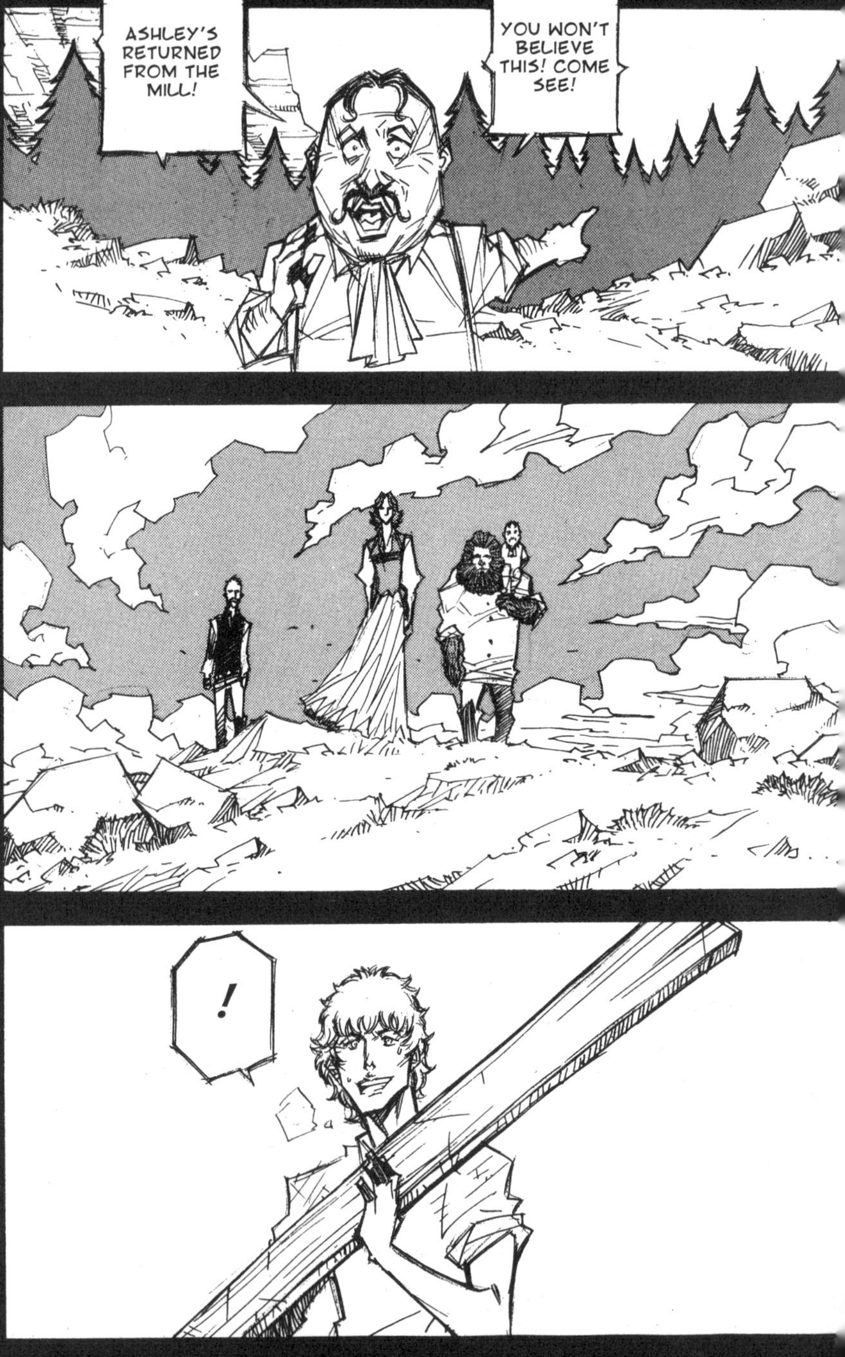
ASHLEY'S RETURNED FROM THE MILL!
YOU WON'T BELIEVE THIS! COME SEE!
!

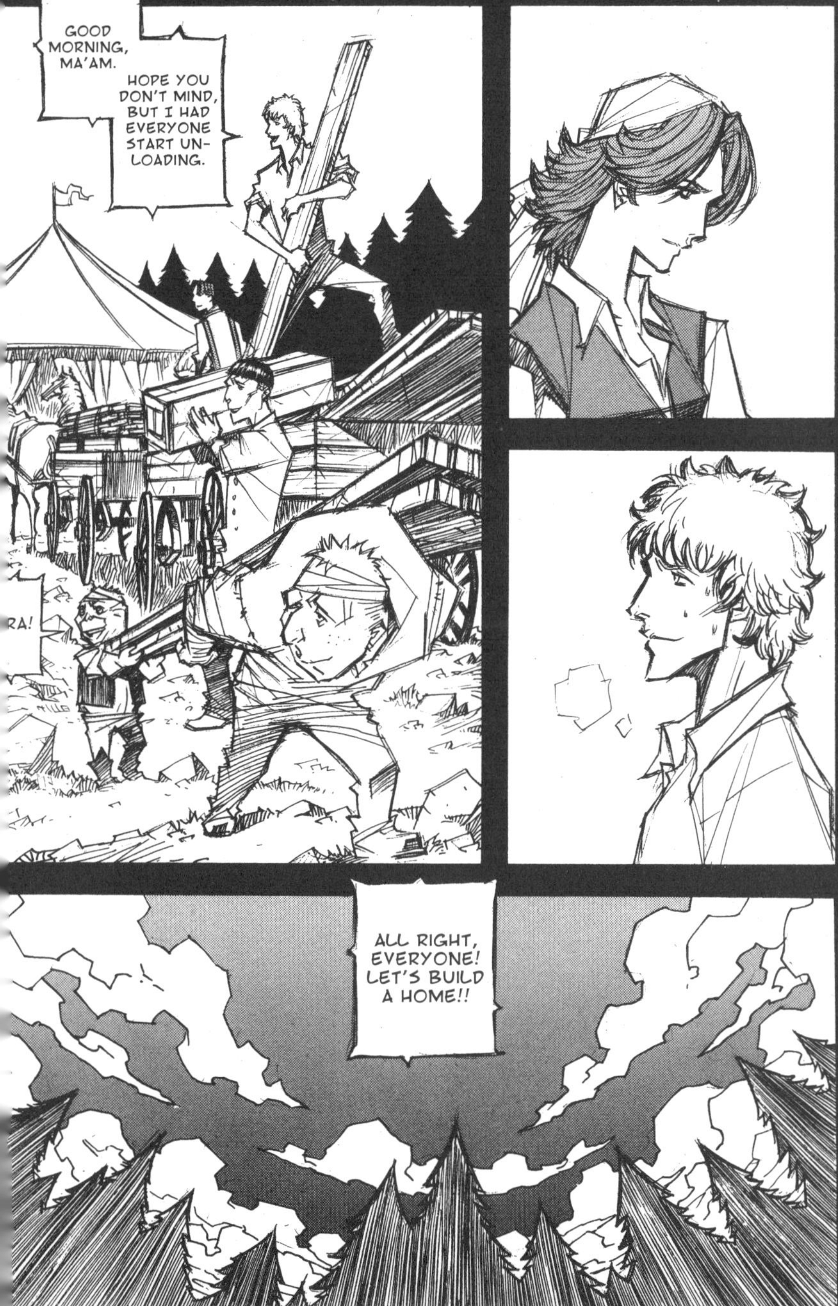
GOOD MORNING, MA'AM.
HOPE YOU DON'T MIND, BUT I HAD EVERYONE START UN-LOADING.
RA!
ALL RIGHT, EVERYONE! LET'S BUILD A HOME!!

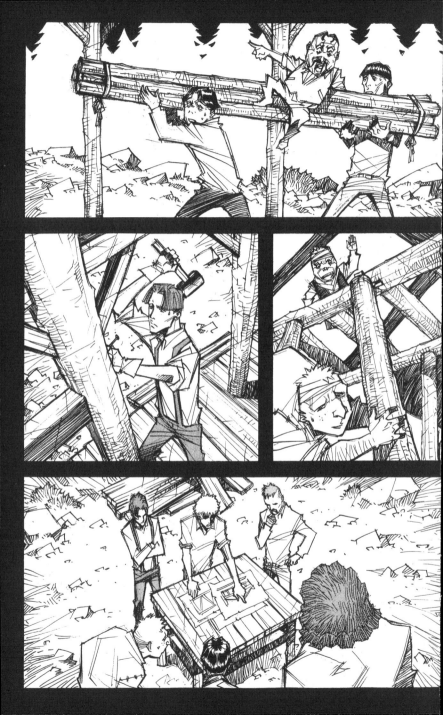

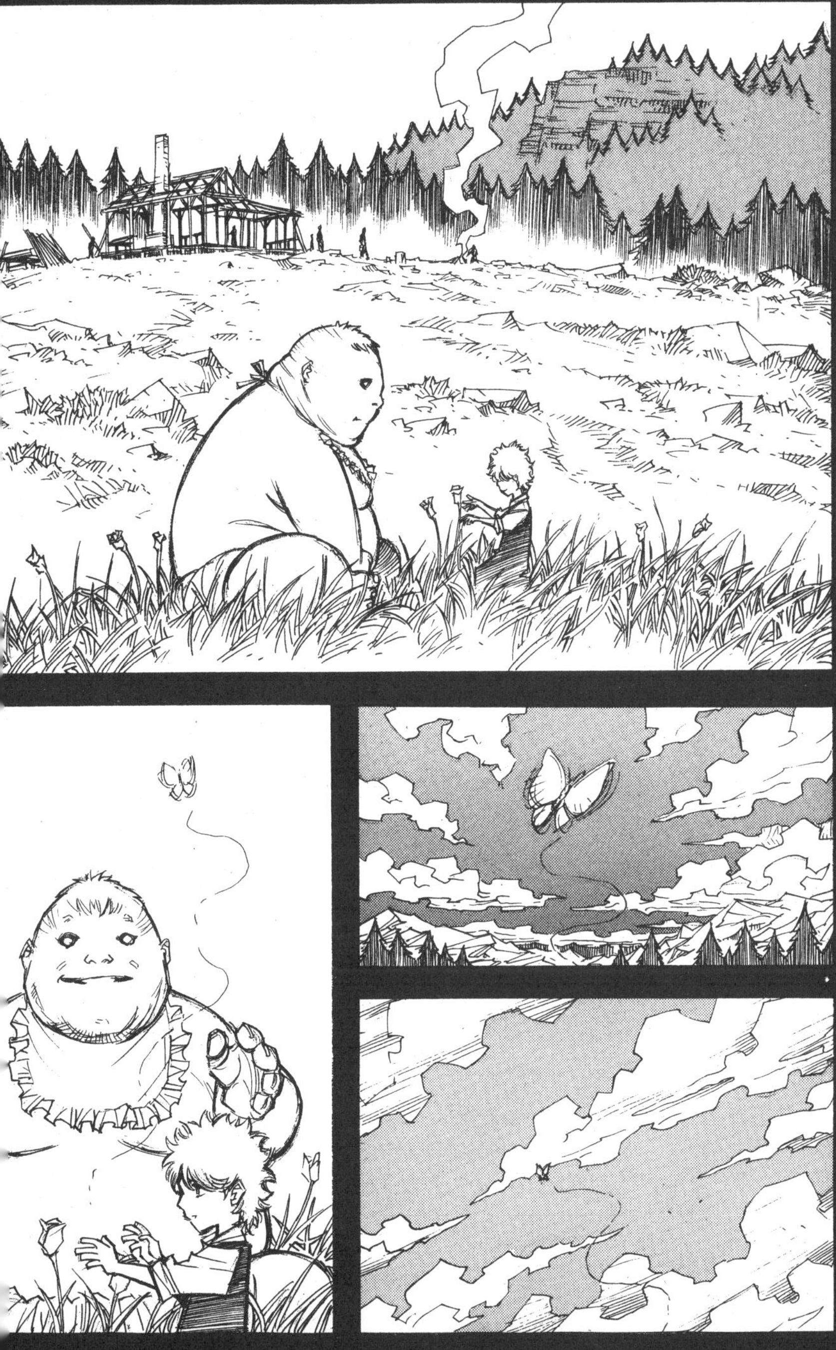

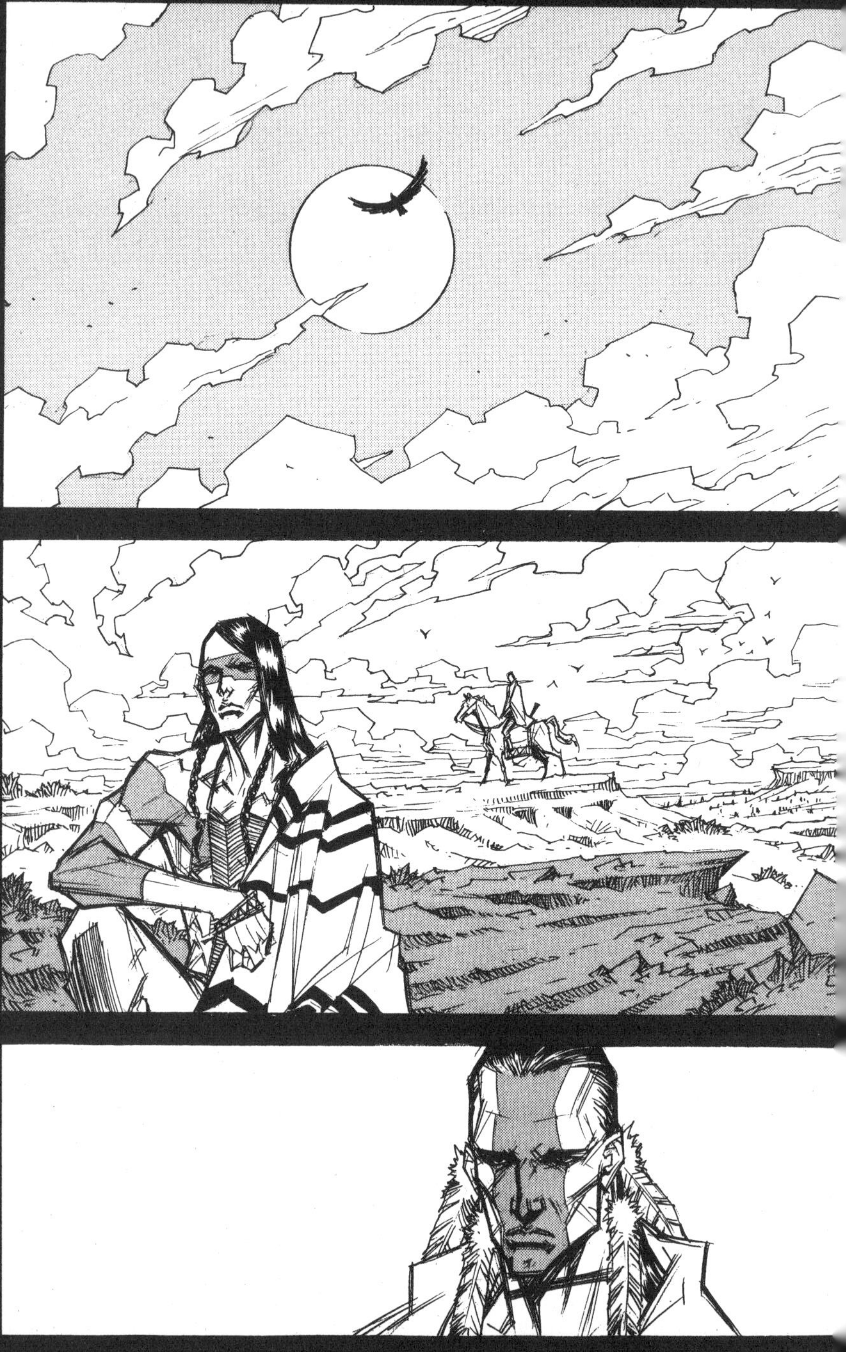

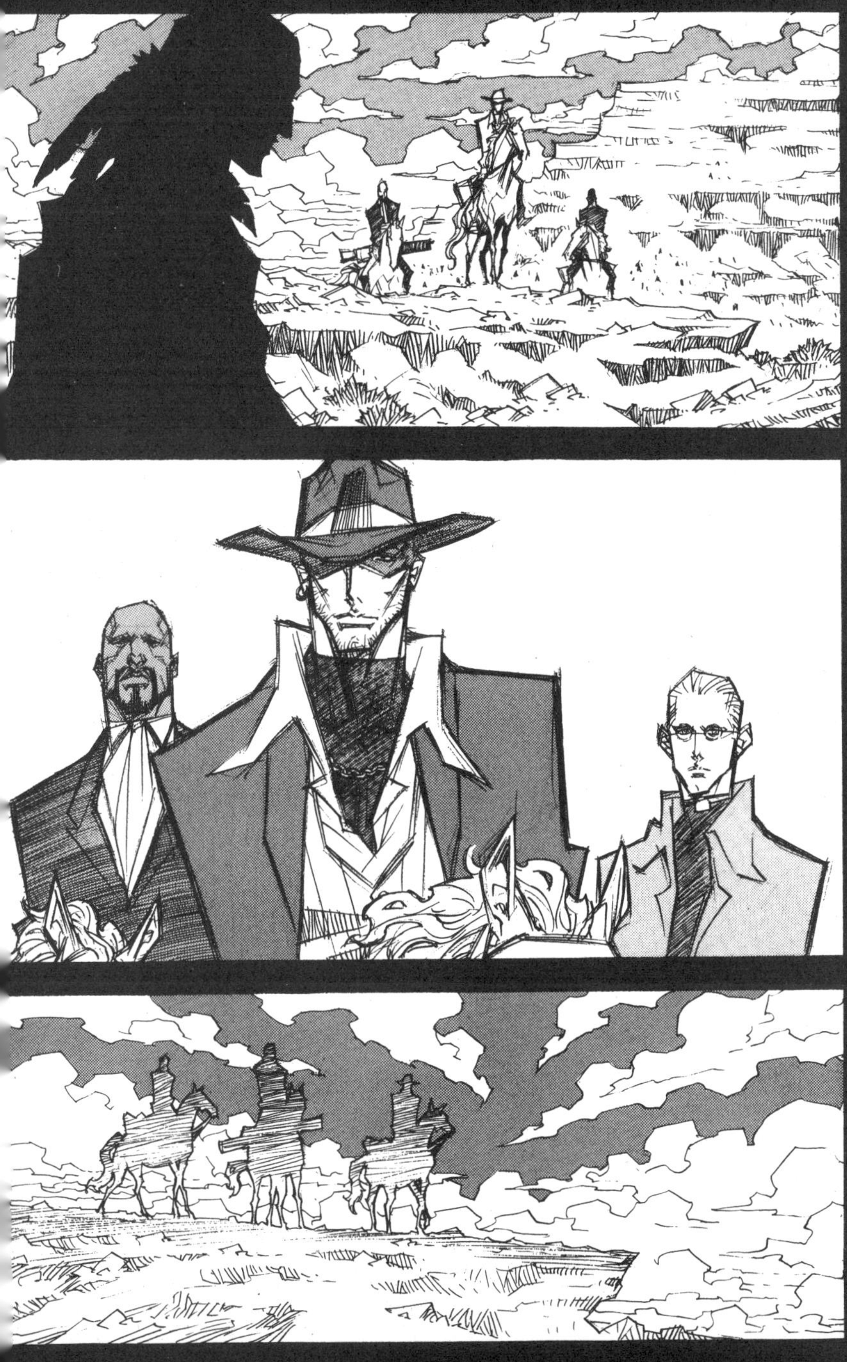

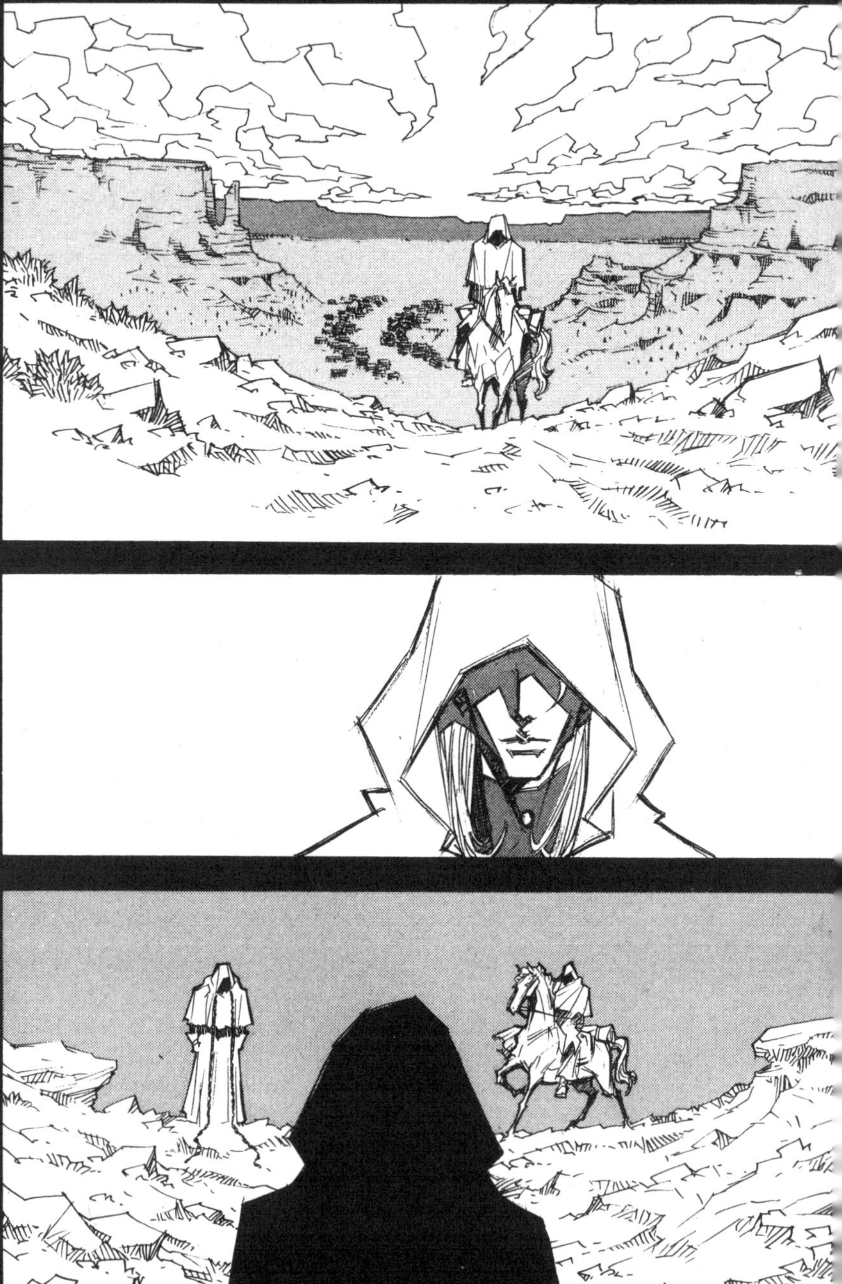

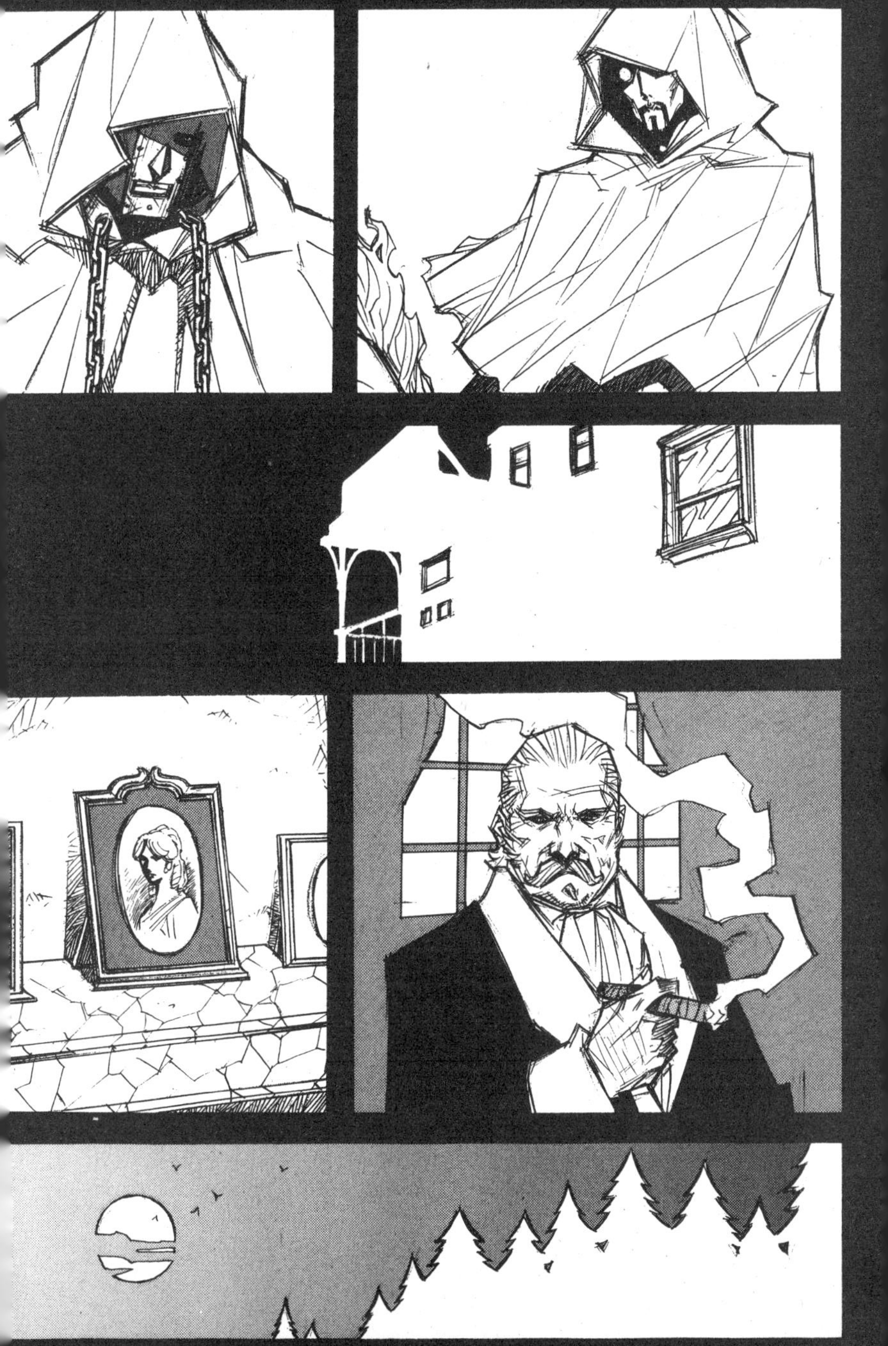

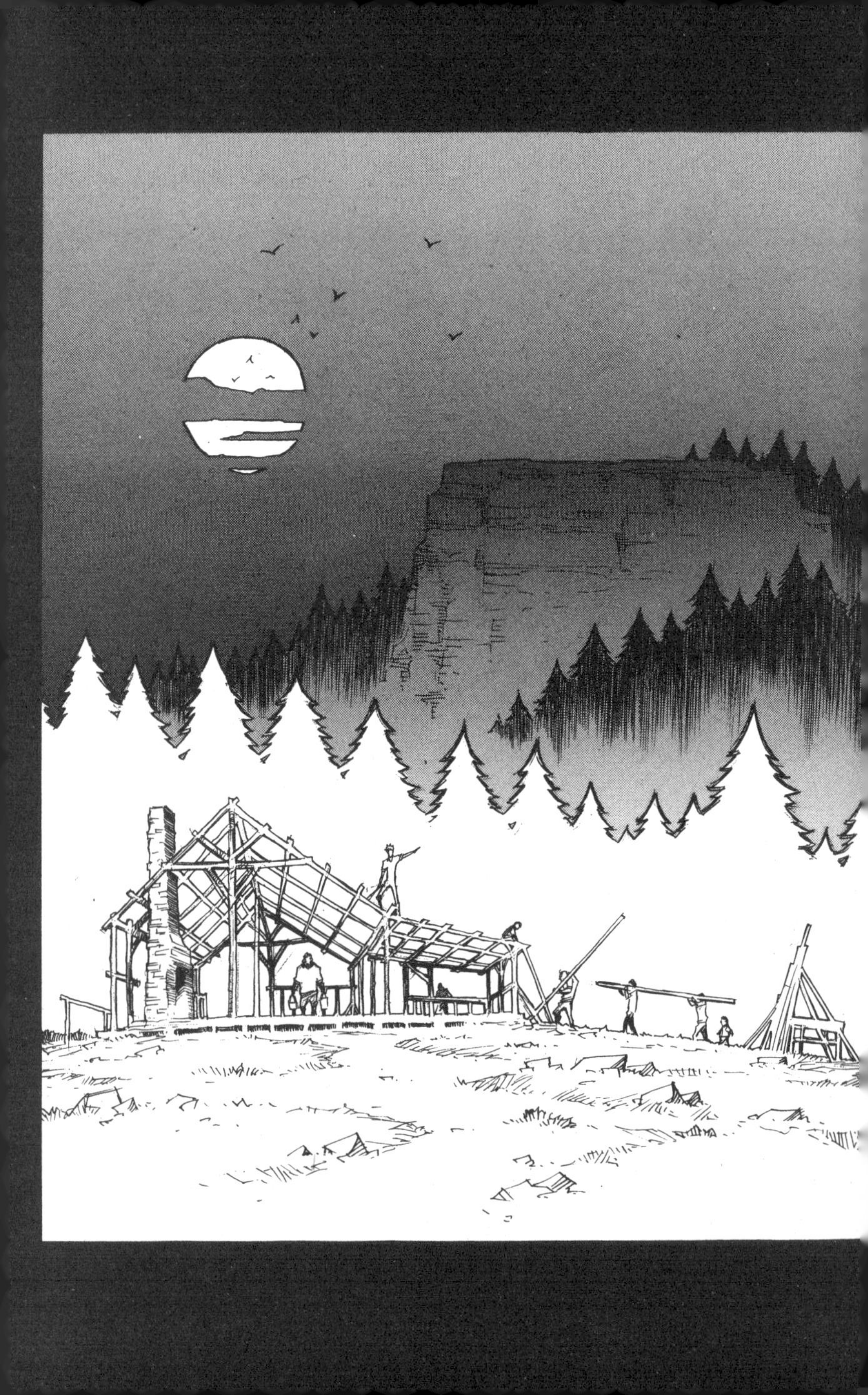

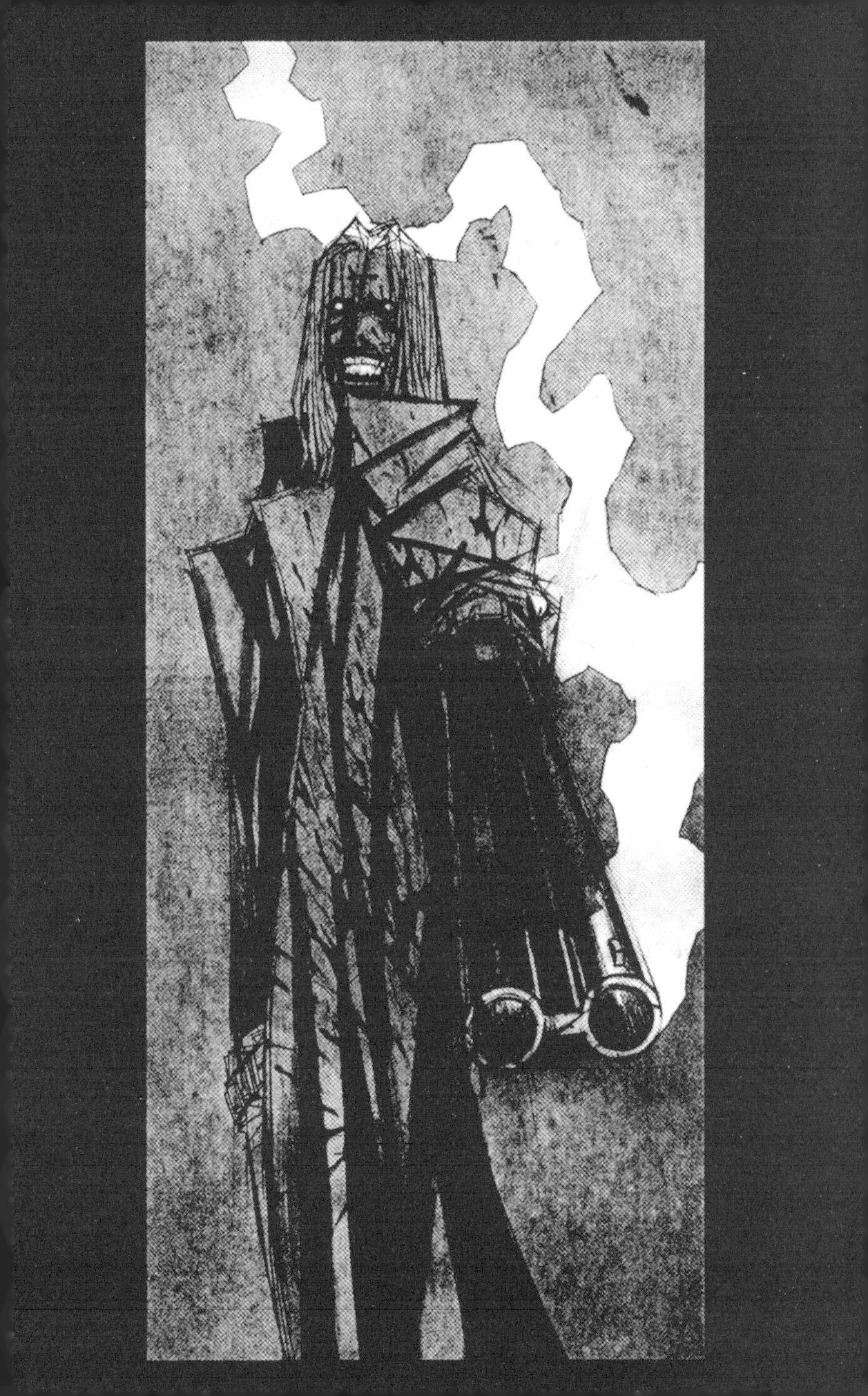

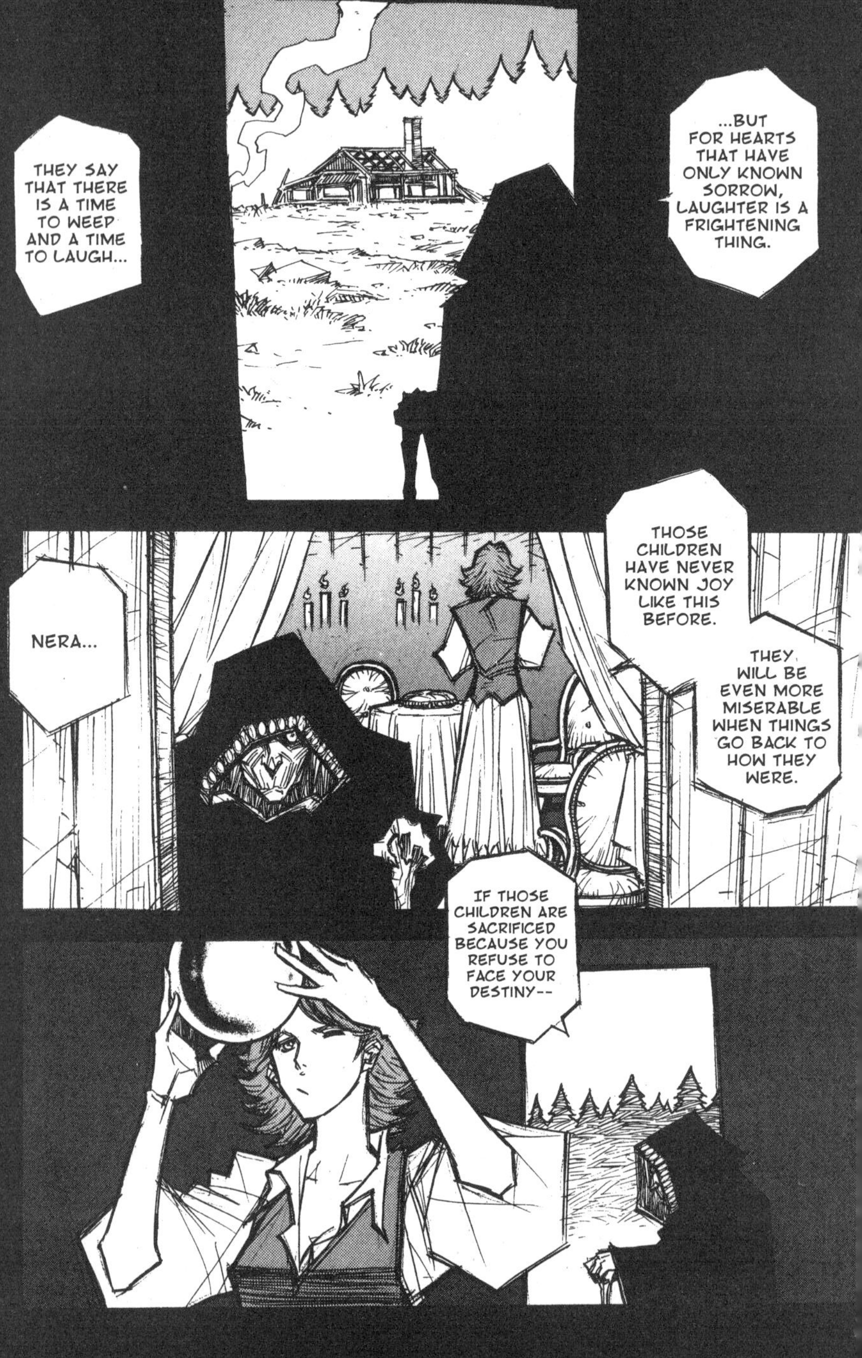
THEY SAY THAT THERE IS A TIME TO WEEP AND A TIME TO LAUGH...
...BUT FOR HEARTS THAT HAVE ONLY KNOWN SORROW, LAUGHTER IS A FRIGHTENING THING.
NERA...
THOSE CHILDREN HAVE NEVER KNOWN JOY LIKE THIS BEFORE.
THEY WILL BE EVEN MORE MISERABLE WHEN THINGS GO BACK TO HOW THEY WERE.
IF THOSE CHILDREN ARE SACRIFICED BECAUSE YOU REFUSE TO FACE YOUR DESTINY--

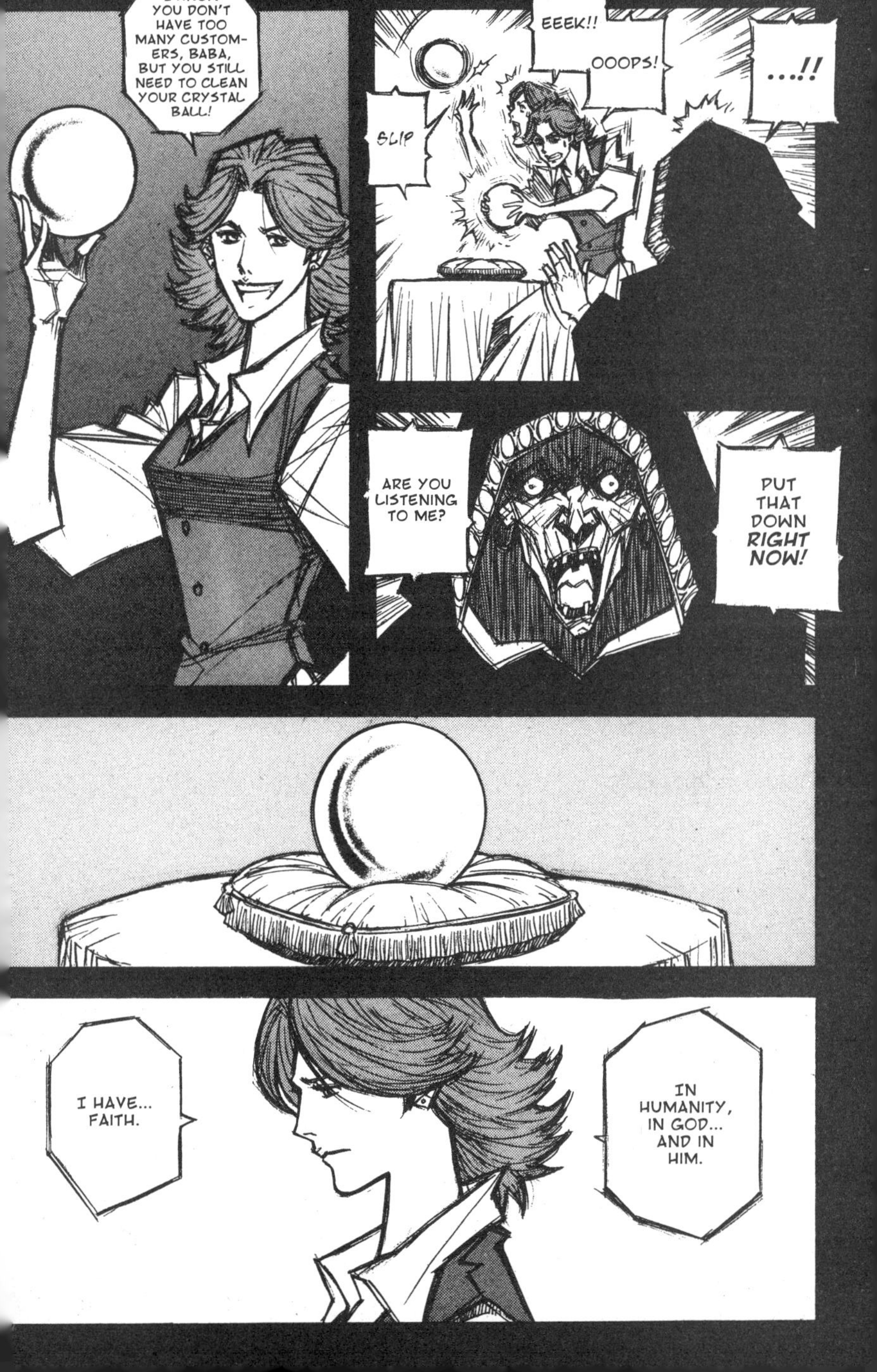
I KNOW YOU DON'T HAVE TOO MANY CUSTOMERS, BABA, BUT YOU STILL NEED TO CLEAN YOUR CRYSTAL BALL!
EEEK!!
SLIP
OOOPS!
...!!
ARE YOU LISTENING TO ME?
PUT THAT DOWN RIGHT NOW!
I HAVE... FAITH.
IN HUMANITY, IN GOD... AND IN HIM.

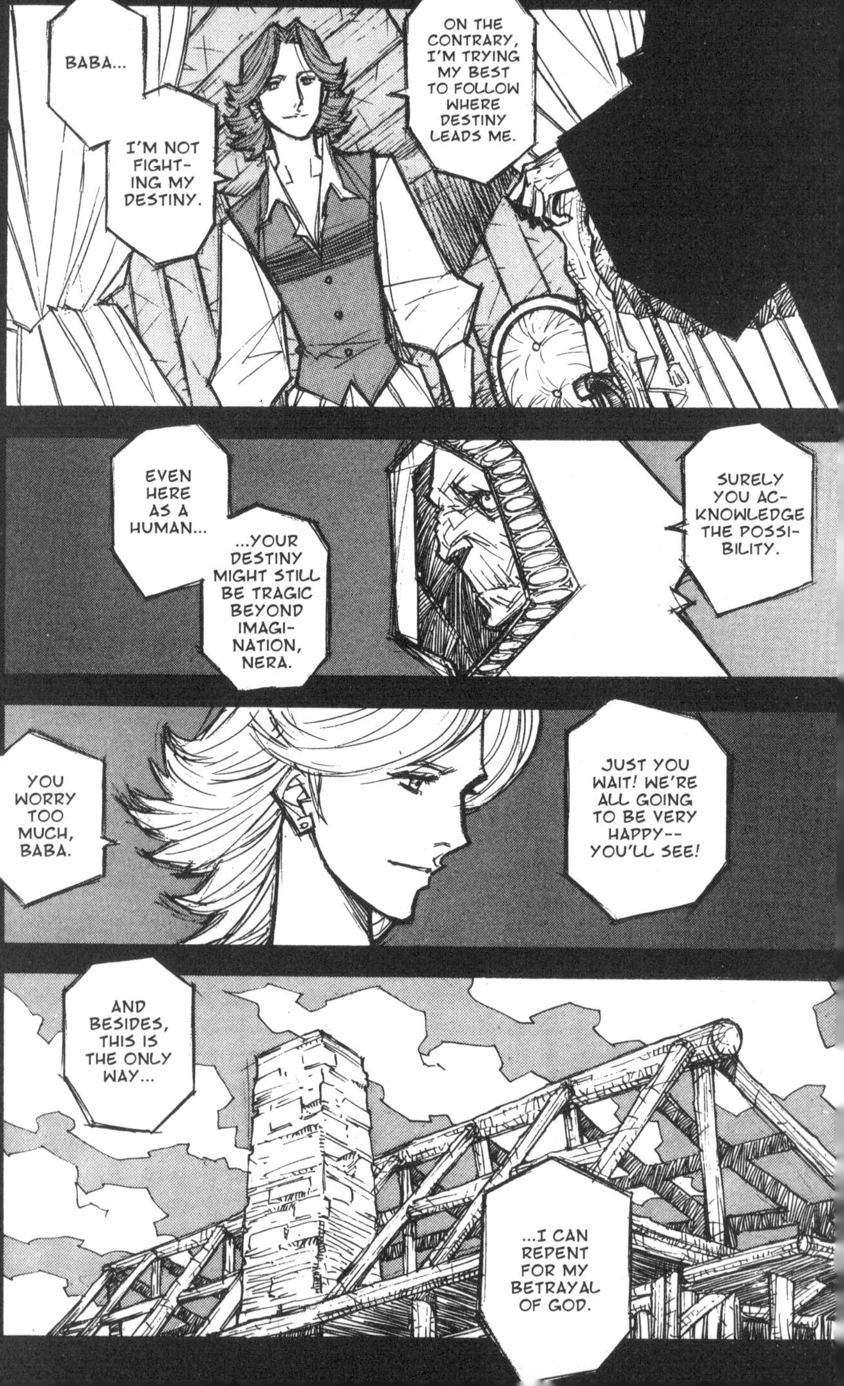
BABA...
I'M NOT FIGHTING MY DESTINY.
ON THE CONTRARY, I'M TRYING MY BEST TO FOLLOW WHERE DESTINY LEADS ME.
EVEN HERE AS A HUMAN...
...YOUR DESTINY MIGHT STILL BE TRAGIC BEYOND IMAGINATION, NERA.
SURELY YOU ACKNOWLEDGE THE POSSIBILITY.
YOU WORRY TOO MUCH, BABA.
JUST YOU WAIT! WE'RE ALL GOING TO BE VERY HAPPY-- YOU'LL SEE!
AND BESIDES, THIS IS THE ONLY WAY...
...I CAN REPENT FOR MY BETRAYAL OF GOD.

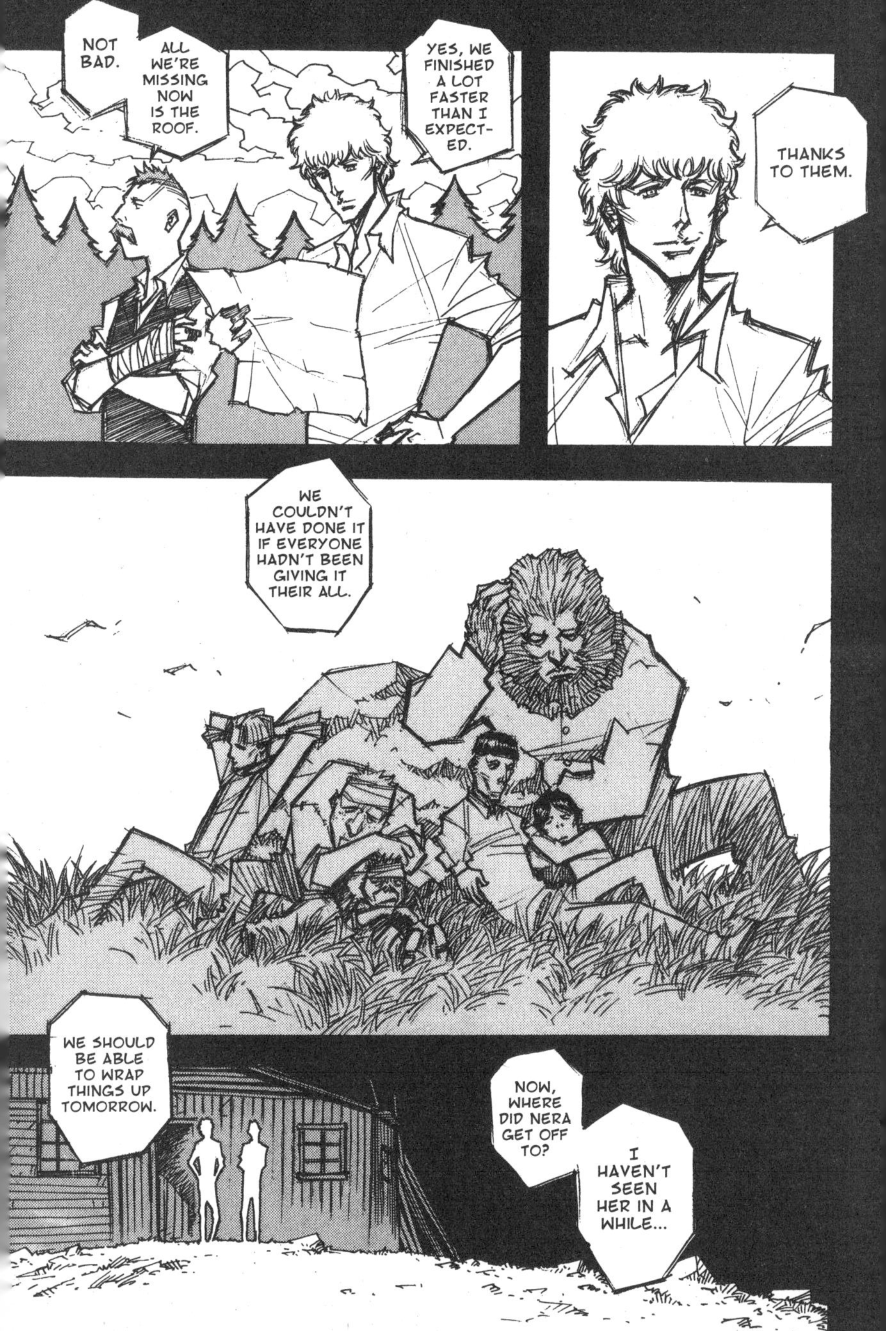
NOT BAD.
ALL WE'RE MISSING NOW IS THE ROOF.
YES, WE FINISHED A LOT FASTER THAN I EXPECTED.
THANKS TO THEM.
WE COULDN'T HAVE DONE IT IF EVERYONE HADN'T BEEN GIVING IT THEIR ALL.
WE SHOULD BE ABLE TO WRAP THINGS UP TOMORROW.
NOW, WHERE DID NERA GET OFF TO?
I HAVEN'T SEEN HER IN A WHILE...

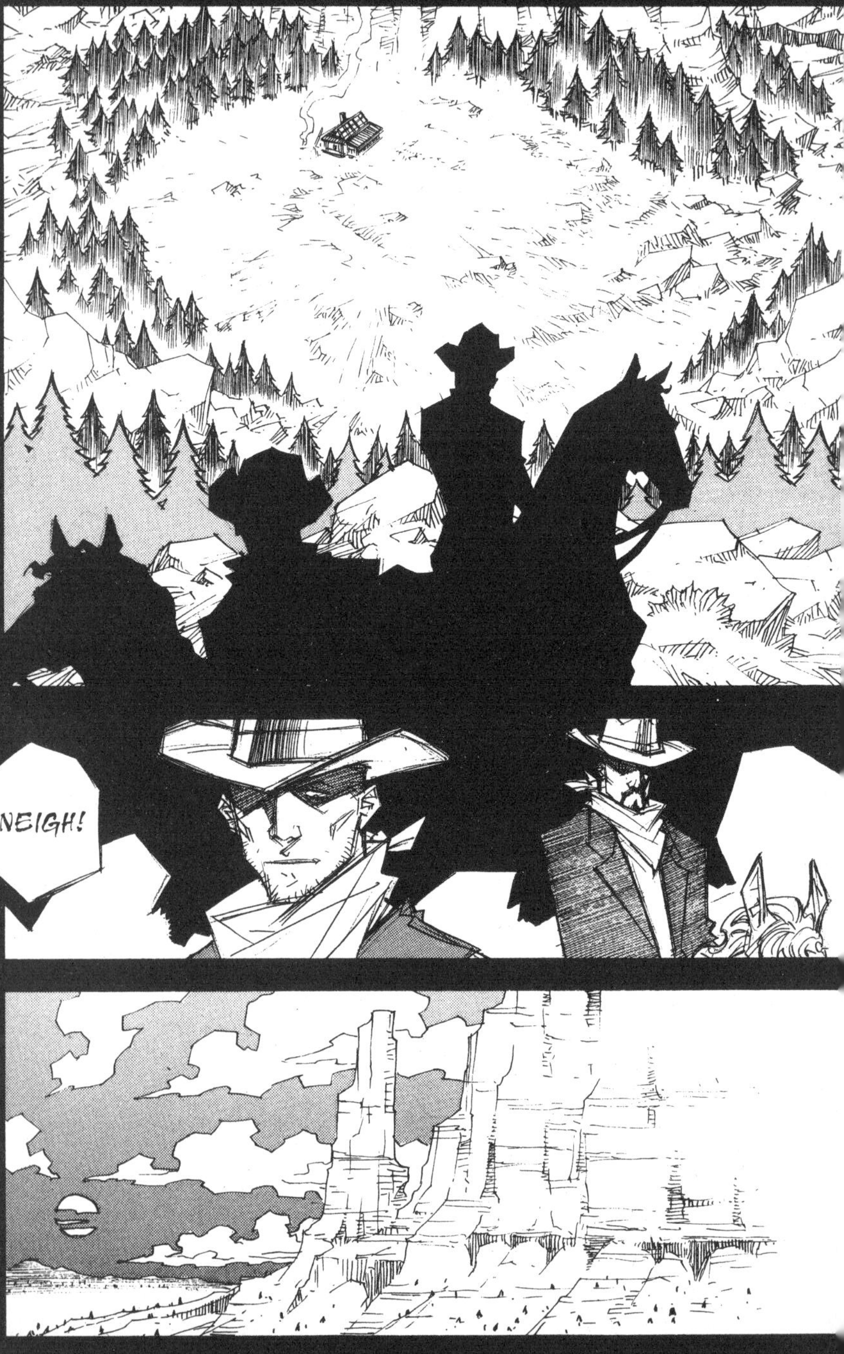
NEIGH!

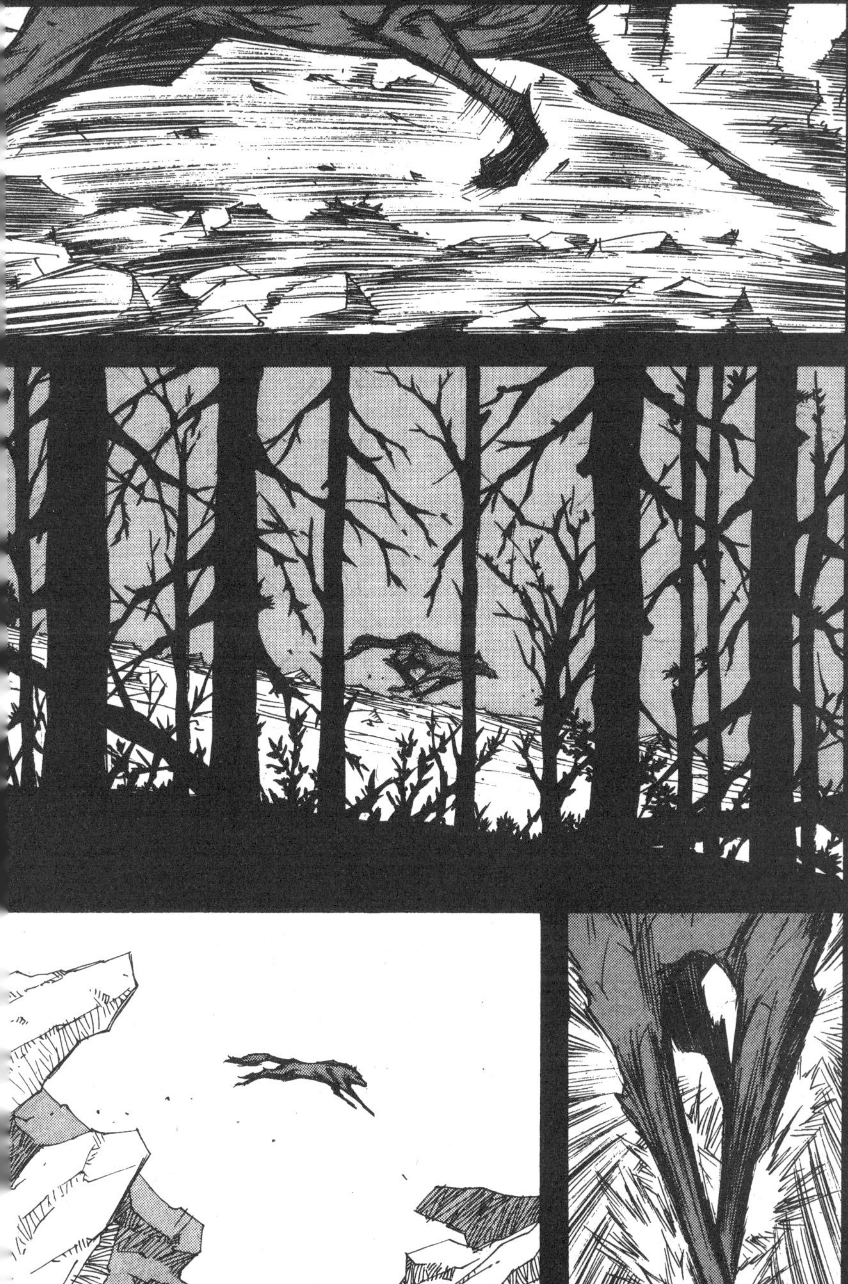

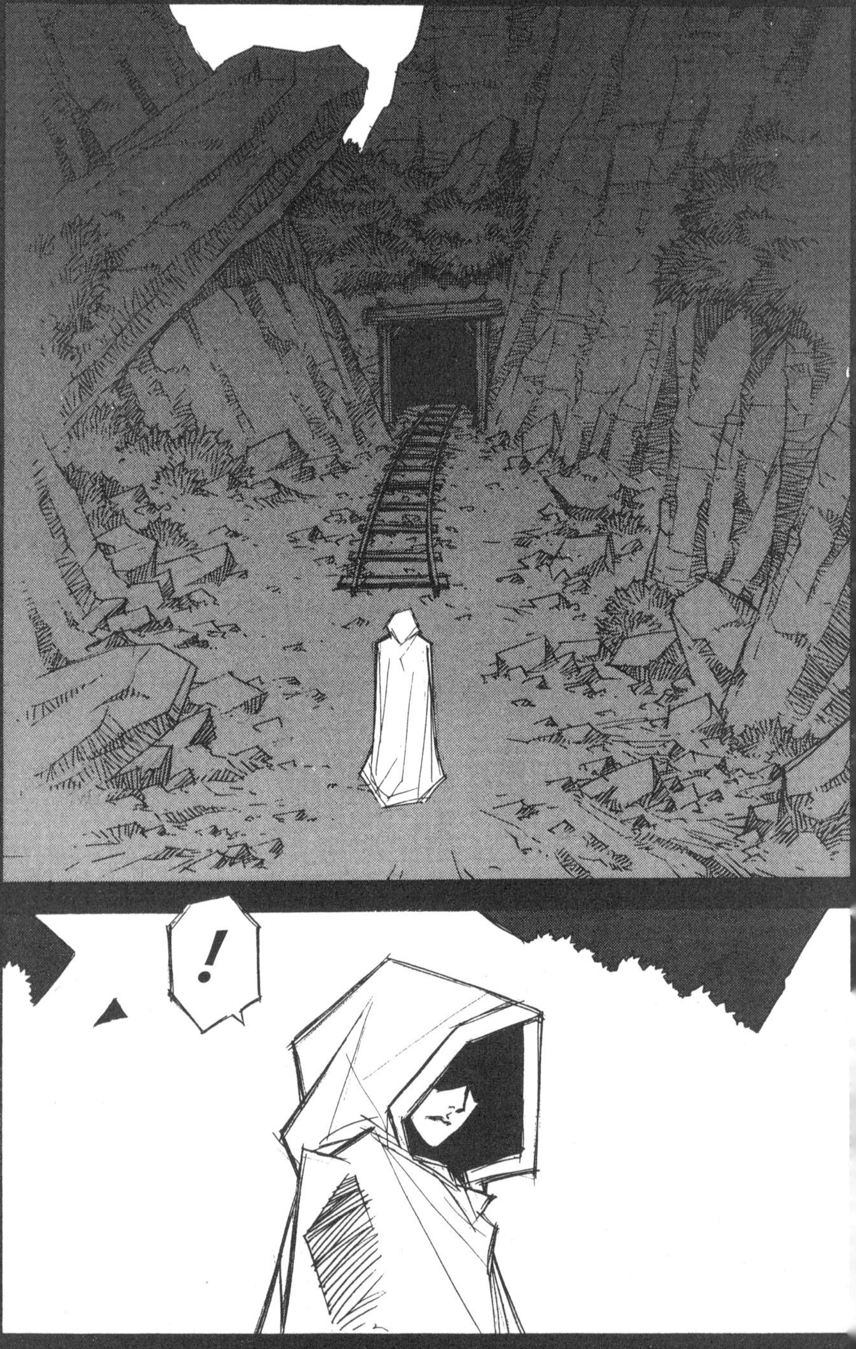
!

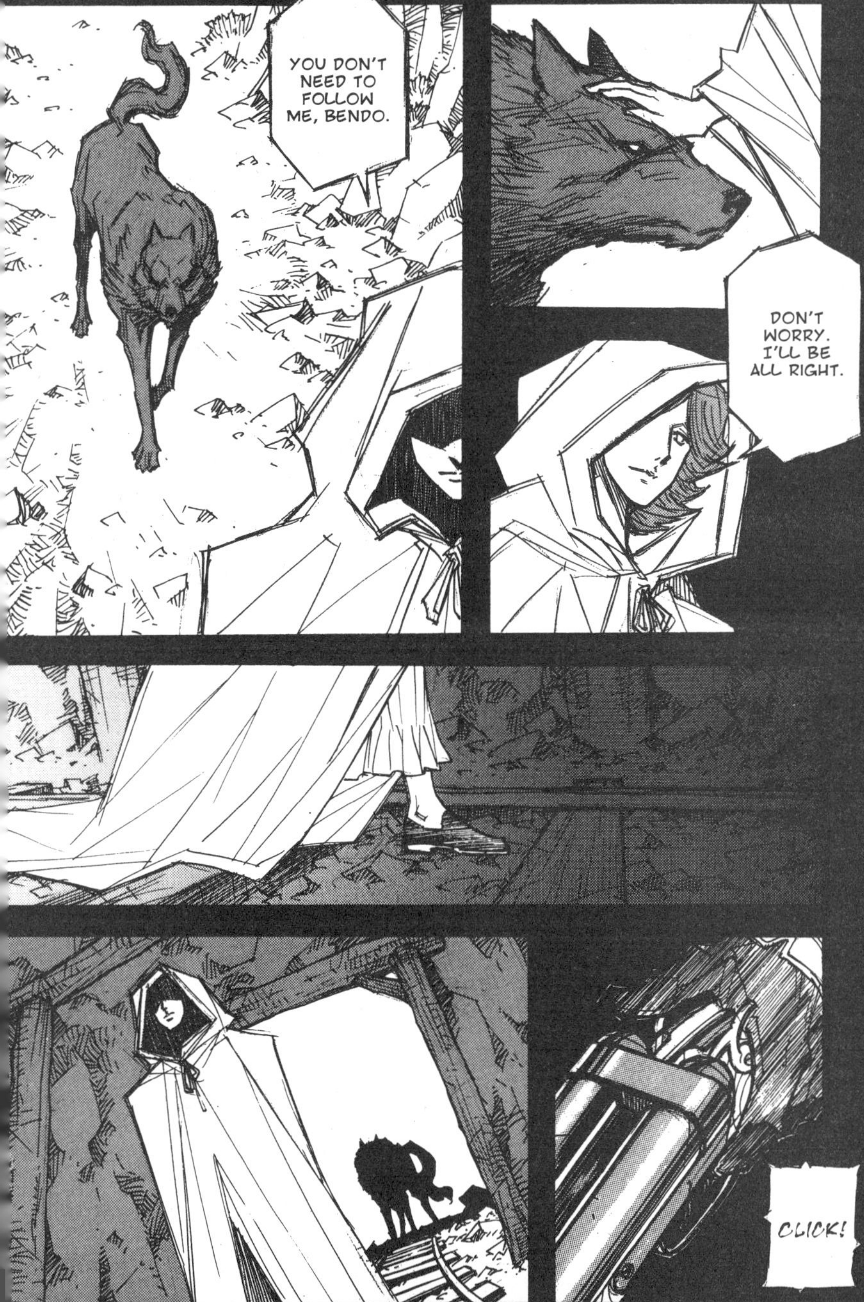
YOU DON'T NEED TO FOLLOW ME, BENDO.
DON'T WORRY. I'LL BE ALL RIGHT.
CLICK!

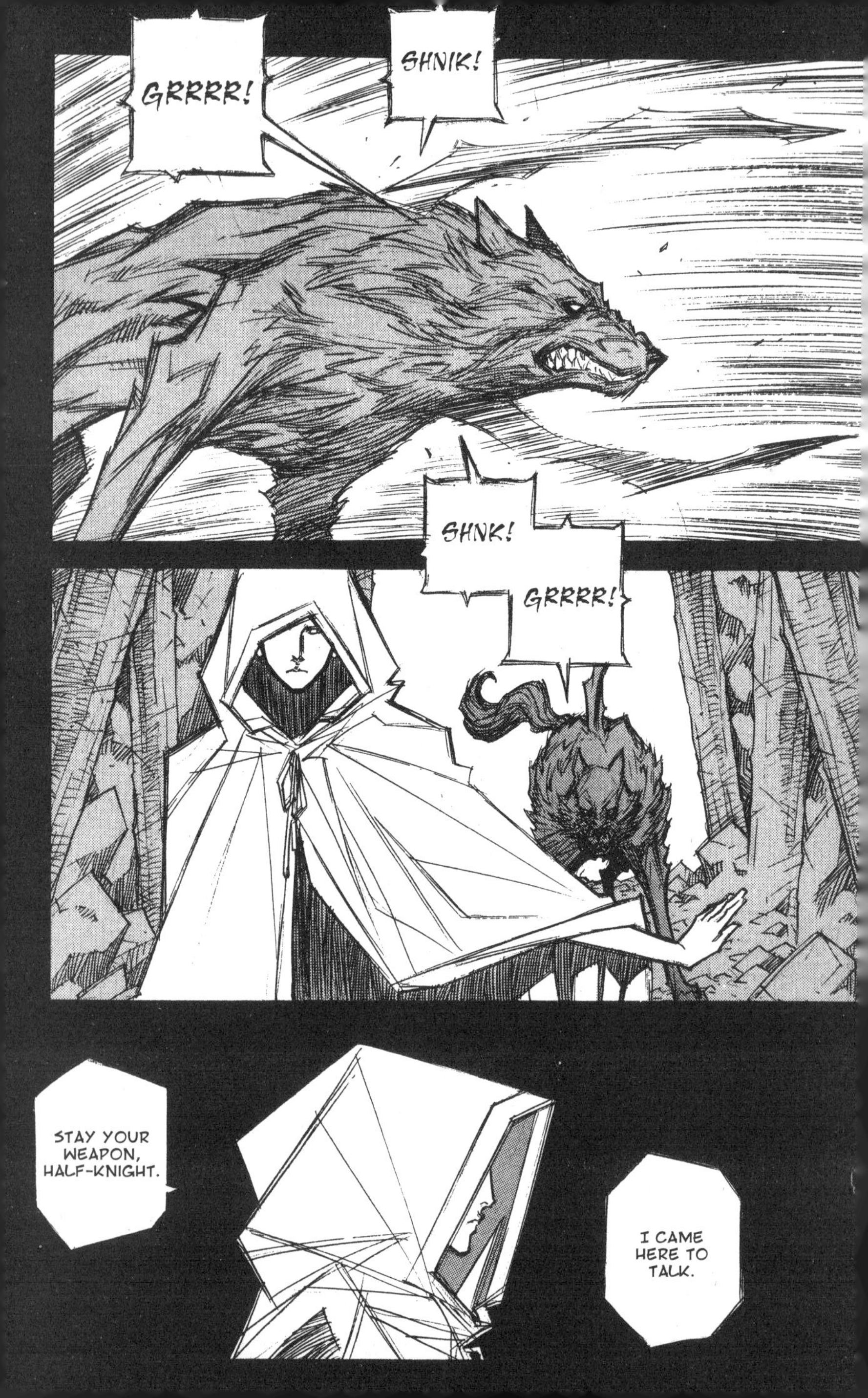
GRRRR!
SHNIK!
SHNK!
GRRRR!
STAY YOUR WEAPON, HALF-KNIGHT.
I CAME HERE TO TALK.

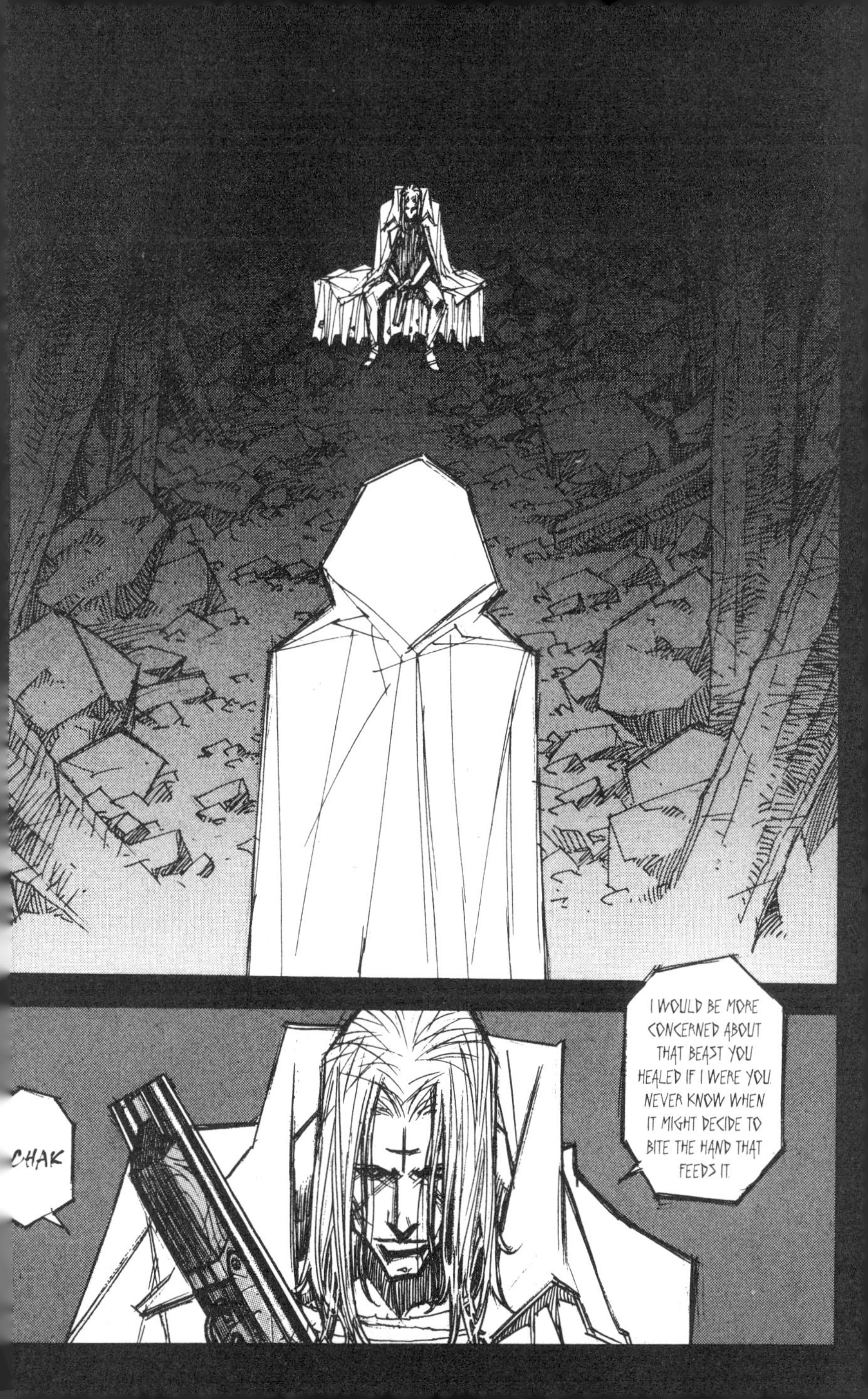
CHAK
I WOULD BE MORE CONCERNED ABOUT THAT BEAST YOU HEALED IF I WERE YOU. NEVER KNOW WHEN IT MIGHT DECIDE TO BITE THE HAND THAT FEEDS IT.

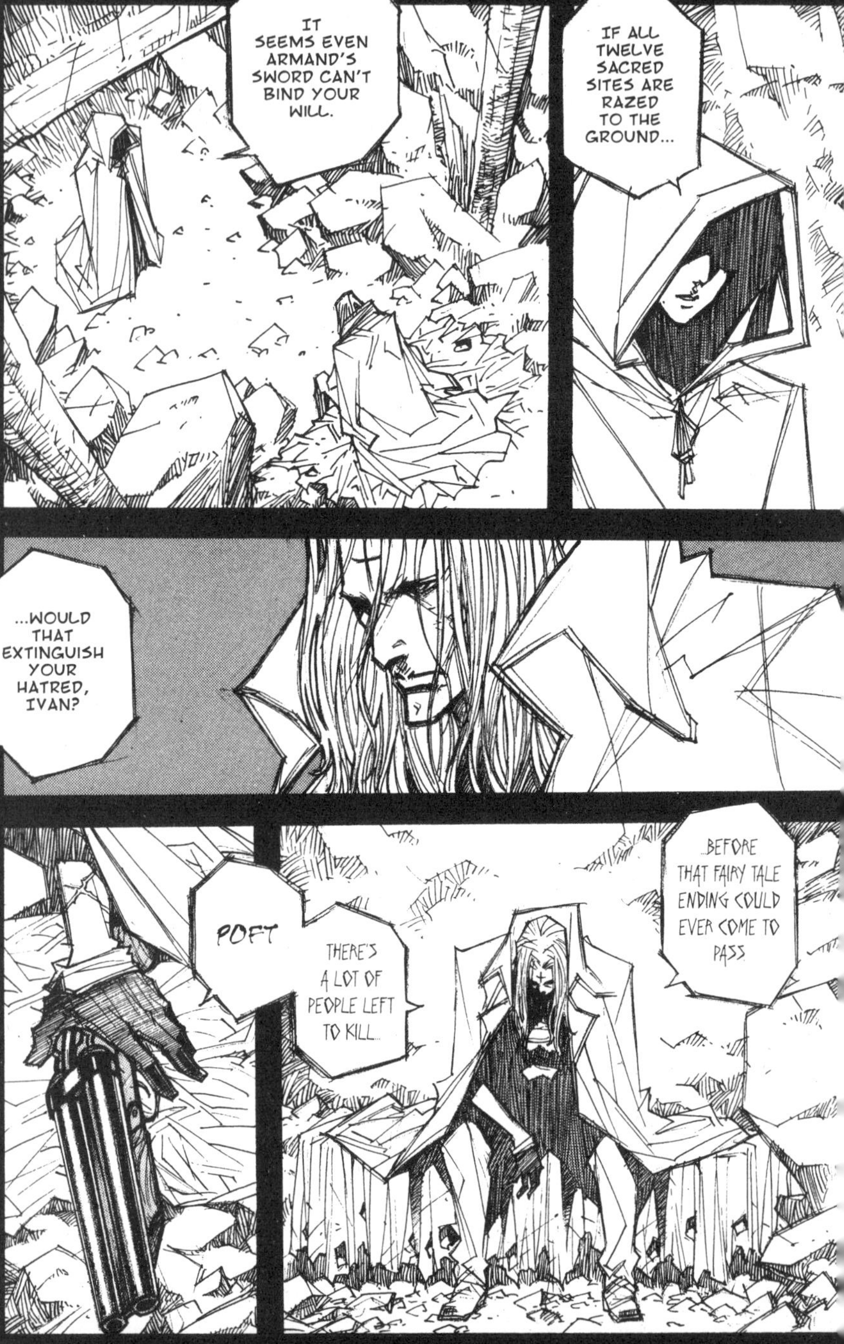
IT SEEMS EVEN ARMAND'S SWORD CAN'T BIND YOUR WILL.
IF ALL TWELVE SACRED SITES ARE RAZED TO THE GROUND...
...WOULD THAT EXTINGUISH YOUR HATRED, IVAN?
POFT
THERE'S A LOT OF PEOPLE LEFT TO KILL...
...BEFORE THAT FAIRY TALE ENDING COULD EVER COME TO PASS

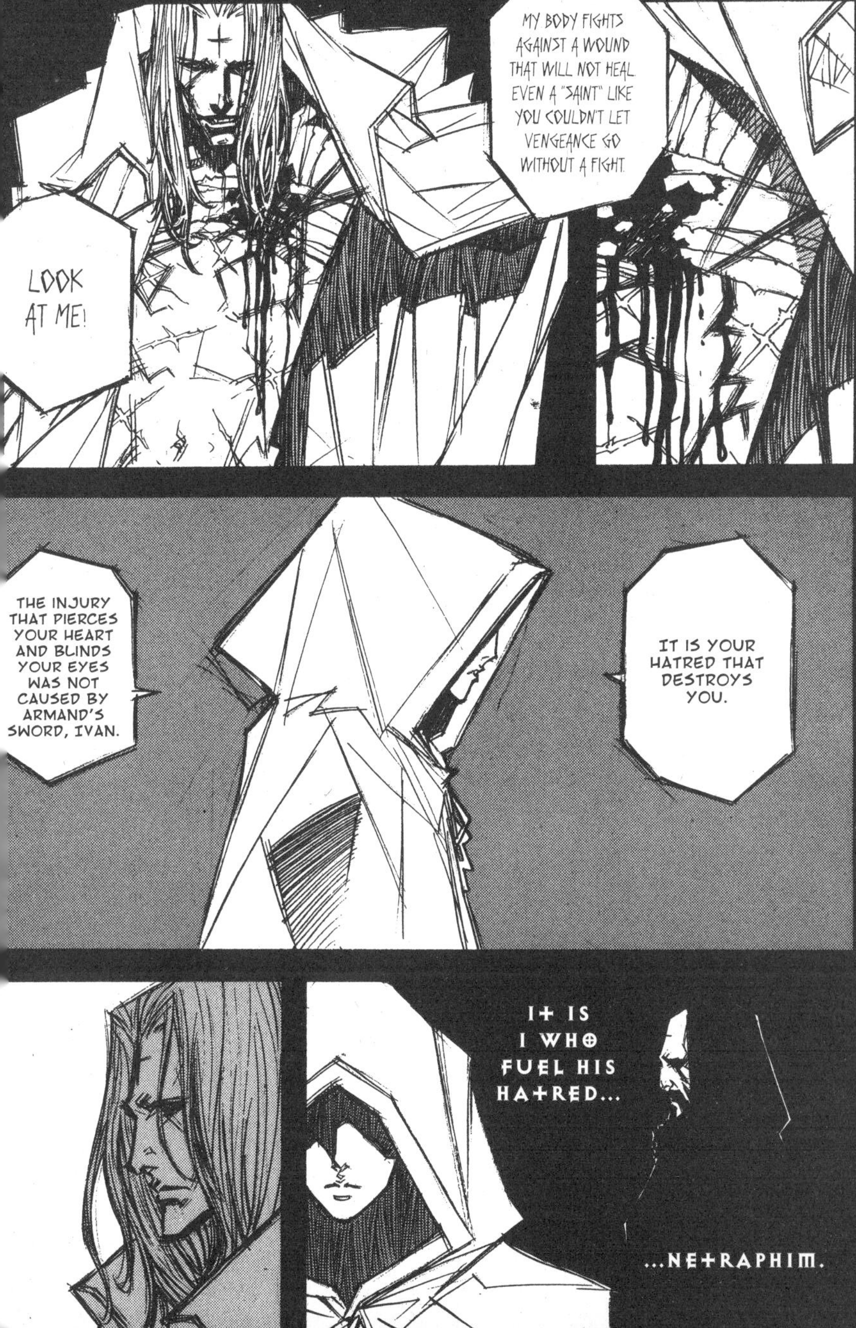
LOOK AT ME!
MY BODY FIGHTS AGAINST A WOUND THAT WILL NOT HEAL. EVEN A "SAINT" LIKE YOU COULDN'T LET VENGEANCE GO WITHOUT A FIGHT.
THE INJURY THAT PIERCES YOUR HEART AND BLINDS YOUR EYES WAS NOT CAUSED BY ARMAND'S SWORD, IVAN.
IT IS YOUR HATRED THAT DESTROYS YOU.
IT IS I WHO FUEL HIS HATRED...
...NETRAPHIM.

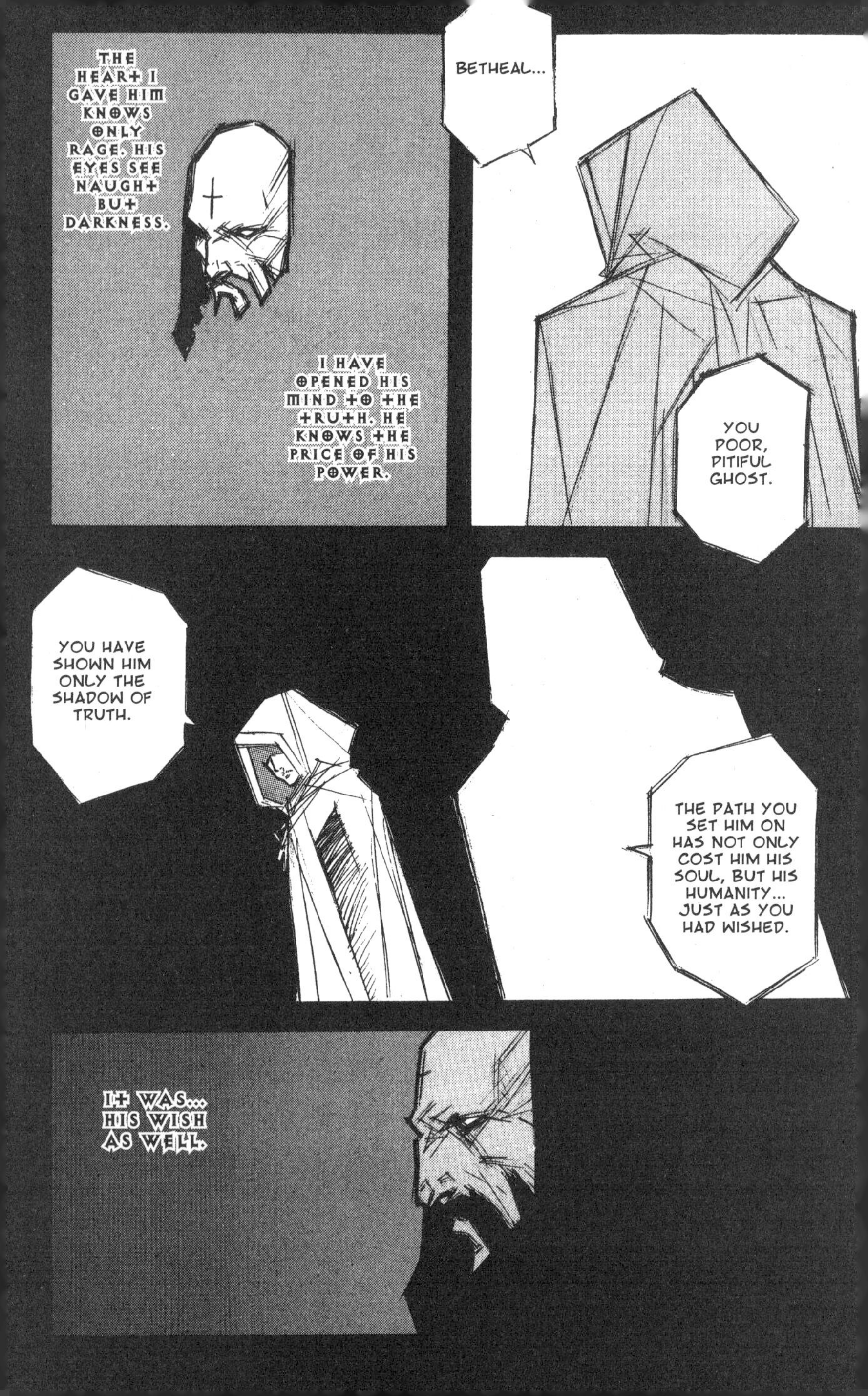
THE HEART I GAVE HIM KNOWS ONLY RAGE. HIS EYES SEE NAUGHT BUT DARKNESS.
I HAVE OPENED HIS MIND TO THE TRUTH. HE KNOWS THE PRICE OF HIS POWER.
BETHEAL...
YOU POOR, PITIFUL GHOST.
YOU HAVE SHOWN HIM ONLY THE SHADOW OF TRUTH.
THE PATH YOU SET HIM ON HAS NOT ONLY COST HIM HIS SOUL, BUT HIS HUMANITY... JUST AS YOU HAD WISHED.
IT WAS... HIS WISH AS WELL.

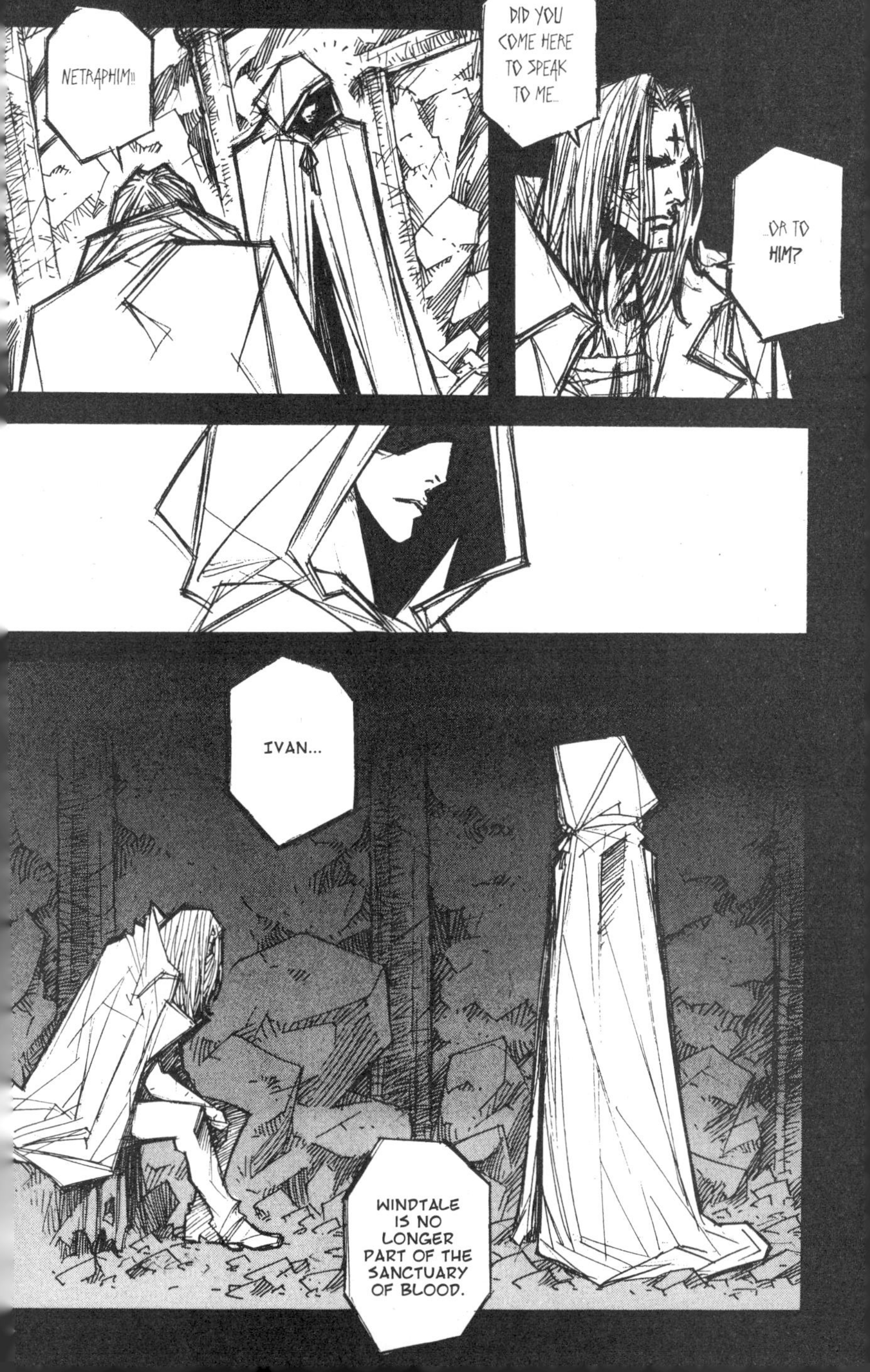
NETRAPHIM!!
DID YOU COME HERE TO SPEAK TO ME...
...OR TO HIM?
IVAN...
WINDTALE IS NO LONGER PART OF THE SANCTUARY OF BLOOD.

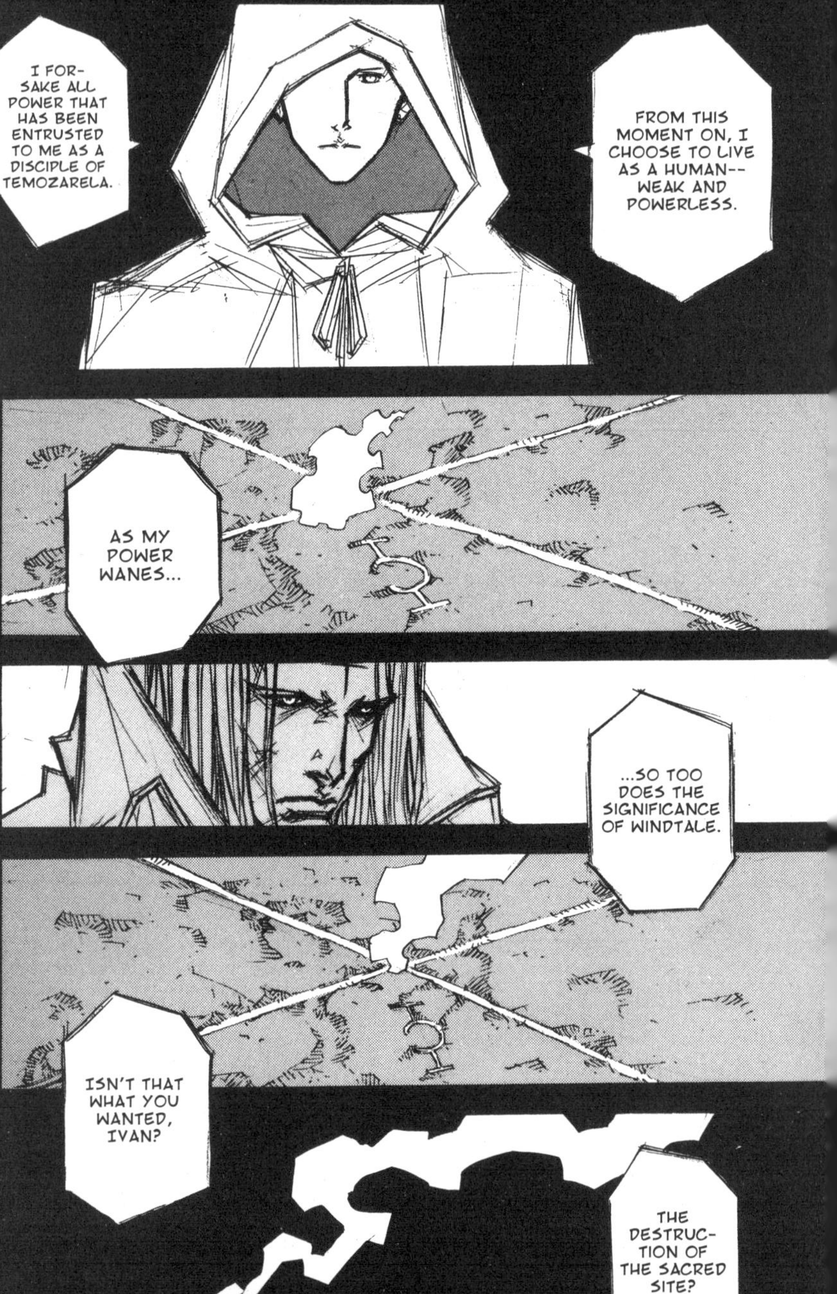
I FOR-SAKE ALL POWER THAT HAS BEEN ENTRUSTED TO ME AS A DISCIPLE OF TEMOZARELA.
FROM THIS MOMENT ON, I CHOOSE TO LIVE AS A HUMAN--WEAK AND POWERLESS.
AS MY POWER WANES...
...SO TOO DOES THE SIGNIFICANCE OF WINDTALE.
ISN'T THAT WHAT YOU WANTED, IVAN?
THE DESTRUC-TION OF THE SACRED SITE?

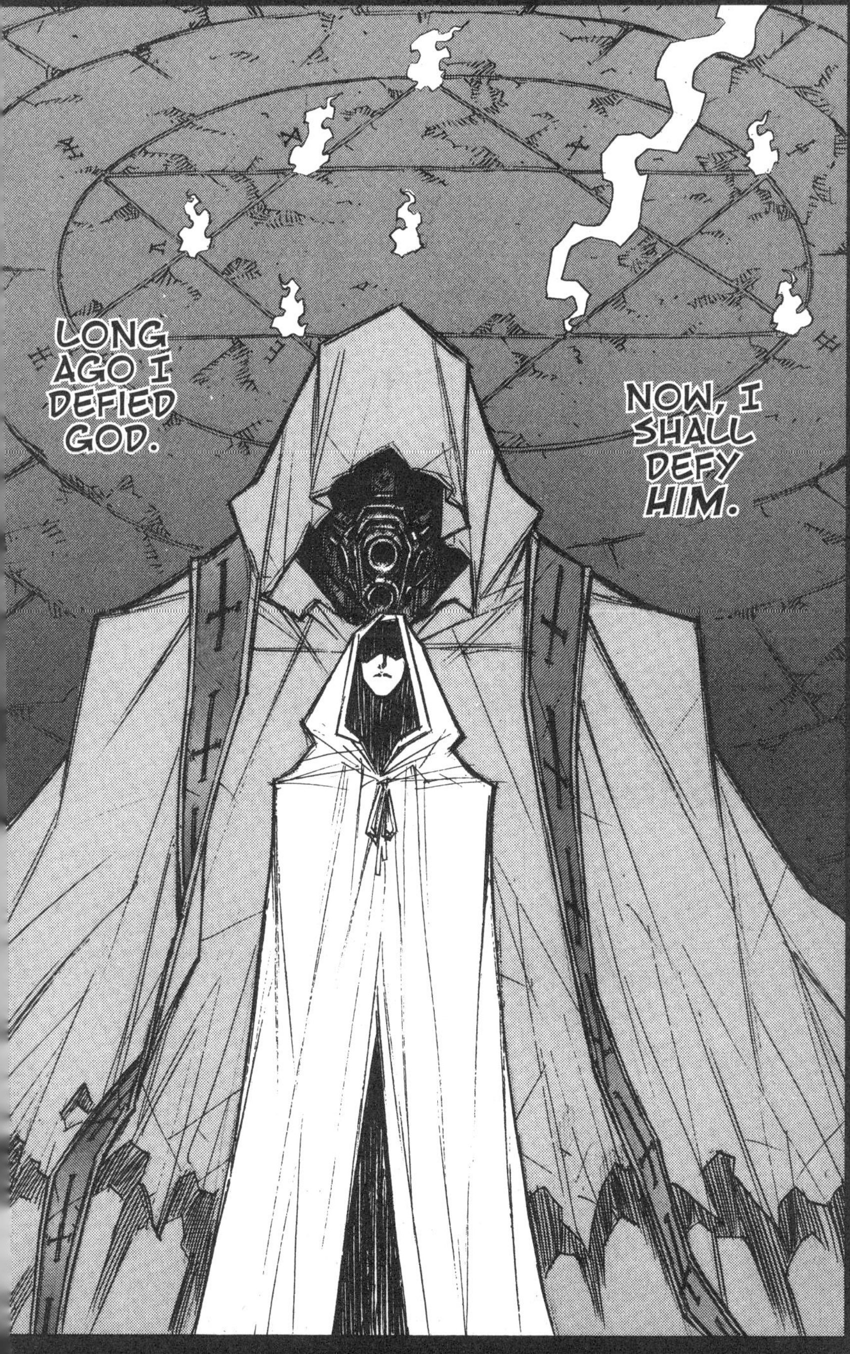
LONG AGO I DEFIED GOD.
NOW, I SHALL DEFY HIM.

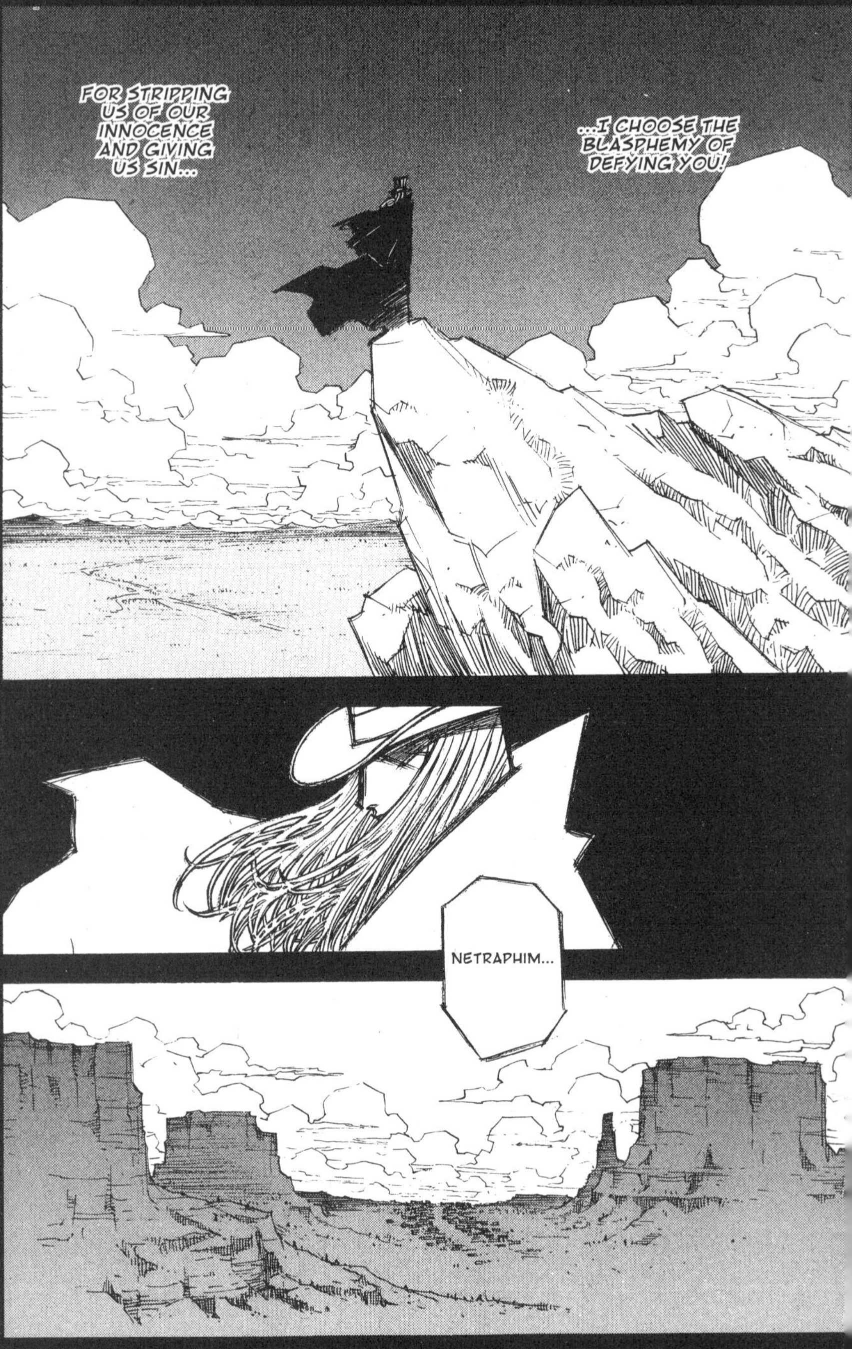
FOR STRIPPING US OF OUR INNOCENCE AND GIVING US SIN...
...I CHOOSE THE BLASPHEMY OF DEFYING YOU!
NETRAPHIM...

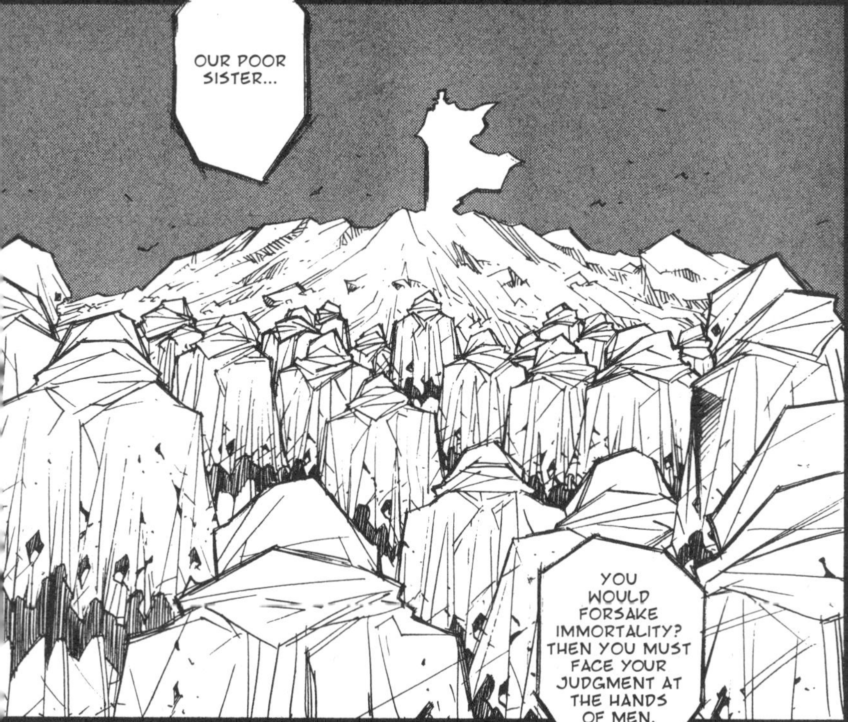
OUR POOR SISTER...
YOU WOULD FORSAKE IMMORTALITY? THEN YOU MUST FACE YOUR JUDGMENT AT THE HANDS OF MEN.
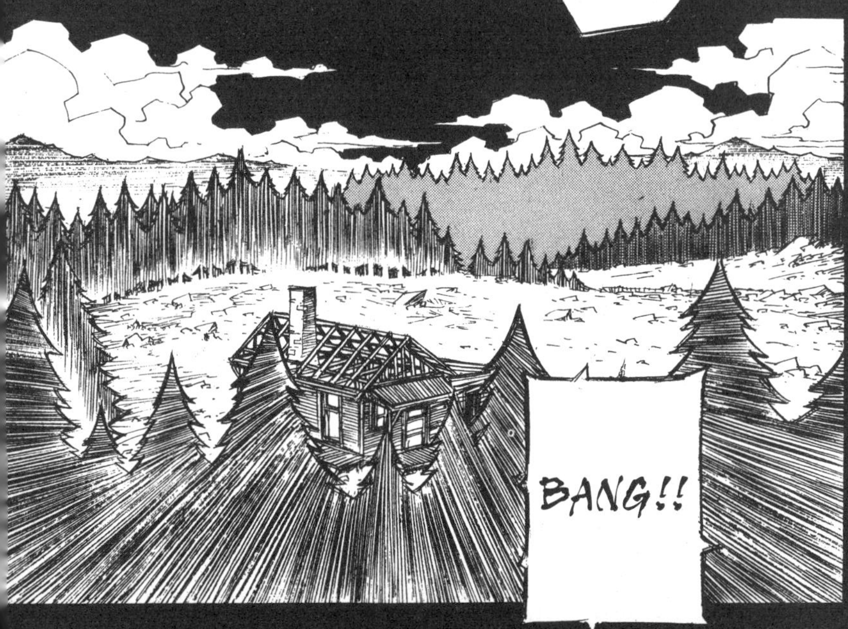
BANG!!

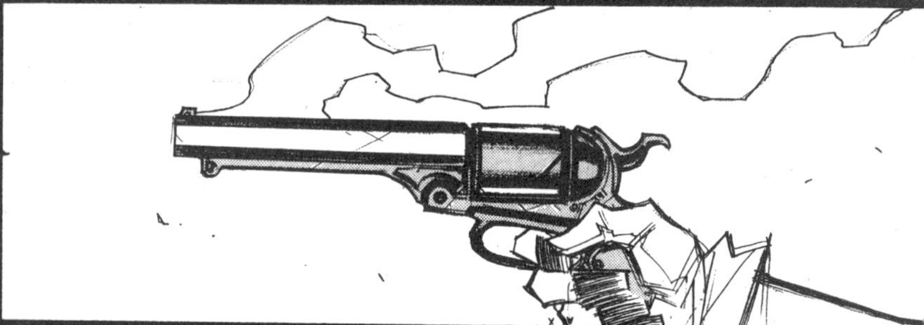
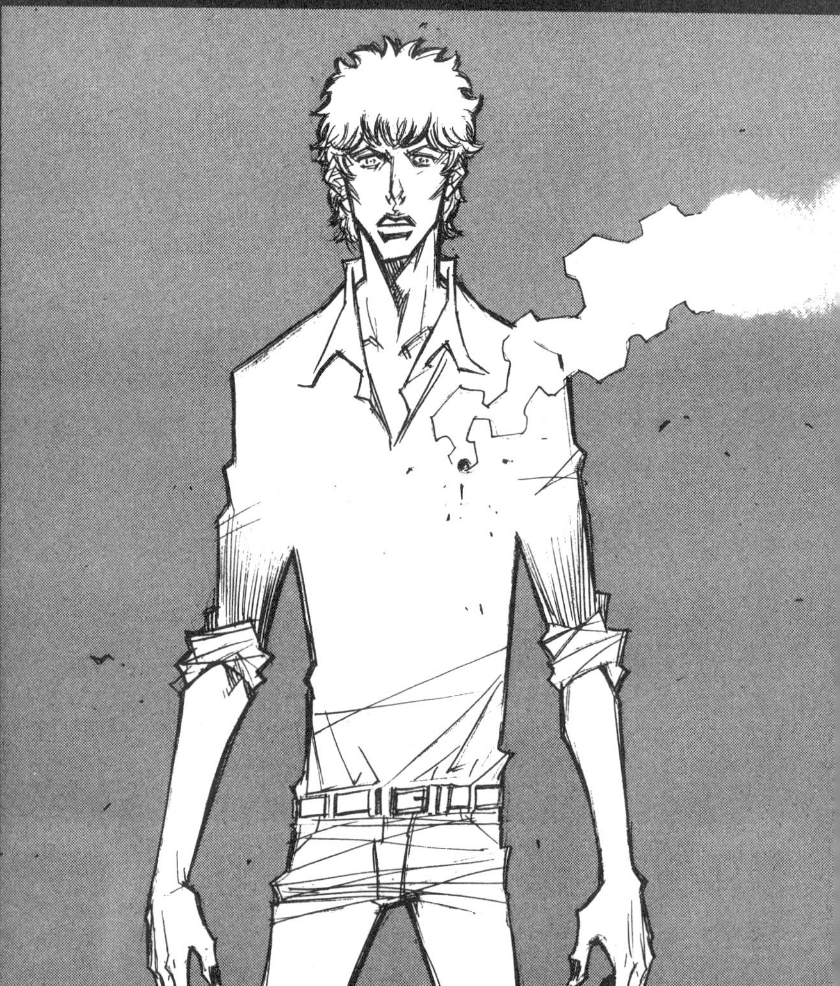

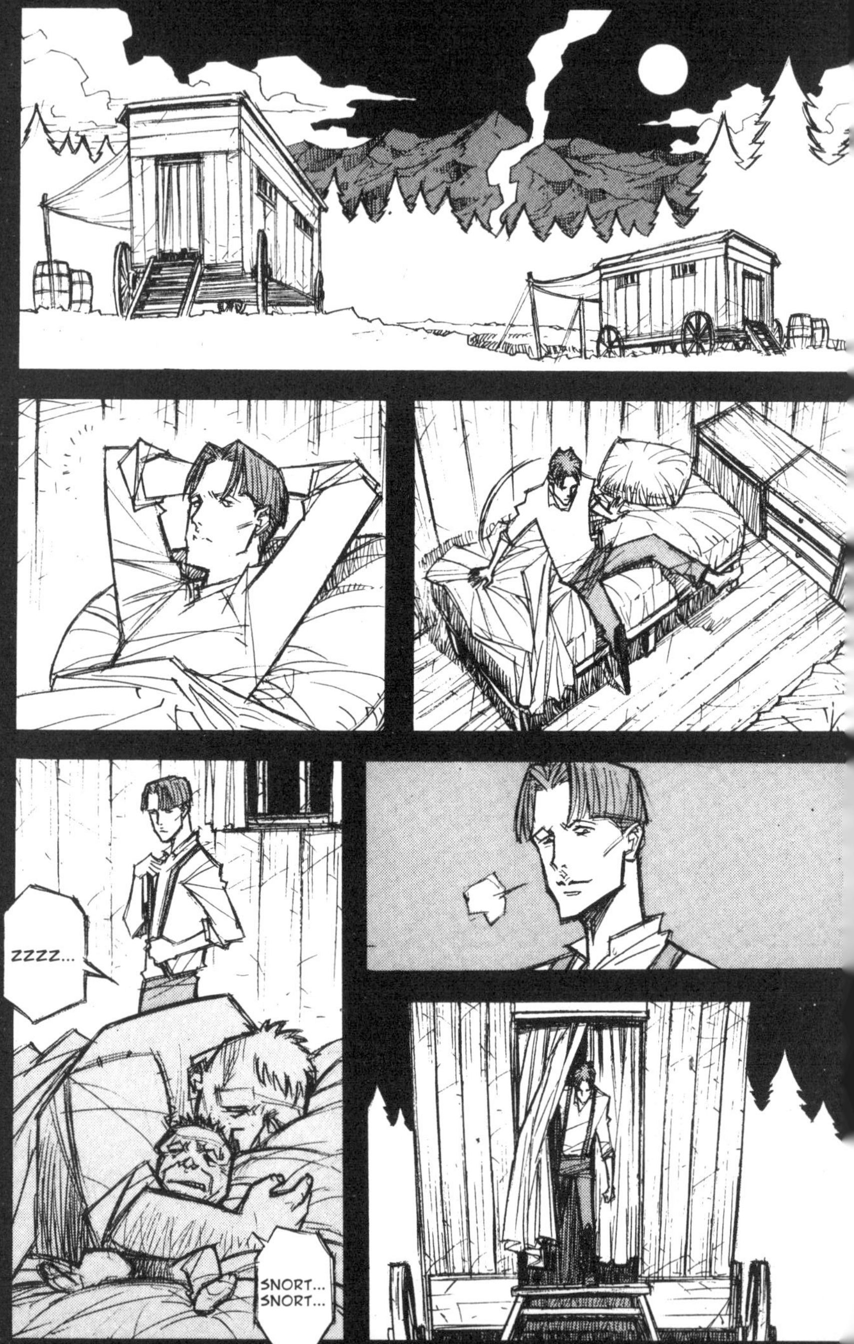
ZZZZ...
SNORT... SNORT...

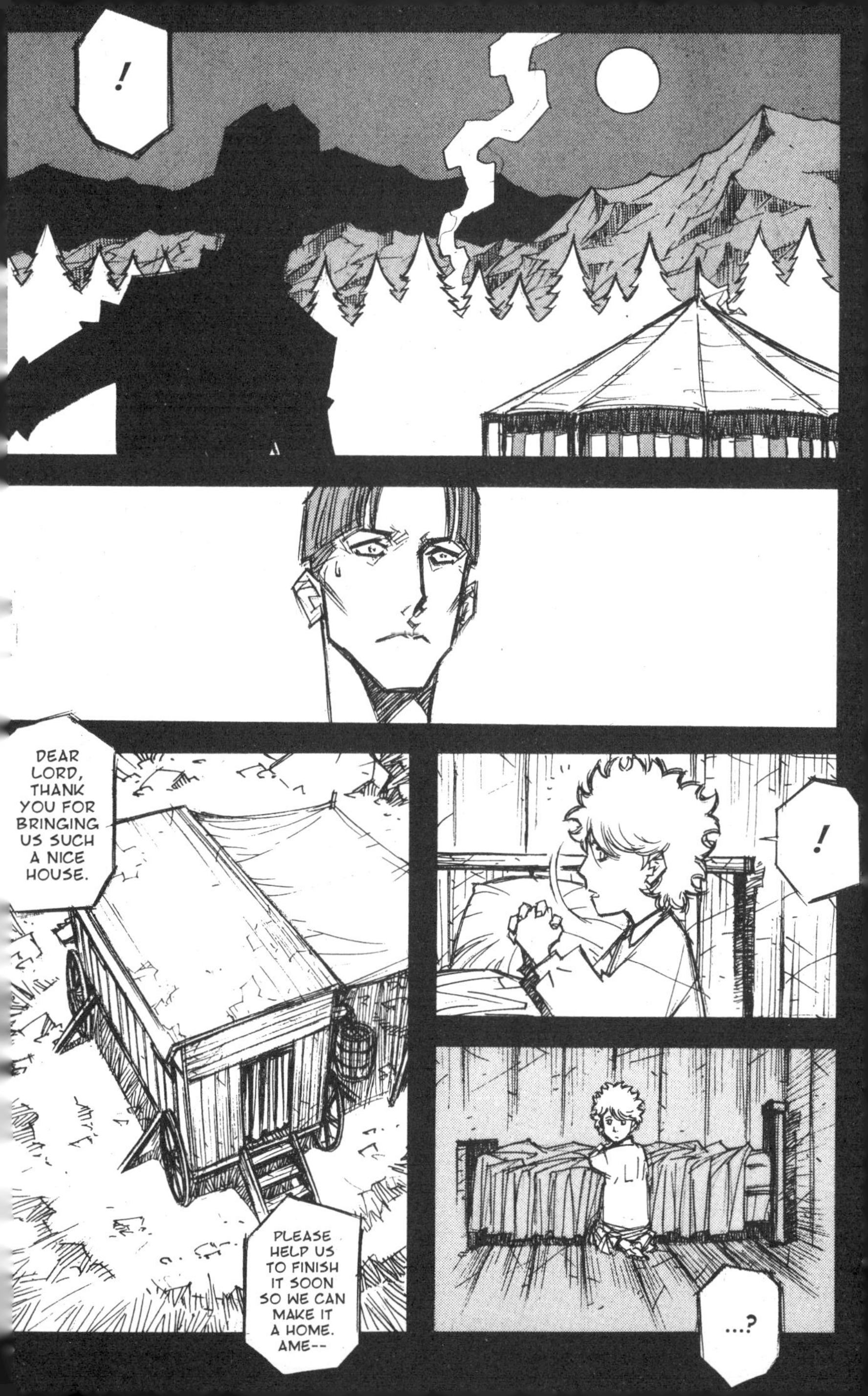
!
DEAR LORD, THANK YOU FOR BRINGING US SUCH A NICE HOUSE.
PLEASE HELP US TO FINISH IT SOON SO WE CAN MAKE IT A HOME. AME--
!
...?

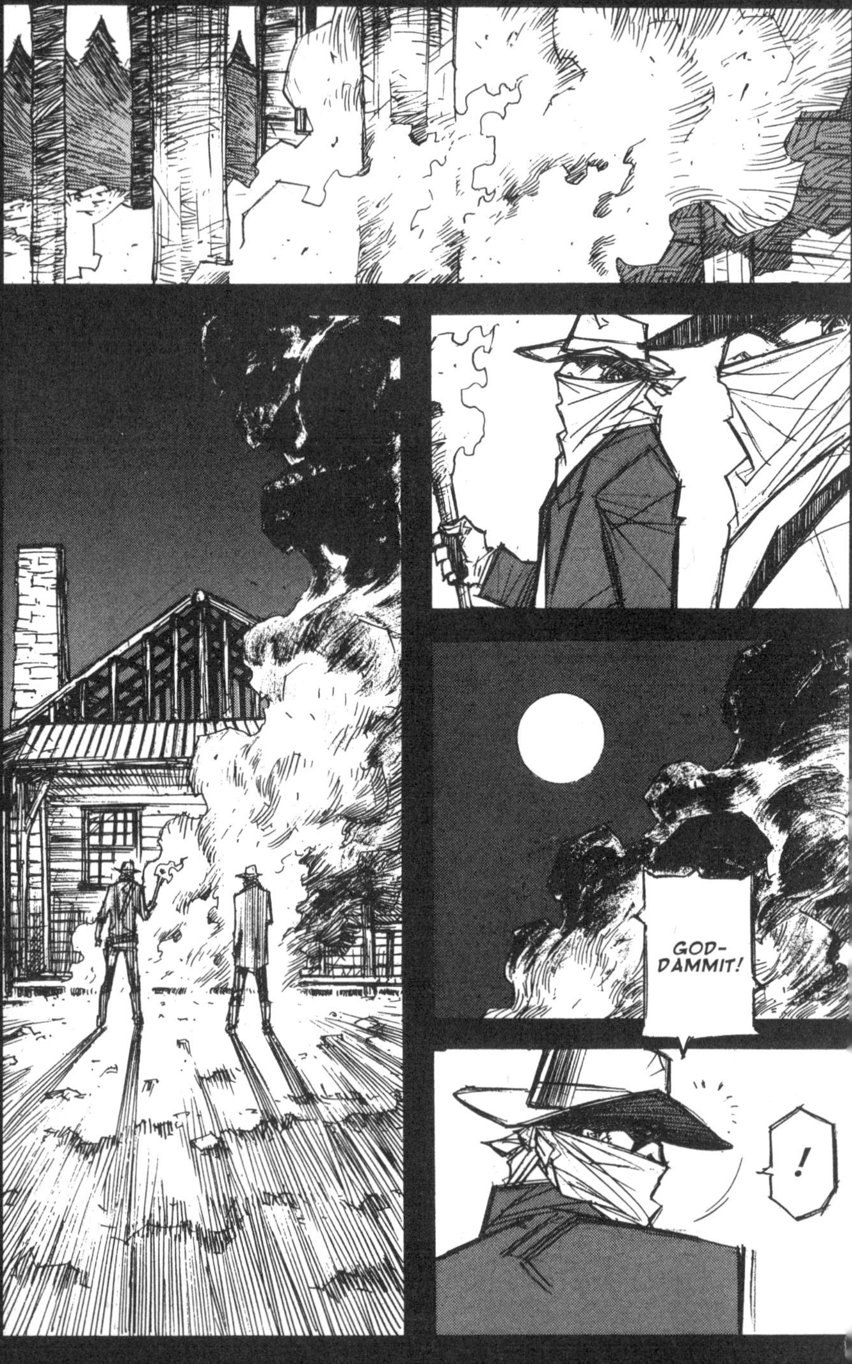
GOD-
DAMMIT!
!

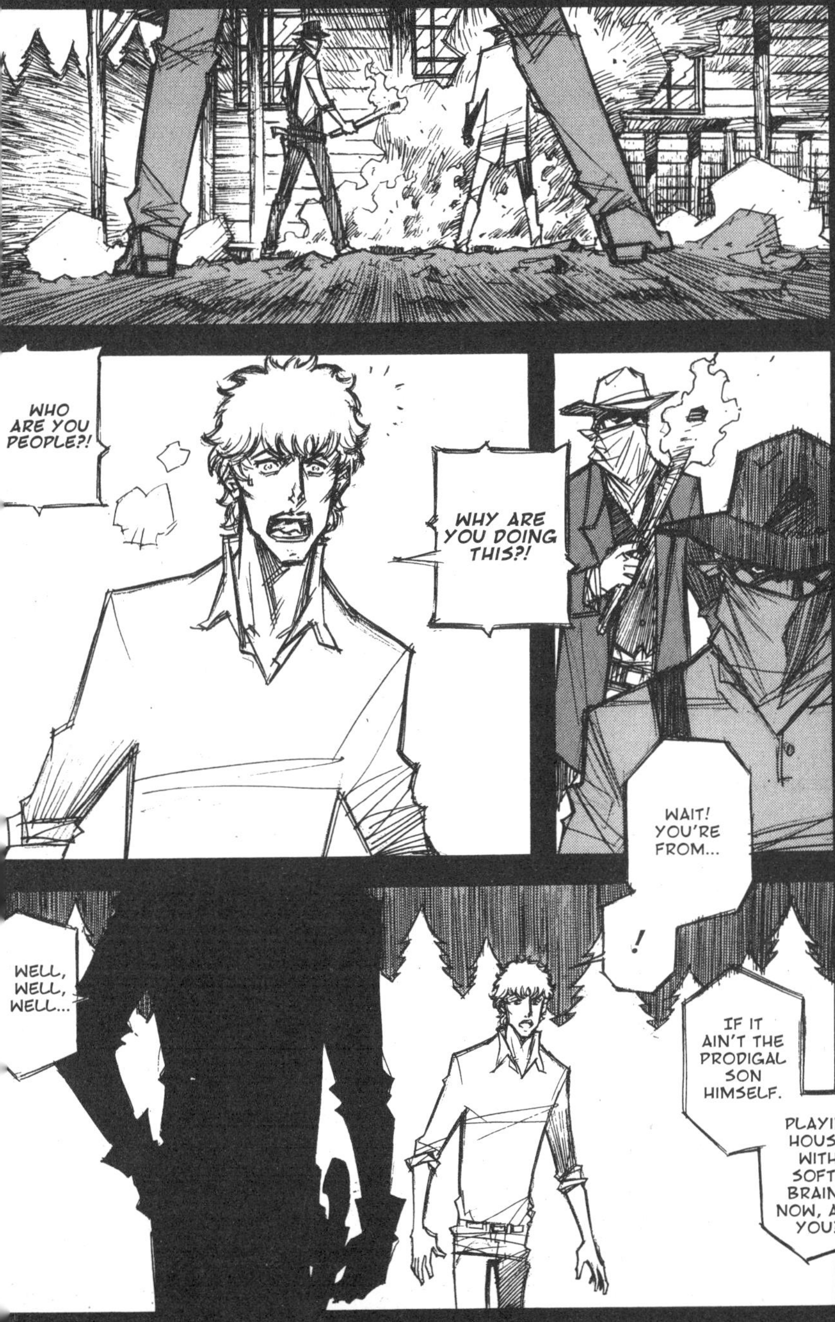
WHO ARE YOU PEOPLE?!
WHY ARE YOU DOING THIS?!
WAIT! YOU'RE FROM...
!
WELL, WELL, WELL...
IF IT AIN'T THE PRODIGAL SON HIMSELF.
PLAYIN' HOUSE WITH SOFT-BRAINS NOW, ARE YOU?

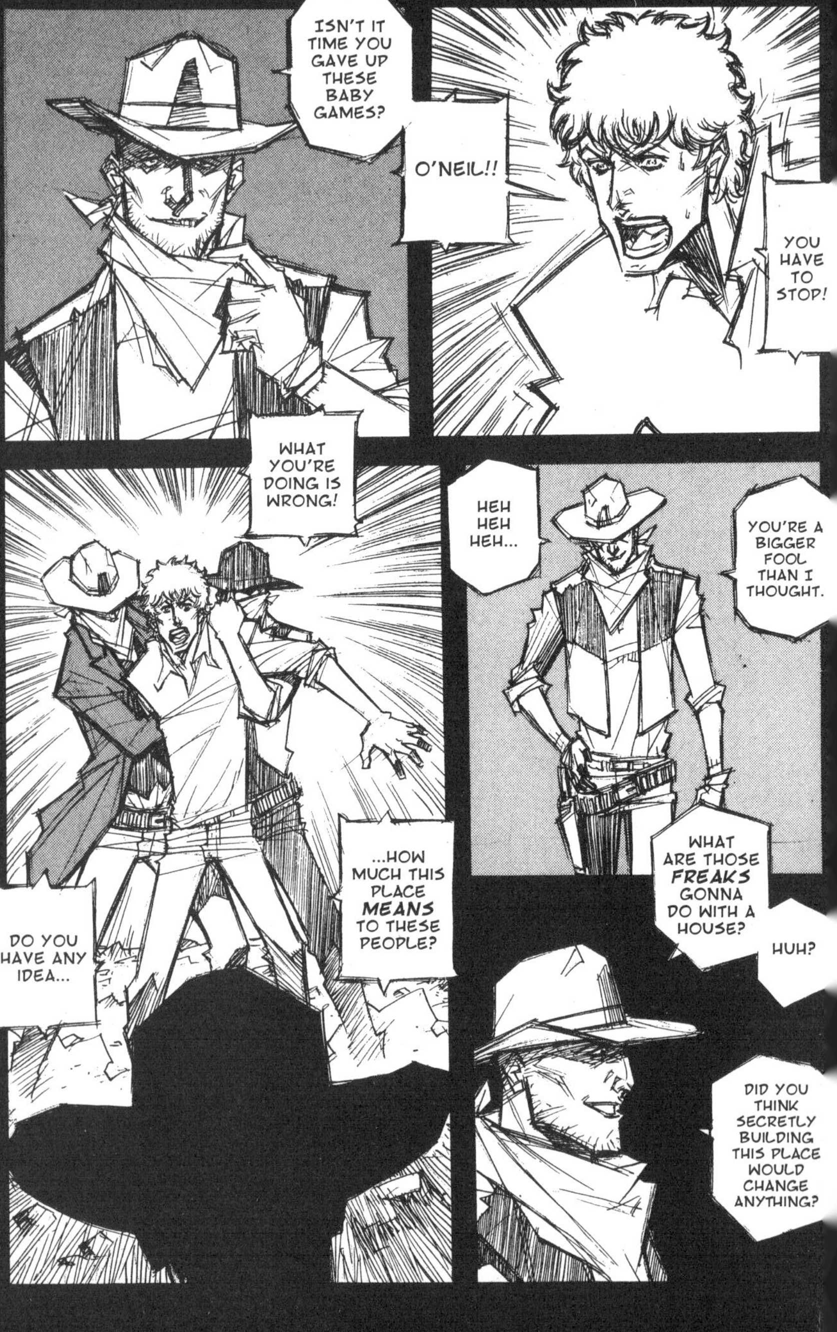
ISN'T IT TIME YOU GAVE UP THESE BABY GAMES?
O'NEIL!!
YOU HAVE TO STOP!
WHAT YOU'RE DOING IS WRONG!
DO YOU HAVE ANY IDEA...
...HOW MUCH THIS PLACE **MEANS** TO THESE PEOPLE?
HEH HEH HEH...
YOU'RE A BIGGER FOOL THAN I THOUGHT.
WHAT ARE THOSE **FREAKS** GONNA DO WITH A HOUSE?
HUH?
DID YOU THINK SECRETLY BUILDING THIS PLACE WOULD CHANGE ANYTHING?

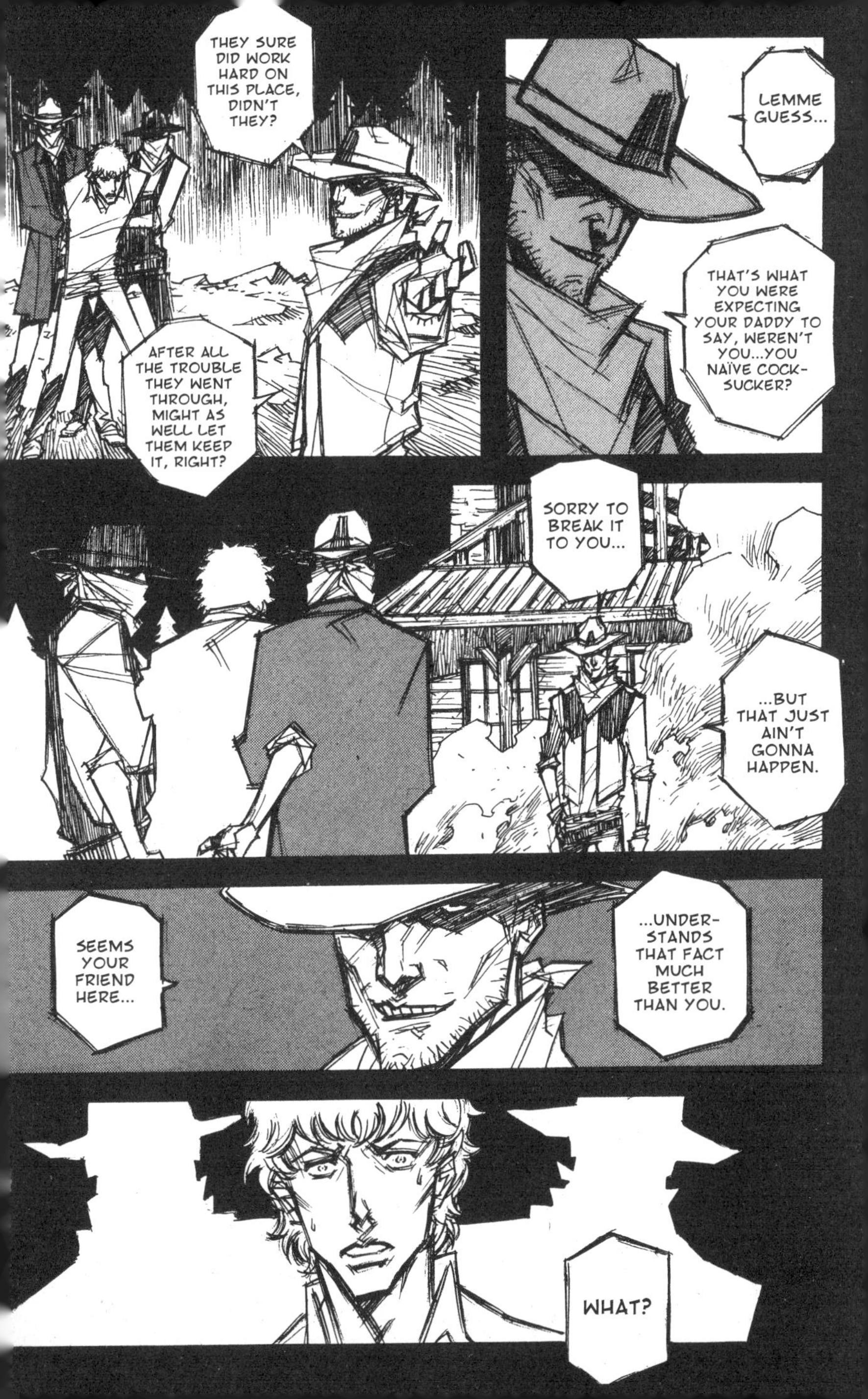
THEY SURE DID WORK HARD ON THIS PLACE, DIDN'T THEY?
AFTER ALL THE TROUBLE THEY WENT THROUGH, MIGHT AS WELL LET THEM KEEP IT, RIGHT?
LEMME GUESS...
THAT'S WHAT YOU WERE EXPECTING YOUR DADDY TO SAY, WEREN'T YOU...YOU NAÏVE COCK-SUCKER?
SORRY TO BREAK IT TO YOU...
...BUT THAT JUST AIN'T GONNA HAPPEN.
SEEMS YOUR FRIEND HERE...
...UNDER-STANDS THAT FACT MUCH BETTER THAN YOU.
WHAT?

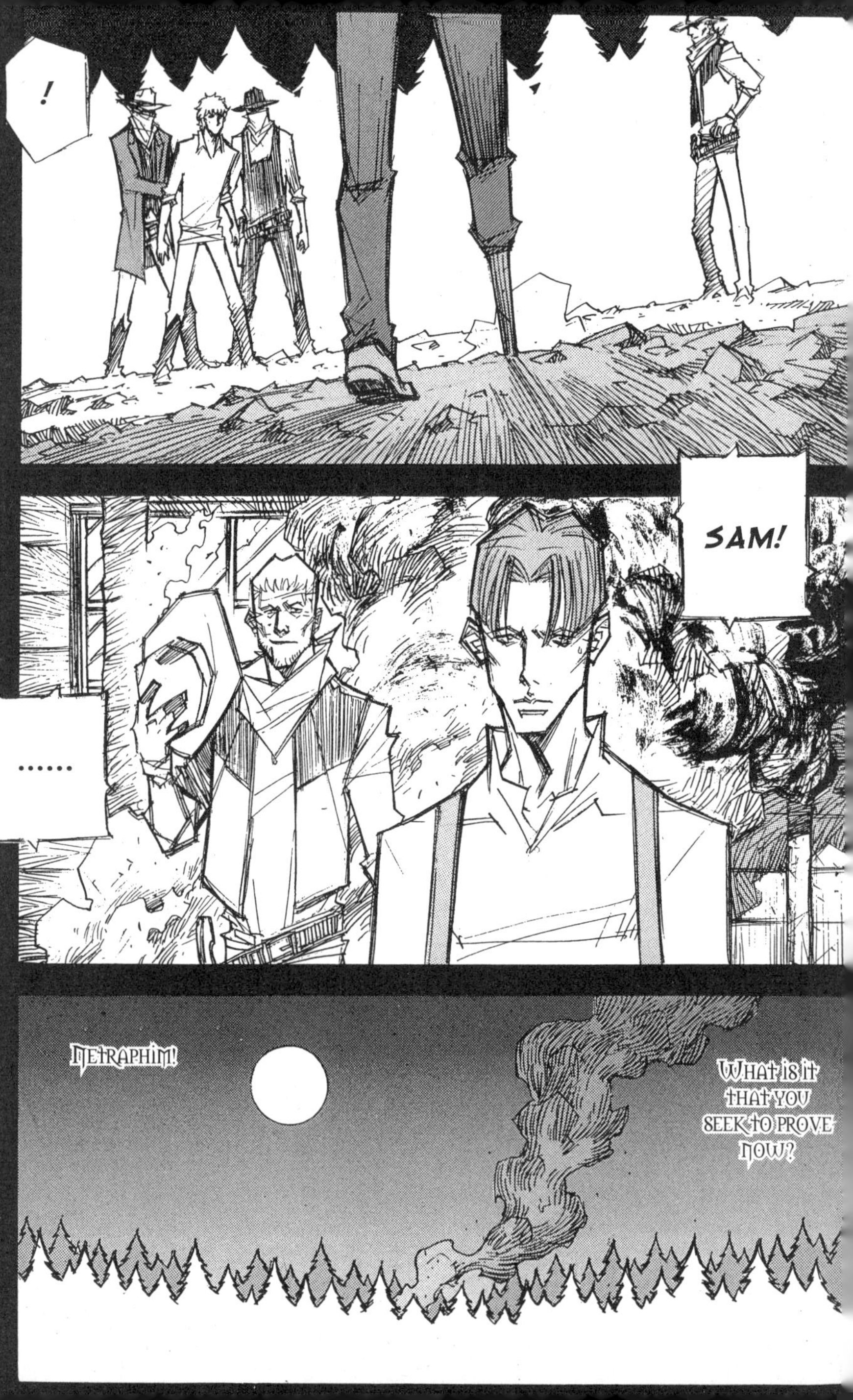
!
SAM!
......
METRAPHIM!
WHAT IS IT THAT YOU SEEK TO PROVE NOW?

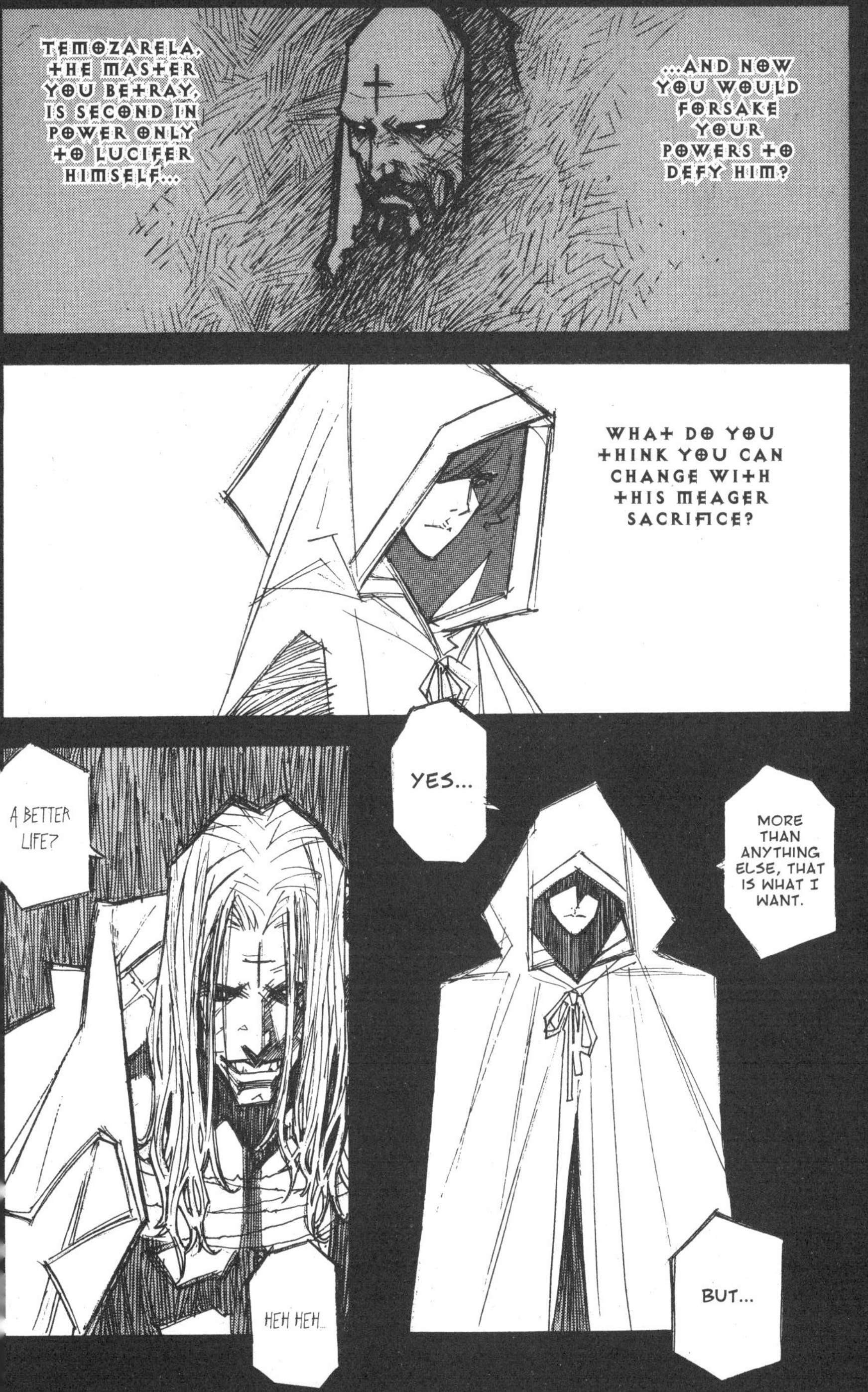

TEMOZARELA, THE MASTER YOU BETRAY, IS SECOND IN POWER ONLY TO LUCIFER HIMSELF...
...AND NOW YOU WOULD FORSAKE YOUR POWERS TO DEFY HIM?
WHAT DO YOU THINK YOU CAN CHANGE WITH THIS MEAGER SACRIFICE?
A BETTER LIFE?
YES...
MORE THAN ANYTHING ELSE, THAT IS WHAT I WANT.
HEH HEH...
BUT...

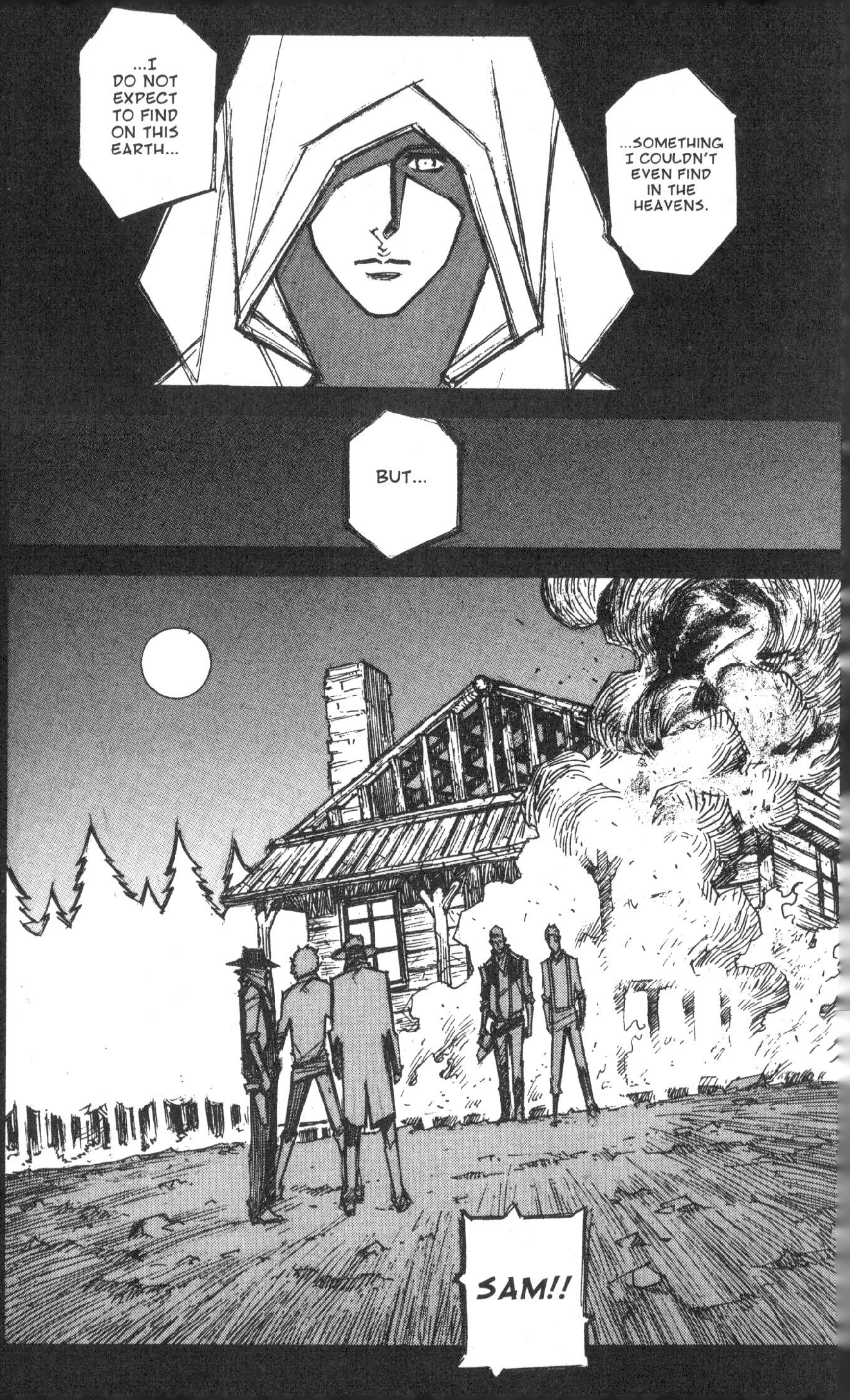
...I DO NOT EXPECT TO FIND ON THIS EARTH...
...SOMETHING I COULDN'T EVEN FIND IN THE HEAVENS.
BUT...
SAM!!

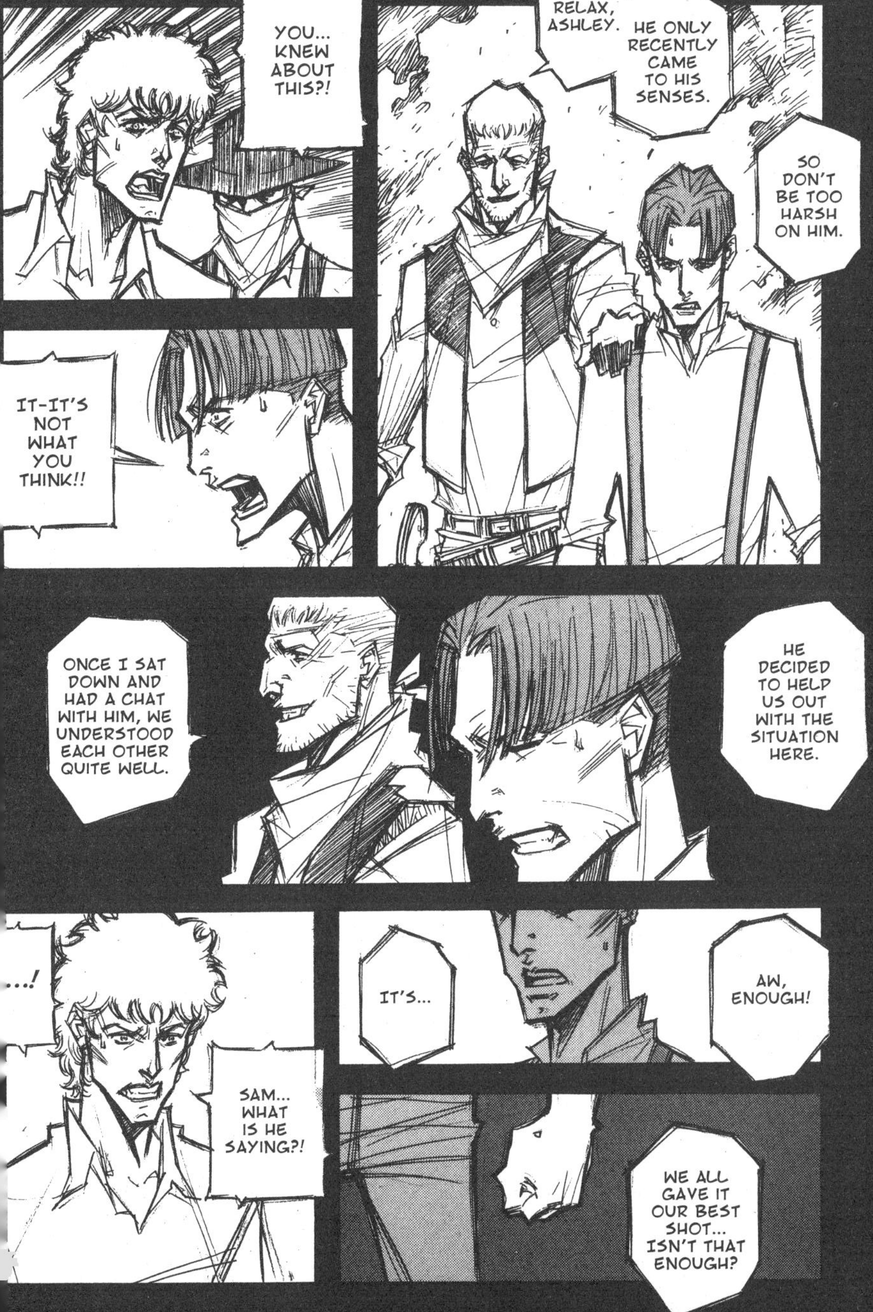
YOU... KNEW ABOUT THIS?!
IT-IT'S NOT WHAT YOU THINK!!
RELAX, ASHLEY.
HE ONLY RECENTLY CAME TO HIS SENSES.
SO DON'T BE TOO HARSH ON HIM.
ONCE I SAT DOWN AND HAD A CHAT WITH HIM, WE UNDERSTOOD EACH OTHER QUITE WELL.
HE DECIDED TO HELP US OUT WITH THE SITUATION HERE.
...!
SAM... WHAT IS HE SAYING?!
IT'S...
AW, ENOUGH!
WE ALL GAVE IT OUR BEST SHOT... ISN'T THAT ENOUGH?

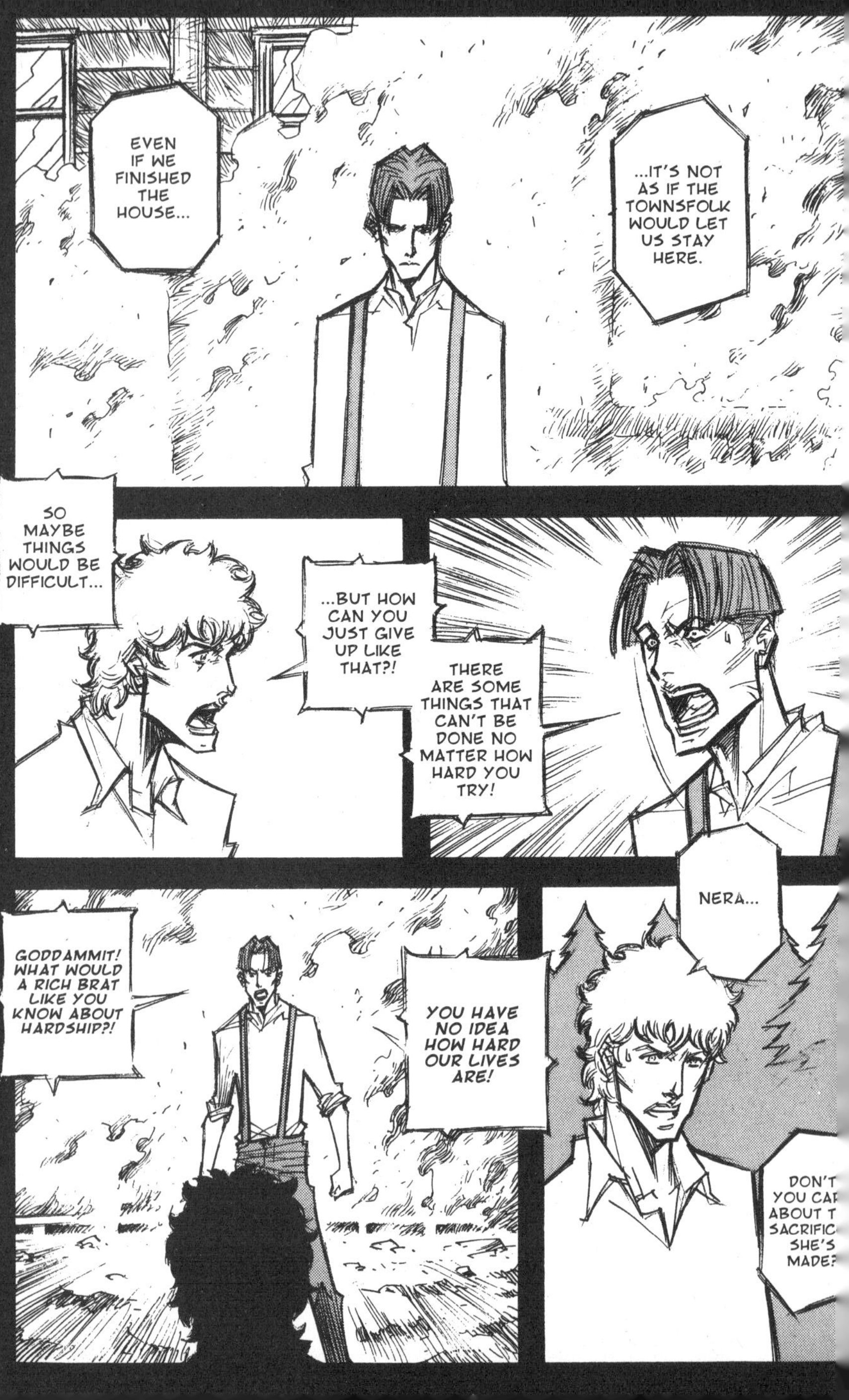
EVEN IF WE FINISHED THE HOUSE...
...IT'S NOT AS IF THE TOWNSFOLK WOULD LET US STAY HERE.
SO MAYBE THINGS WOULD BE DIFFICULT...
...BUT HOW CAN YOU JUST GIVE UP LIKE THAT?!
THERE ARE SOME THINGS THAT CAN'T BE DONE NO MATTER HOW HARD YOU TRY!
GODDAMMIT! WHAT WOULD A RICH BRAT LIKE YOU KNOW ABOUT HARDSHIP?!
YOU HAVE NO IDEA HOW HARD OUR LIVES ARE!
NERA...
DON'T YOU CA ABOUT T SACRIFIC SHE'S MADE?

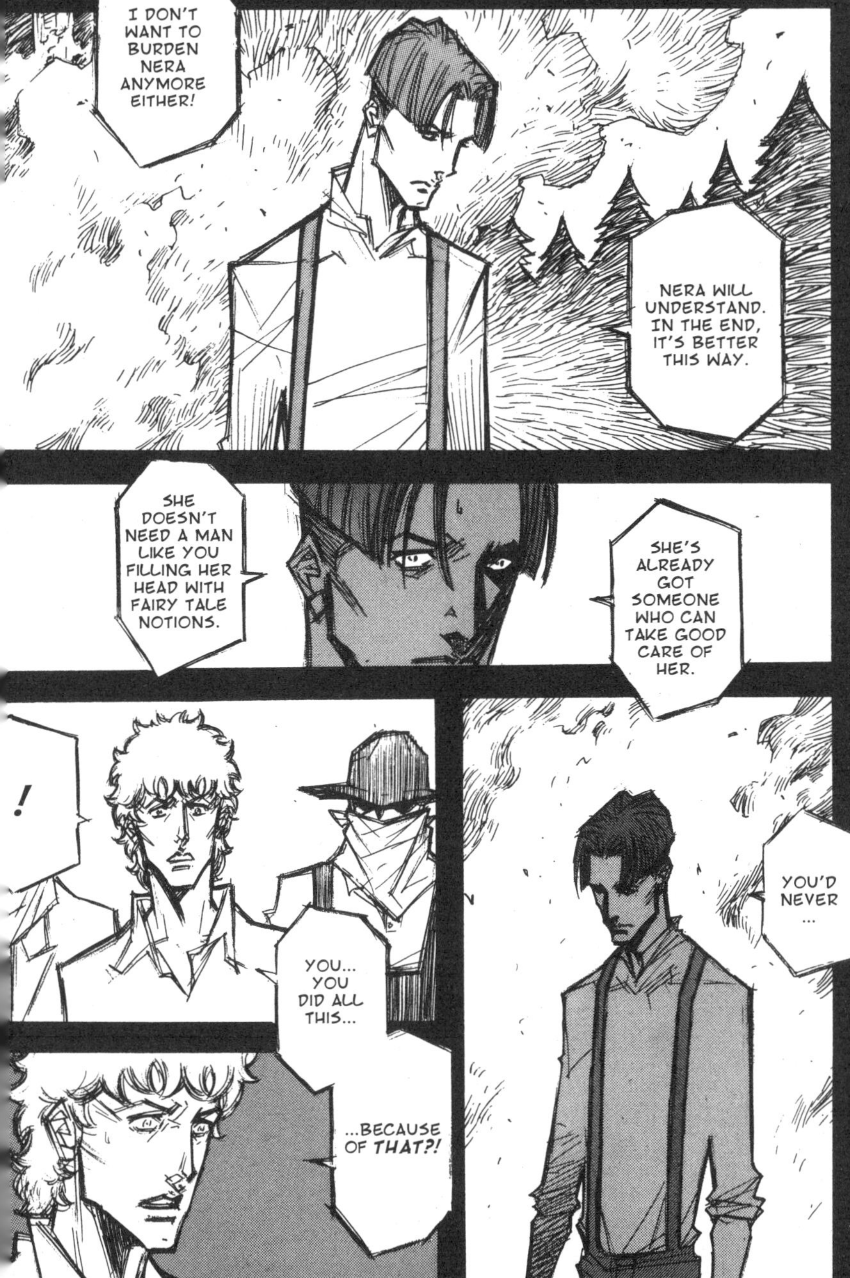
I DON'T WANT TO BURDEN NERA ANYMORE EITHER!
NERA WILL UNDERSTAND. IN THE END, IT'S BETTER THIS WAY.
SHE DOESN'T NEED A MAN LIKE YOU FILLING HER HEAD WITH FAIRY TALE NOTIONS.
SHE'S ALREADY GOT SOMEONE WHO CAN TAKE GOOD CARE OF HER.
!
YOU... YOU DID ALL THIS...
...BECAUSE OF *THAT?!*
YOU'D NEVER ...

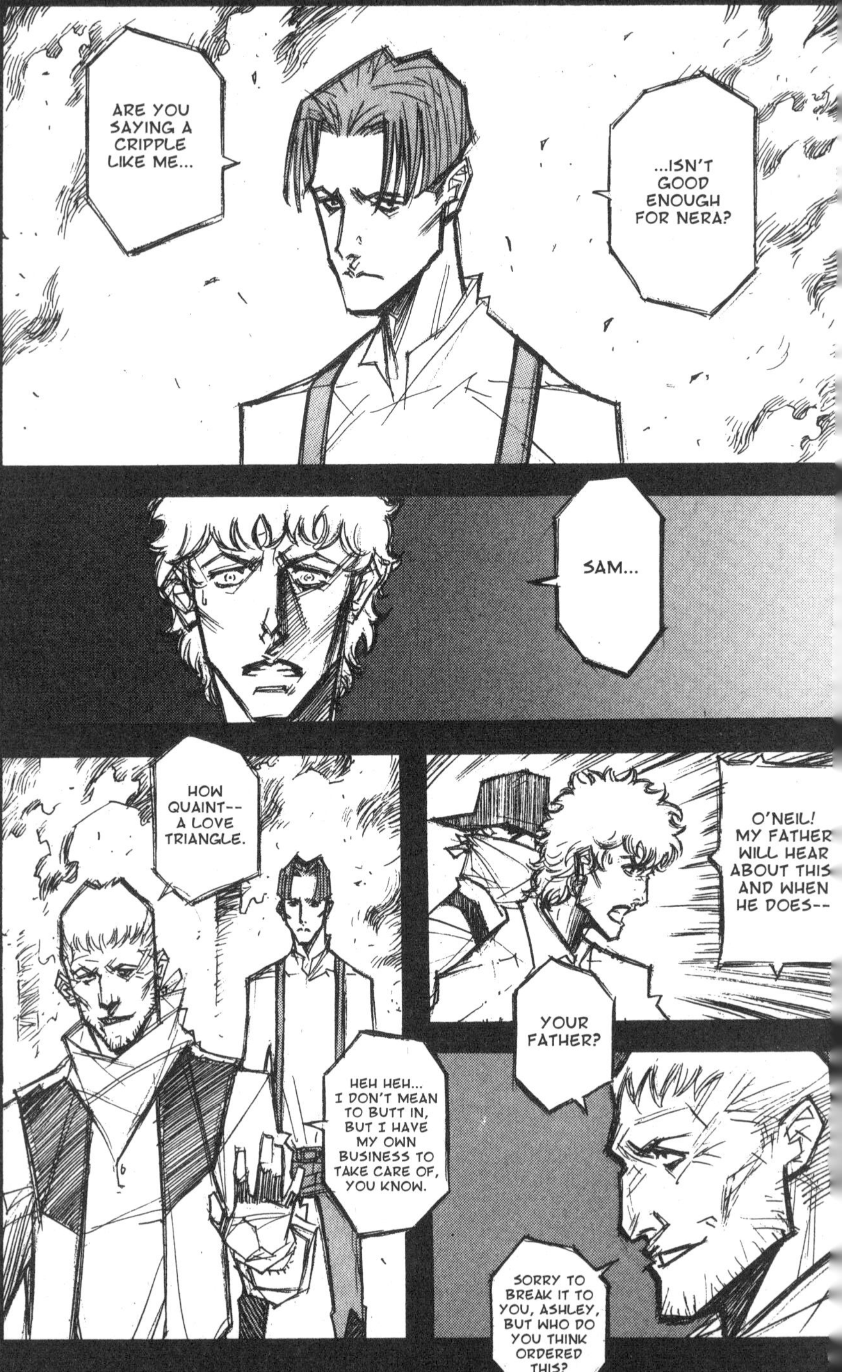
ARE YOU SAYING A CRIPPLE LIKE ME...
...ISN'T GOOD ENOUGH FOR NERA?
SAM...
HOW QUAINT--A LOVE TRIANGLE.
O'NEIL! MY FATHER WILL HEAR ABOUT THIS AND WHEN HE DOES--
HEH HEH... I DON'T MEAN TO BUTT IN, BUT I HAVE MY OWN BUSINESS TO TAKE CARE OF, YOU KNOW.
YOUR FATHER?
SORRY TO BREAK IT TO YOU, ASHLEY, BUT WHO DO YOU THINK ORDERED THIS?

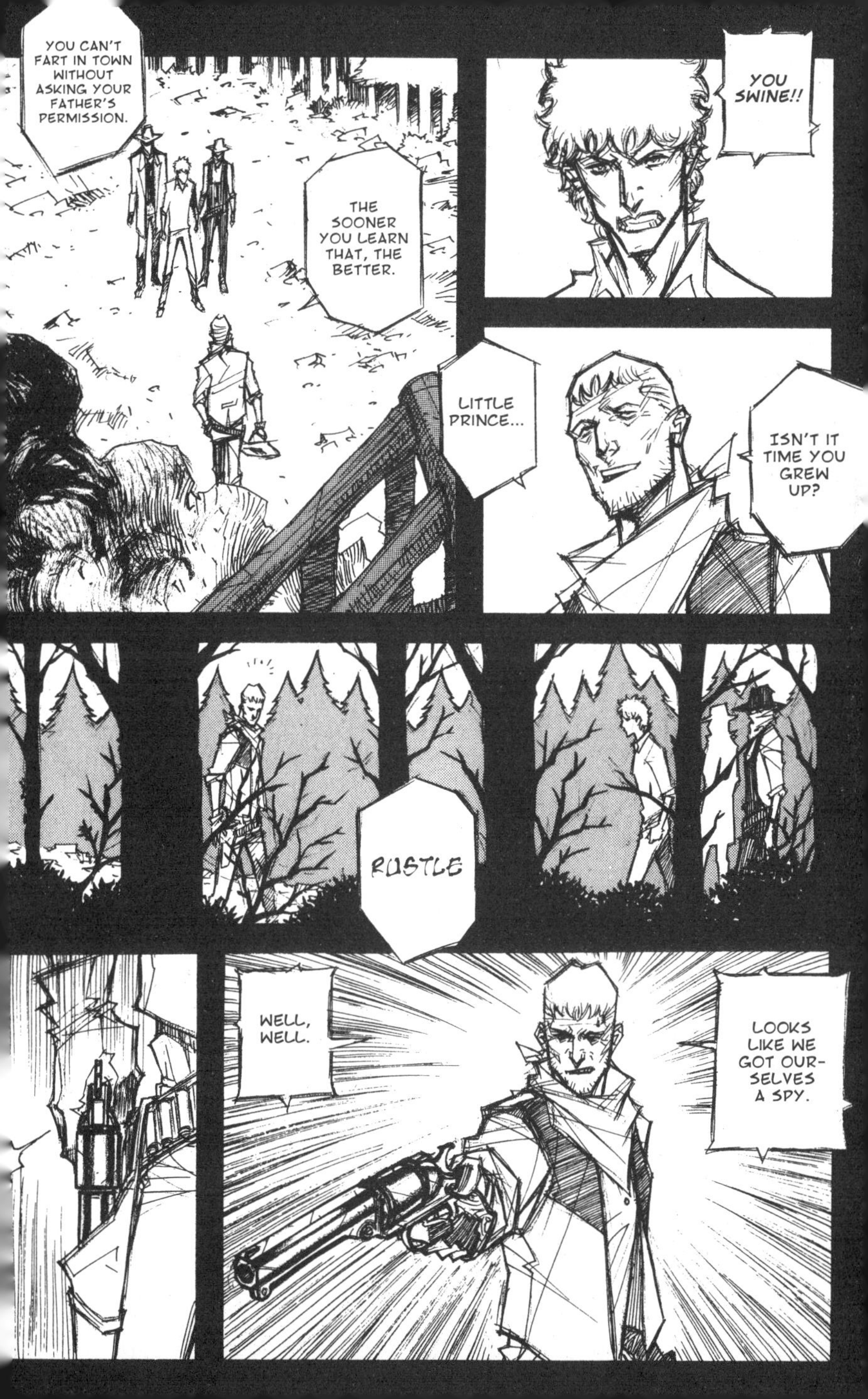
YOU CAN'T FART IN TOWN WITHOUT ASKING YOUR FATHER'S PERMISSION.
THE SOONER YOU LEARN THAT, THE BETTER.
YOU SWINE!!
LITTLE PRINCE...
ISN'T IT TIME YOU GREW UP?
RUSTLE
WELL, WELL.
LOOKS LIKE WE GOT OURSELVES A SPY.

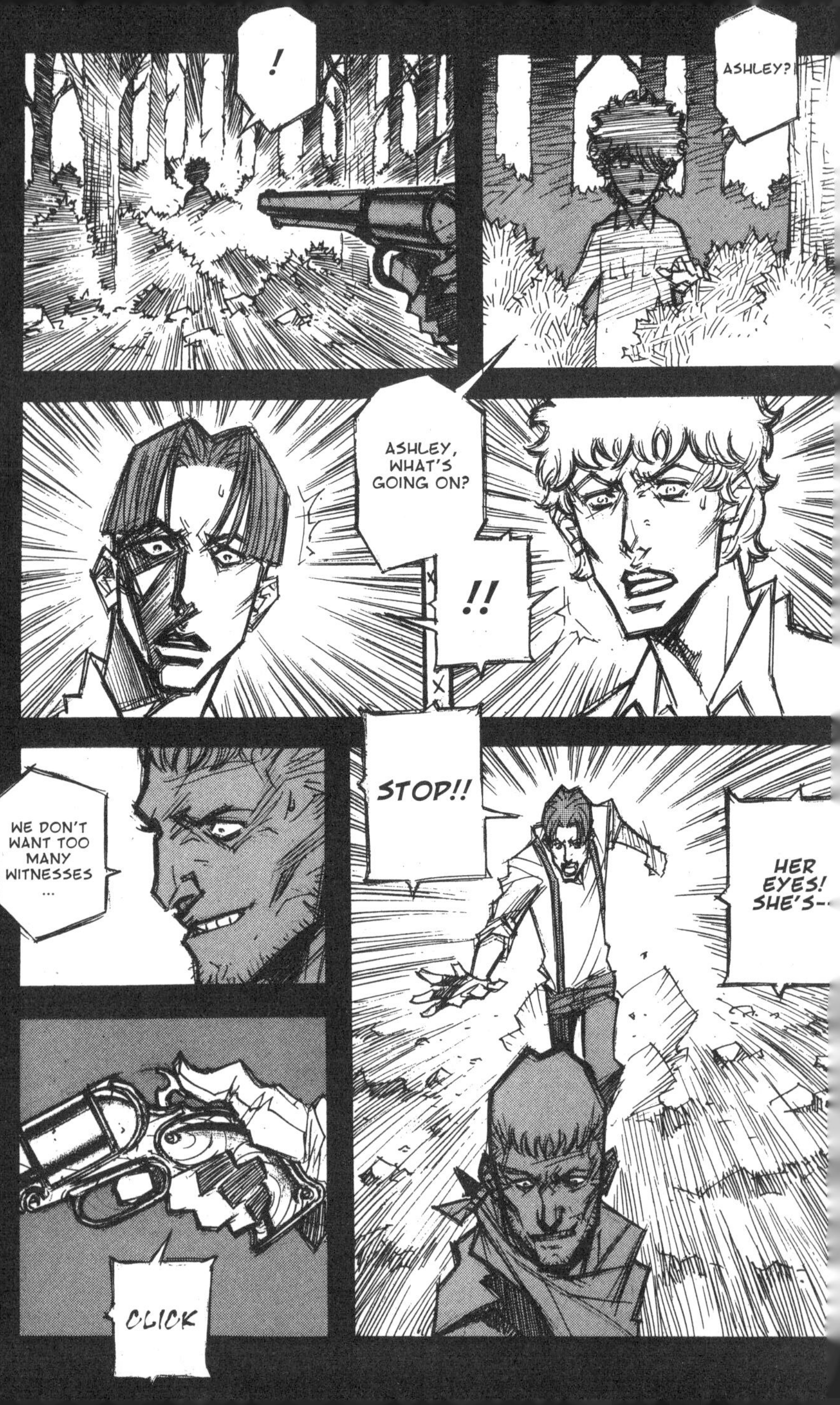
!
ASHLEY?!
ASHLEY, WHAT'S GOING ON?
!!
WE DON'T WANT TOO MANY WITNESSES ...
STOP!!
HER EYES! SHE'S--
CLICK

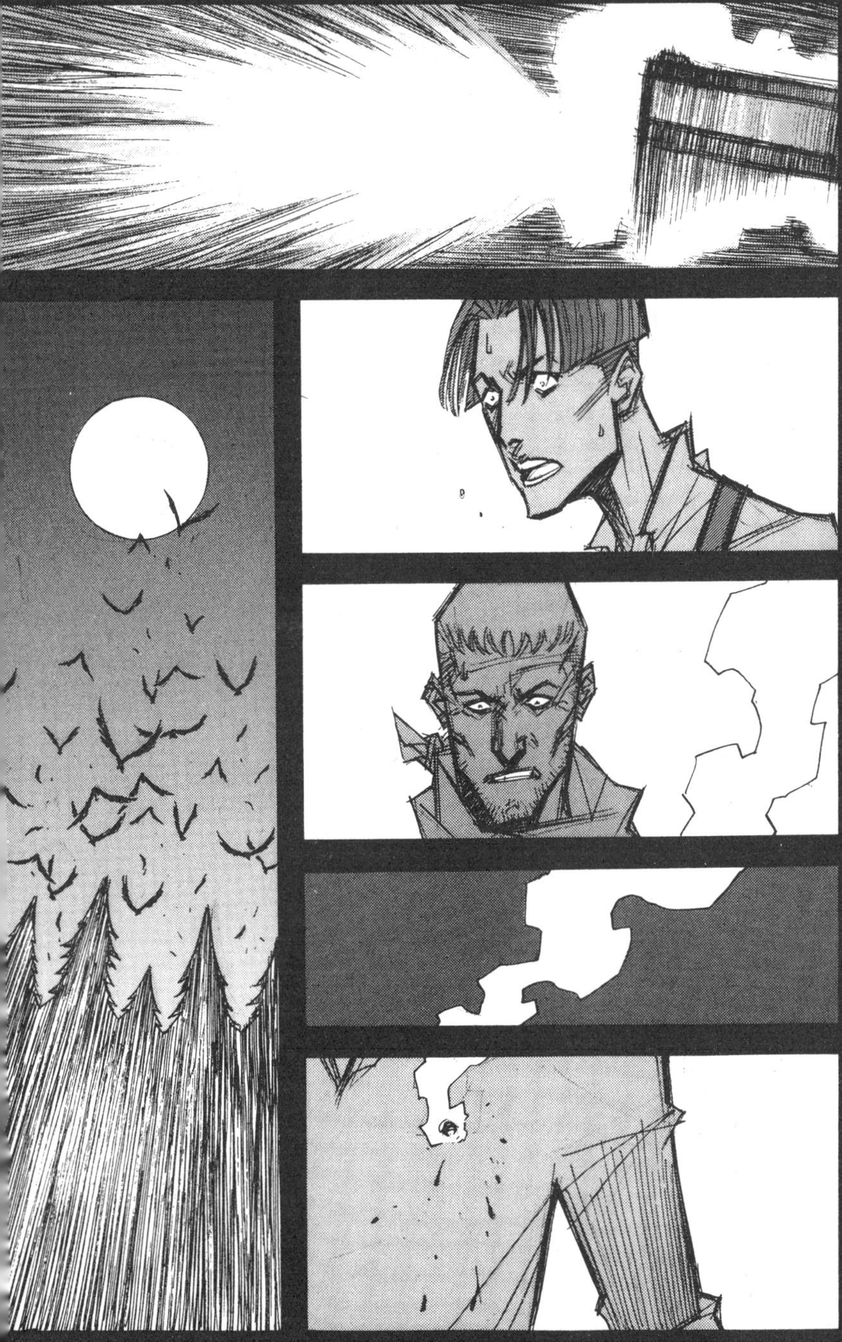

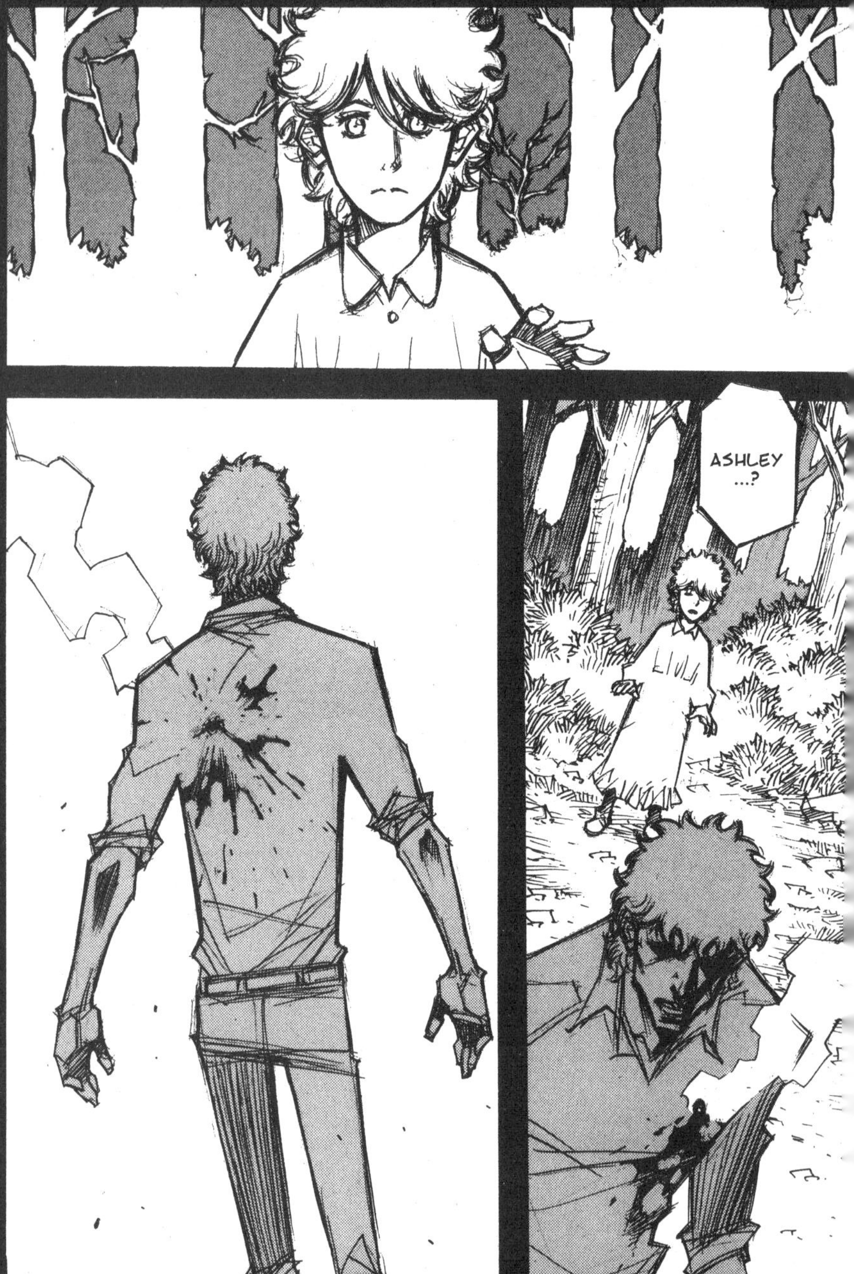
ASHLEY
...?

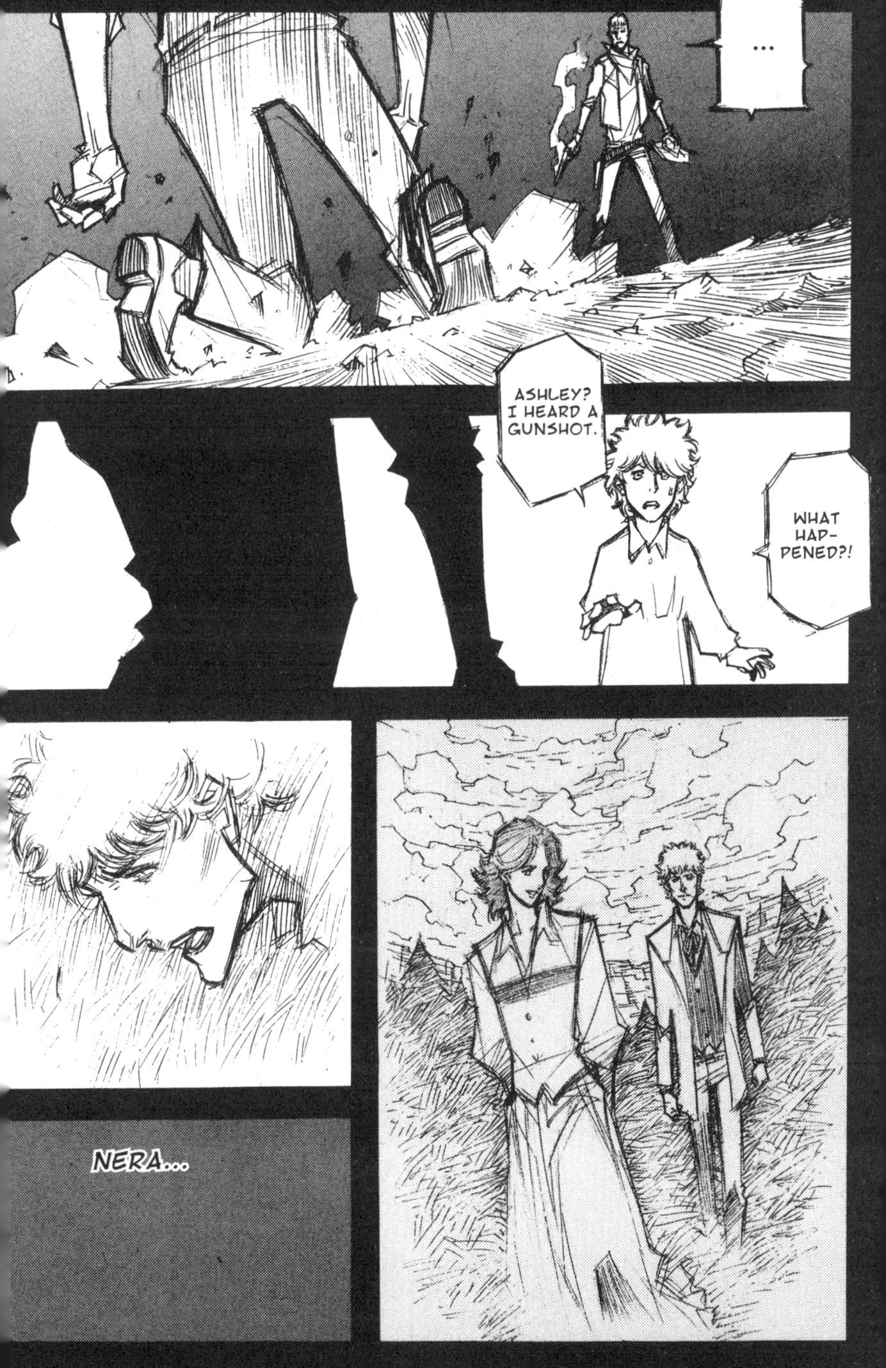
...
ASHLEY? I HEARD A GUNSHOT.
WHAT HAP-PENED?!
NERA...

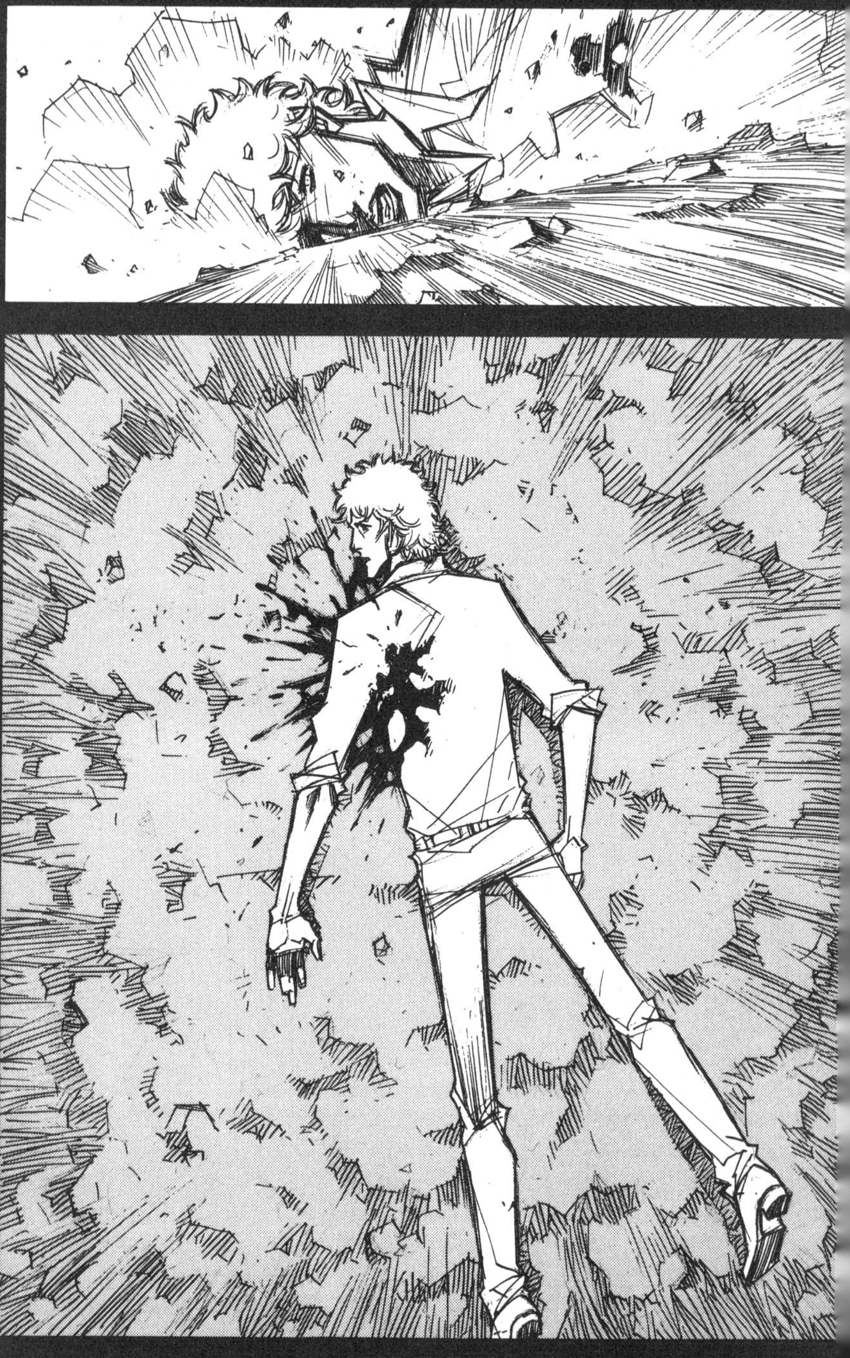

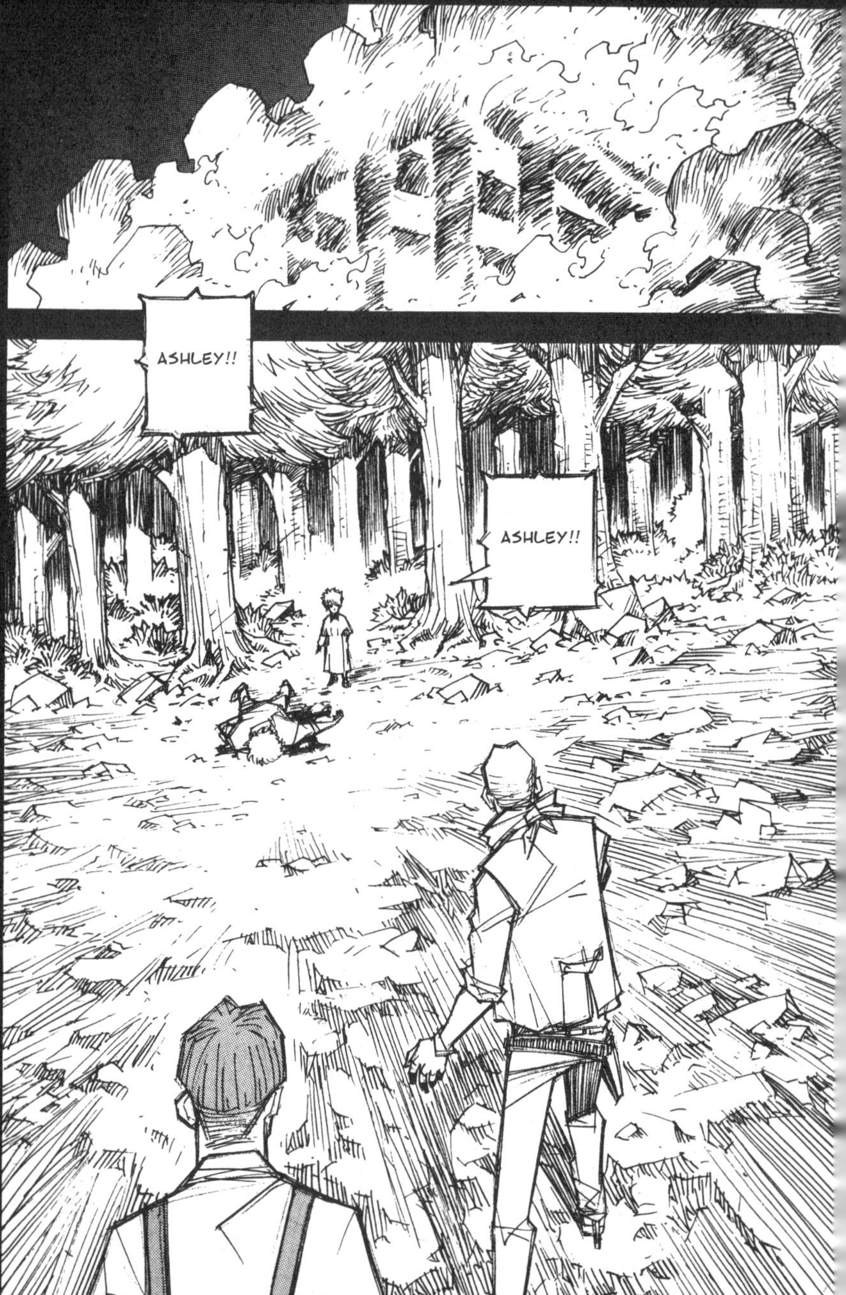
ASHLEY!!
ASHLEY!!

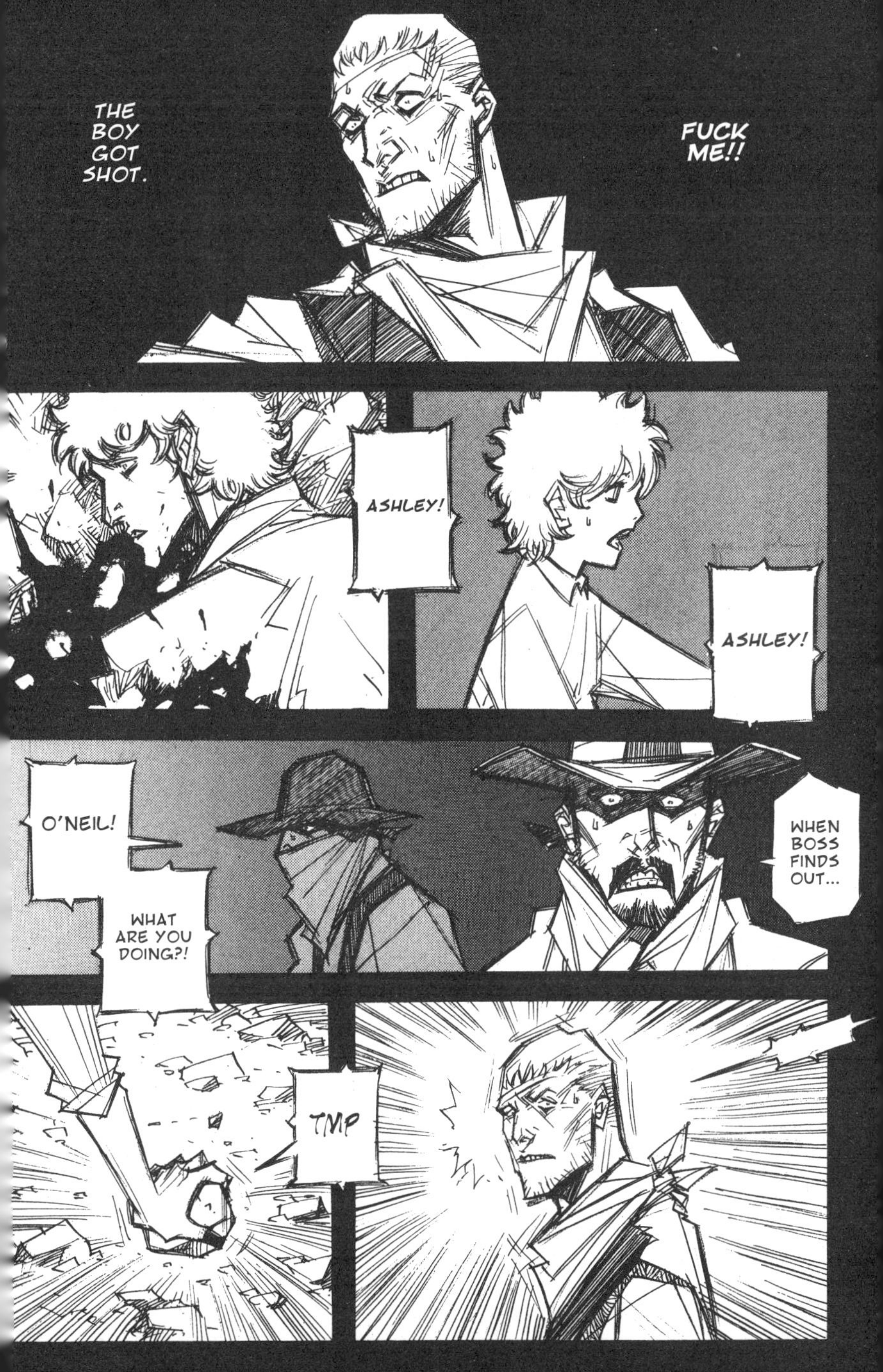
THE BOY GOT SHOT.
FUCK ME!!
ASHLEY!
ASHLEY!
O'NEIL!
WHAT ARE YOU DOING?!
WHEN BOSS FINDS OUT...
TMP

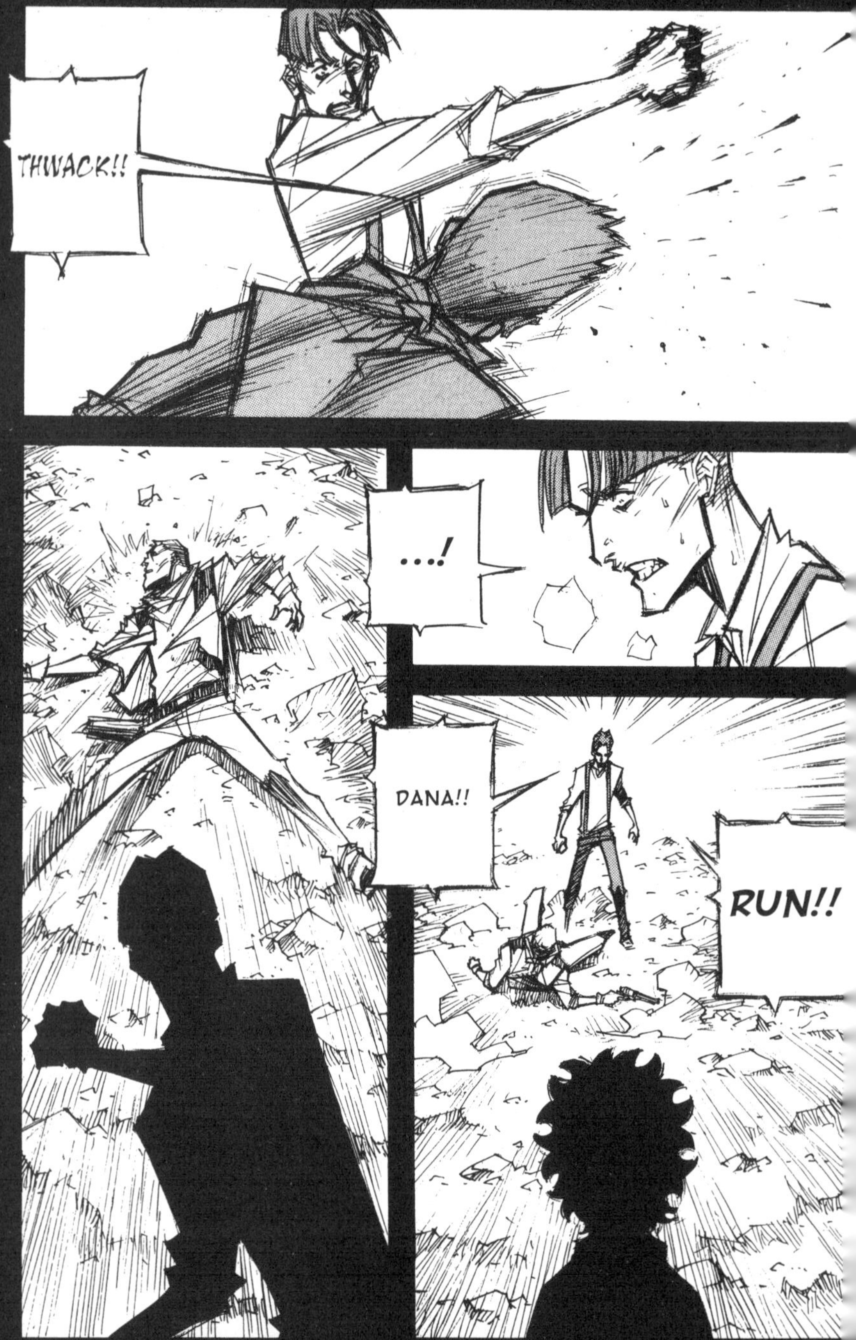
THWACK!!
...!
DANA!!
RUN!!

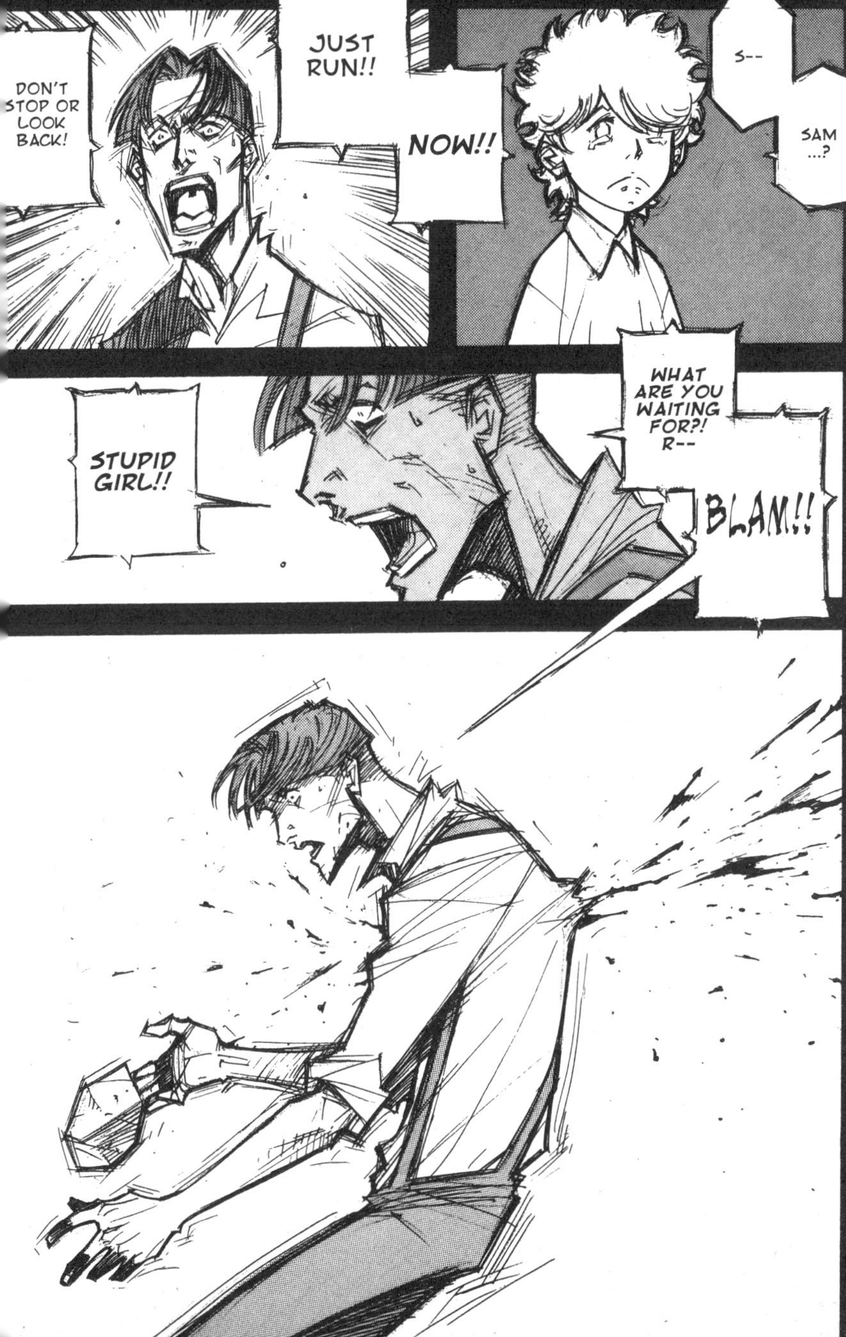
DON'T STOP OR LOOK BACK!
JUST RUN!!
NOW!!
S--
SAM ...?
STUPID GIRL!!
WHAT ARE YOU WAITING FOR?! R--
BLAM!!

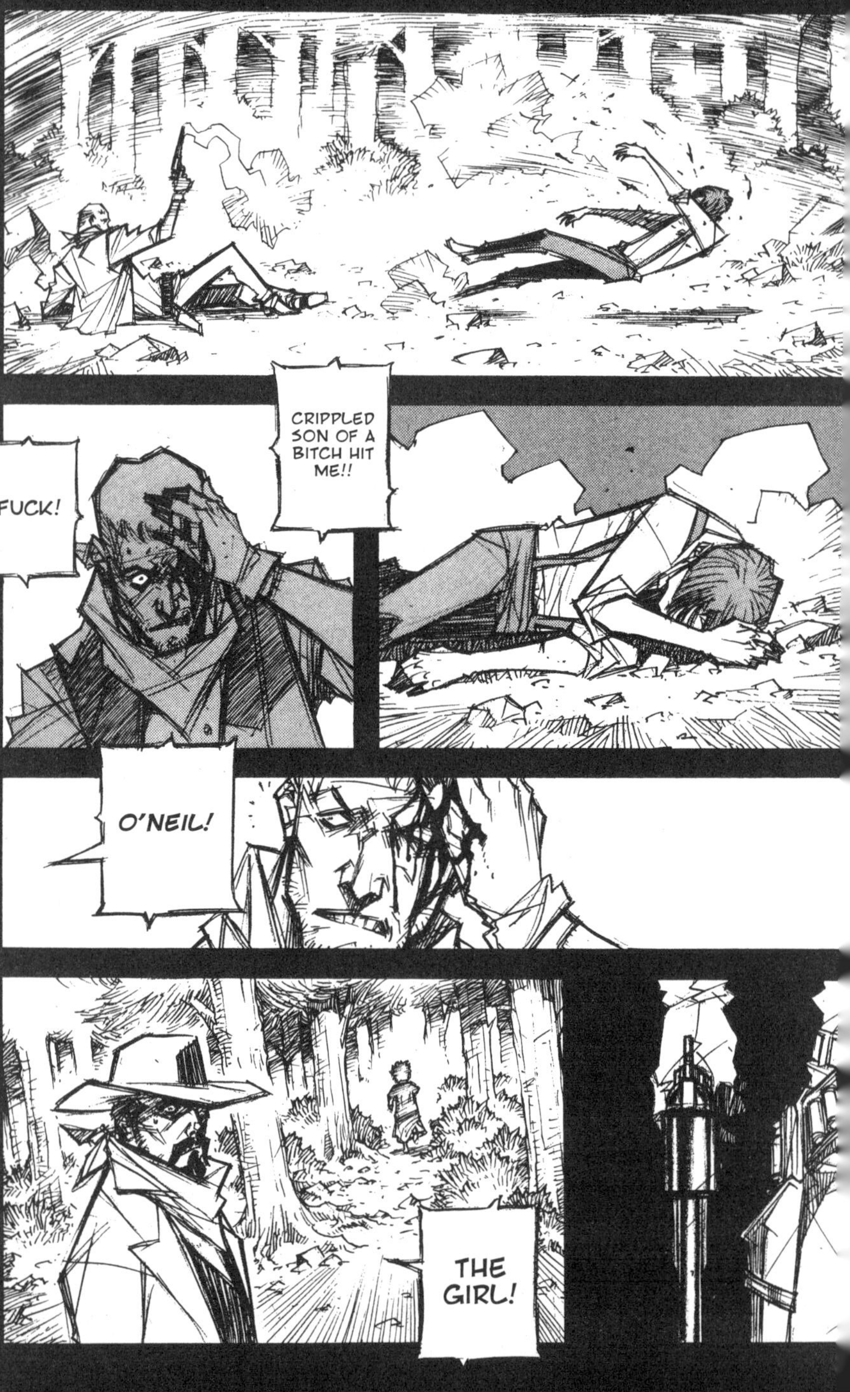
FUCK!
CRIPPLED SON OF A BITCH HIT ME!!
O'NEIL!
THE GIRL!

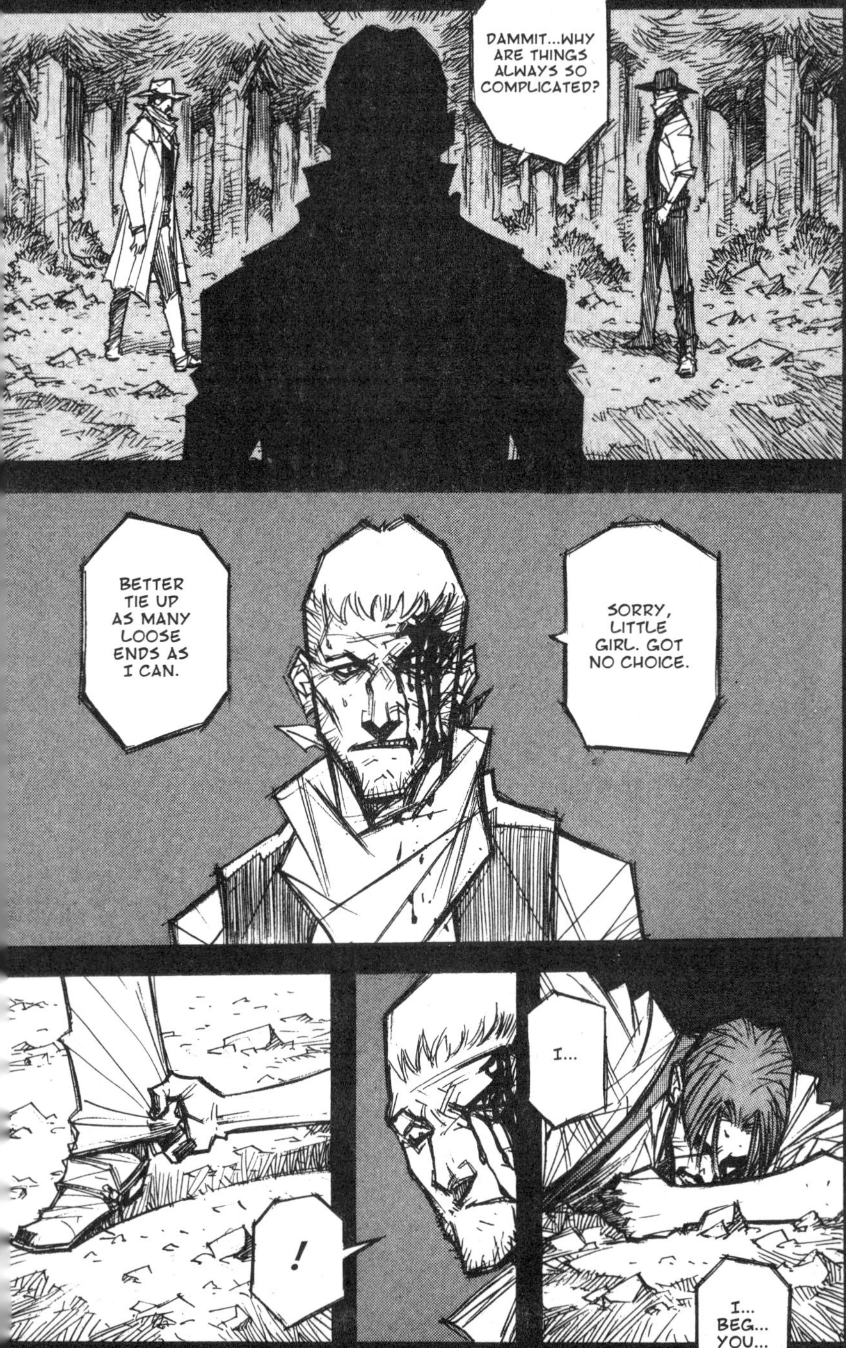
DAMMIT...WHY ARE THINGS ALWAYS SO COMPLICATED?
BETTER TIE UP AS MANY LOOSE ENDS AS I CAN.
SORRY, LITTLE GIRL. GOT NO CHOICE.
!
I...
I... BEG... YOU...

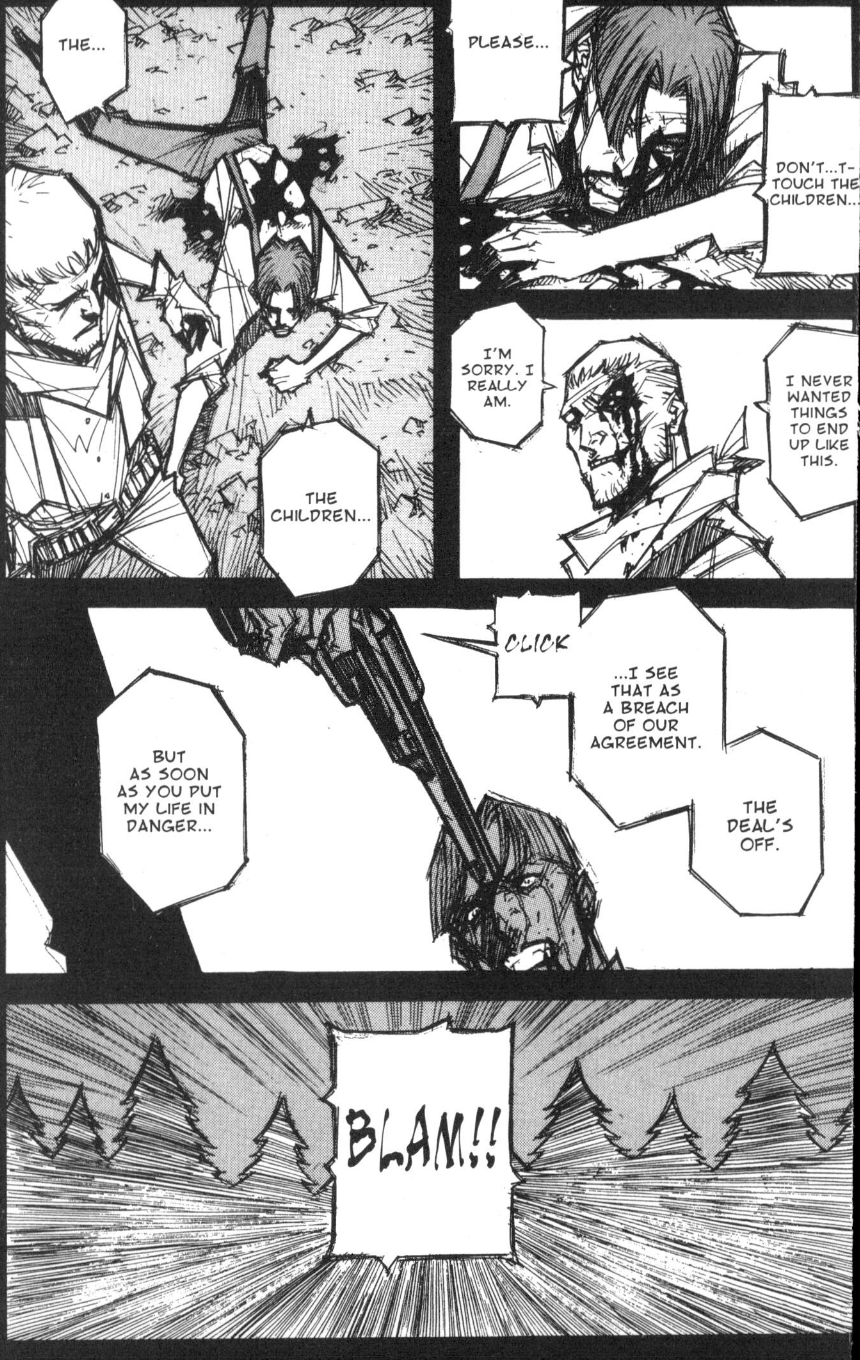
THE...
THE CHILDREN...
PLEASE...
DON'T...T-TOUCH THE CHILDREN...
I'M SORRY. I REALLY AM.
I NEVER WANTED THINGS TO END UP LIKE THIS.
BUT AS SOON AS YOU PUT MY LIFE IN DANGER...
CLICK
...I SEE THAT AS A BREACH OF OUR AGREEMENT.
THE DEAL'S OFF.
BLAM!!

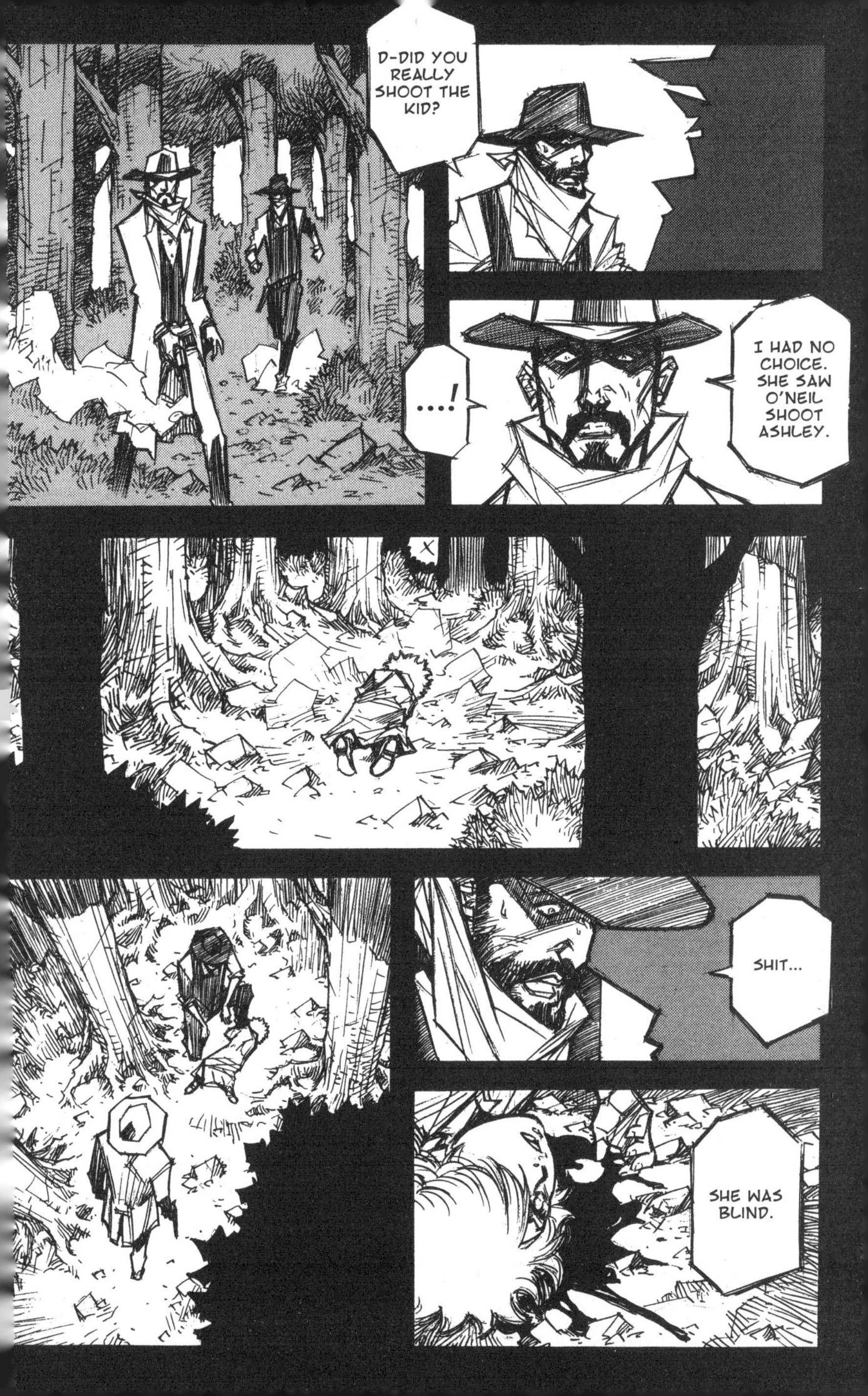
D-DID YOU REALLY SHOOT THE KID?
...!
I HAD NO CHOICE. SHE SAW O'NEIL SHOOT ASHLEY.
SHIT...
SHE WAS BLIND.

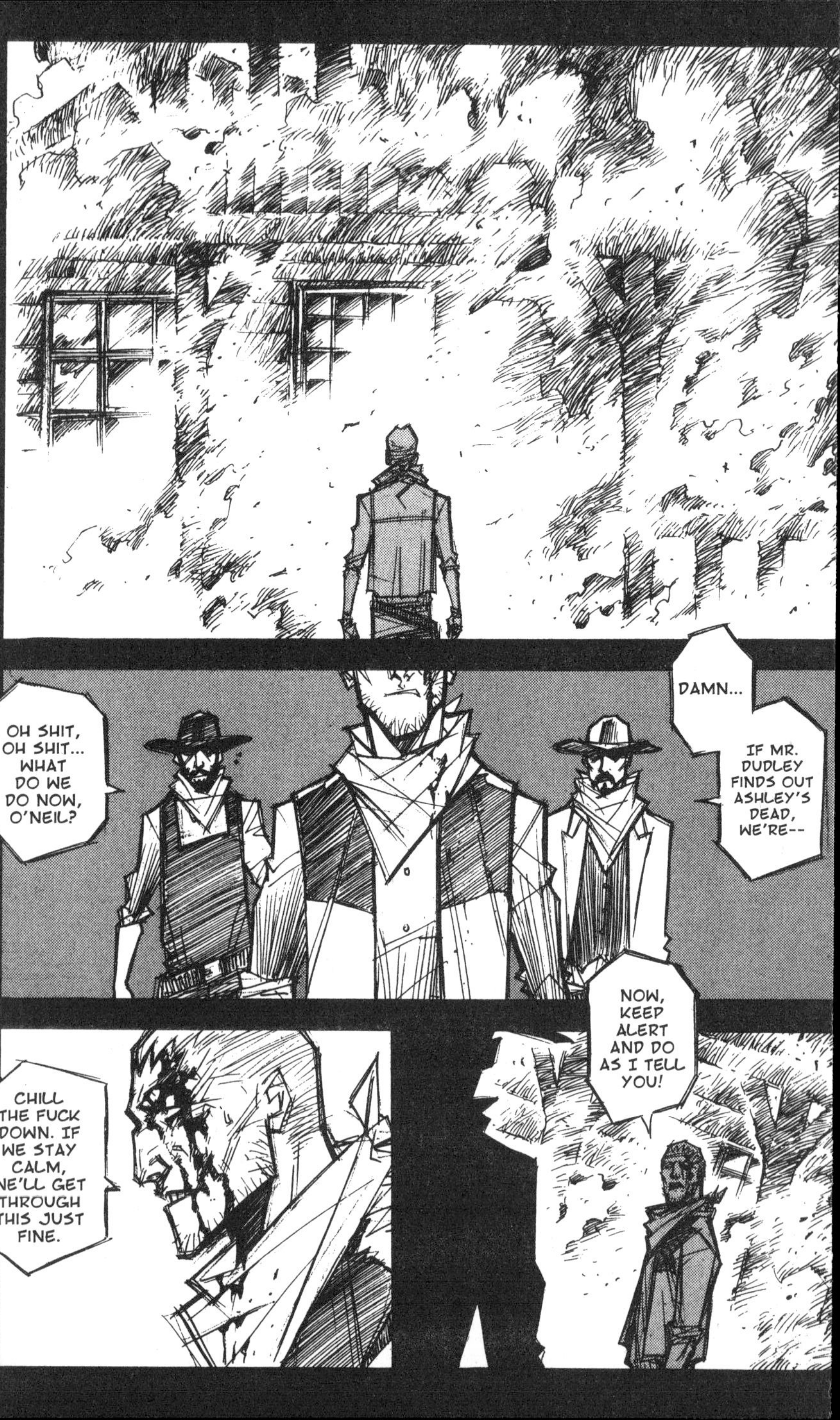
OH SHIT, OH SHIT... WHAT DO WE DO NOW, O'NEIL?
DAMN...
IF MR. DUDLEY FINDS OUT ASHLEY'S DEAD, WE'RE--
CHILL THE FUCK DOWN. IF WE STAY CALM, WE'LL GET THROUGH THIS JUST FINE.
NOW, KEEP ALERT AND DO AS I TELL YOU!

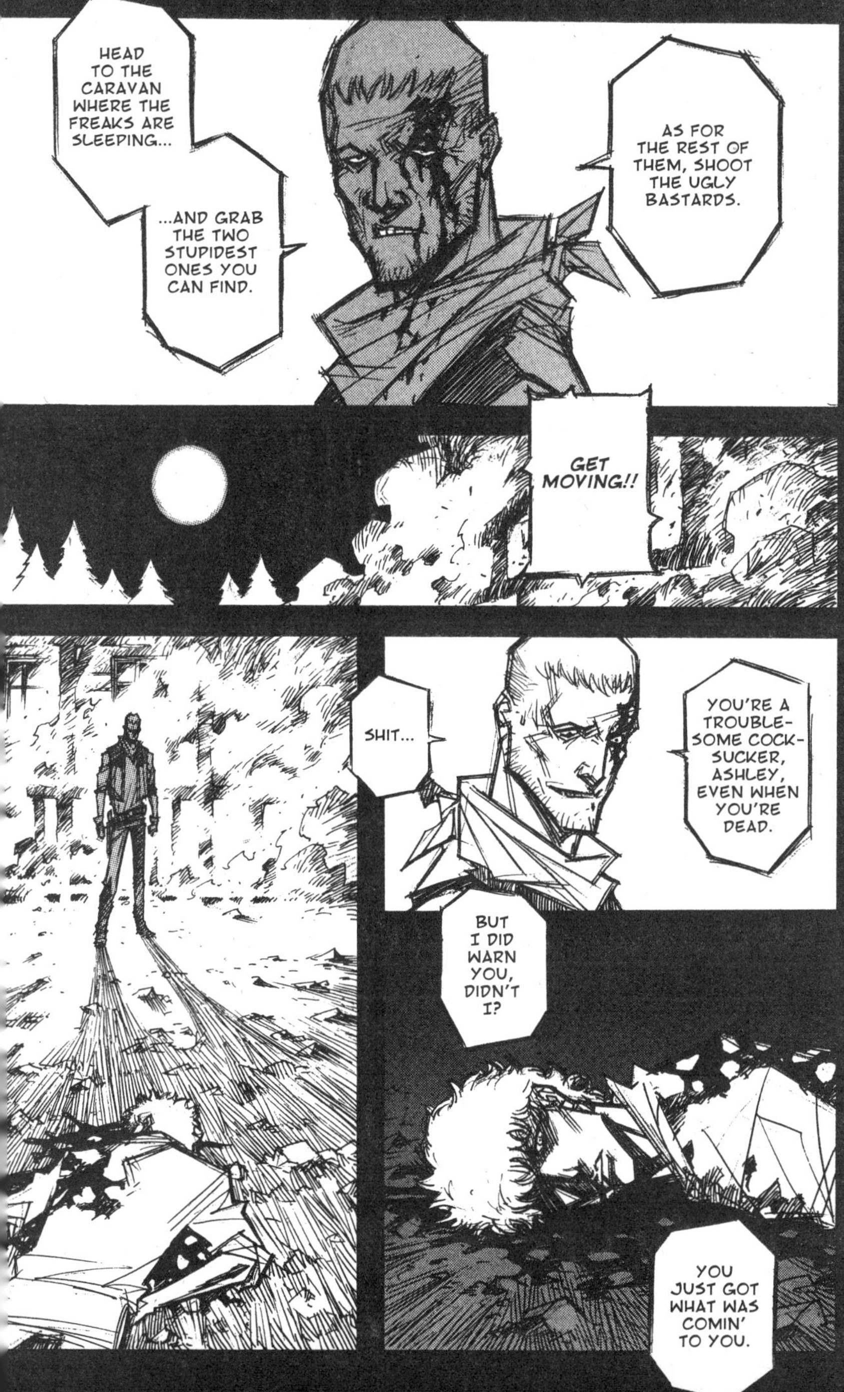
HEAD TO THE CARAVAN WHERE THE FREAKS ARE SLEEPING...
...AND GRAB THE TWO STUPIDEST ONES YOU CAN FIND.
AS FOR THE REST OF THEM, SHOOT THE UGLY BASTARDS.
GET MOVING!!
SHIT...
YOU'RE A TROUBLE-SOME COCK-SUCKER, ASHLEY, EVEN WHEN YOU'RE DEAD.
BUT I DID WARN YOU, DIDN'T I?
YOU JUST GOT WHAT WAS COMIN' TO YOU.

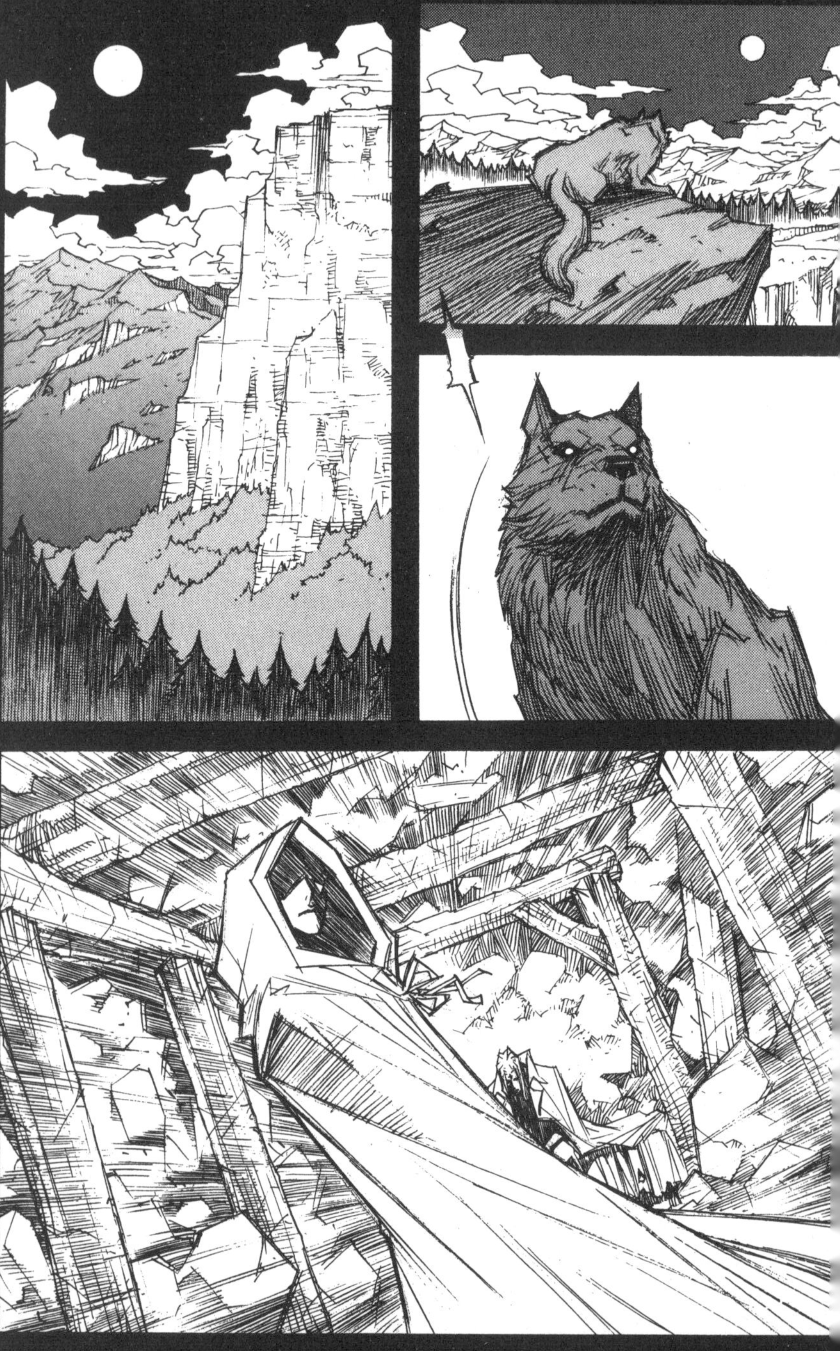

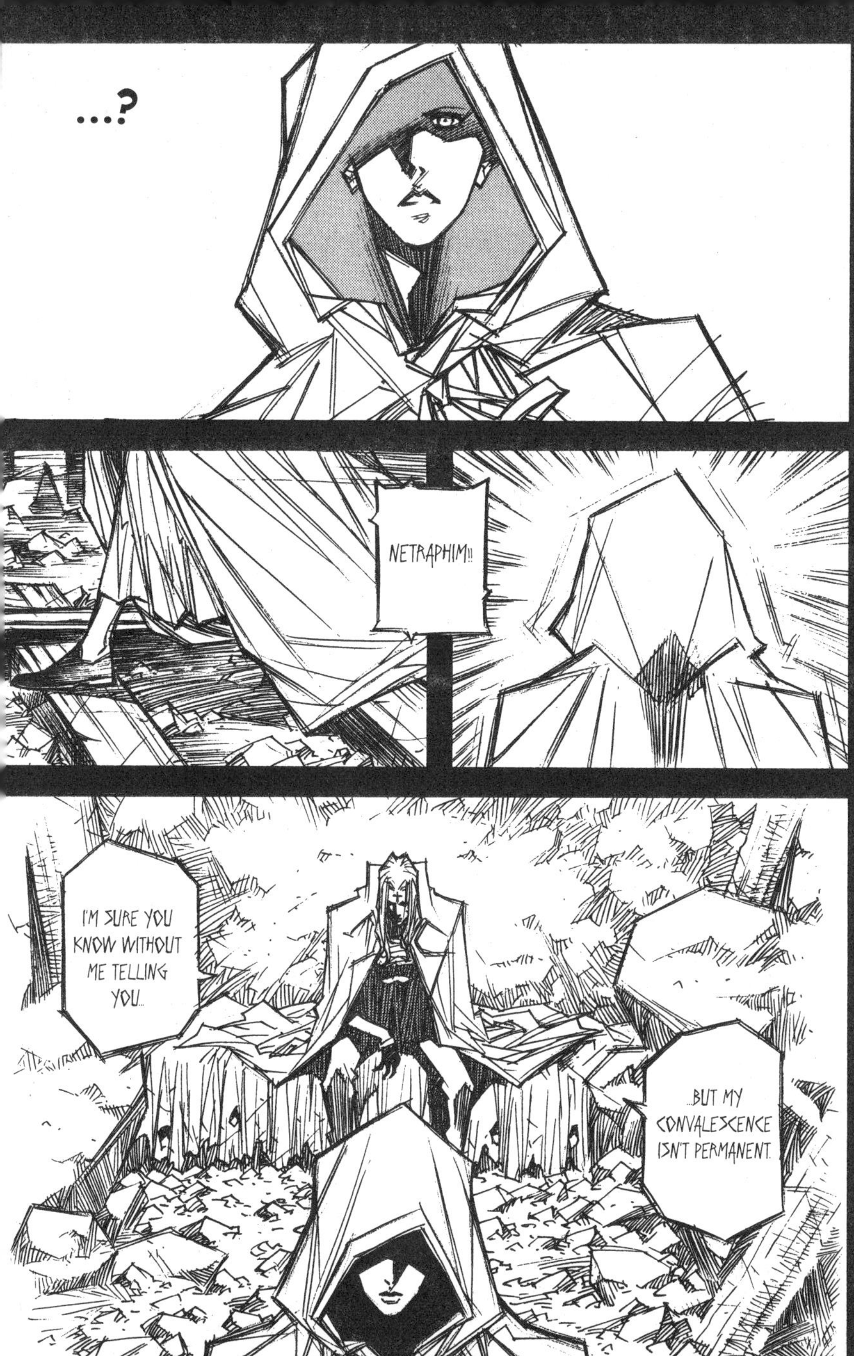
...?
NETRAPHIM!!
I'M SURE YOU KNOW WITHOUT ME TELLING YOU...
...BUT MY CONVALESCENCE ISN'T PERMANENT.

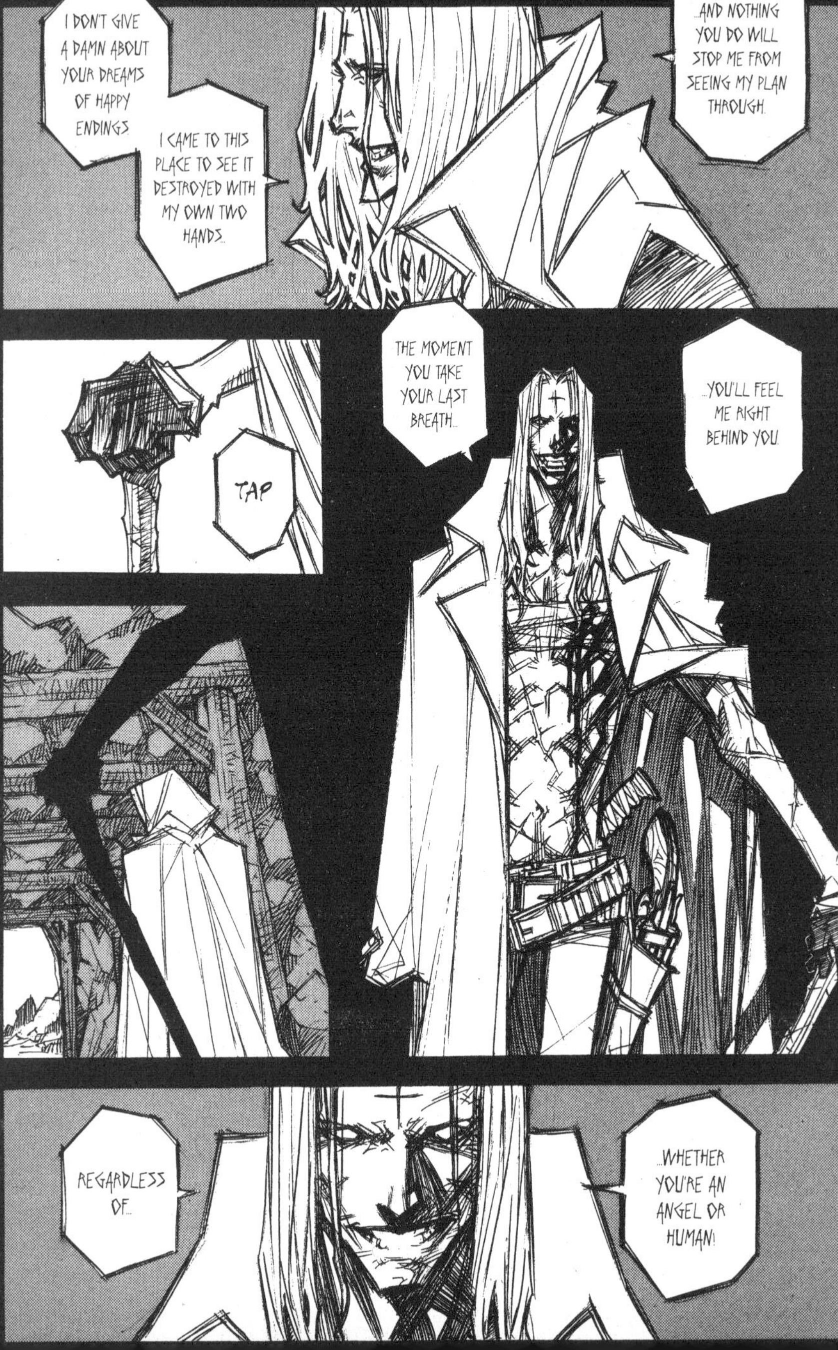
I DON'T GIVE A DAMN ABOUT YOUR DREAMS OF HAPPY ENDINGS.
I CAME TO THIS PLACE TO SEE IT DESTROYED WITH MY OWN TWO HANDS...
...AND NOTHING YOU DO WILL STOP ME FROM SEEING MY PLAN THROUGH.
TAP
THE MOMENT YOU TAKE YOUR LAST BREATH...
...YOU'LL FEEL ME RIGHT BEHIND YOU.
REGARDLESS OF...
...WHETHER YOU'RE AN ANGEL OR HUMAN!

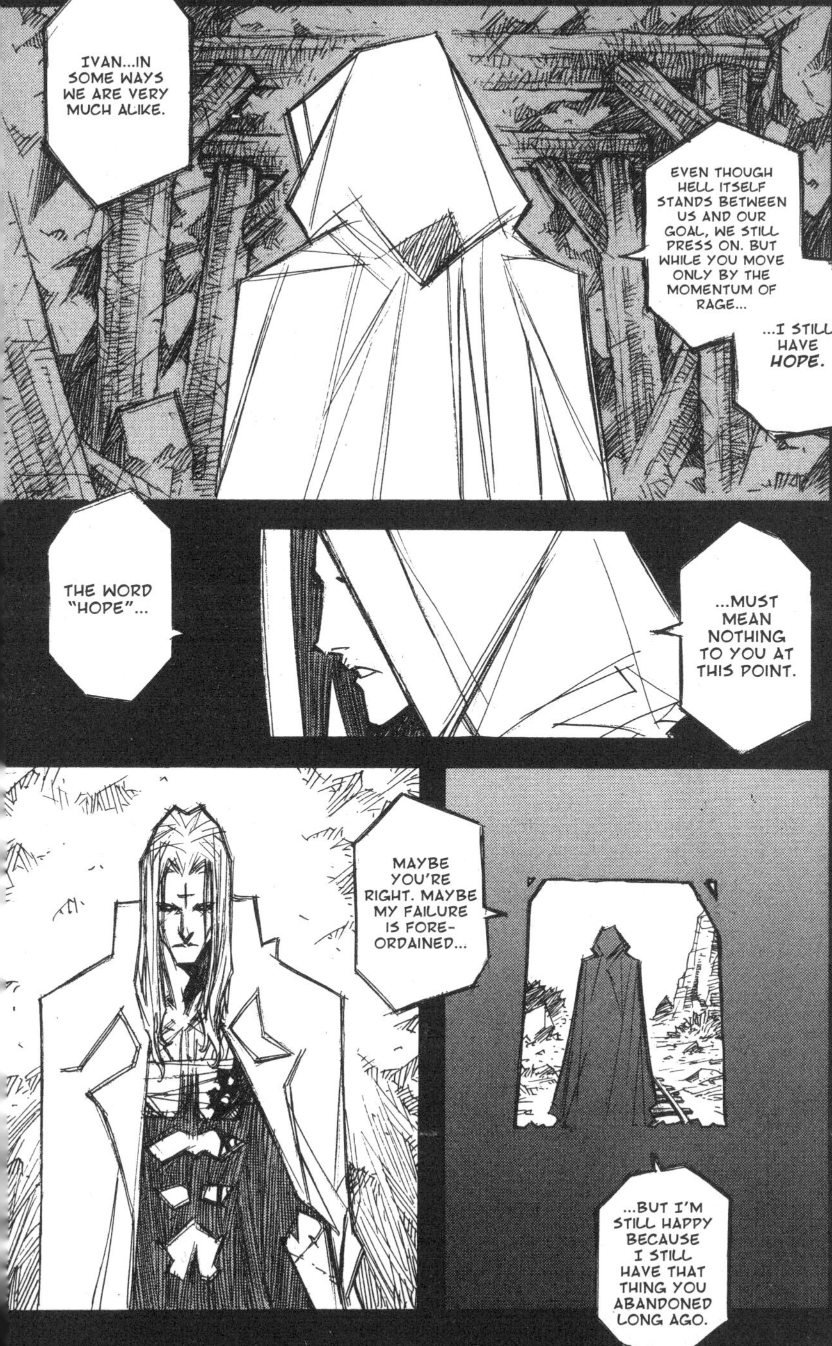
IVAN...IN SOME WAYS WE ARE VERY MUCH ALIKE.
EVEN THOUGH HELL ITSELF STANDS BETWEEN US AND OUR GOAL, WE STILL PRESS ON. BUT WHILE YOU MOVE ONLY BY THE MOMENTUM OF RAGE...
...I STILL HAVE HOPE.
THE WORD "HOPE"...
...MUST MEAN NOTHING TO YOU AT THIS POINT.
MAYBE YOU'RE RIGHT. MAYBE MY FAILURE IS FORE-ORDAINED...
...BUT I'M STILL HAPPY BECAUSE I STILL HAVE THAT THING YOU ABANDONED LONG AGO.

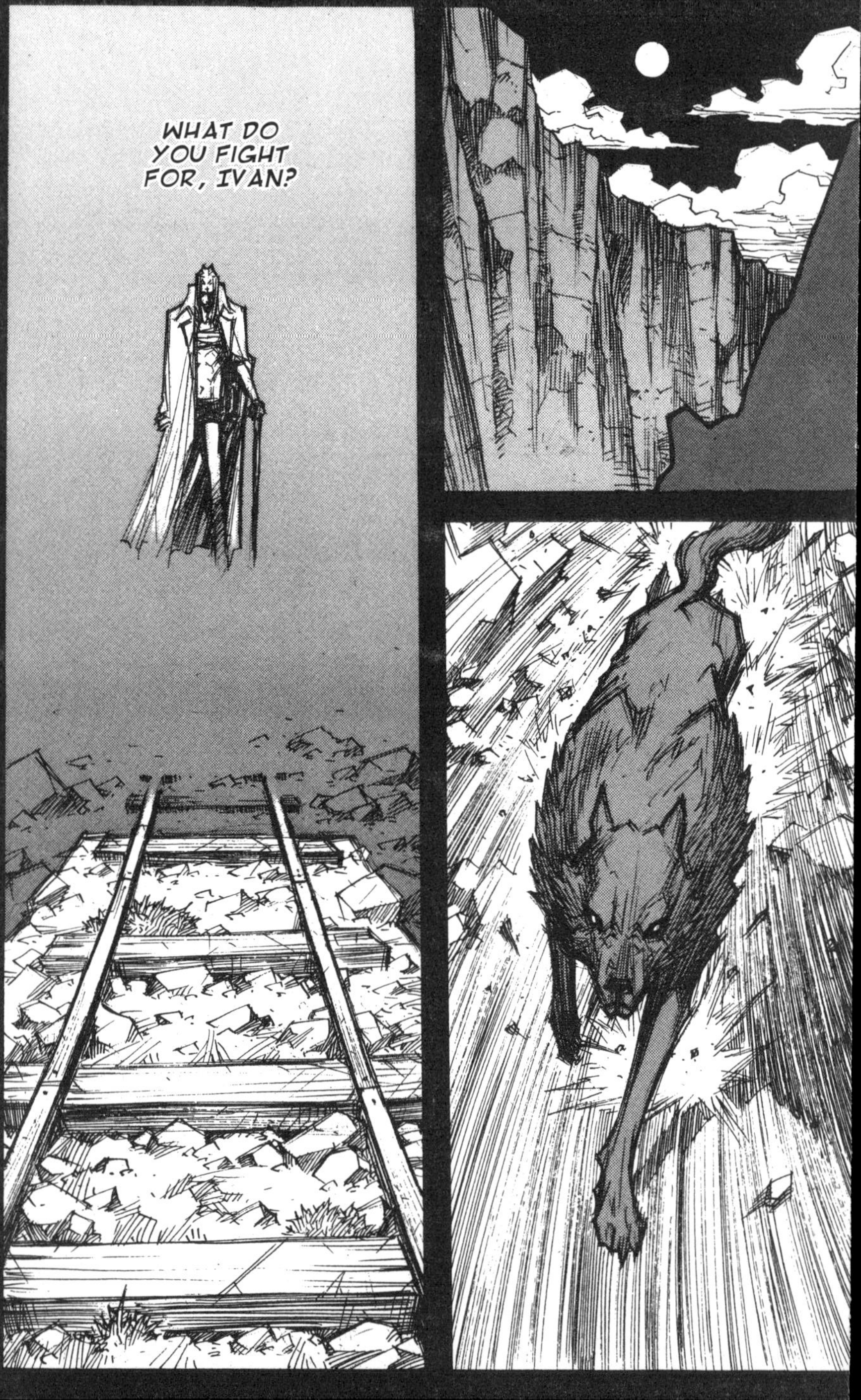
WHAT DO YOU FIGHT FOR, IVAN?

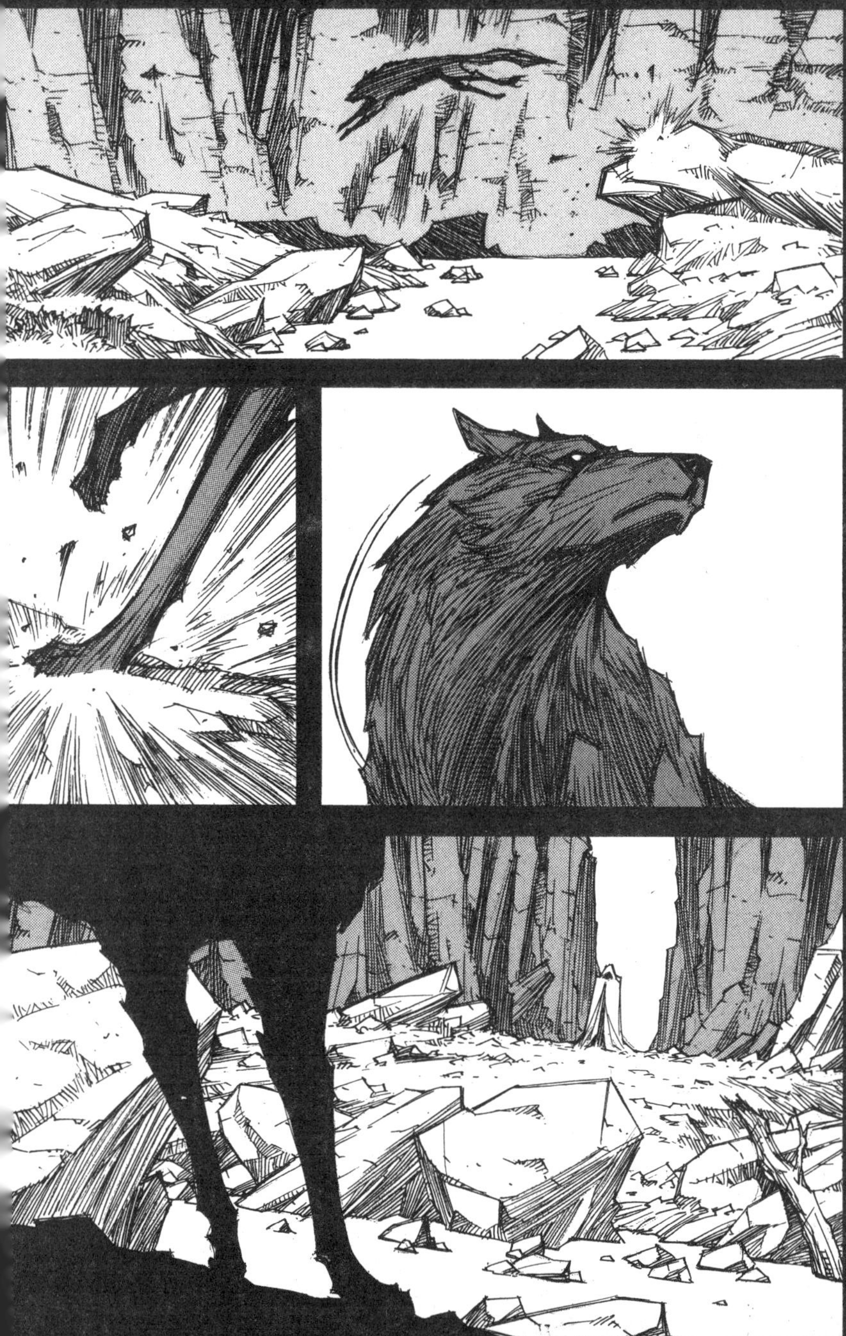

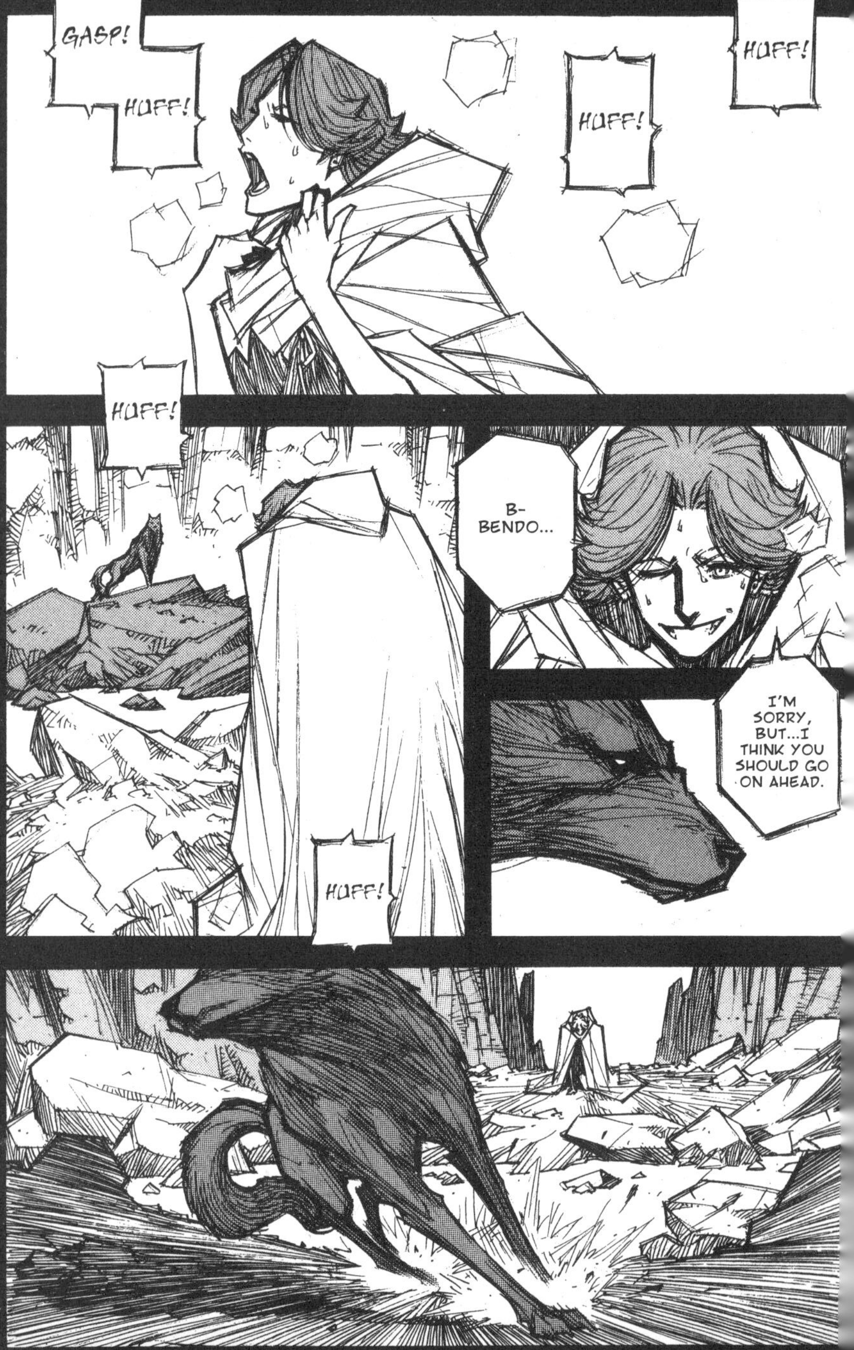
GASP!
HUFF!
HUFF!
HUFF!
HUFF!
HUFF!
B-BENDO...
I'M SORRY, BUT...I THINK YOU SHOULD GO ON AHEAD.

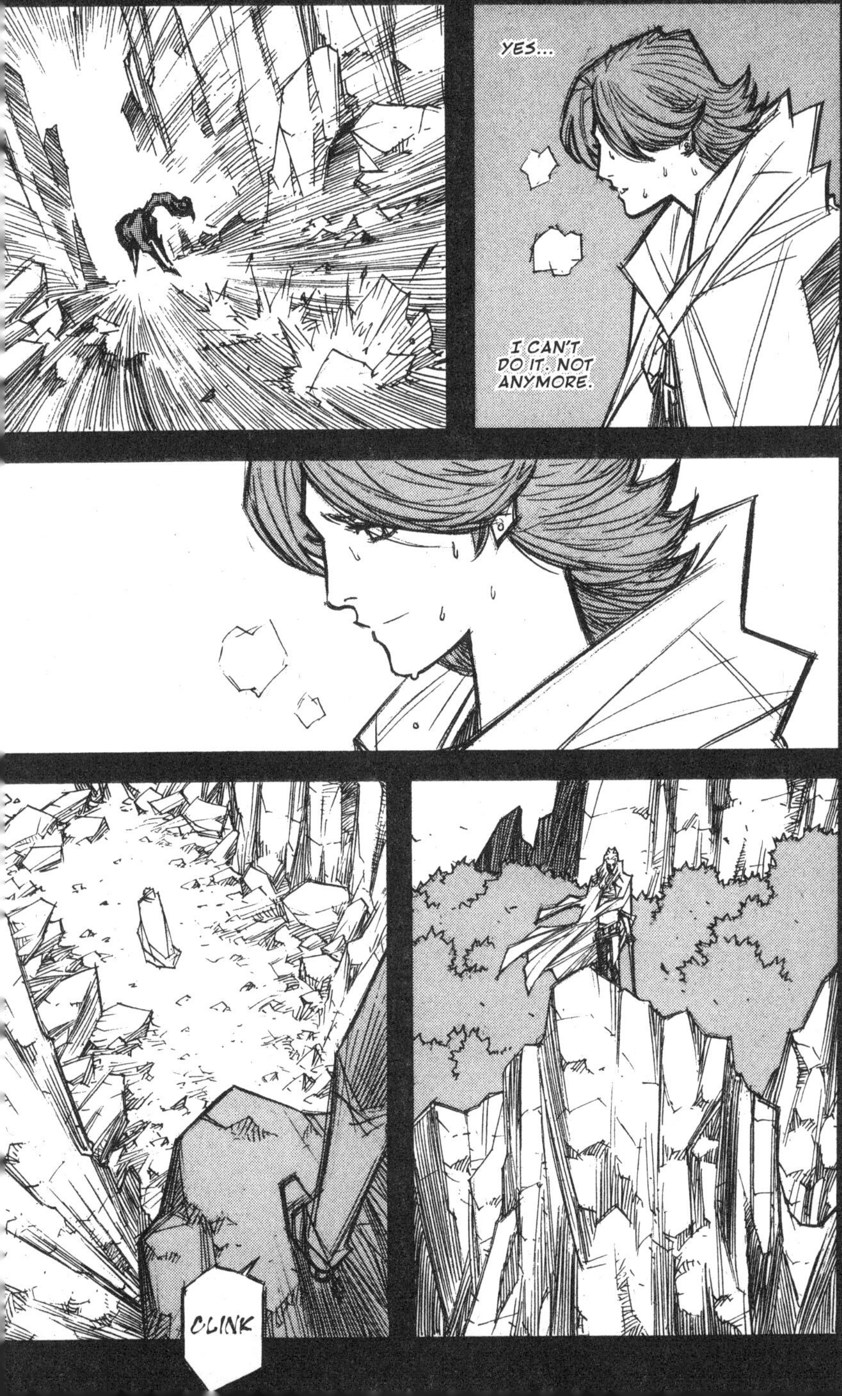
YES...
I CAN'T DO IT. NOT ANYMORE.
CLINK

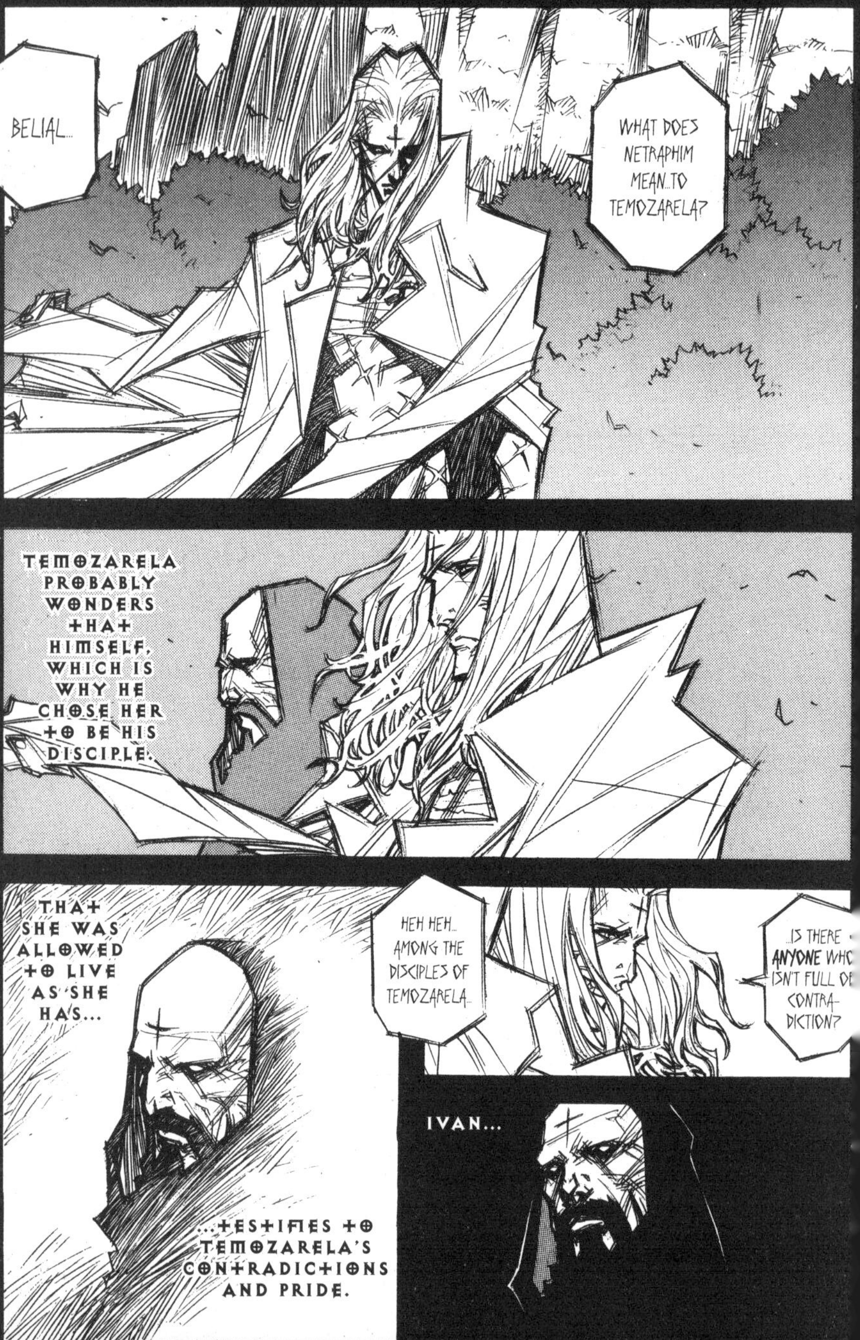
BELIAL...
WHAT DOES NETRAPHIM MEAN...TO TEMOZARELA?
TEMOZARELA PROBABLY WONDERS THAT HIMSELF, WHICH IS WHY HE CHOSE HER TO BE HIS DISCIPLE.
THAT SHE WAS ALLOWED TO LIVE AS SHE HAS...
...TESTIFIES TO TEMOZARELA'S CONTRADICTIONS AND PRIDE.
HEH HEH... AMONG THE DISCIPLES OF TEMOZARELA...
...IS THERE ANYONE WHO ISN'T FULL OF CONTRA-DICTION?
IVAN...

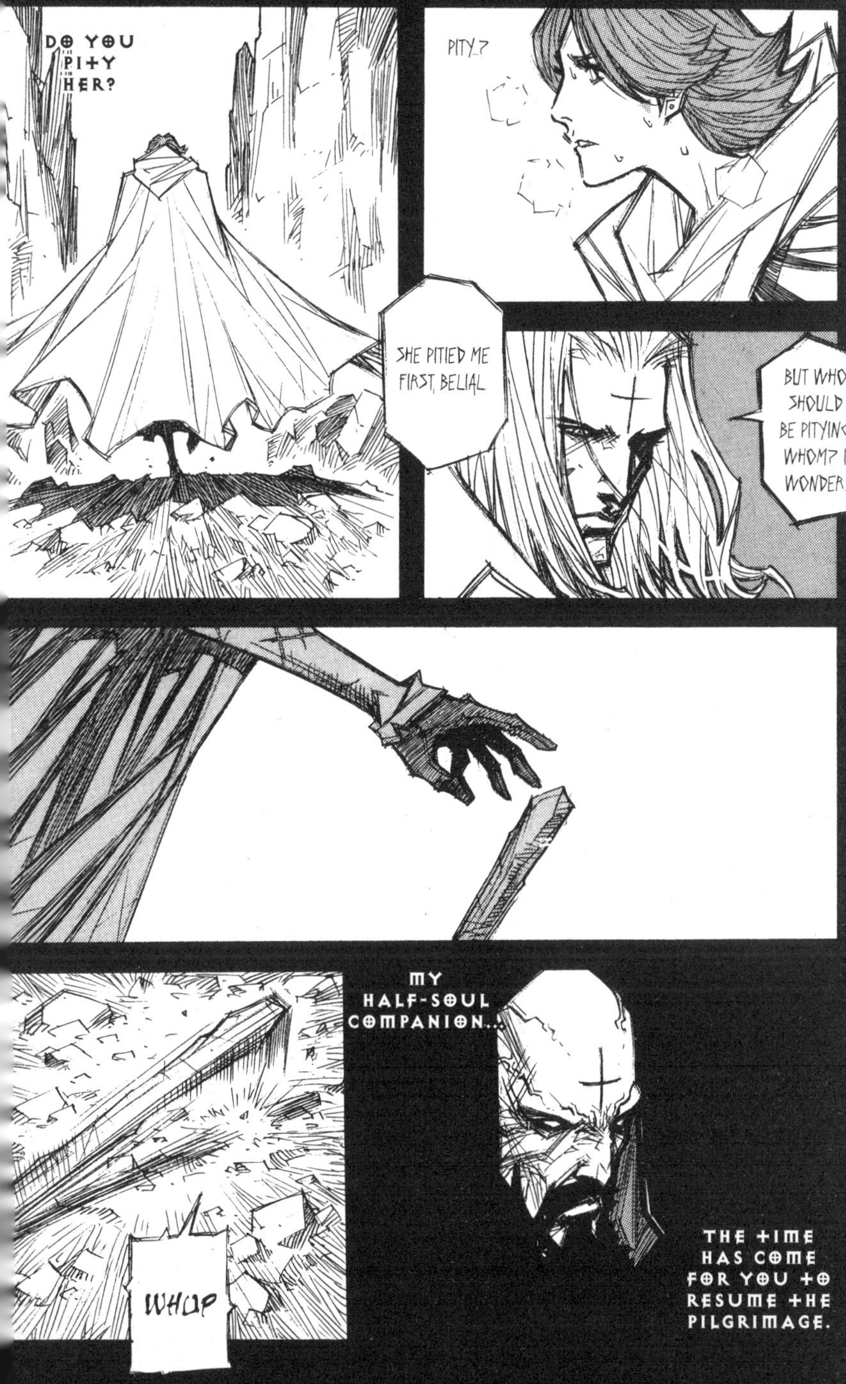
DO YOU PITY HER?
PITY...?
SHE PITIED ME FIRST, BELIAL.
BUT WHO SHOULD BE PITYING WHOM? I WONDER.
MY HALF-SOUL COMPANION...!
WHUP
THE TIME HAS COME FOR YOU TO RESUME THE PILGRIMAGE.

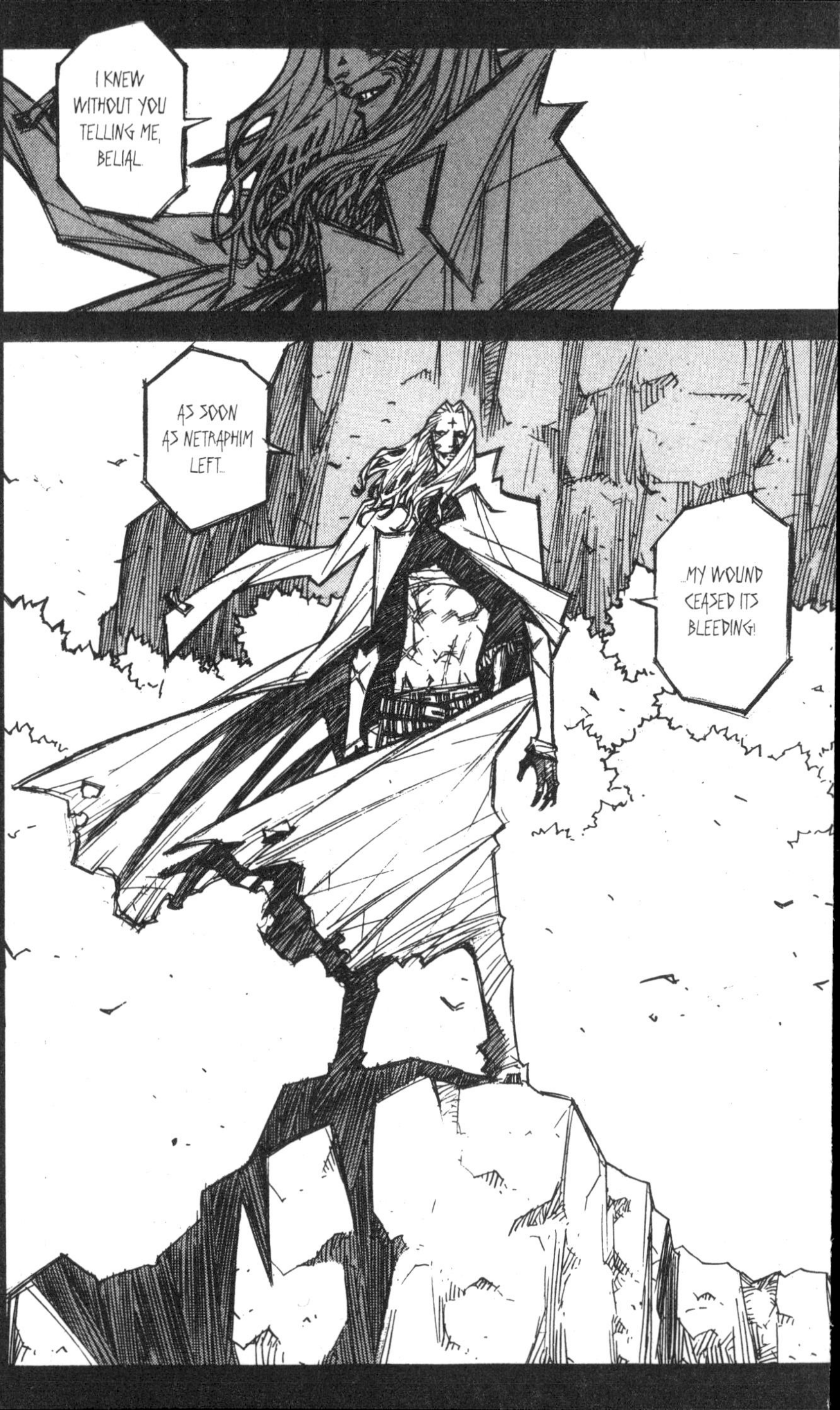
I KNEW WITHOUT YOU TELLING ME, BELIAL.
AS SOON AS NETRAPHIM LEFT...
...MY WOUND CEASED ITS BLEEDING!

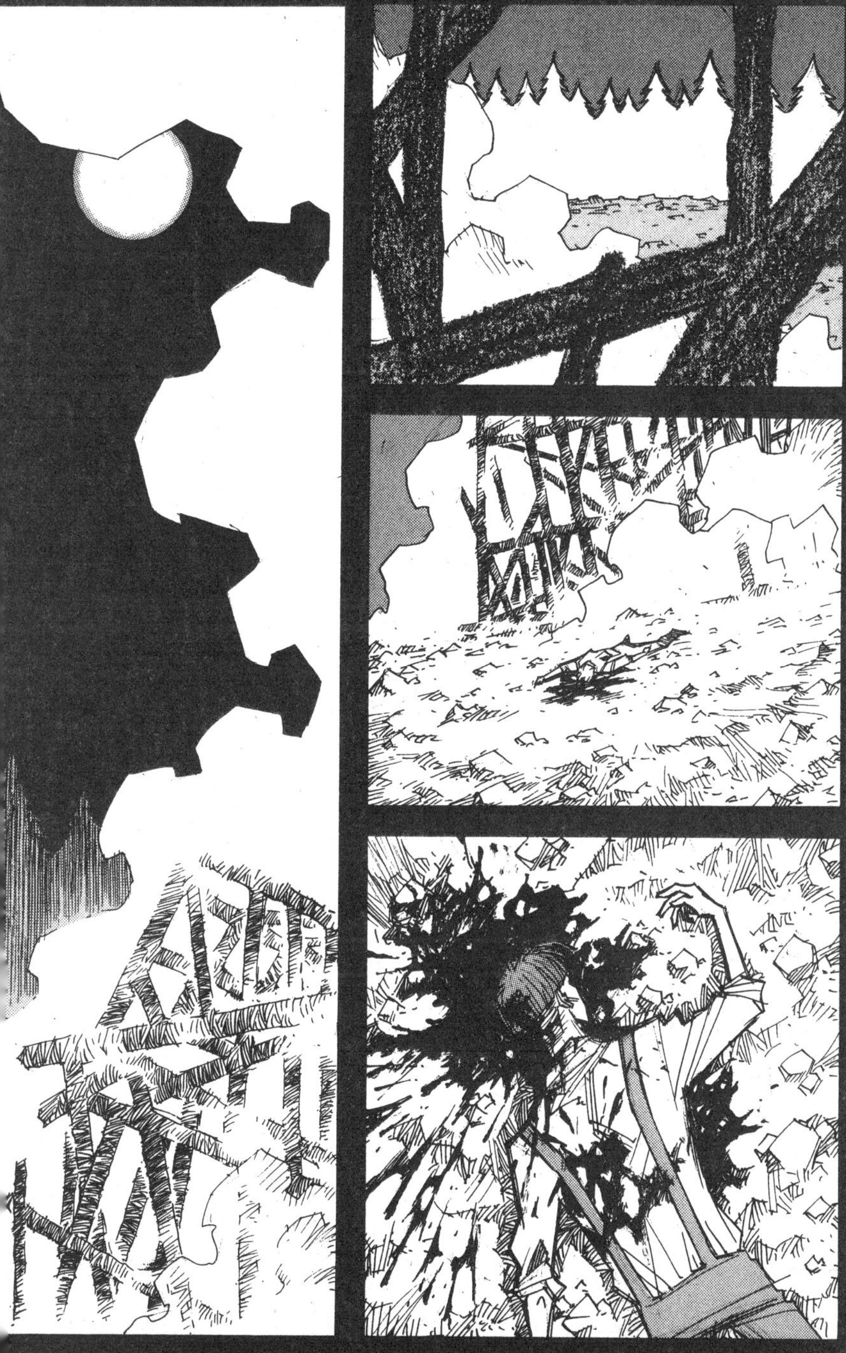

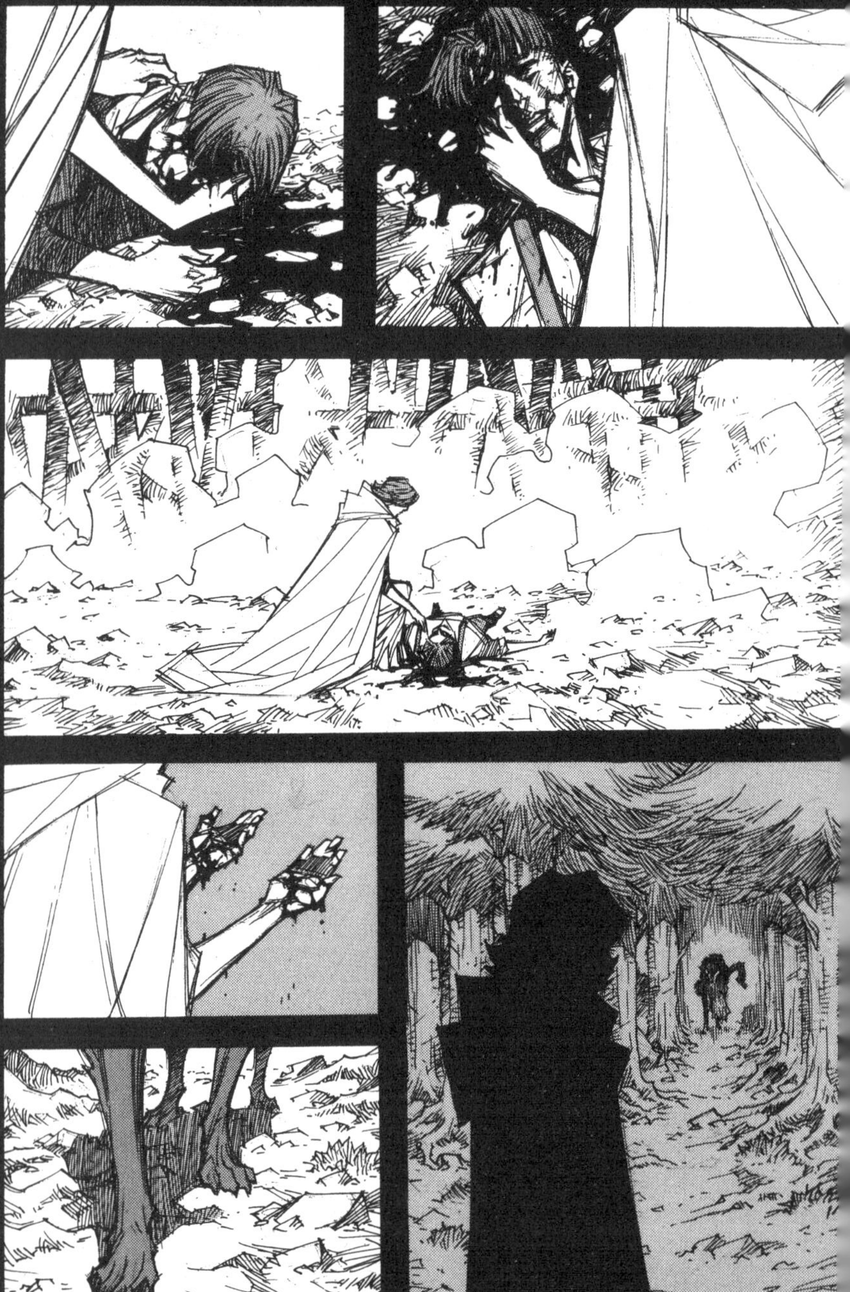

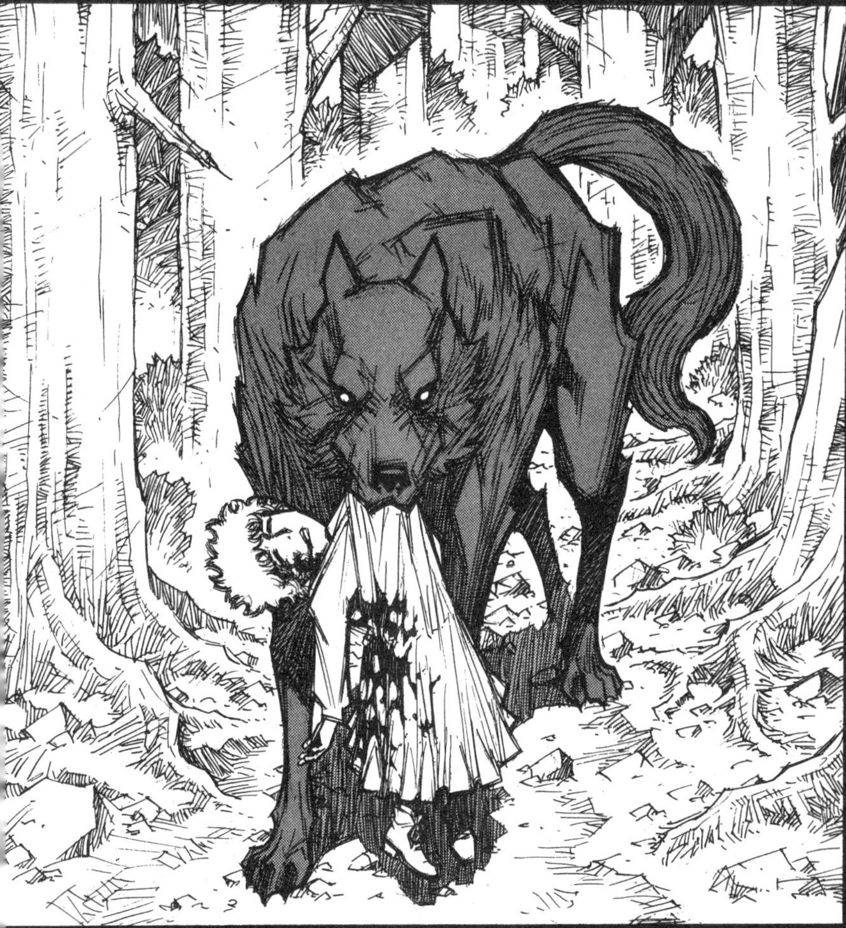
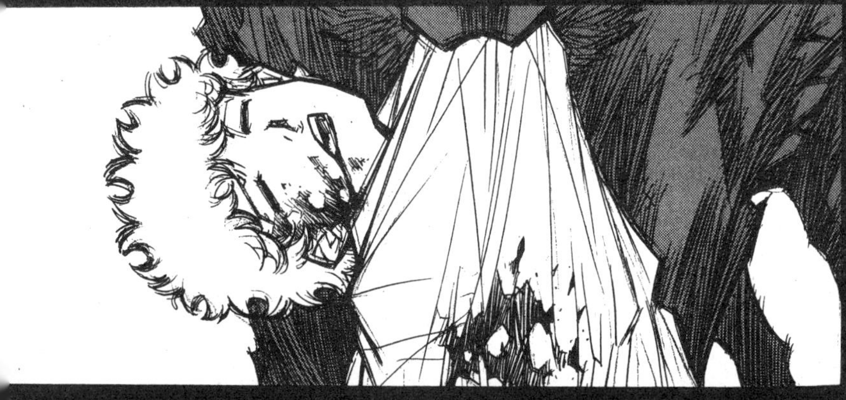

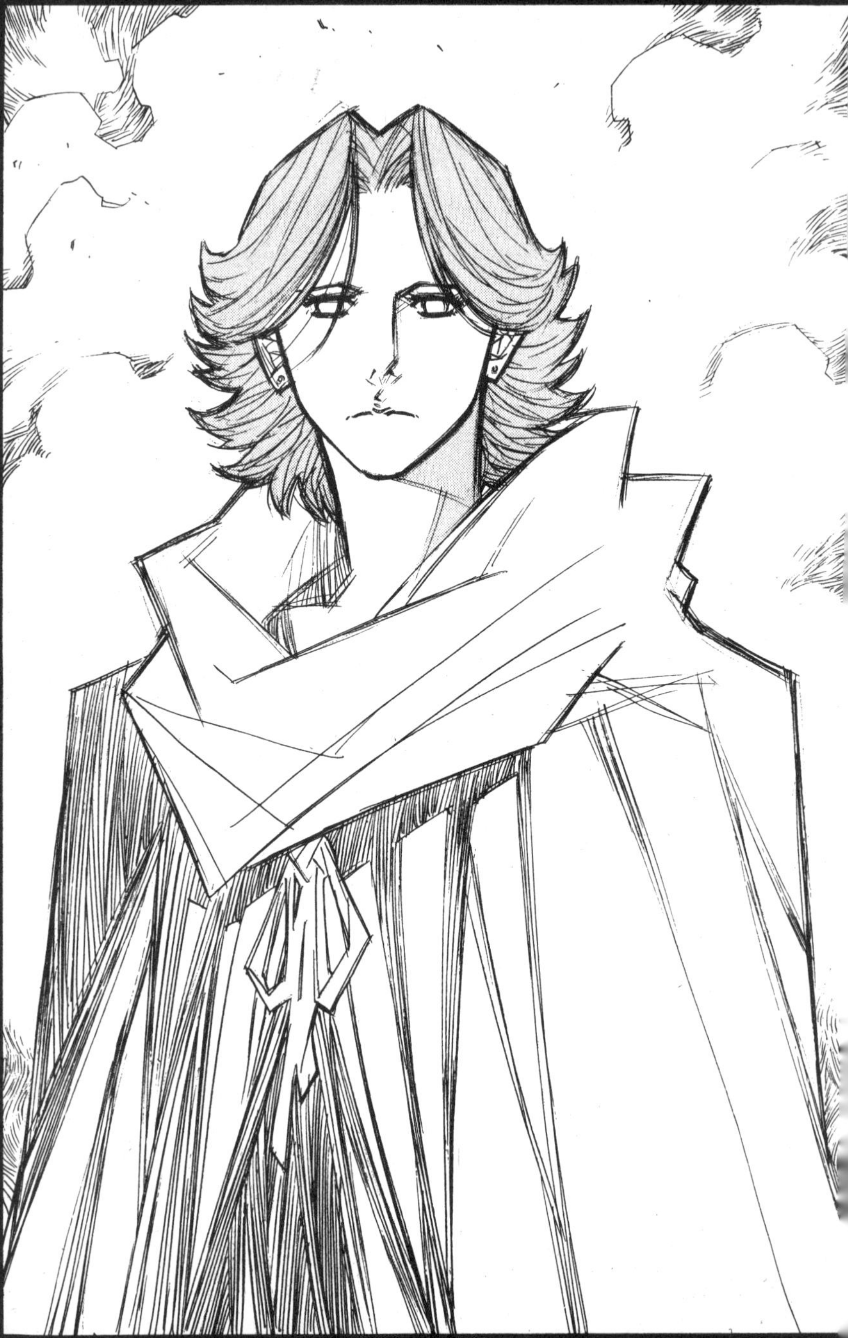

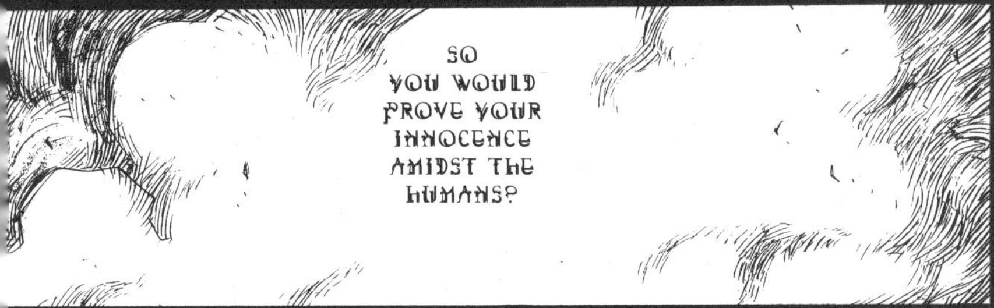
SO YOU WOULD PROVE YOUR INNOCENCE AMIDST THE HUMANS?
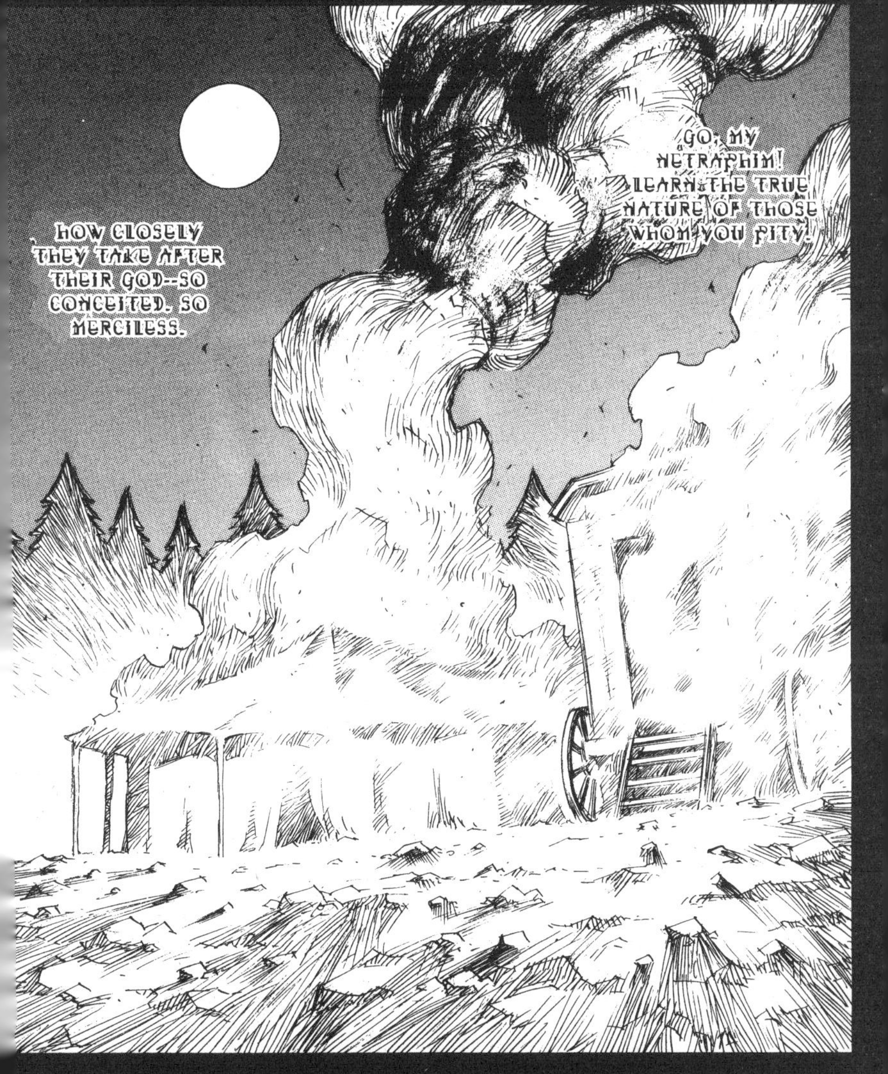
HOW CLOSELY THEY TAKE AFTER THEIR GOD--SO CONCEITED. SO MERCILESS.
GO, MY NETRAPHIM! LEARN THE TRUE NATURE OF THOSE WHOM YOU PITY!

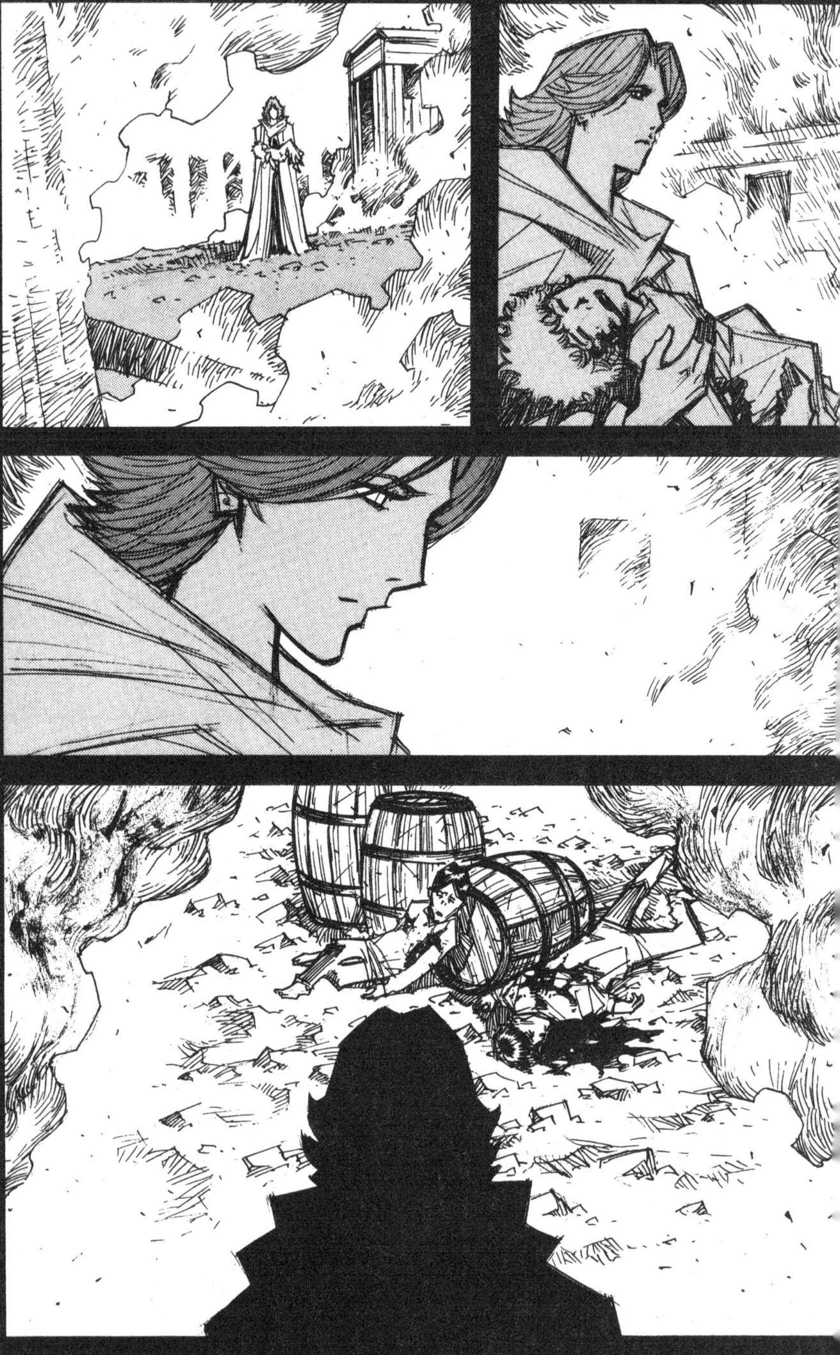

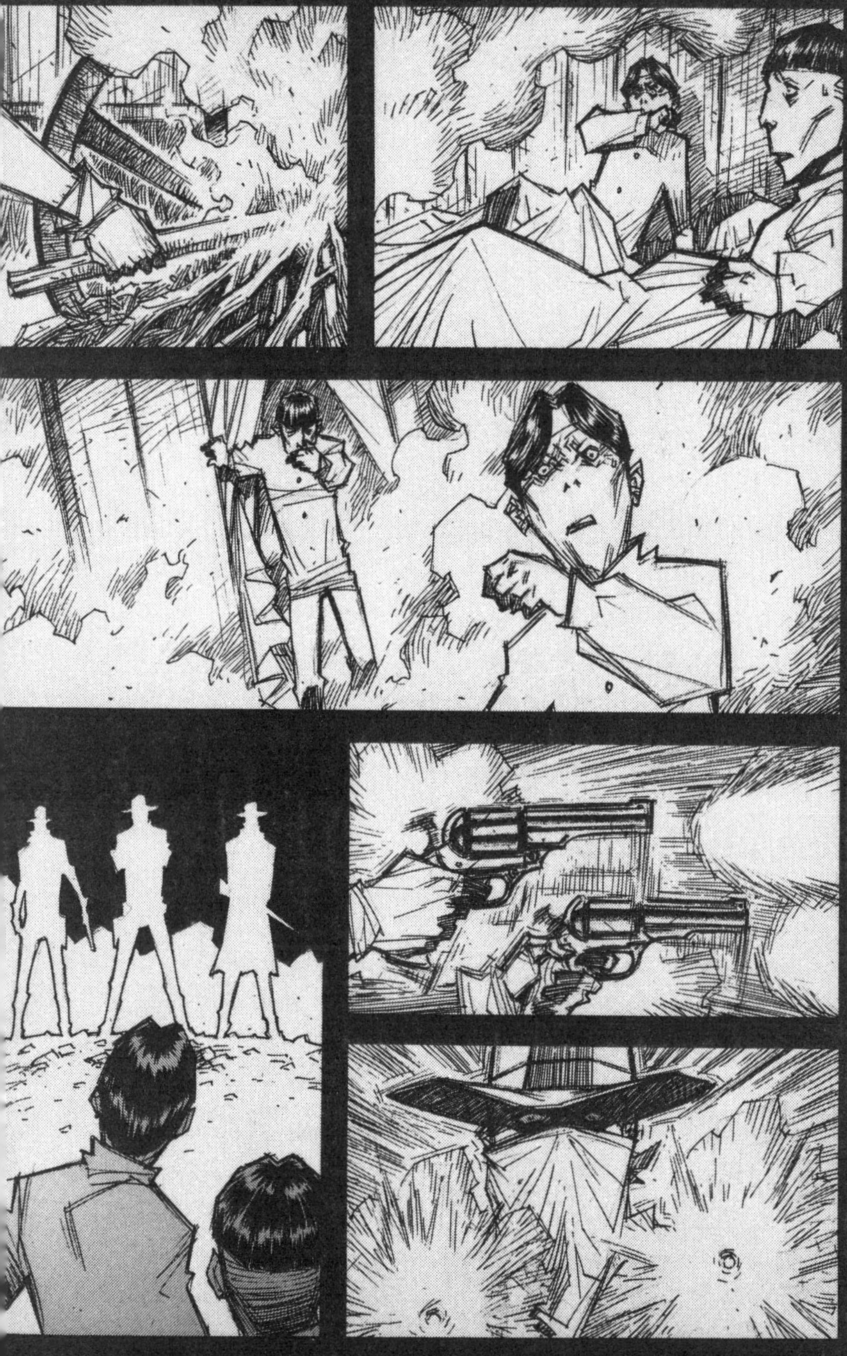

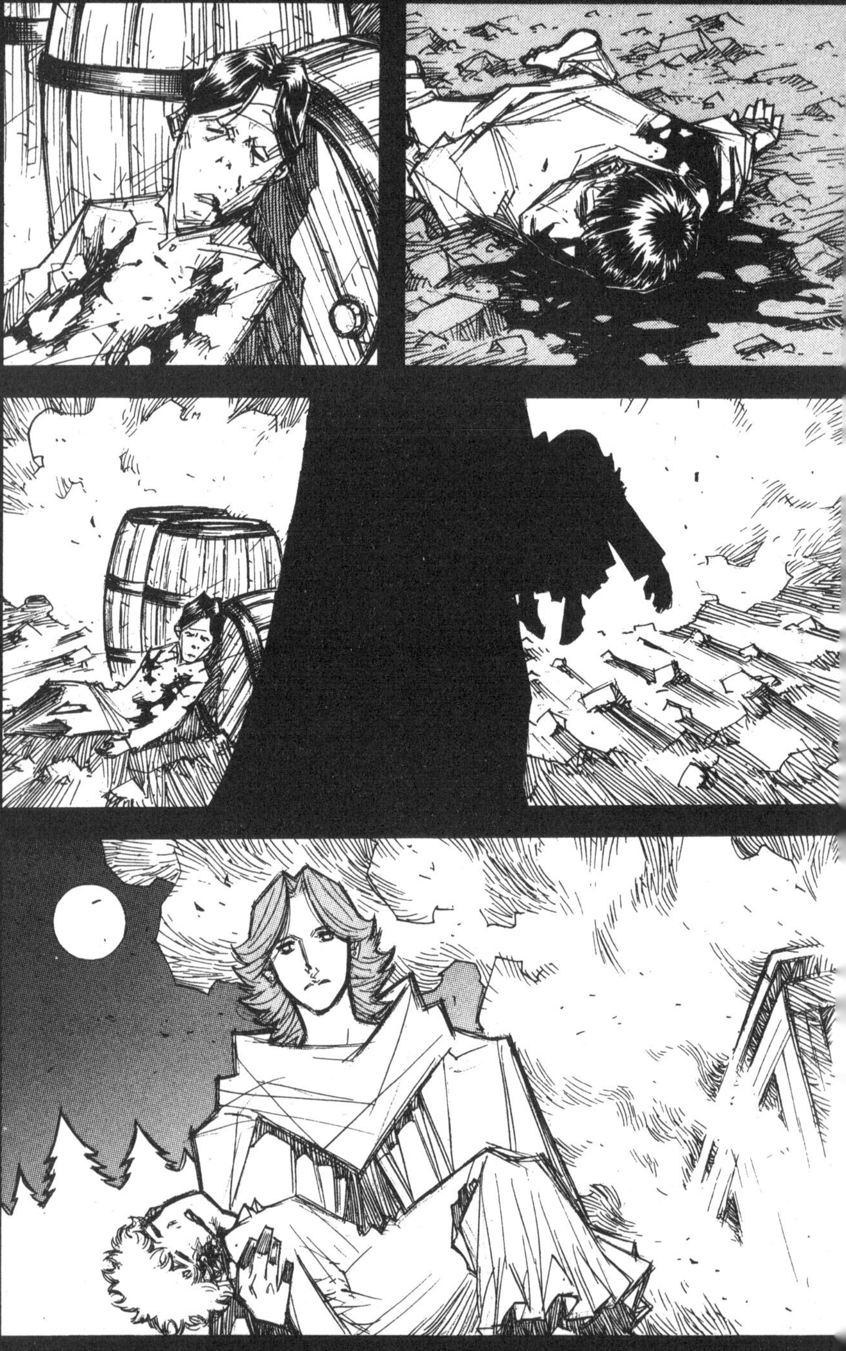

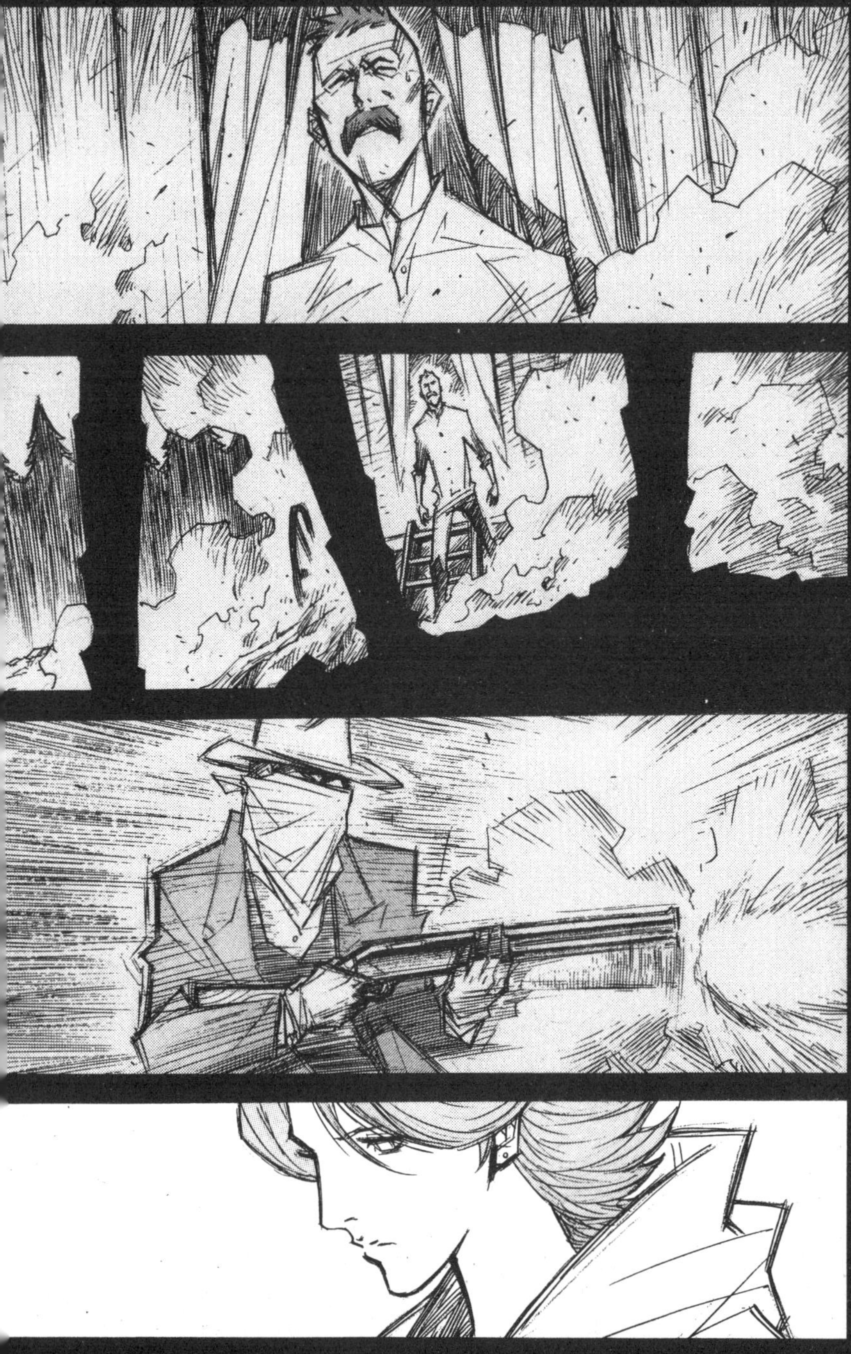

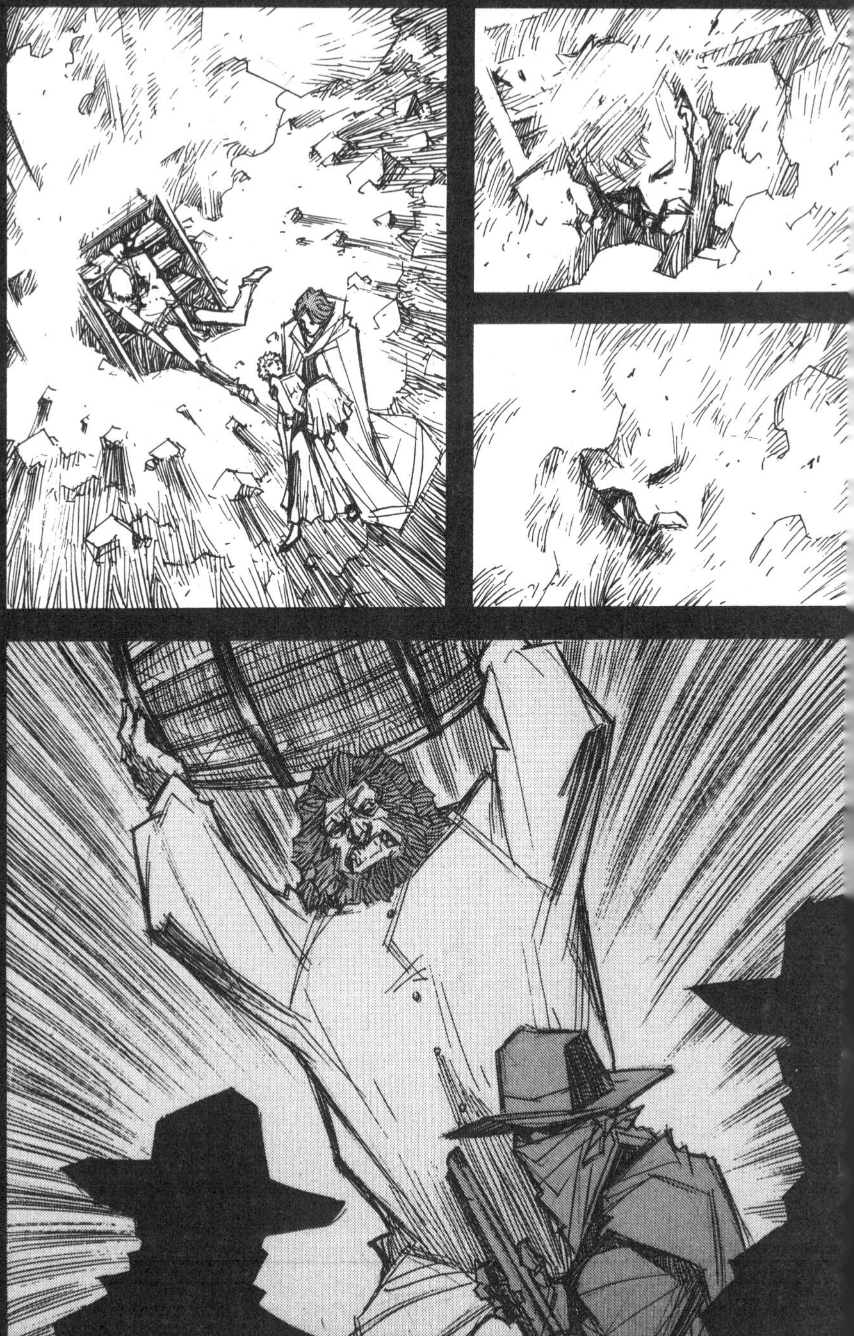

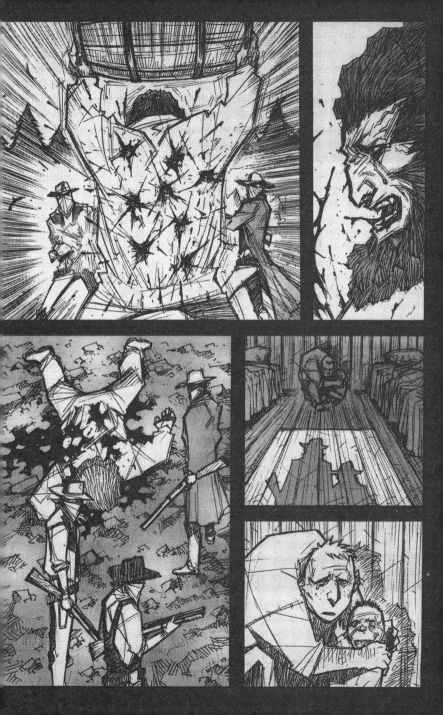

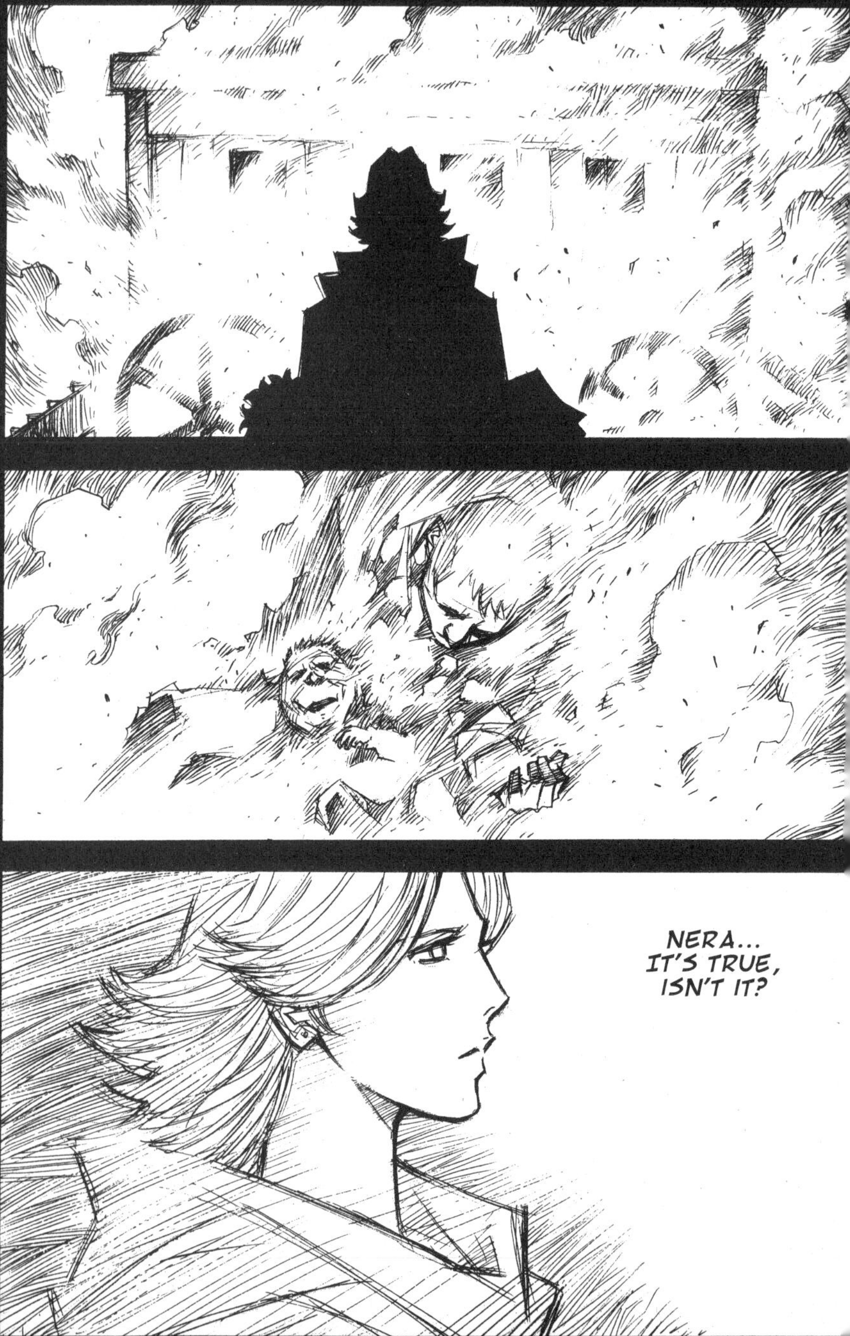
NERA... IT'S TRUE, ISN'T IT?

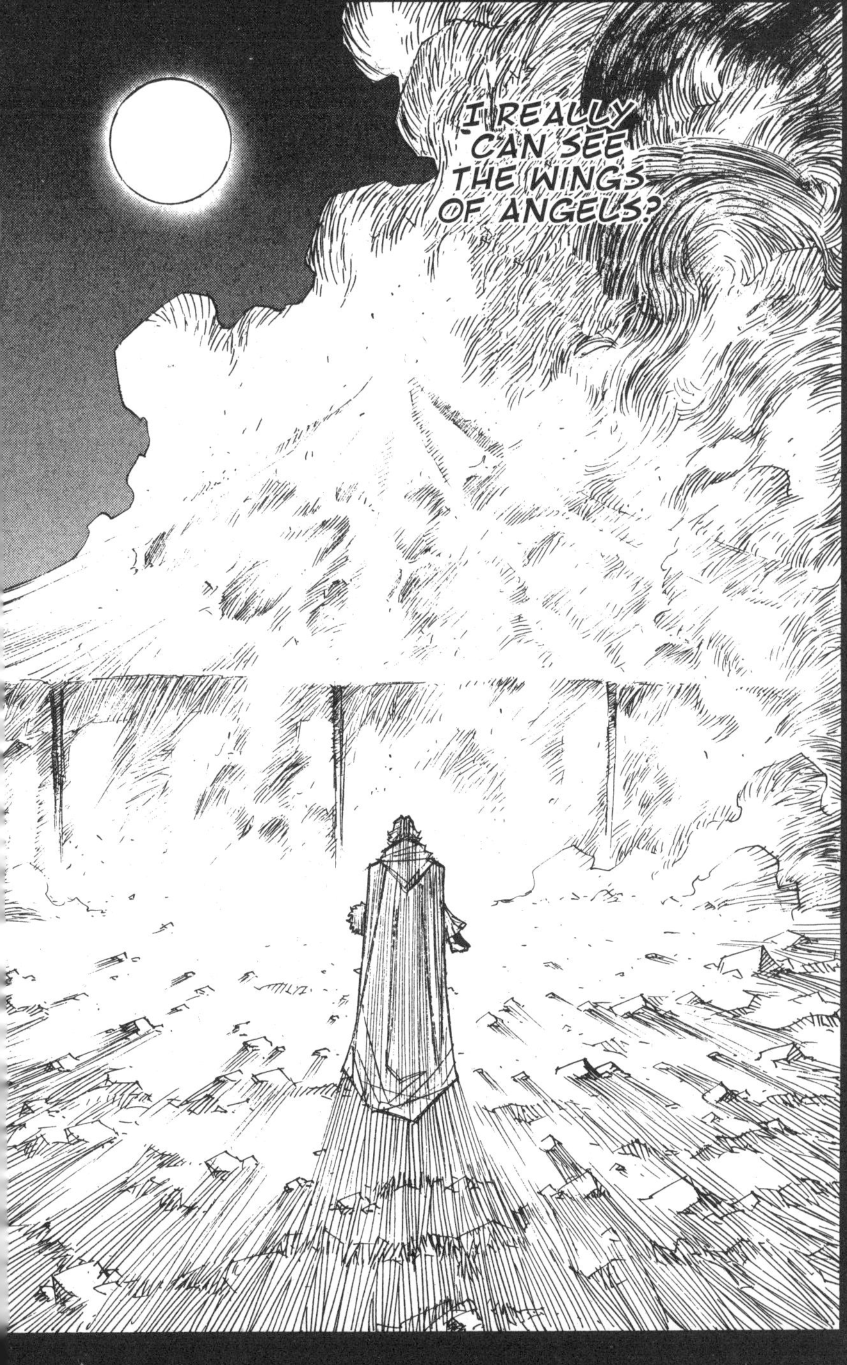
I REALLY CAN SEE THE WINGS OF ANGELS?

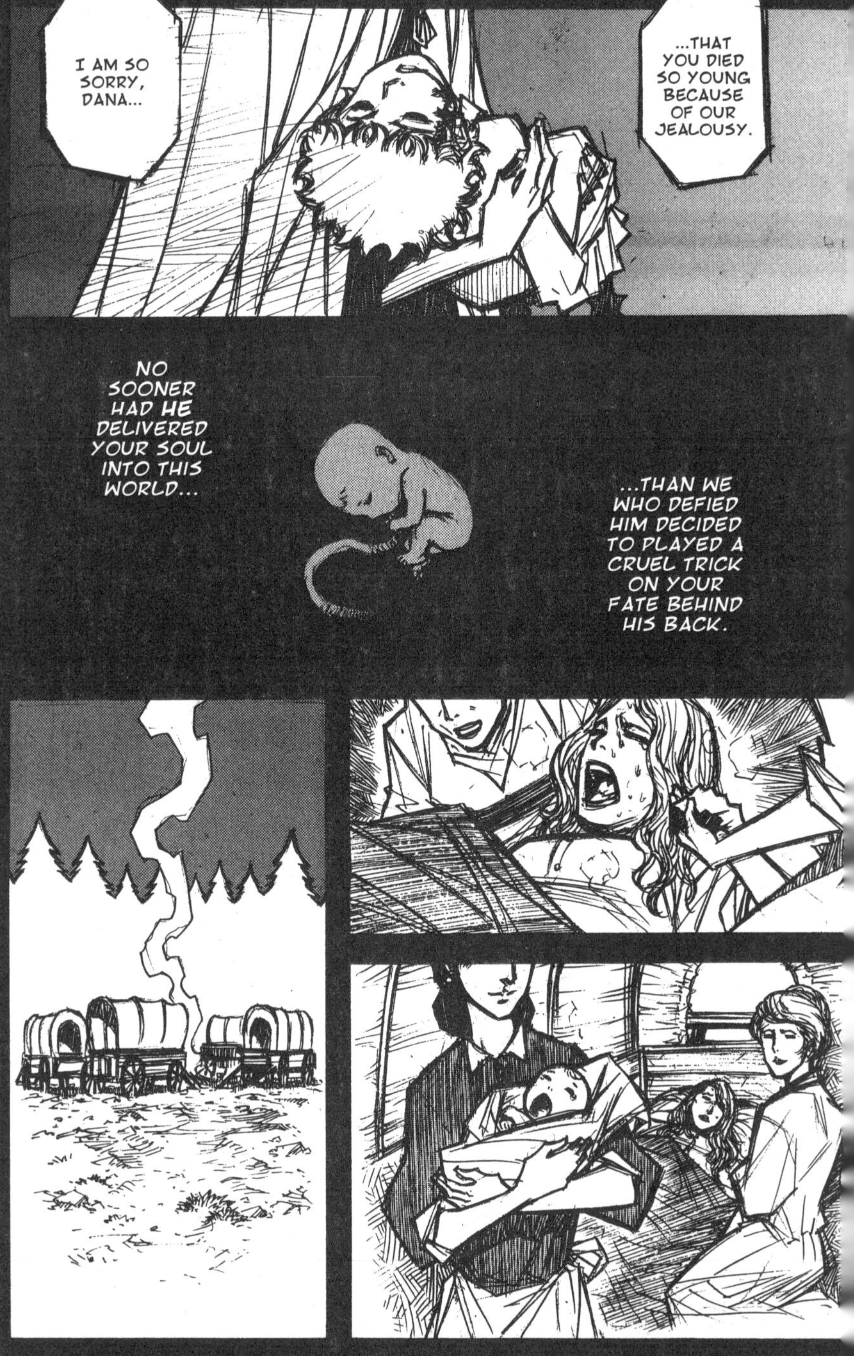
I AM SO SORRY, DANA...
...THAT YOU DIED SO YOUNG BECAUSE OF OUR JEALOUSY.
NO SOONER HAD HE DELIVERED YOUR SOUL INTO THIS WORLD...
...THAN WE WHO DEFIED HIM DECIDED TO PLAYED A CRUEL TRICK ON YOUR FATE BEHIND HIS BACK.

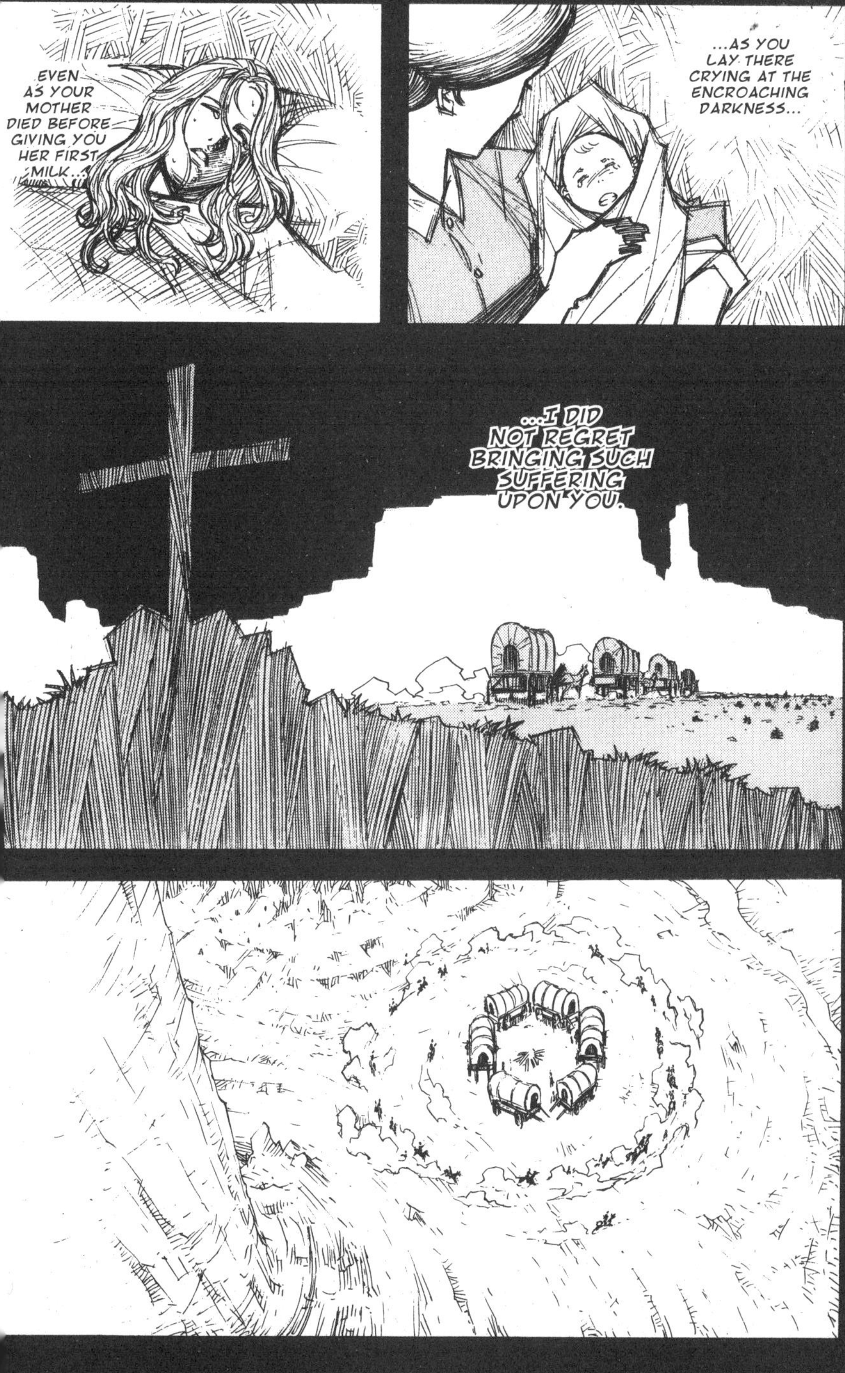

EVEN AS YOUR MOTHER DIED BEFORE GIVING YOU HER FIRST MILK...
...AS YOU LAY THERE CRYING AT THE ENCROACHING DARKNESS...
...I DID NOT REGRET BRINGING SUCH SUFFERING UPON YOU.

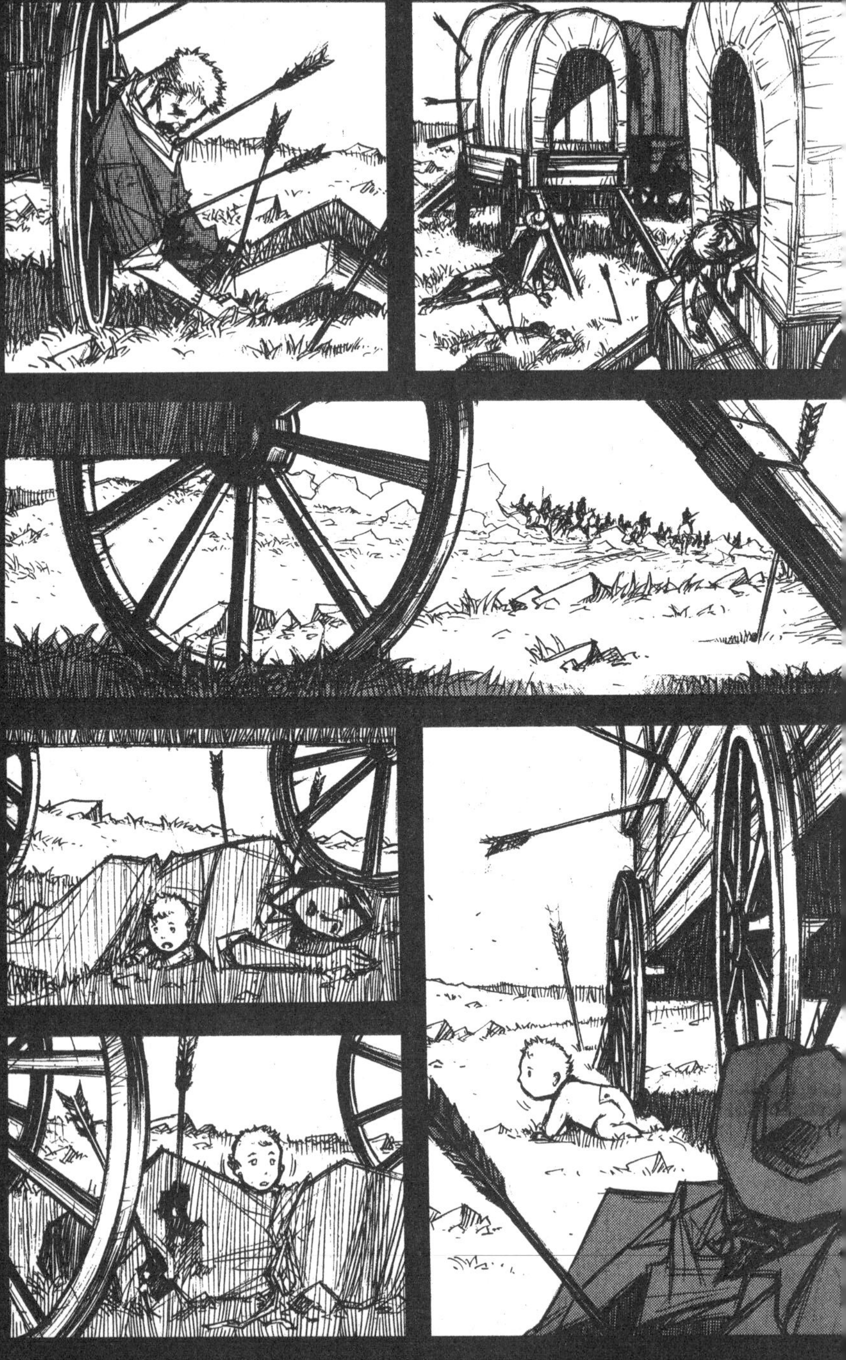

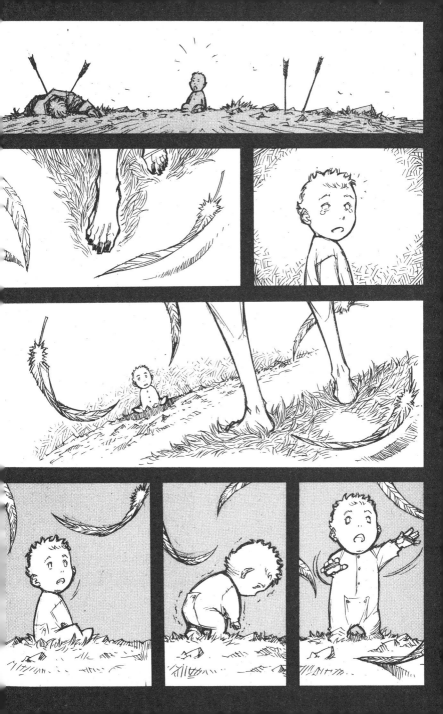

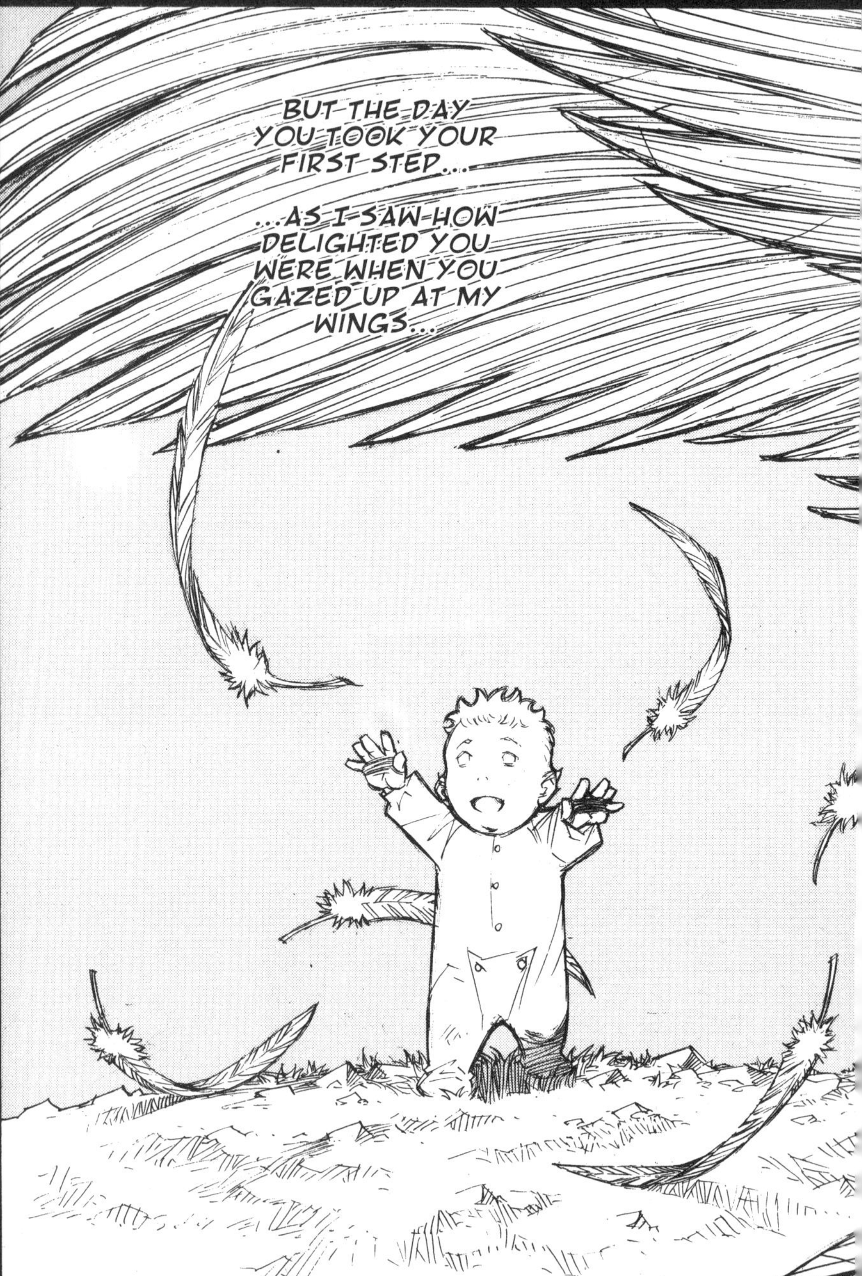
BUT THE DAY YOU TOOK YOUR FIRST STEP...
...AS I SAW HOW DELIGHTED YOU WERE WHEN YOU GAZED UP AT MY WINGS...

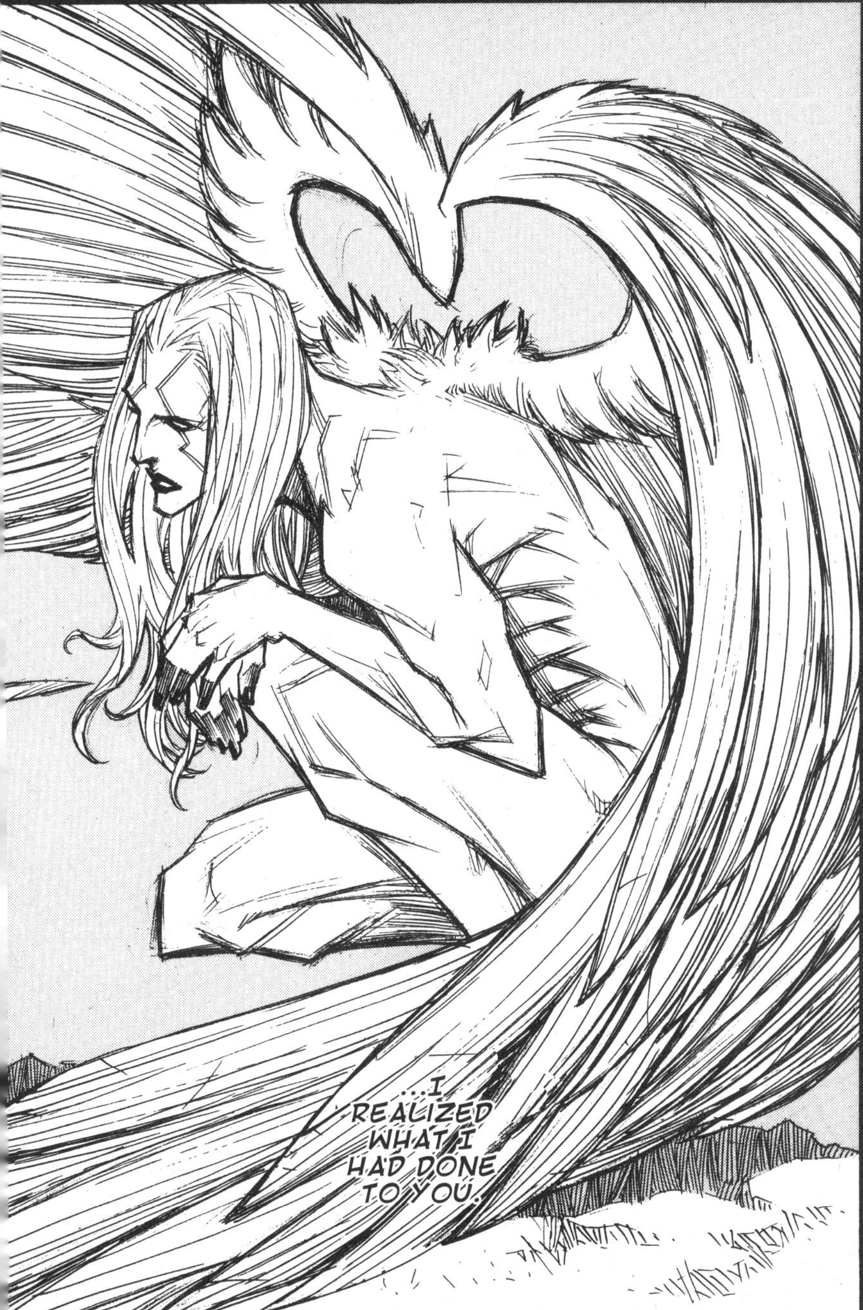
...I REALIZED WHAT I HAD DONE TO YOU.

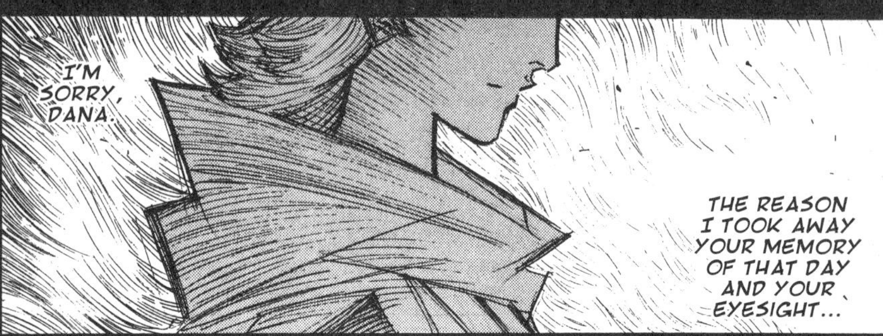
I'M SORRY, DANA.
THE REASON I TOOK AWAY YOUR MEMORY OF THAT DAY AND YOUR EYESIGHT...

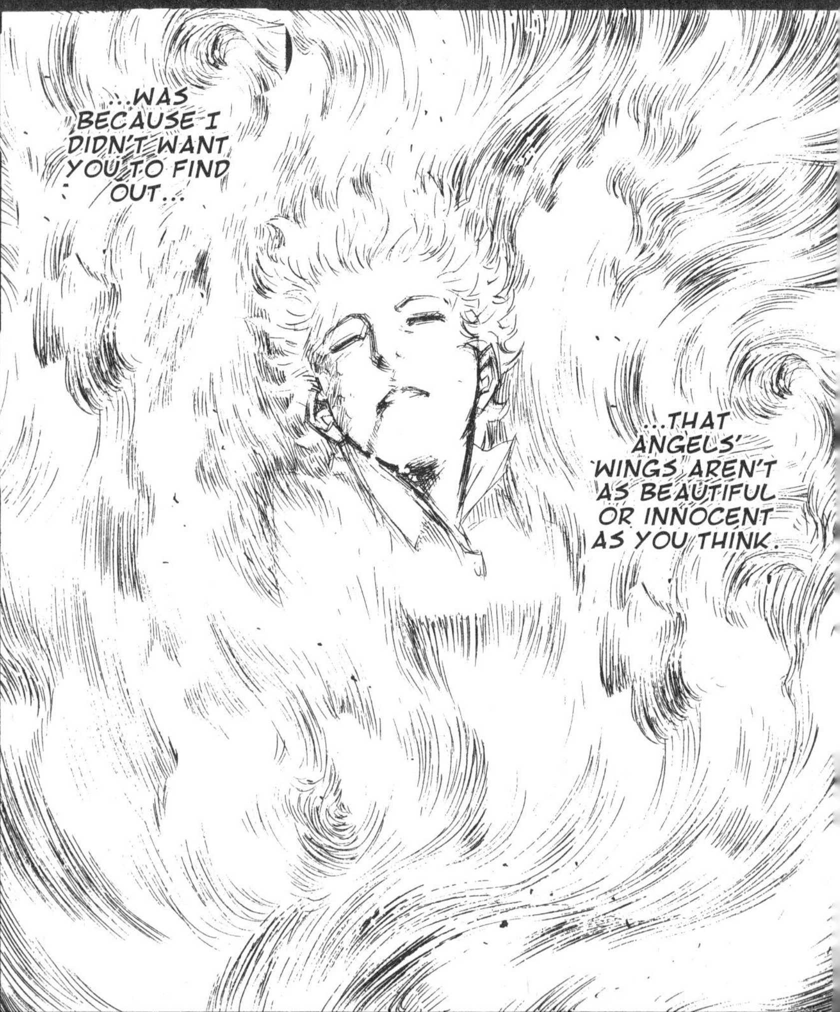
...WAS BECAUSE I DIDN'T WANT YOU TO FIND OUT...
...THAT ANGELS' WINGS AREN'T AS BEAUTIFUL OR INNOCENT AS YOU THINK.

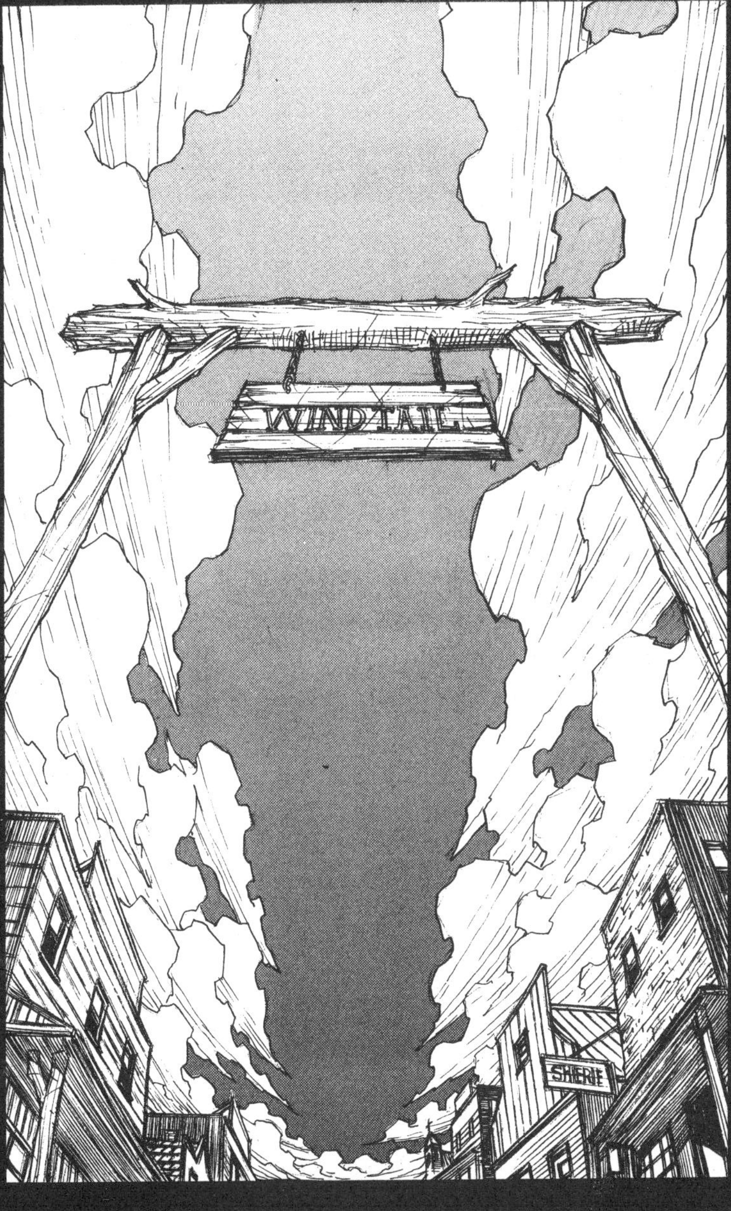
WIND TAIL
SHERIF

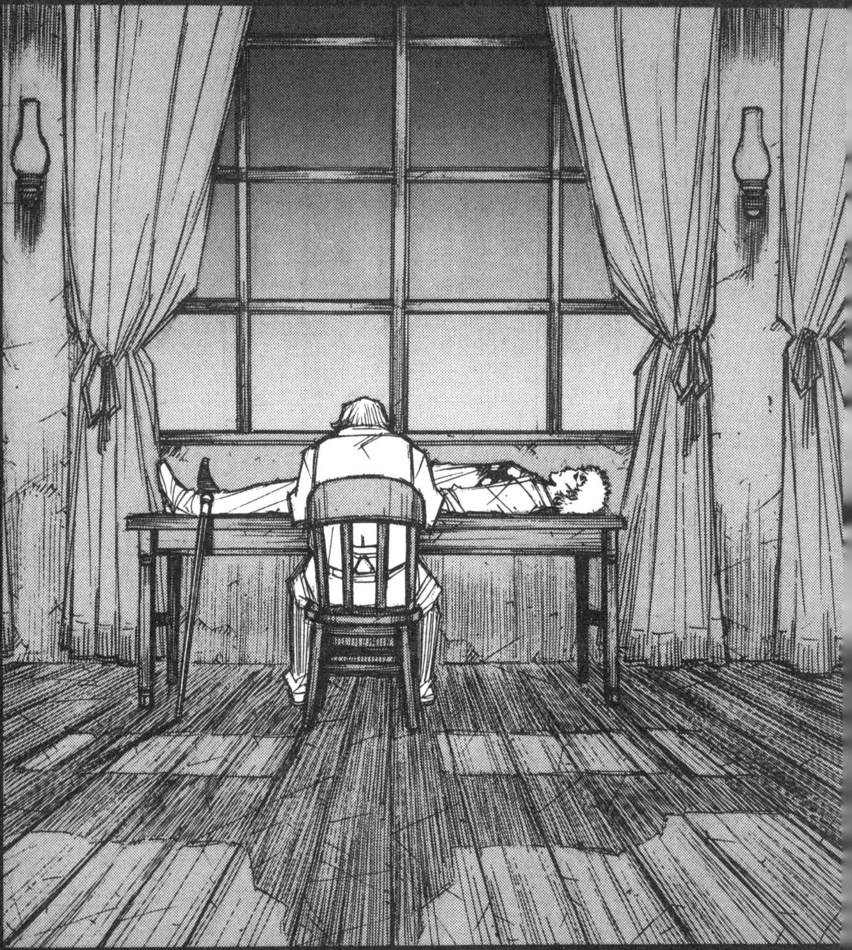
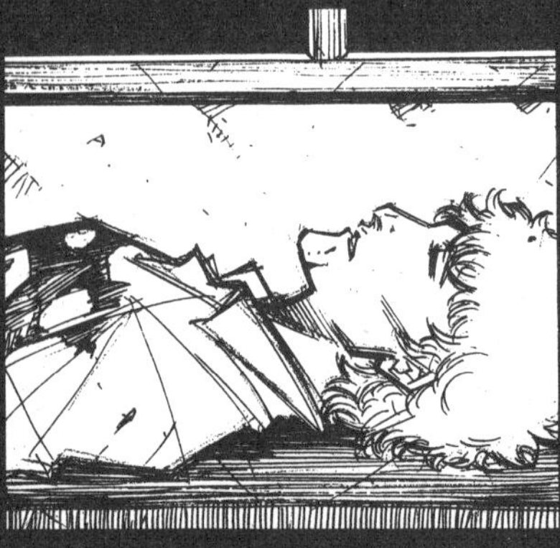
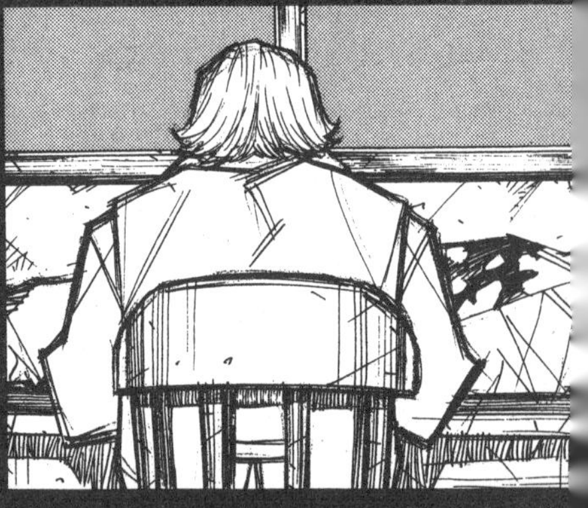

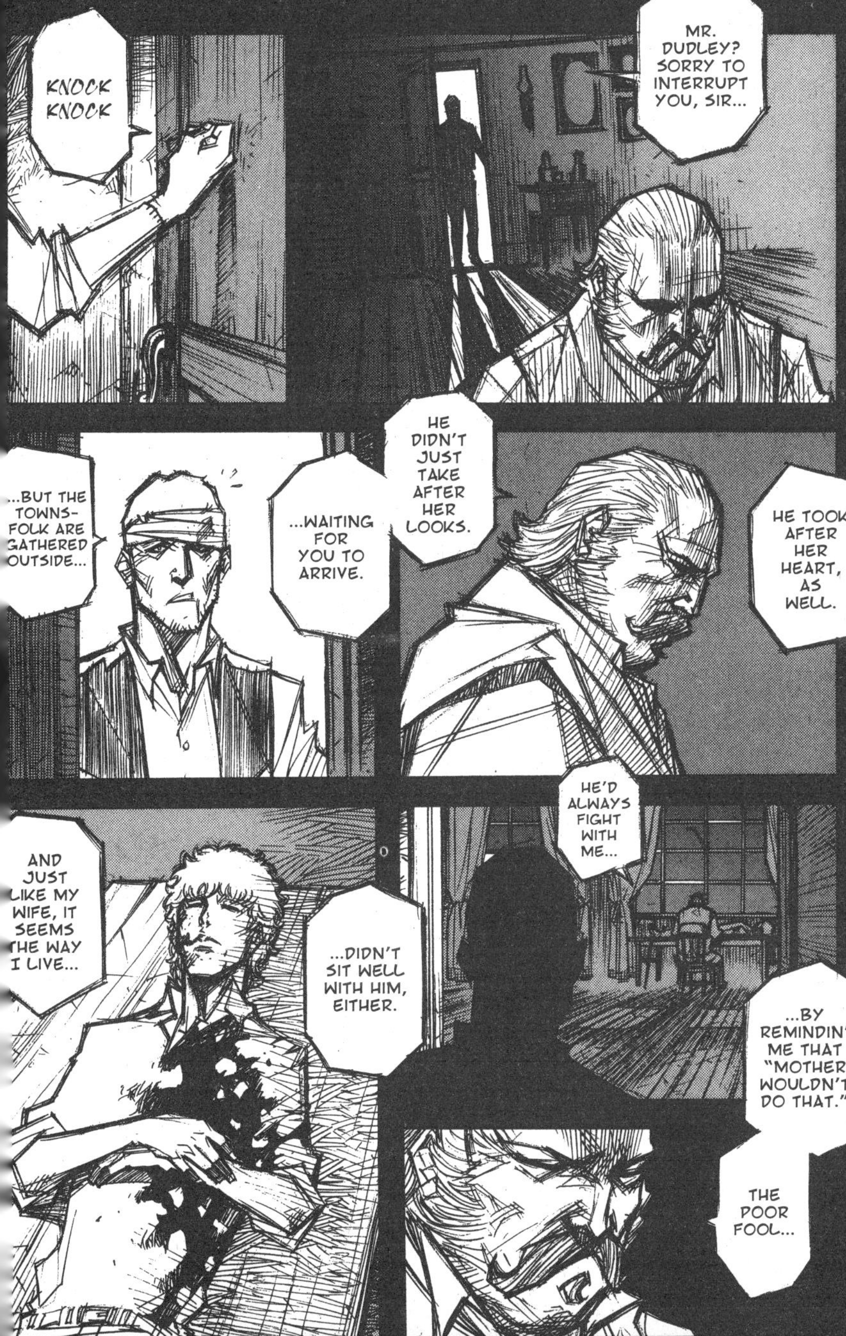
KNOCK KNOCK
MR. DUDLEY? SORRY TO INTERRUPT YOU, SIR...
...BUT THE TOWNS-FOLK ARE GATHERED OUTSIDE...
...WAITING FOR YOU TO ARRIVE.
HE DIDN'T JUST TAKE AFTER HER LOOKS.
HE TOOK AFTER HER HEART, AS WELL.
AND JUST LIKE MY WIFE, IT SEEMS THE WAY I LIVE...
...DIDN'T SIT WELL WITH HIM, EITHER.
HE'D ALWAYS FIGHT WITH ME...
...BY REMINDIN' ME THAT "MOTHER WOULDN'T DO THAT."
THE POOR FOOL...

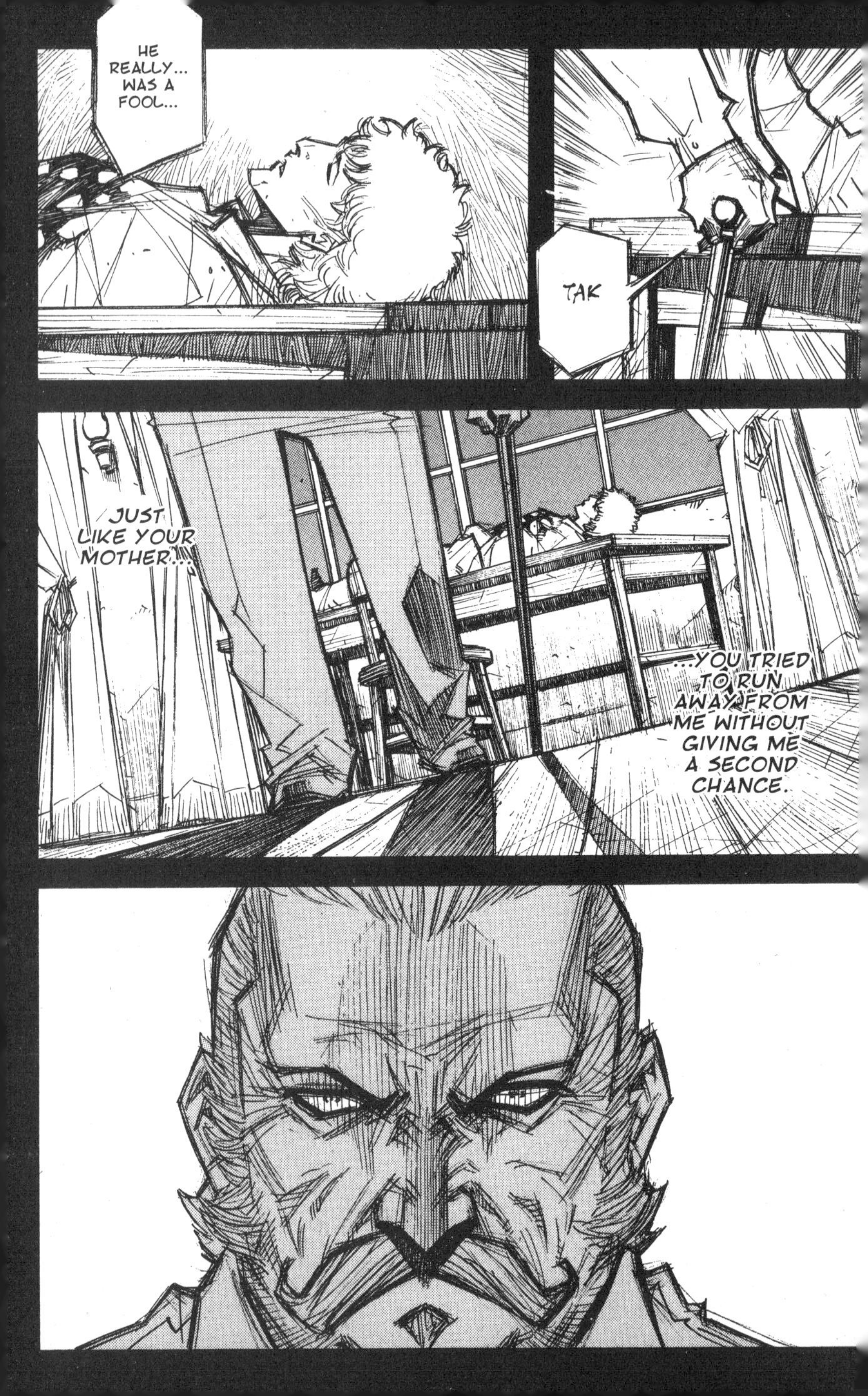
HE REALLY... WAS A FOOL...
TAK
JUST LIKE YOUR MOTHER...
...YOU TRIED TO RUN AWAY FROM ME WITHOUT GIVING ME A SECOND CHANCE.

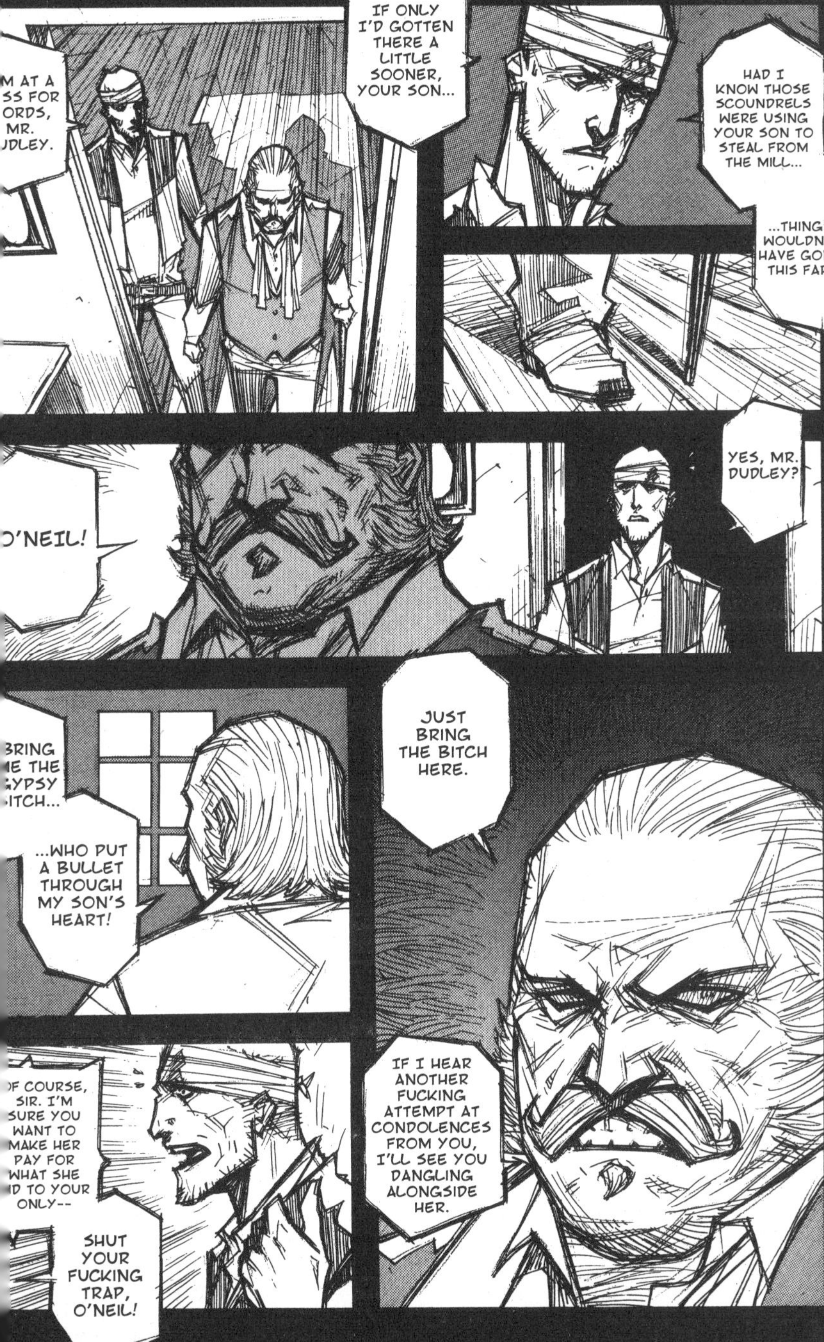
M AT A SS FOR ORDS, MR. UDLEY.
IF ONLY I'D GOTTEN THERE A LITTLE SOONER, YOUR SON...
HAD I KNOW THOSE SCOUNDRELS WERE USING YOUR SON TO STEAL FROM THE MILL...
...THINGS WOULDN'T HAVE GONE THIS FAR.
'NEIL!
YES, MR. DUDLEY?
BRING IE THE GYPSY ITCH...
...WHO PUT A BULLET THROUGH MY SON'S HEART!
F COURSE, SIR. I'M SURE YOU WANT TO MAKE HER PAY FOR WHAT SHE D TO YOUR ONLY--
SHUT YOUR FUCKING TRAP, O'NEIL!
JUST BRING THE BITCH HERE.
IF I HEAR ANOTHER FUCKING ATTEMPT AT CONDOLENCES FROM YOU, I'LL SEE YOU DANGLING ALONGSIDE HER.

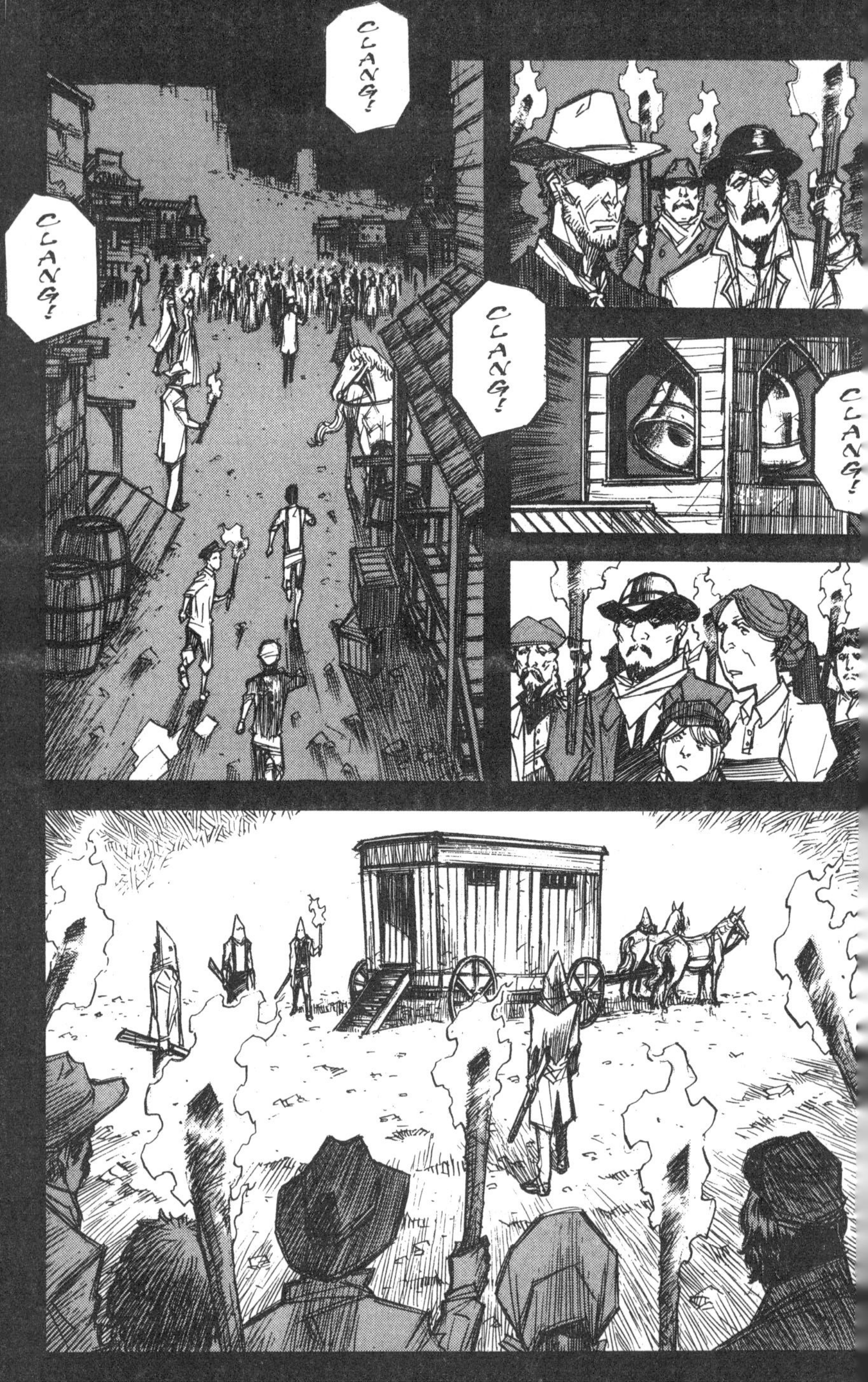
CLANG!
CLANG!
CLANG!
CLANG!

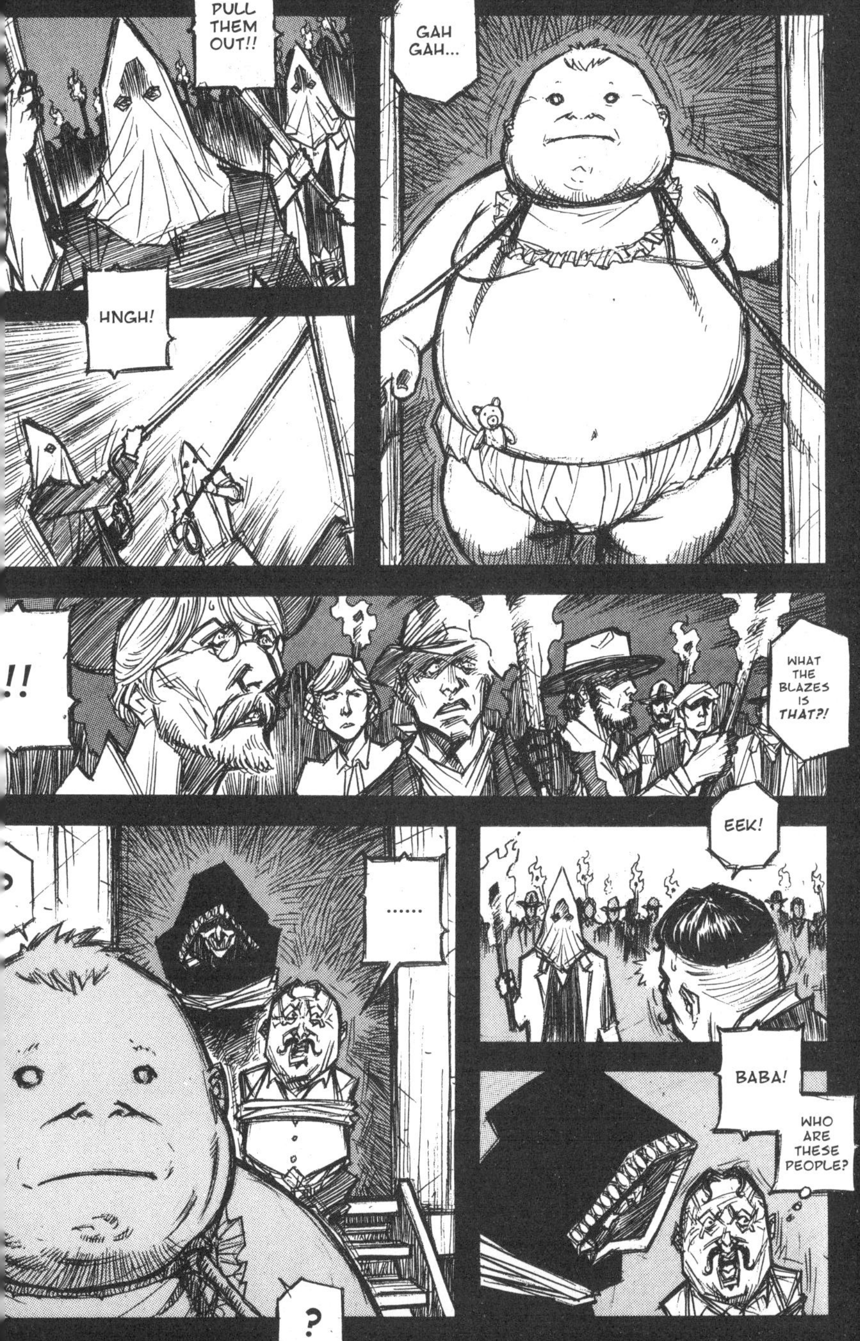
PULL THEM OUT!!
HNGH!
GAH GAH...
!!
WHAT THE BLAZES IS *THAT?!*
......
?
EEK!
BABA!
WHO ARE THESE PEOPLE?

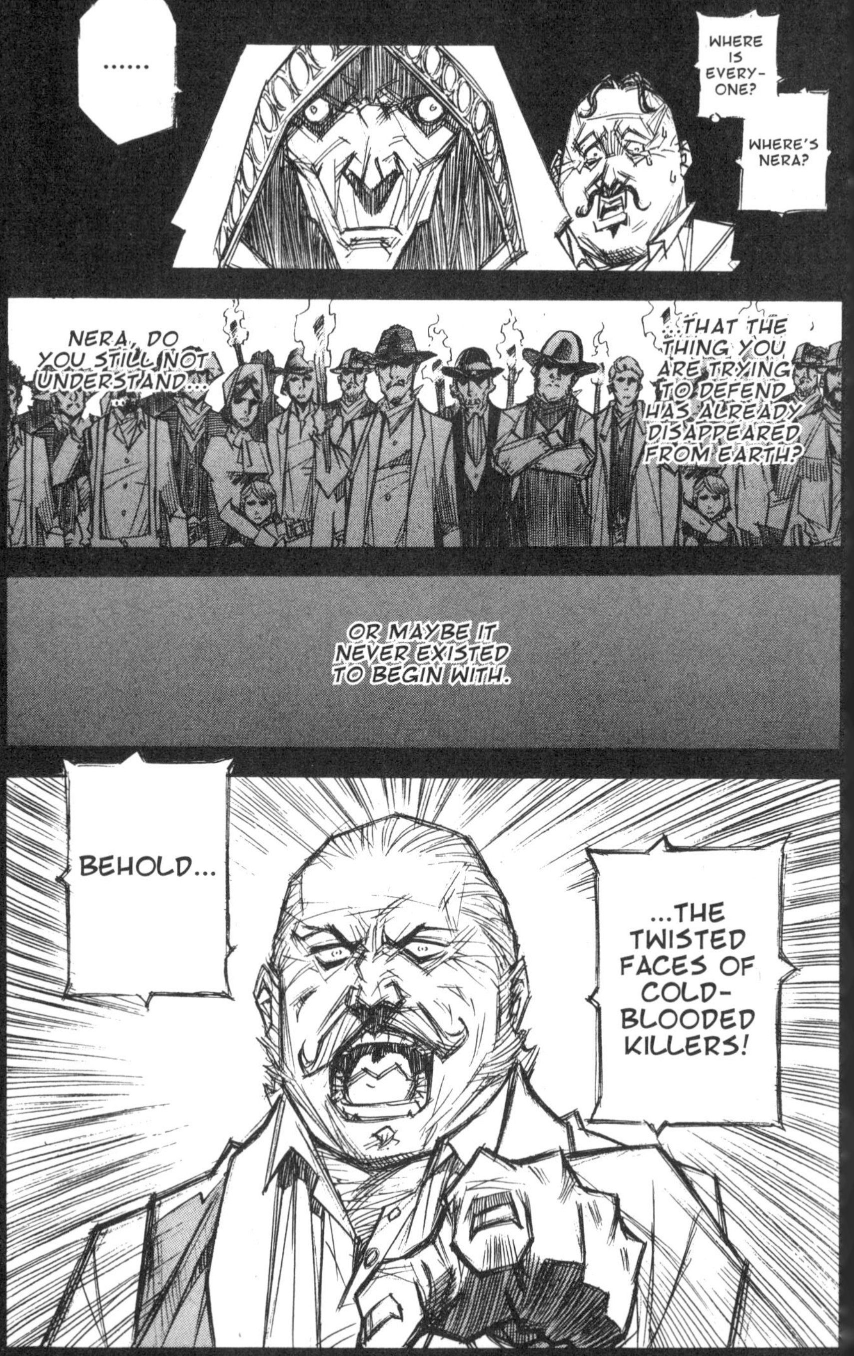
......
WHERE IS EVERY-ONE?
WHERE'S NERA?
NERA, DO YOU STILL NOT UNDERSTAND...
...THAT THE THING YOU ARE TRYING TO DEFEND HAS ALREADY DISAPPEARED FROM EARTH?
OR MAYBE IT NEVER EXISTED TO BEGIN WITH.
BEHOLD...
...THE TWISTED FACES OF COLD-BLOODED KILLERS!

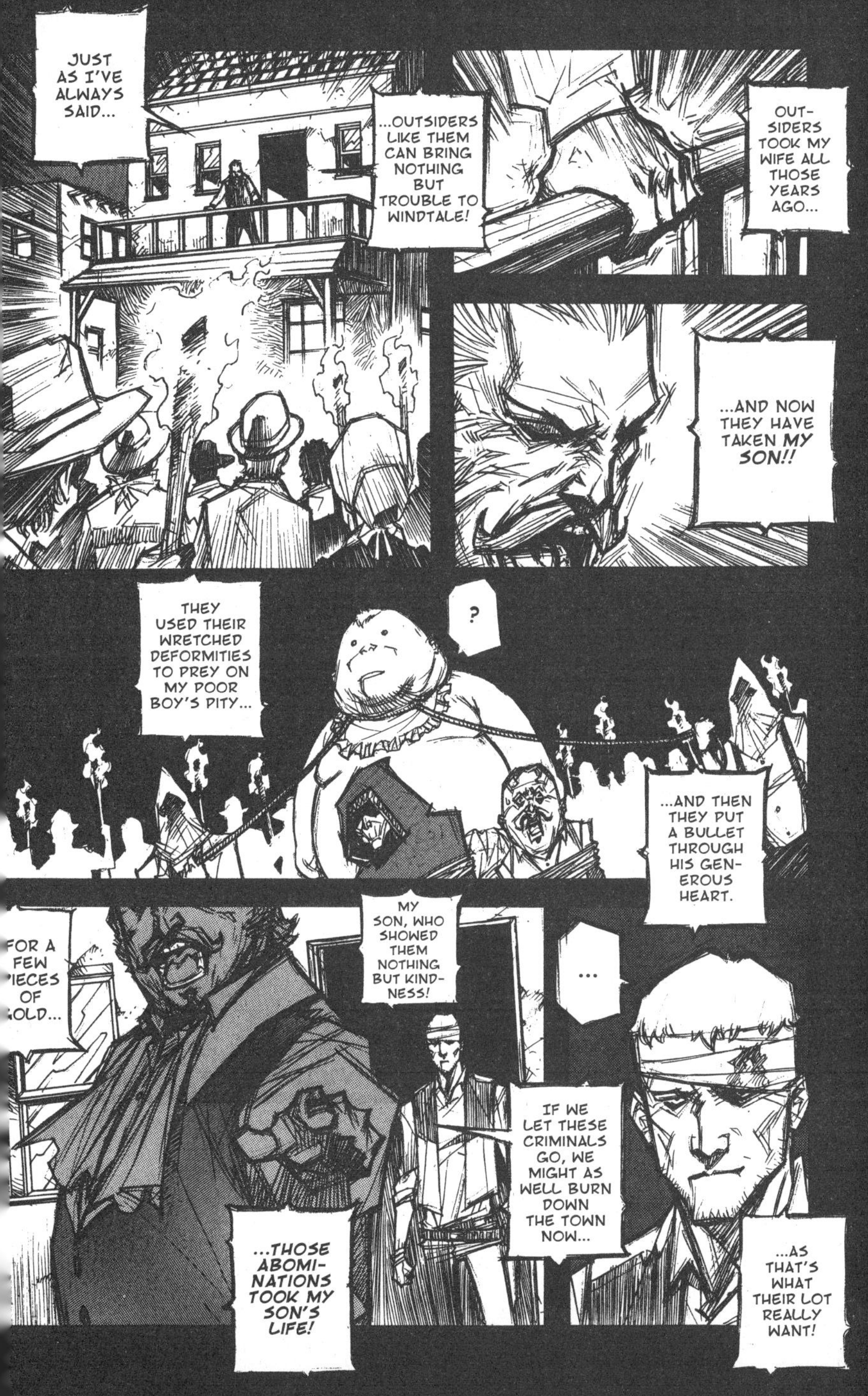
JUST AS I'VE ALWAYS SAID...
...OUTSIDERS LIKE THEM CAN BRING NOTHING BUT TROUBLE TO WINDTALE!
OUT-SIDERS TOOK MY WIFE ALL THOSE YEARS AGO...
...AND NOW THEY HAVE TAKEN MY SON!!
THEY USED THEIR WRETCHED DEFORMITIES TO PREY ON MY POOR BOY'S PITY...
?
...AND THEN THEY PUT A BULLET THROUGH HIS GEN-EROUS HEART.
FOR A FEW PIECES OF GOLD...
MY SON, WHO SHOWED THEM NOTHING BUT KIND-NESS!
...THOSE ABOMI-NATIONS TOOK MY SON'S LIFE!
...
IF WE LET THESE CRIMINALS GO, WE MIGHT AS WELL BURN DOWN THE TOWN NOW...
...AS THAT'S WHAT THEIR LOT REALLY WANT!

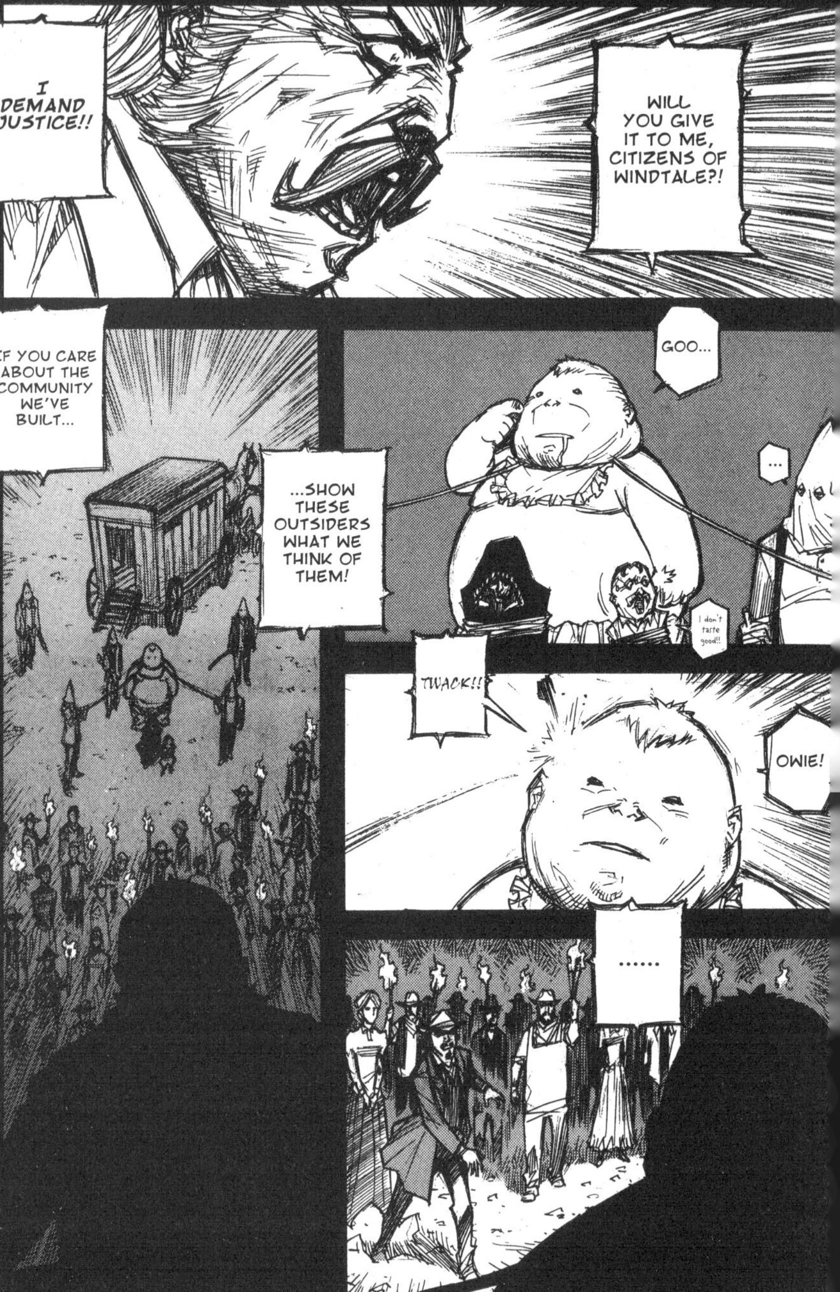
I DEMAND JUSTICE!!
WILL YOU GIVE IT TO ME, CITIZENS OF WINDTALE?!
IF YOU CARE ABOUT THE COMMUNITY WE'VE BUILT...
...SHOW THESE OUTSIDERS WHAT WE THINK OF THEM!
GOO...
...
I don't taste good!!
TWACK!!
OWIE!
......

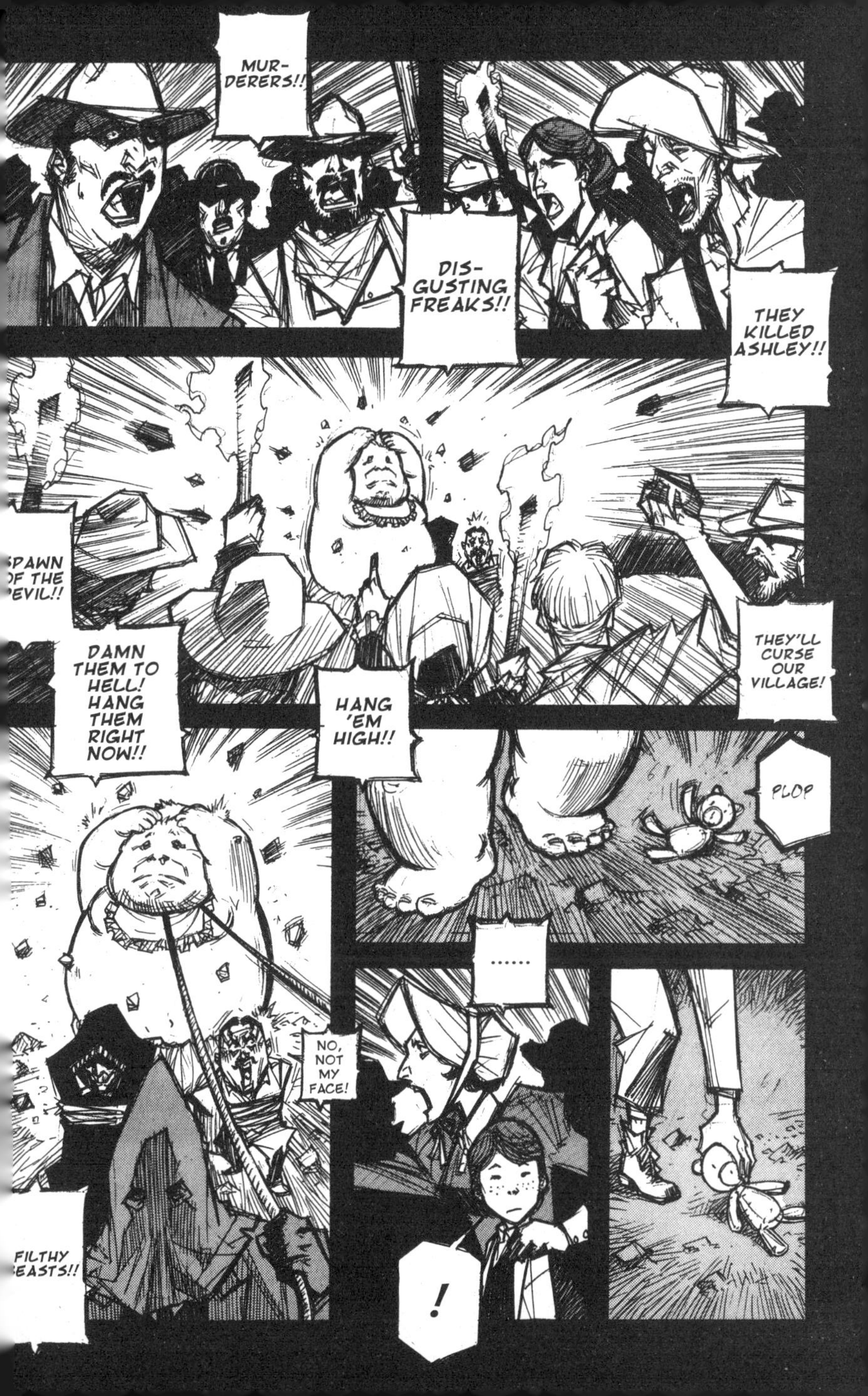
MURDERERS!!
DISGUSTING FREAKS!!
THEY KILLED ASHLEY!!
SPAWN OF THE DEVIL!!
DAMN THEM TO HELL! HANG THEM RIGHT NOW!!
HANG 'EM HIGH!!
THEY'LL CURSE OUR VILLAGE!
NO, NOT MY FACE!
FILTHY BEASTS!!
PLOP
......
!

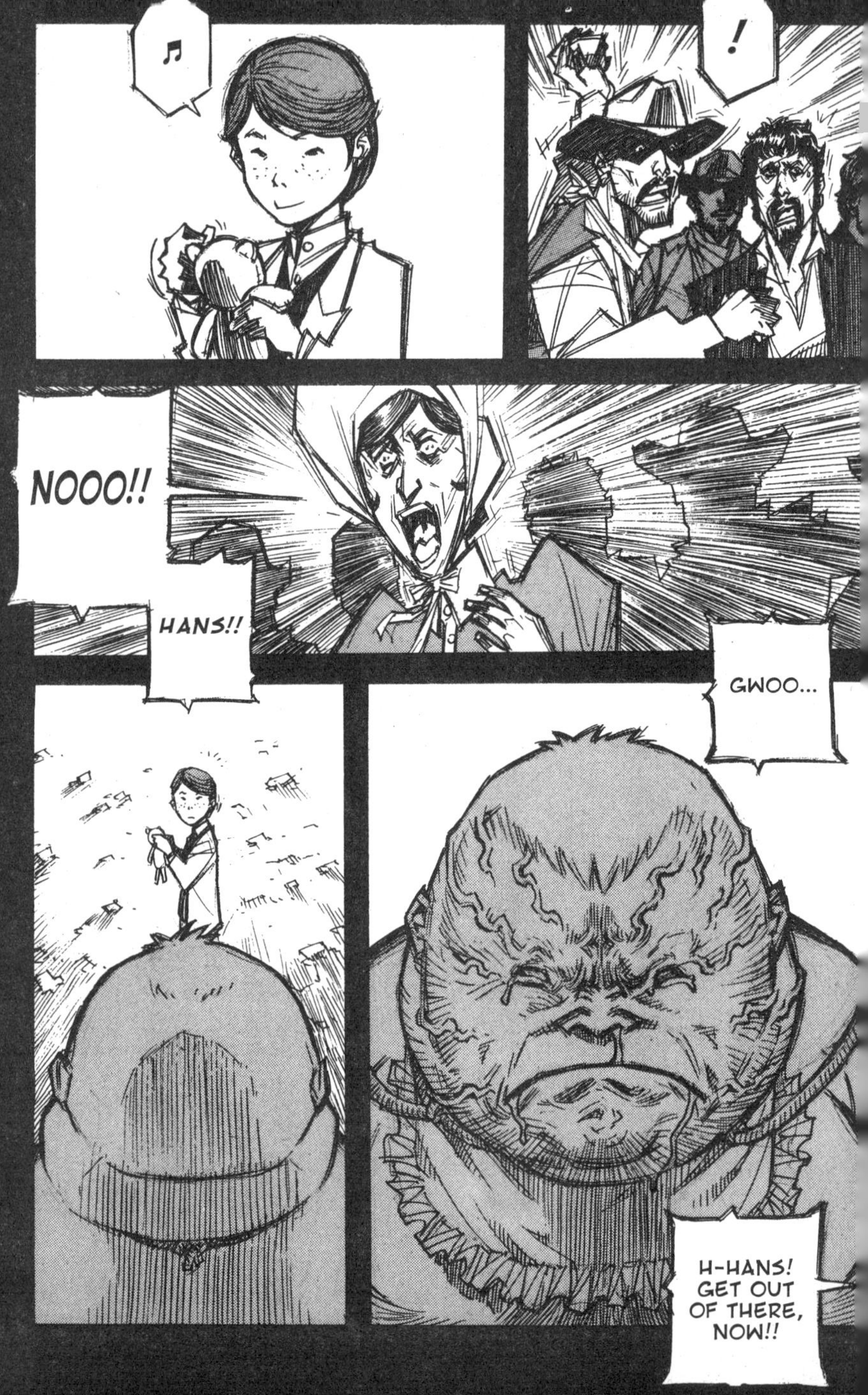
♫
!
NOOO!!
HANS!!
GWOO...
H-HANS! GET OUT OF THERE, NOW!!

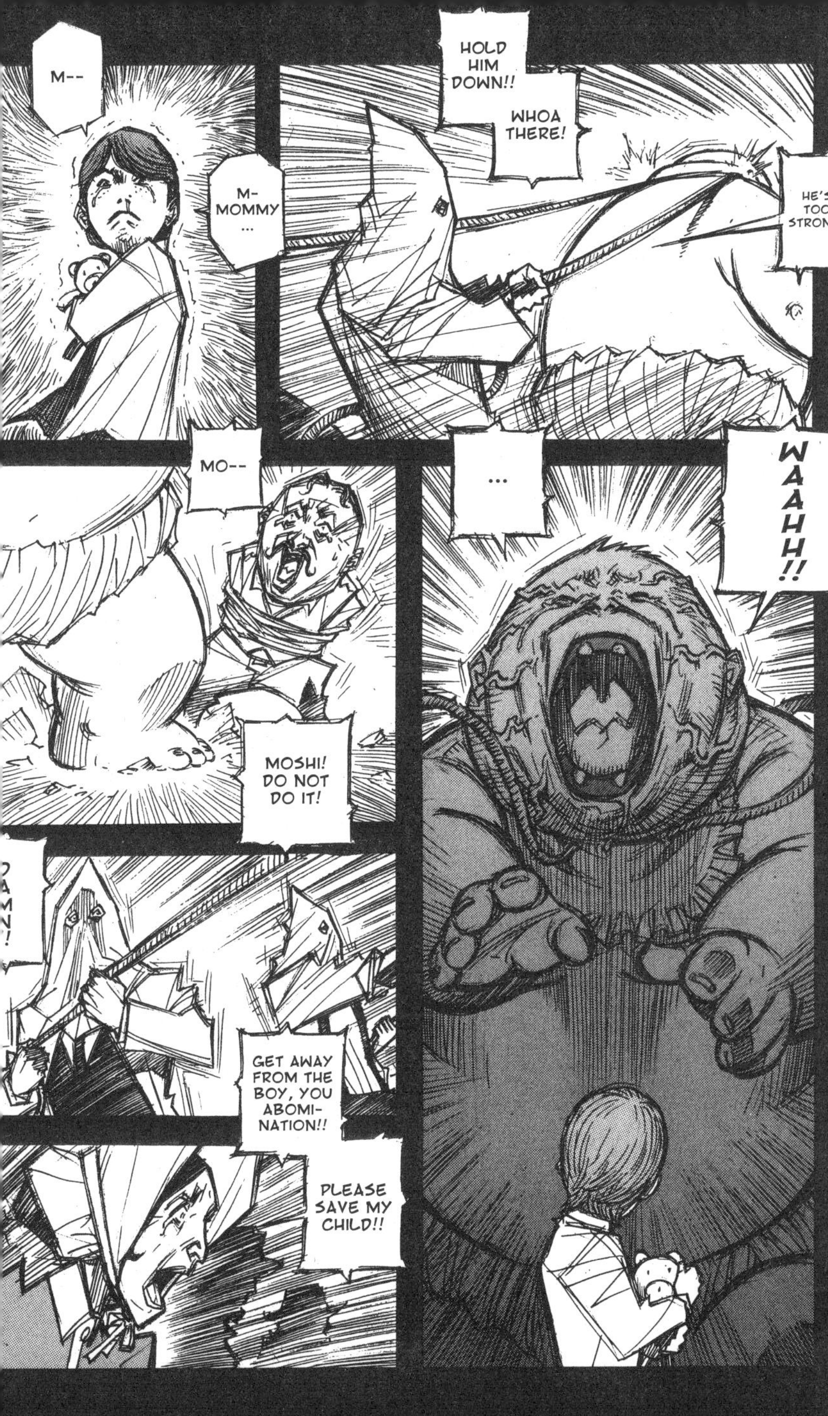
M--
M-MOMMY...
HOLD HIM DOWN!!
WHOA THERE!
HE'S TOO STRONG!
MO--
MOSHI! DO NOT DO IT!
DAMN!
GET AWAY FROM THE BOY, YOU ABOMINATION!!
PLEASE SAVE MY CHILD!!
...
WAAHH!!

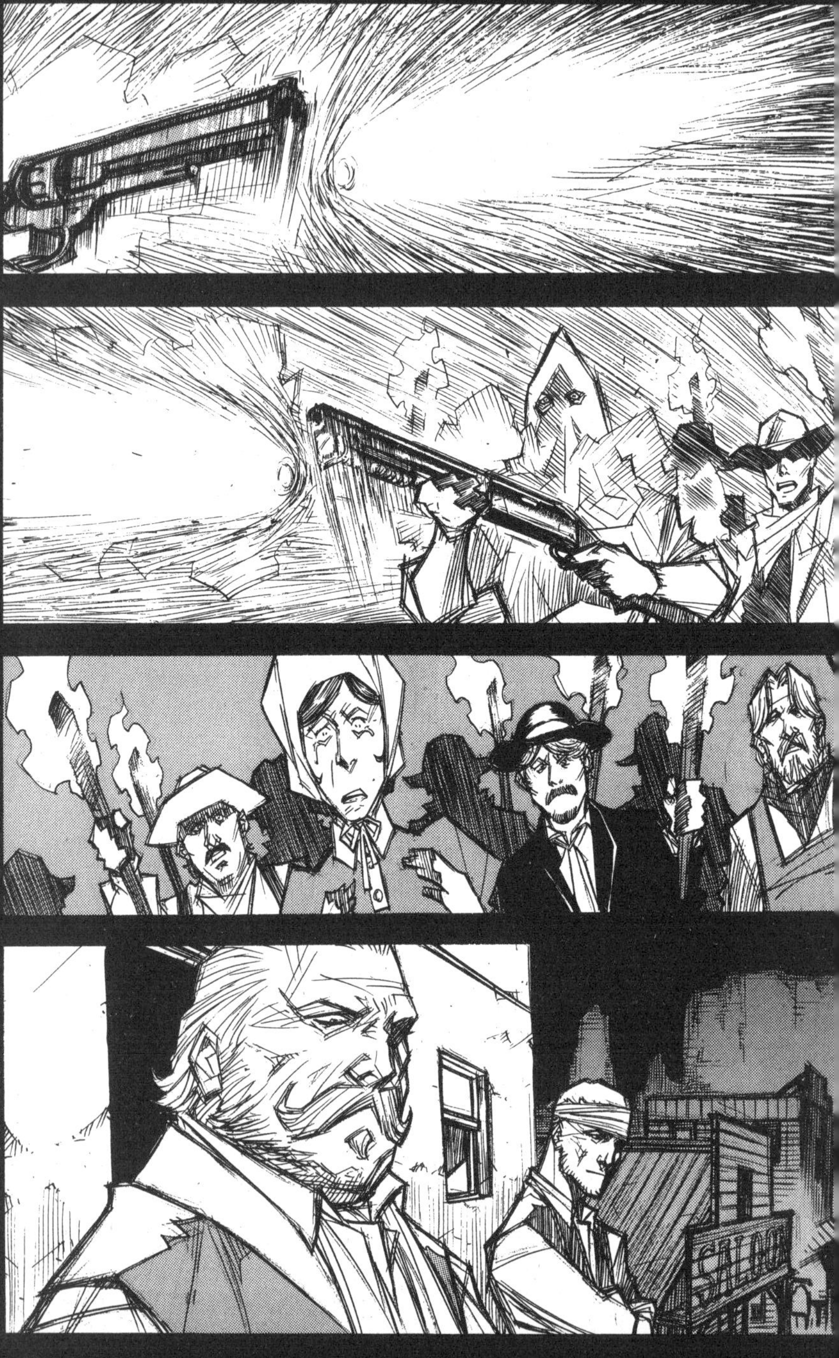
SALOO

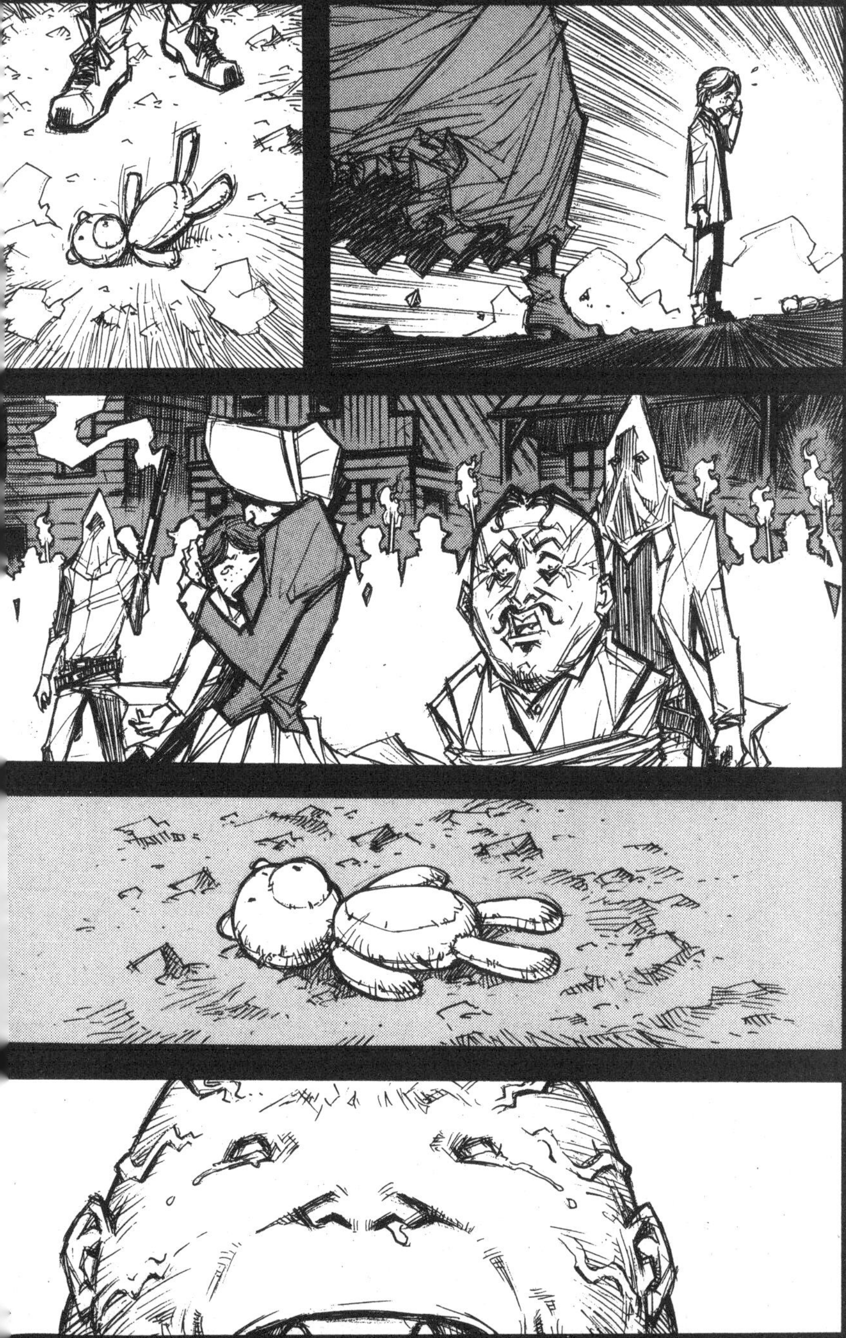

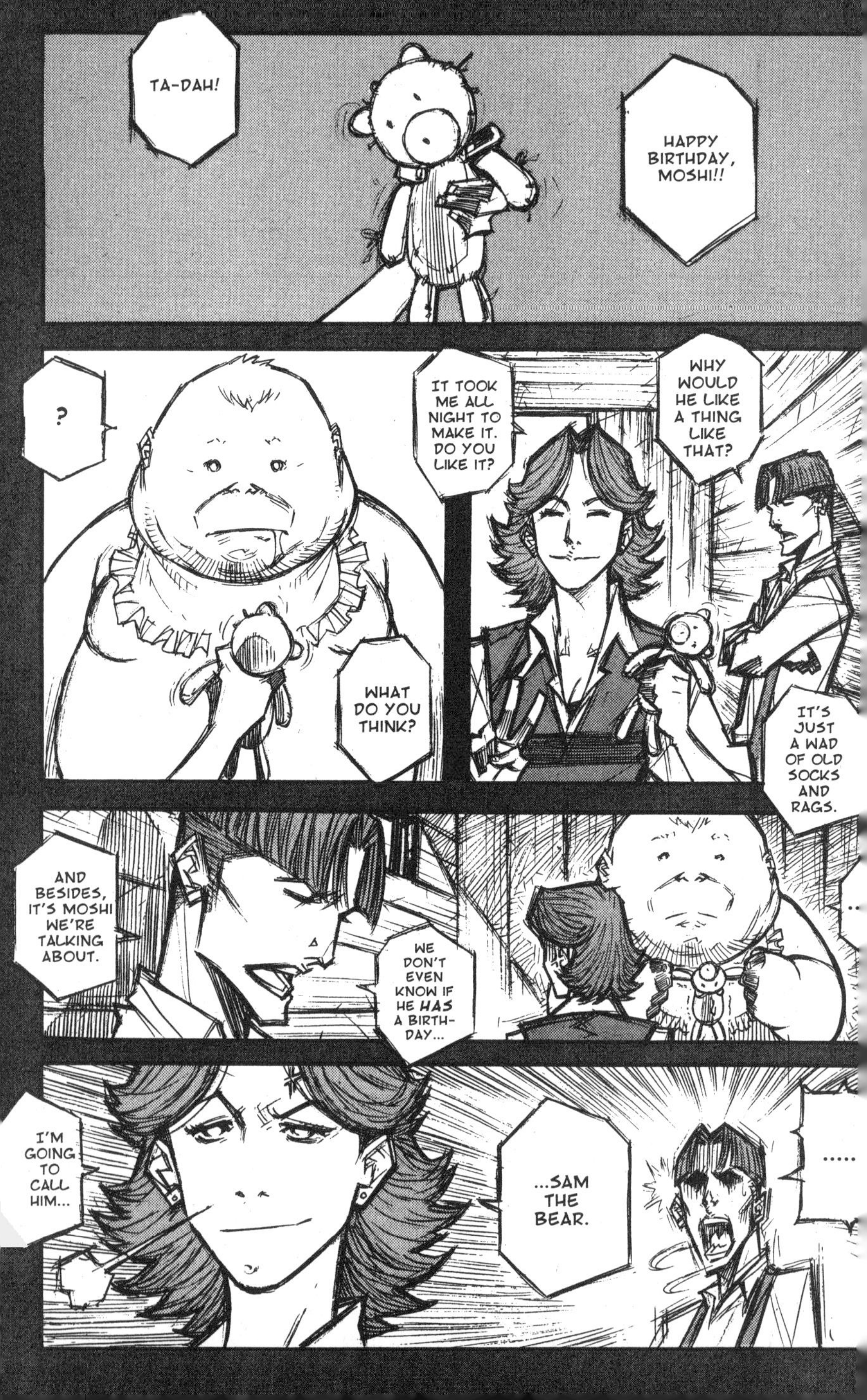

TA-DAH!
HAPPY BIRTHDAY, MOSHI!!
?
WHAT DO YOU THINK?
IT TOOK ME ALL NIGHT TO MAKE IT. DO YOU LIKE IT?
WHY WOULD HE LIKE A THING LIKE THAT?
IT'S JUST A WAD OF OLD SOCKS AND RAGS.
AND BESIDES, IT'S MOSHI WE'RE TALKING ABOUT.
WE DON'T EVEN KNOW IF HE **HAS** A BIRTH-DAY...
...
I'M GOING TO CALL HIM...
...SAM THE BEAR.
.....

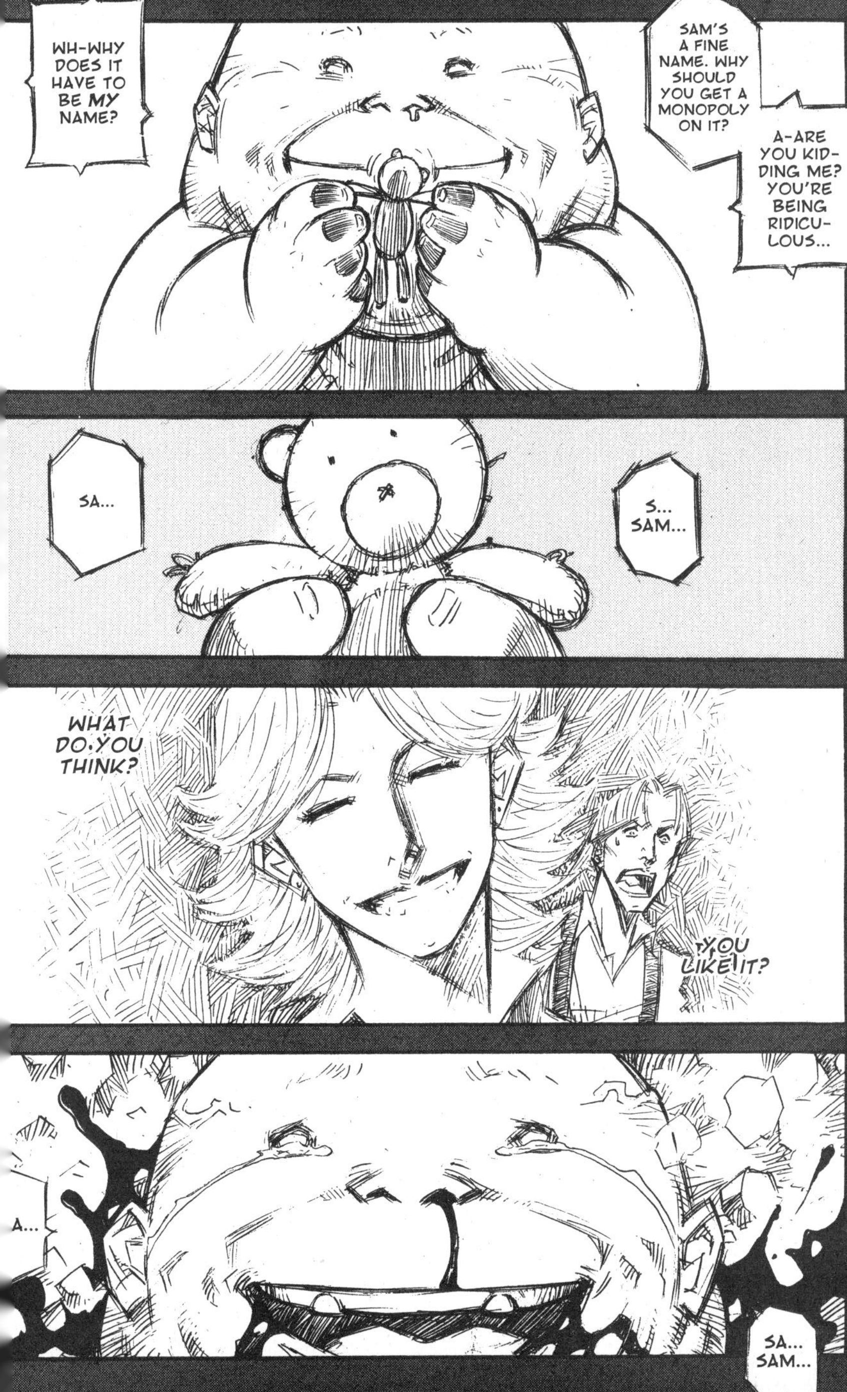
WH-WHY DOES IT HAVE TO BE MY NAME?
SAM'S A FINE NAME. WHY SHOULD YOU GET A MONOPOLY ON IT?
A-ARE YOU KID-DING ME? YOU'RE BEING RIDICU-LOUS...
SA...
S... SAM...
WHAT DO YOU THINK?
Y-YOU LIKE IT?
A...
SA... SAM...

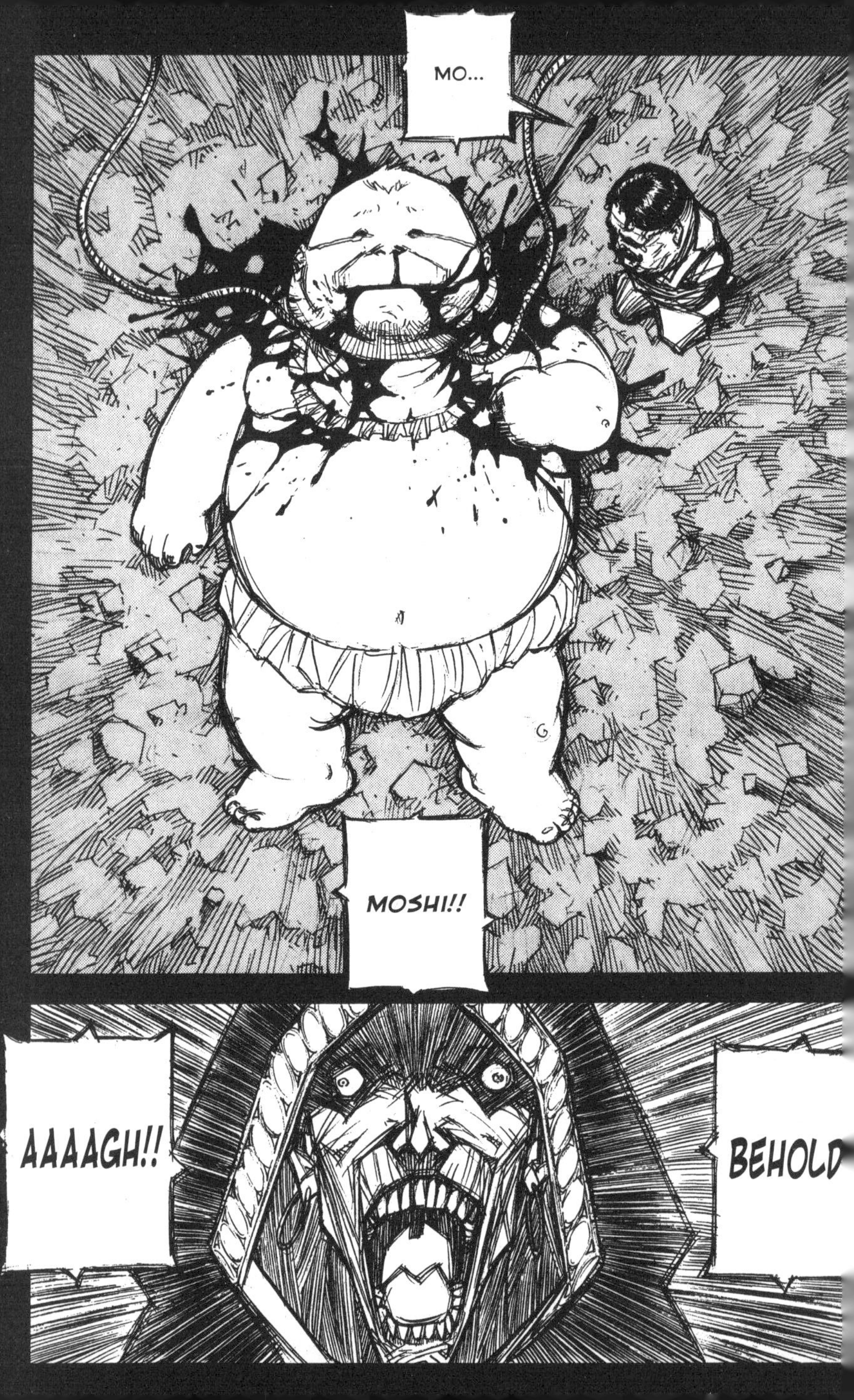
MO...
MOSHI!!
AAAAGH!!
BEHOLD

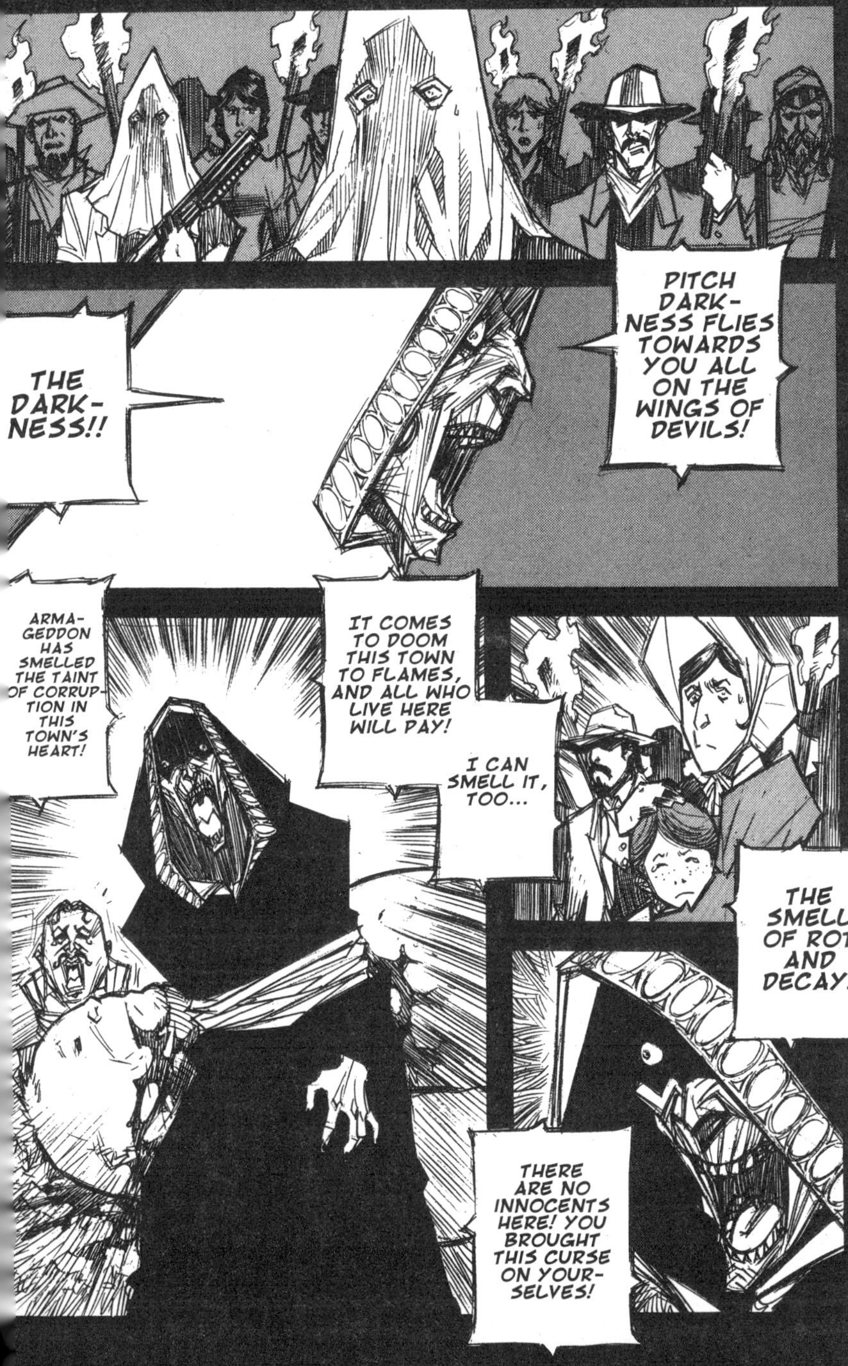
THE DARK-NESS!!
PITCH DARK-NESS FLIES TOWARDS YOU ALL ON THE WINGS OF DEVILS!
ARMA-GEDDON HAS SMELLED THE TAINT OF CORRUP-TION IN THIS TOWN'S HEART!
IT COMES TO DOOM THIS TOWN TO FLAMES, AND ALL WHO LIVE HERE WILL PAY!
I CAN SMELL IT, TOO...
THE SMELL OF ROT AND DECAY!
THERE ARE NO INNOCENTS HERE! YOU BROUGHT THIS CURSE ON YOUR-SELVES!

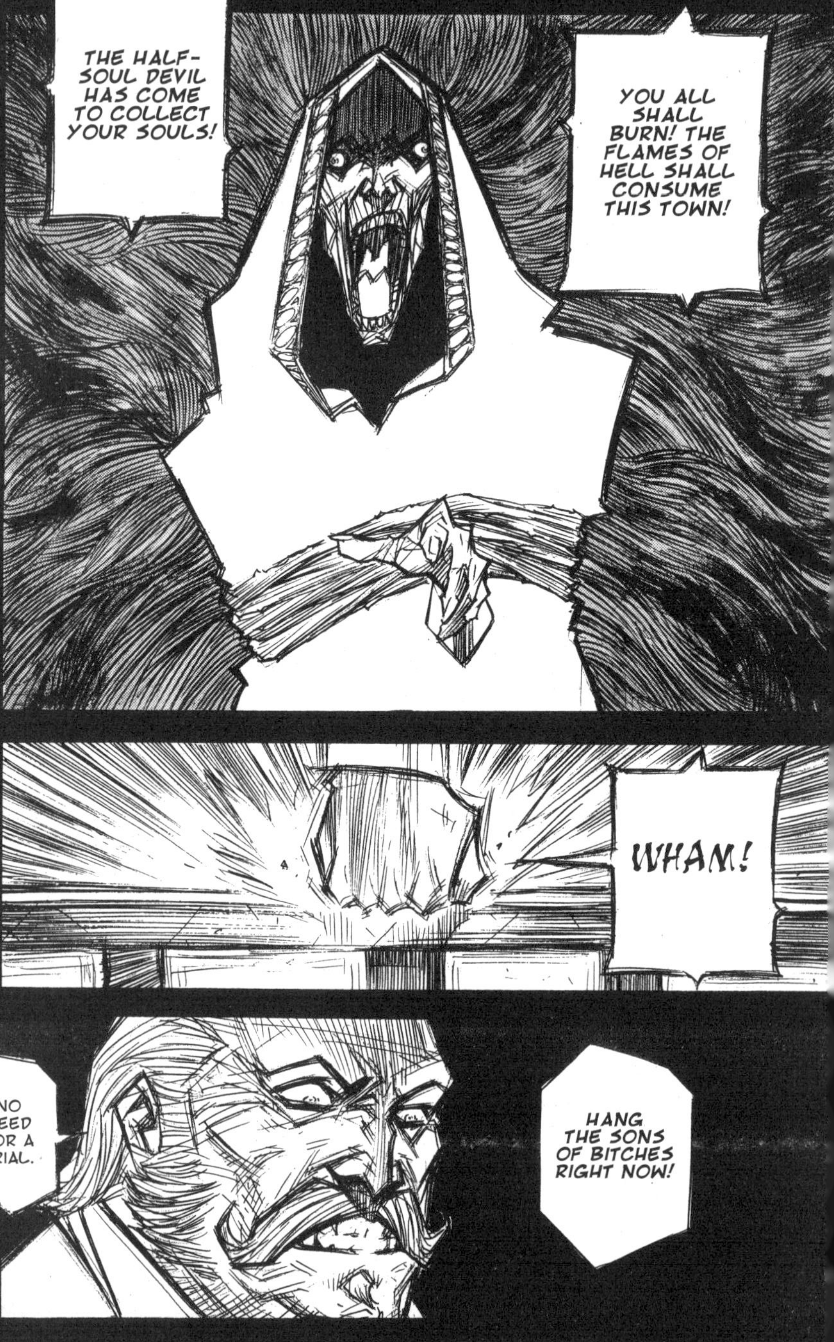
THE HALF-SOUL DEVIL HAS COME TO COLLECT YOUR SOULS!
YOU ALL SHALL BURN! THE FLAMES OF HELL SHALL CONSUME THIS TOWN!
WHAM!
NO NEED FOR A TRIAL.
HANG THE SONS OF BITCHES RIGHT NOW!

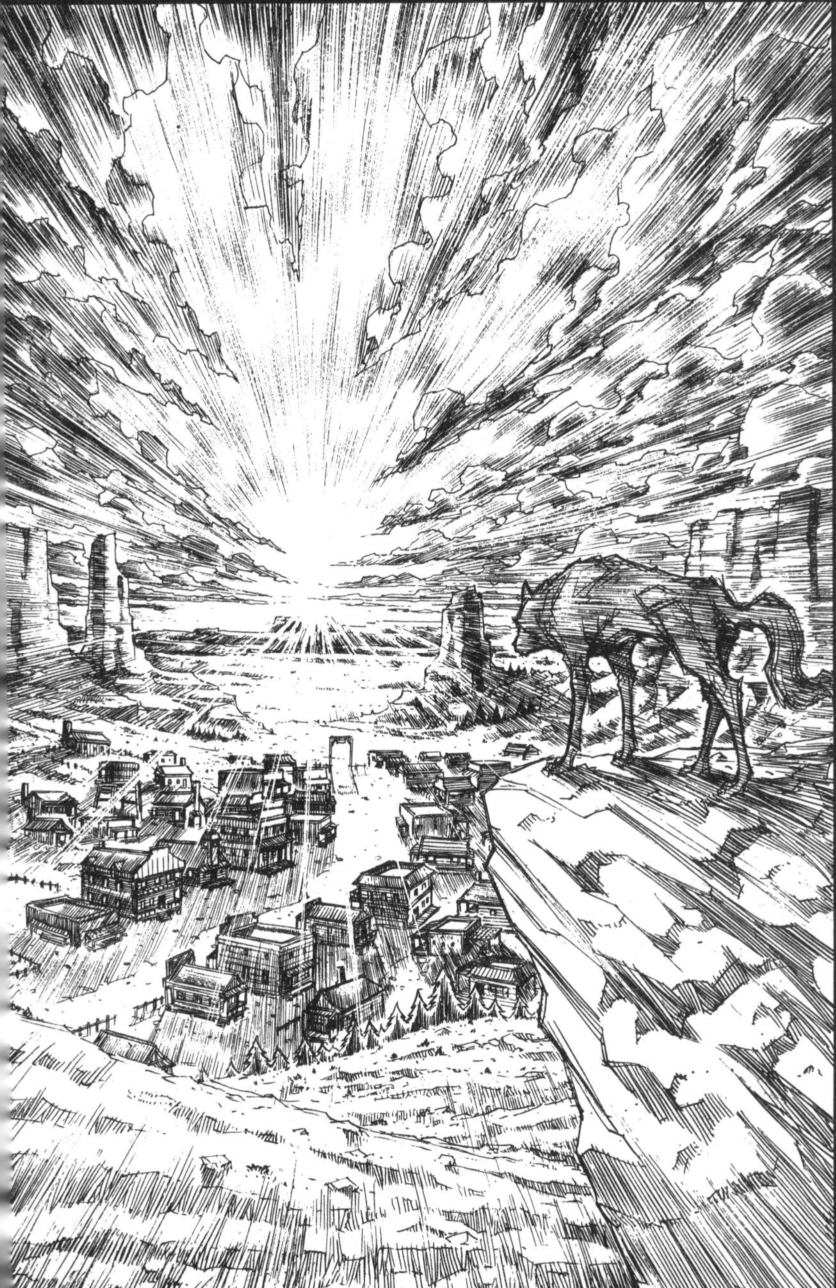

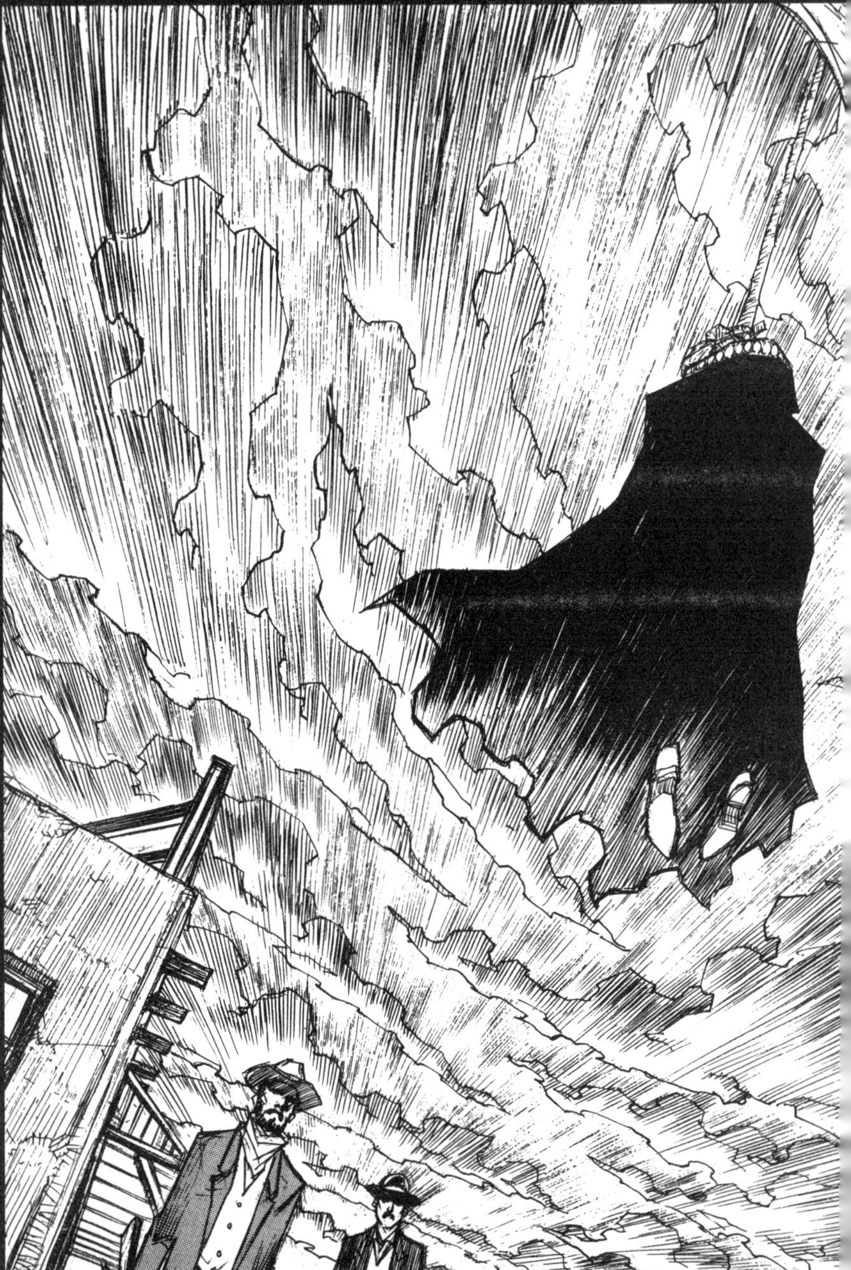

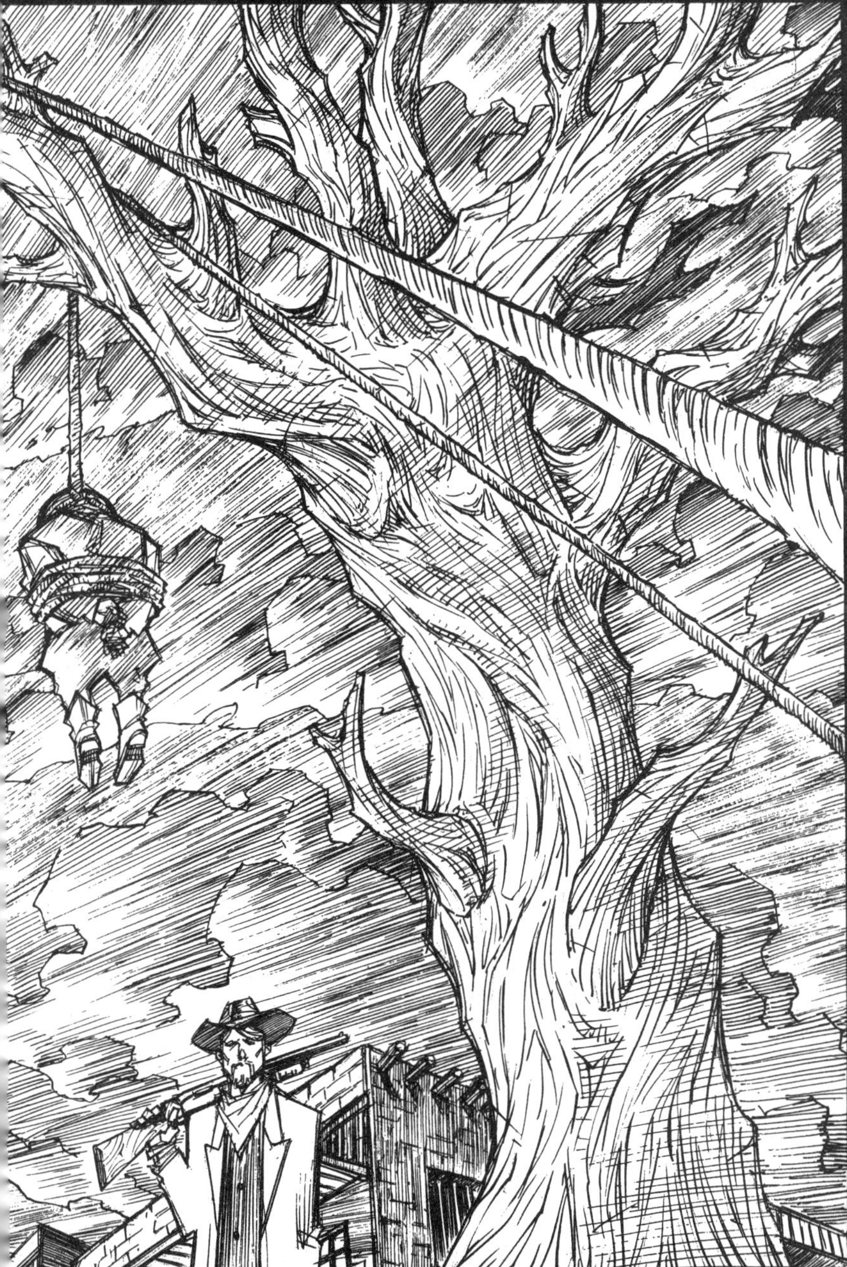

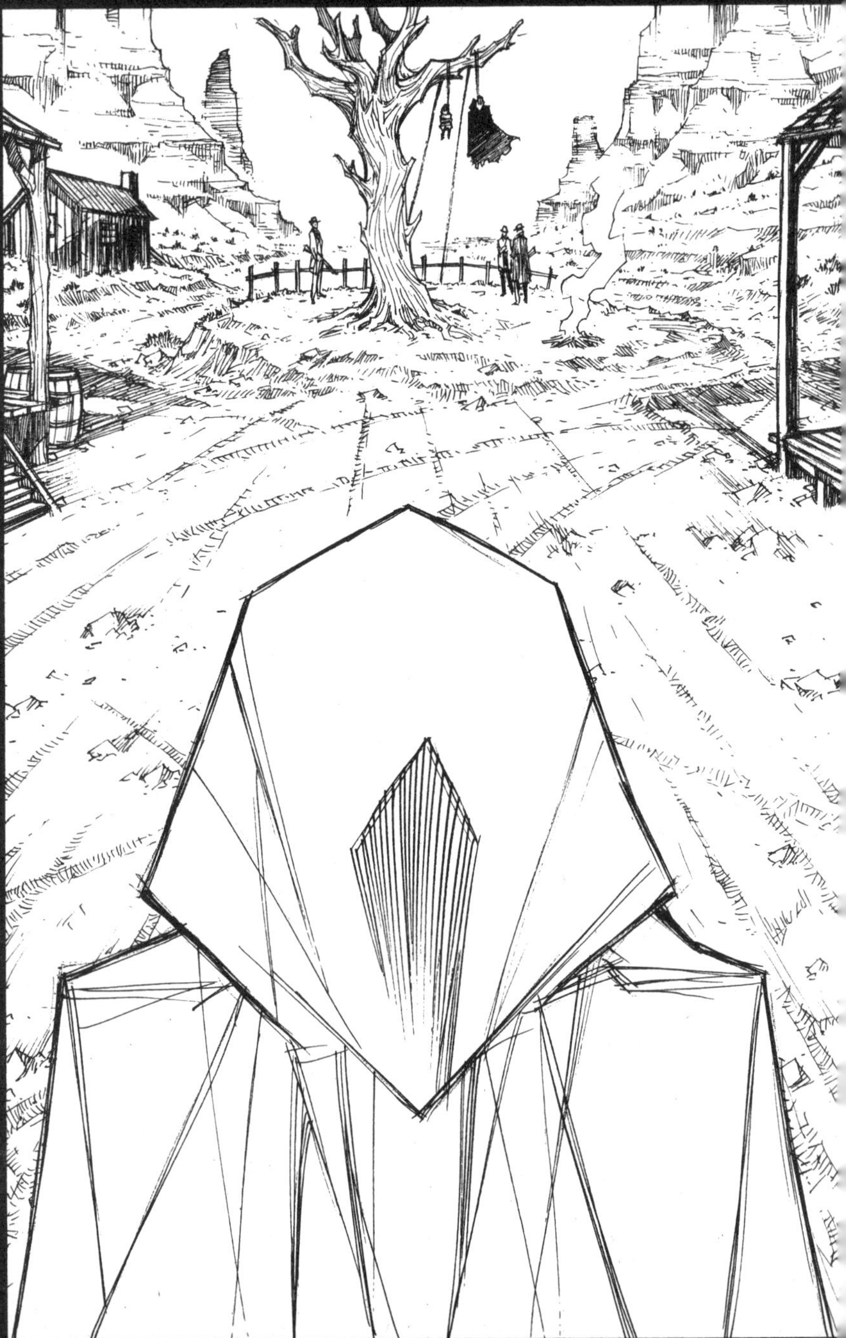

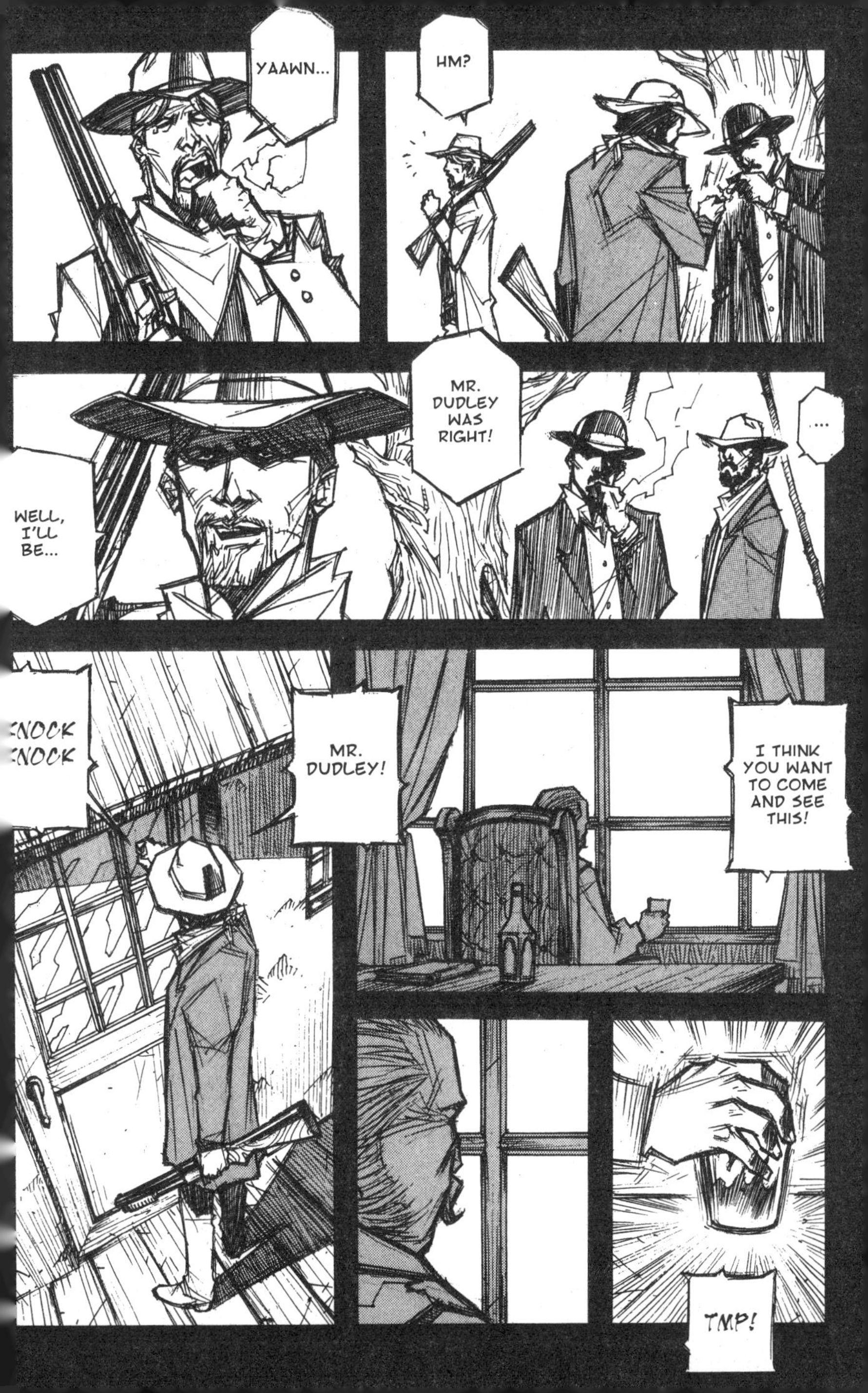
YAAWN...
HM?
WELL, I'LL BE...
MR. DUDLEY WAS RIGHT!
....
KNOCK KNOCK
MR. DUDLEY!
I THINK YOU WANT TO COME AND SEE THIS!
TMP!

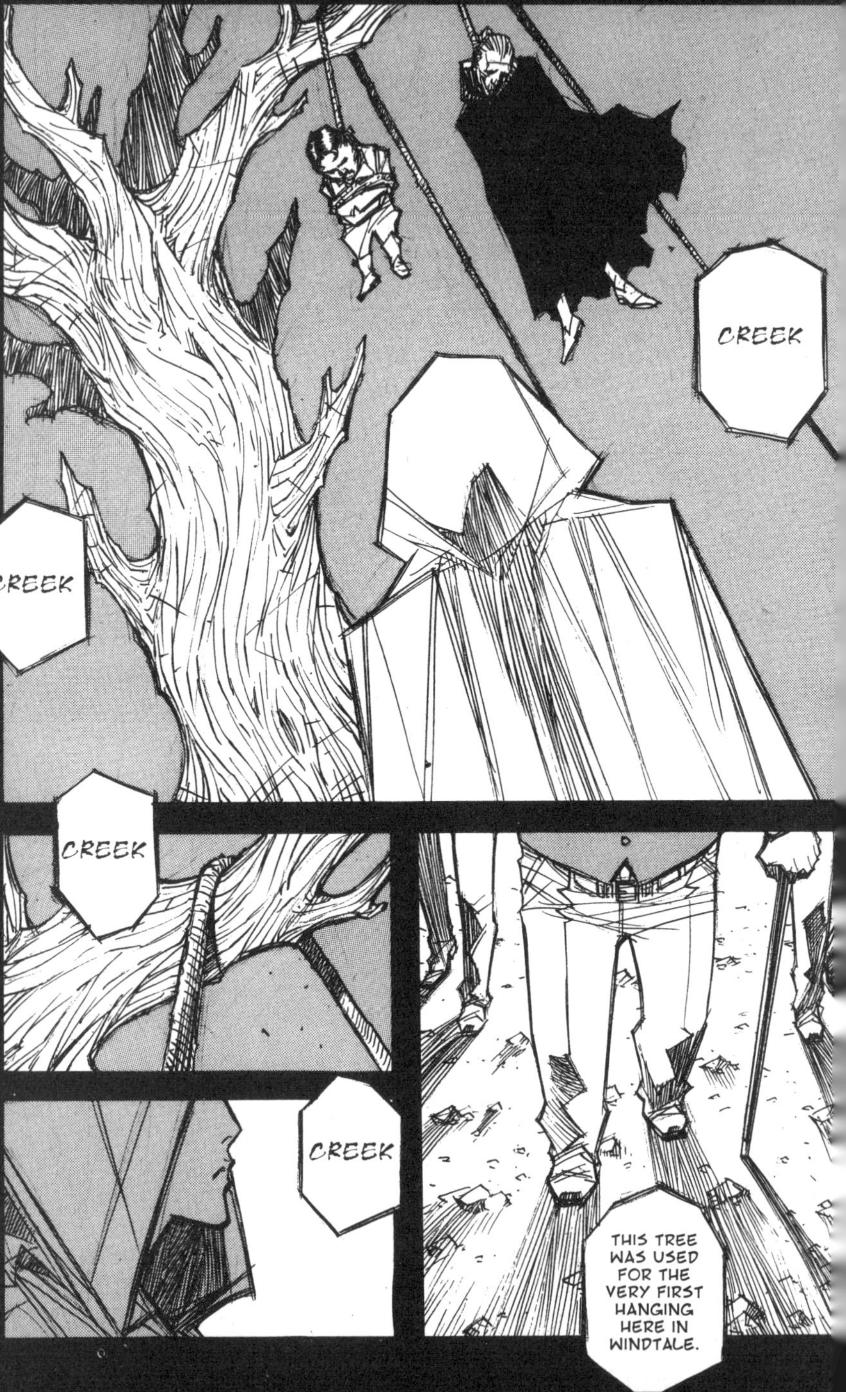
CREEK
CREEK
CREEK
CREEK
THIS TREE WAS USED FOR THE VERY FIRST HANGING HERE IN WINDTALE.

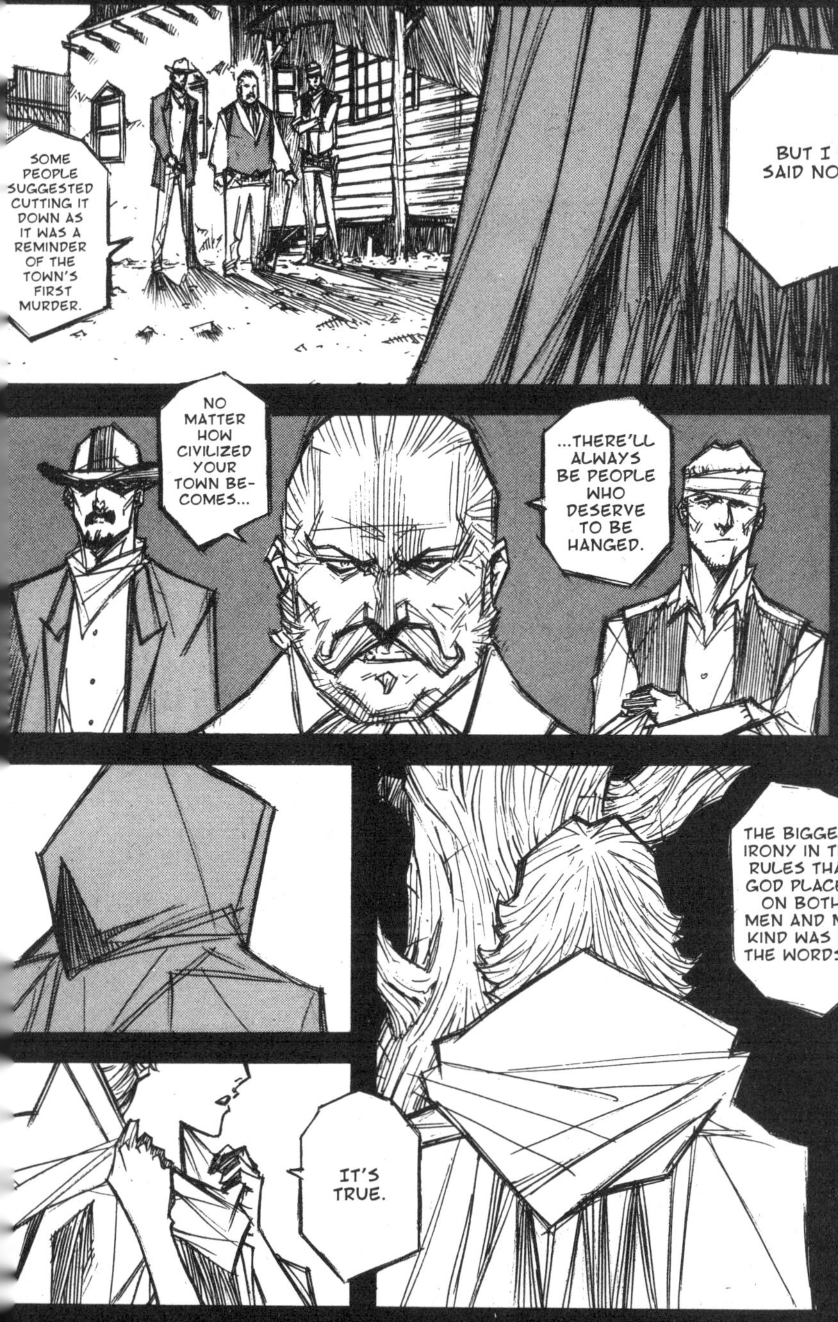
SOME PEOPLE SUGGESTED CUTTING IT DOWN AS IT WAS A REMINDER OF THE TOWN'S FIRST MURDER.
BUT I SAID NO.
NO MATTER HOW CIVILIZED YOUR TOWN BE-COMES...
...THERE'LL ALWAYS BE PEOPLE WHO DESERVE TO BE HANGED.
THE BIGGEST IRONY IN THE RULES THAT GOD PLACED ON BOTH MEN AND MY KIND WAS IN THE WORDS...
IT'S TRUE.

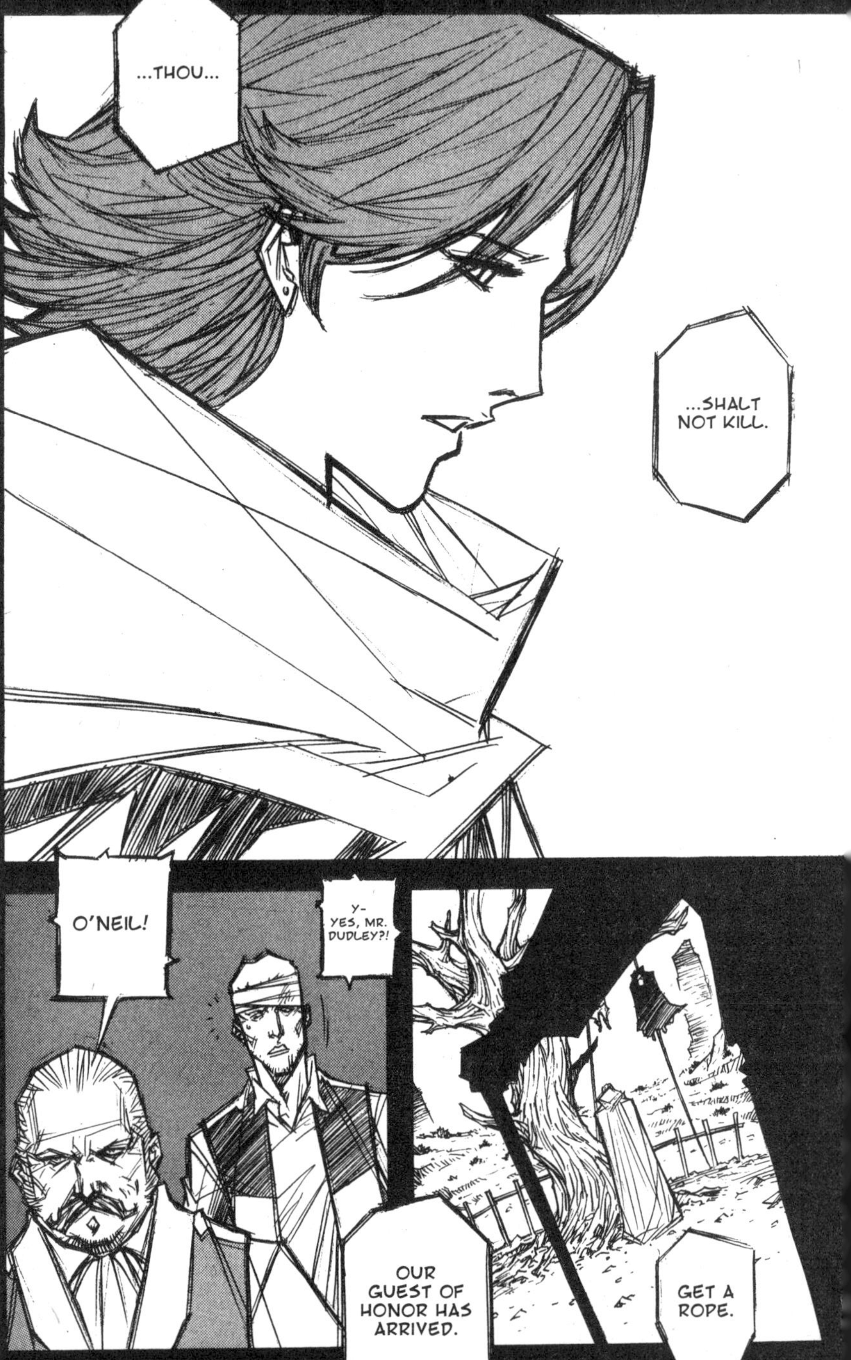
...THOU...
...SHALT NOT KILL.
O'NEIL!
Y- YES, MR. DUDLEY?!
OUR GUEST OF HONOR HAS ARRIVED.
GET A ROPE.

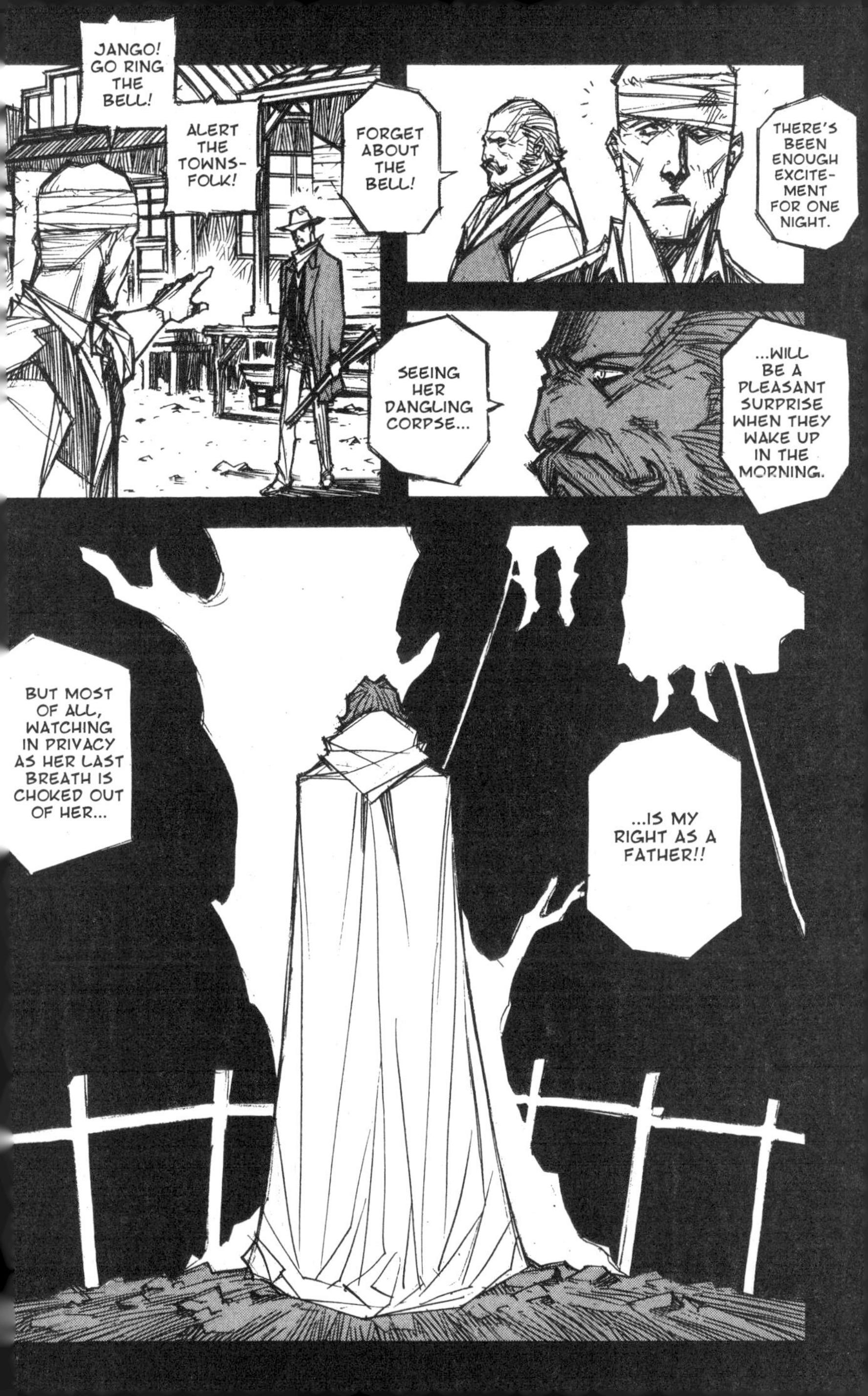
JANGO! GO RING THE BELL!
ALERT THE TOWNS-FOLK!
FORGET ABOUT THE BELL!
THERE'S BEEN ENOUGH EXCITE-MENT FOR ONE NIGHT.
SEEING HER DANGLING CORPSE...
...WILL BE A PLEASANT SURPRISE WHEN THEY WAKE UP IN THE MORNING.
BUT MOST OF ALL, WATCHING IN PRIVACY AS HER LAST BREATH IS CHOKED OUT OF HER...
...IS MY RIGHT AS A FATHER!!

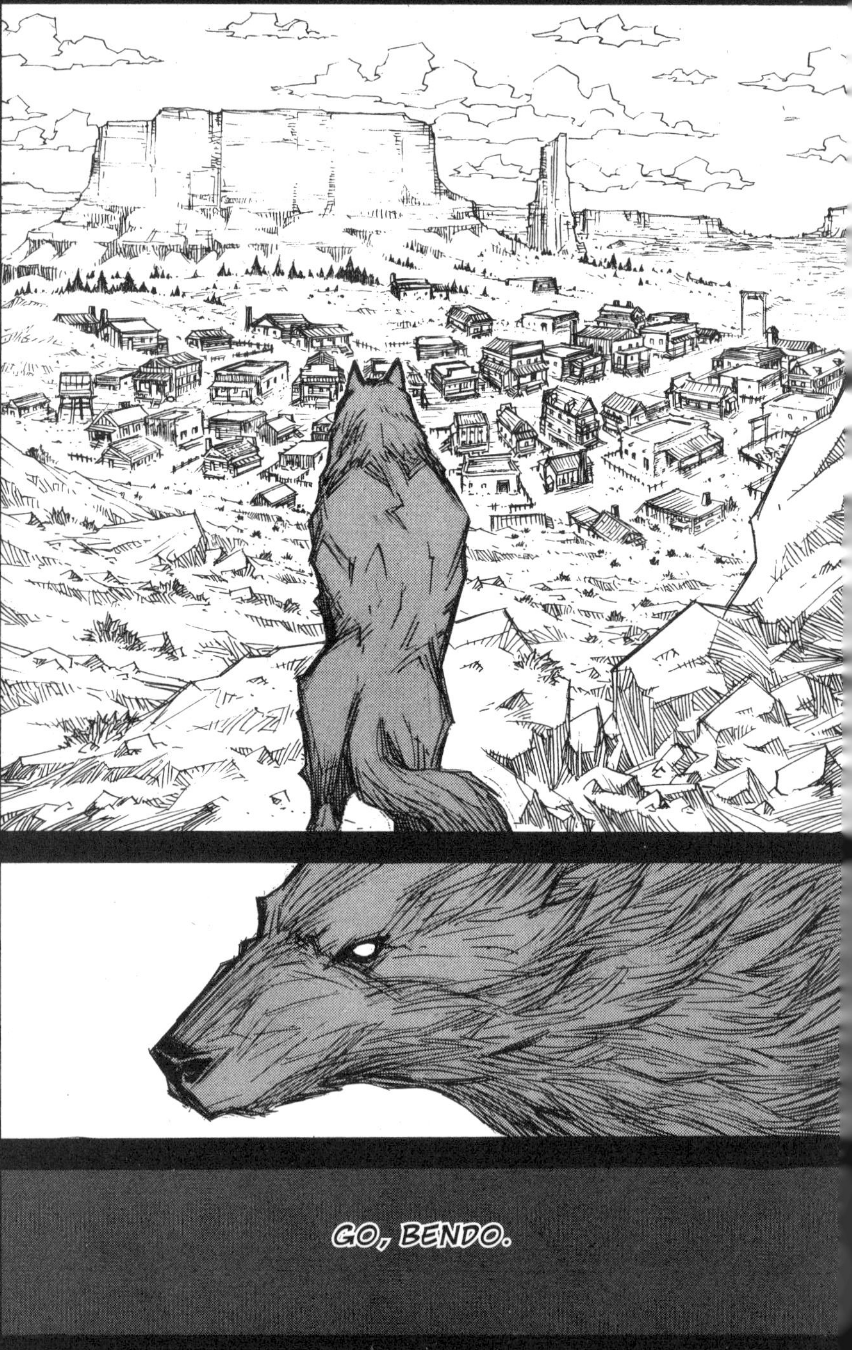
GO, BENDO.

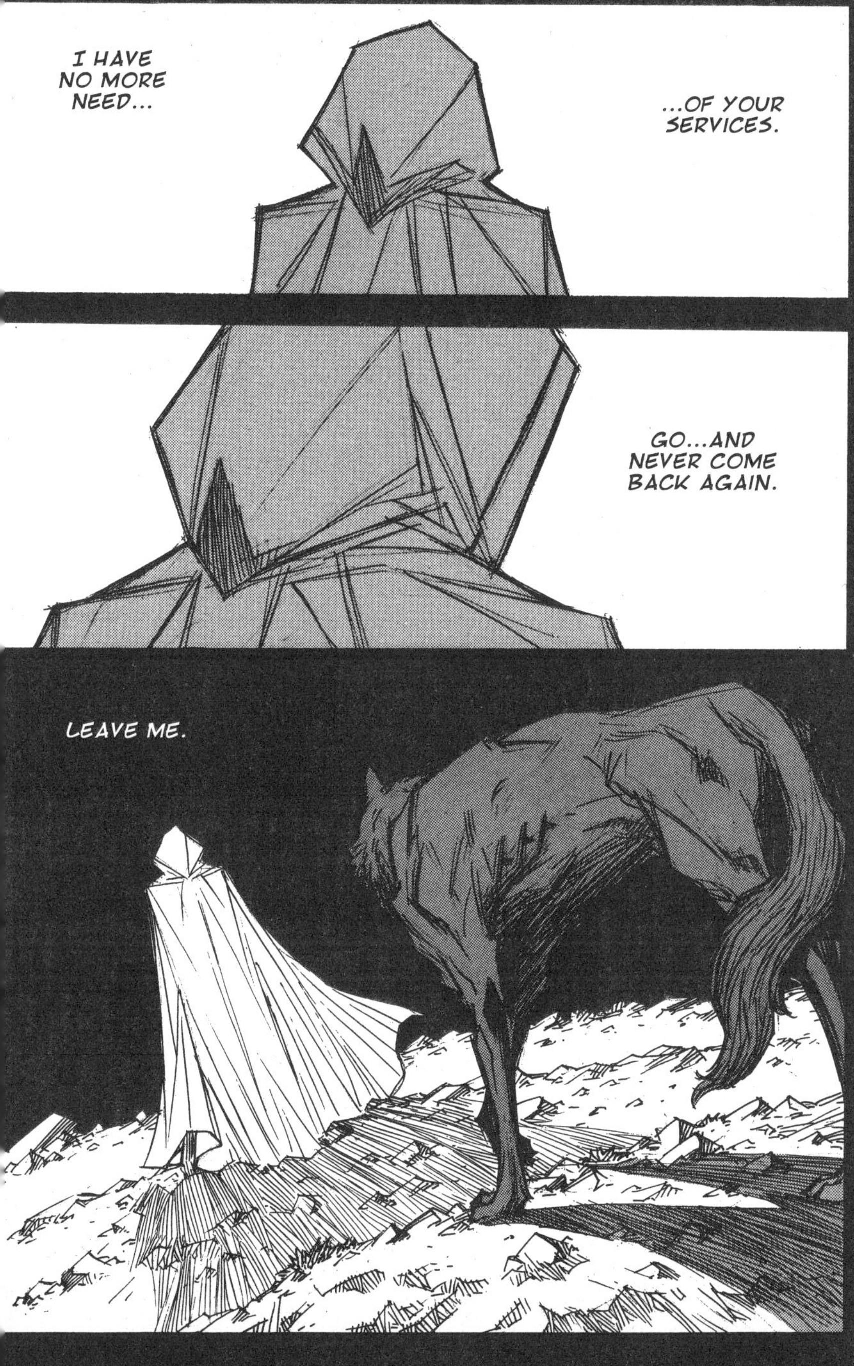
I HAVE NO MORE NEED...
...OF YOUR SERVICES.
GO...AND NEVER COME BACK AGAIN.
LEAVE ME.

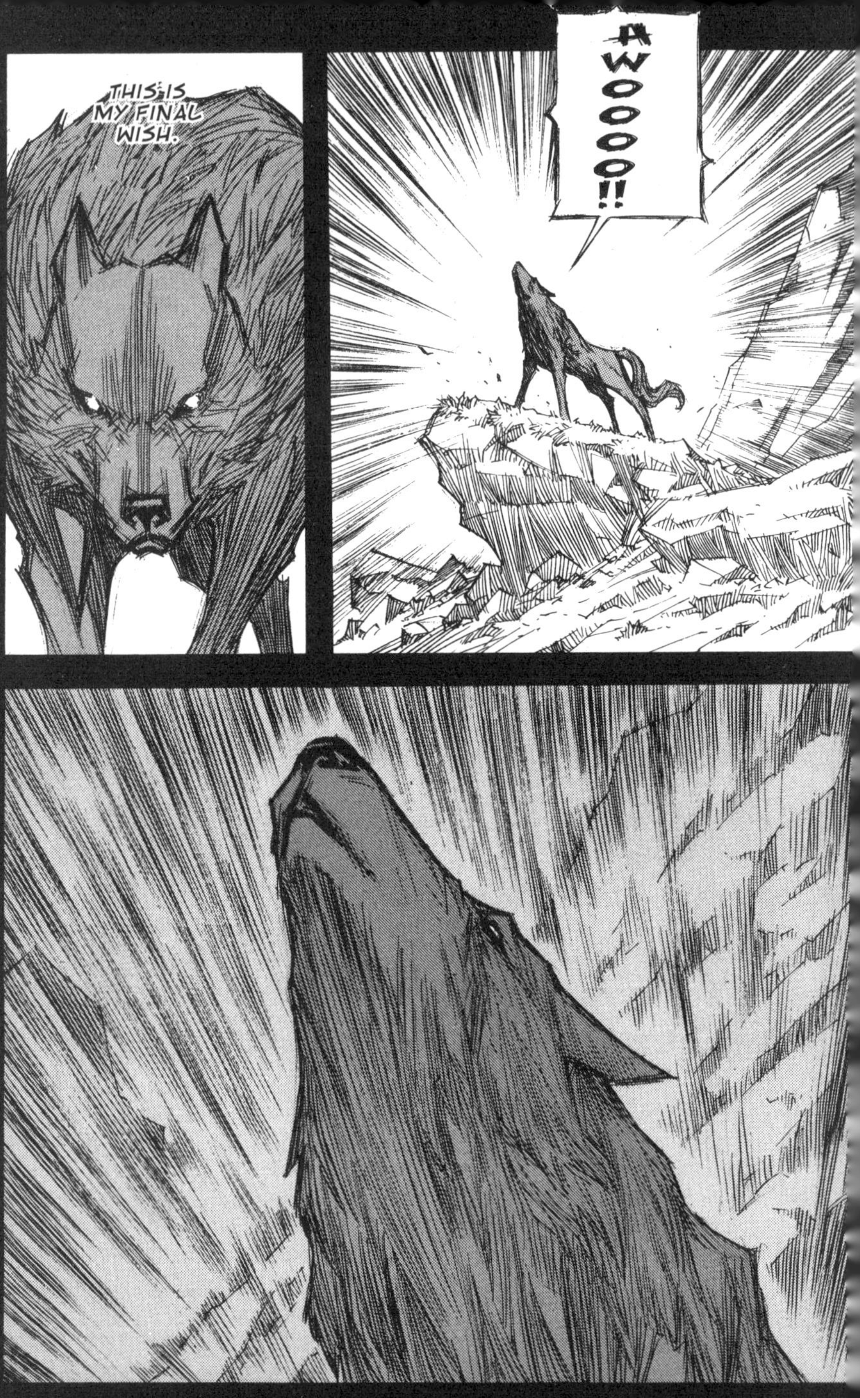
THIS IS MY FINAL WISH.
AWOOOOO!!

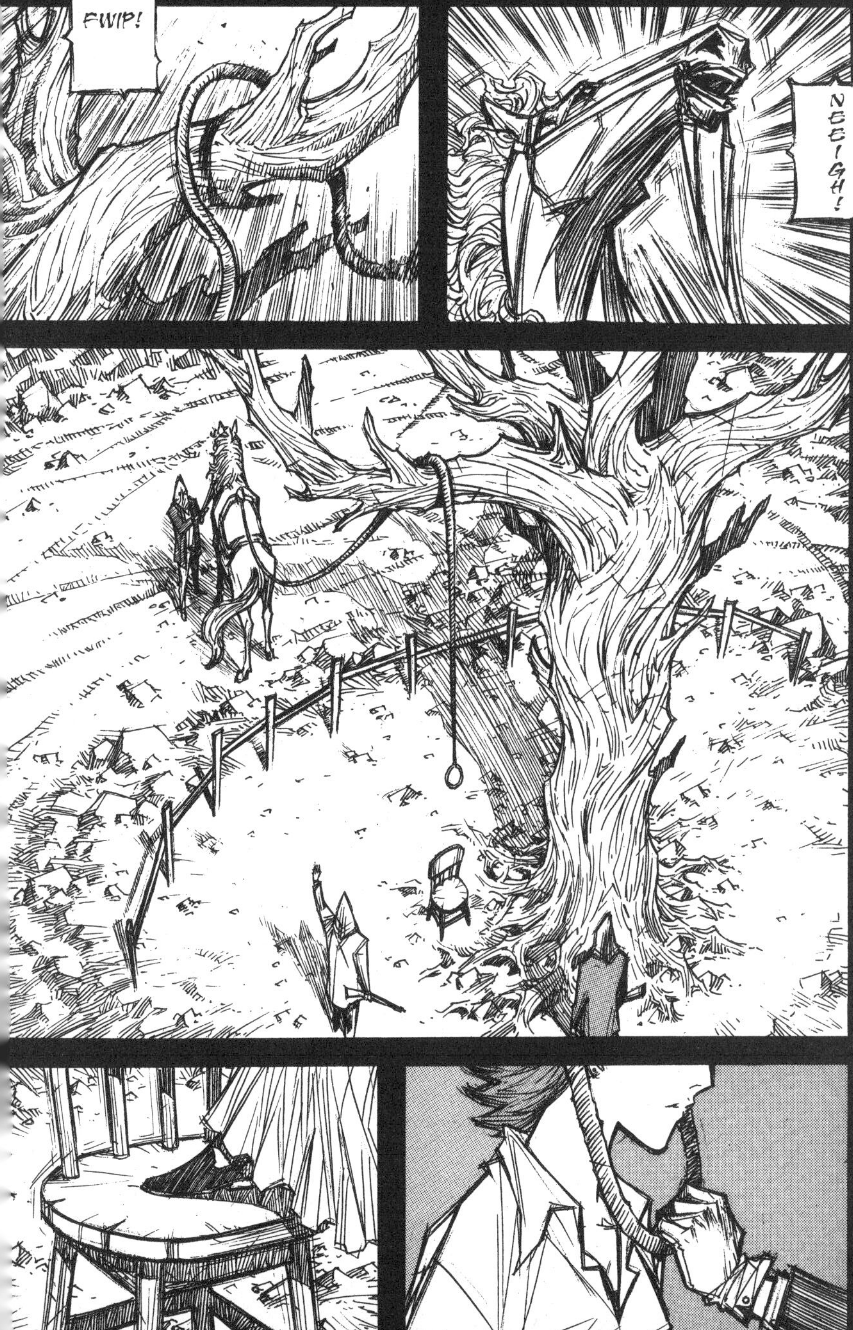
FWIP!
NEEIGH!

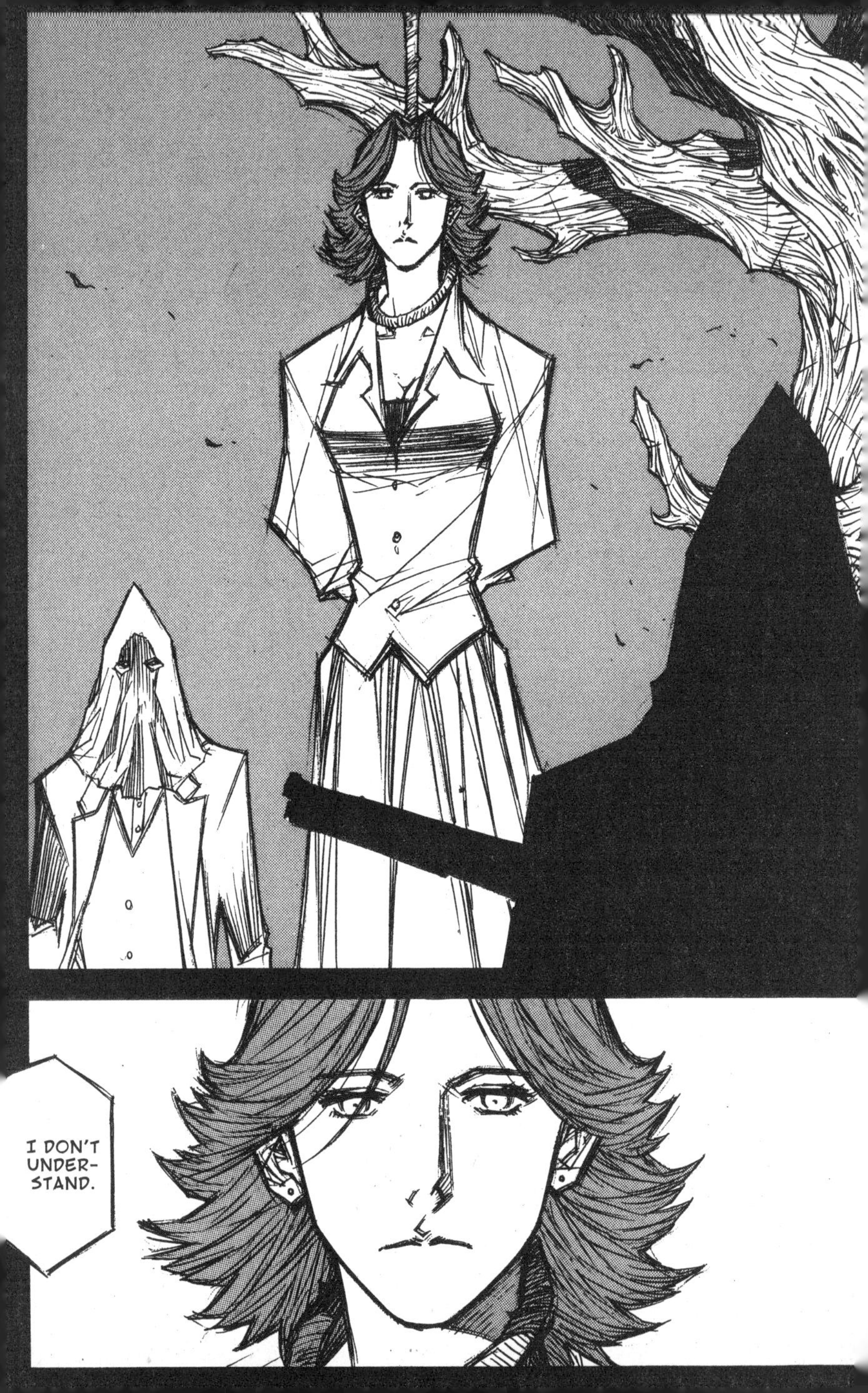
I DON'T UNDER- STAND.

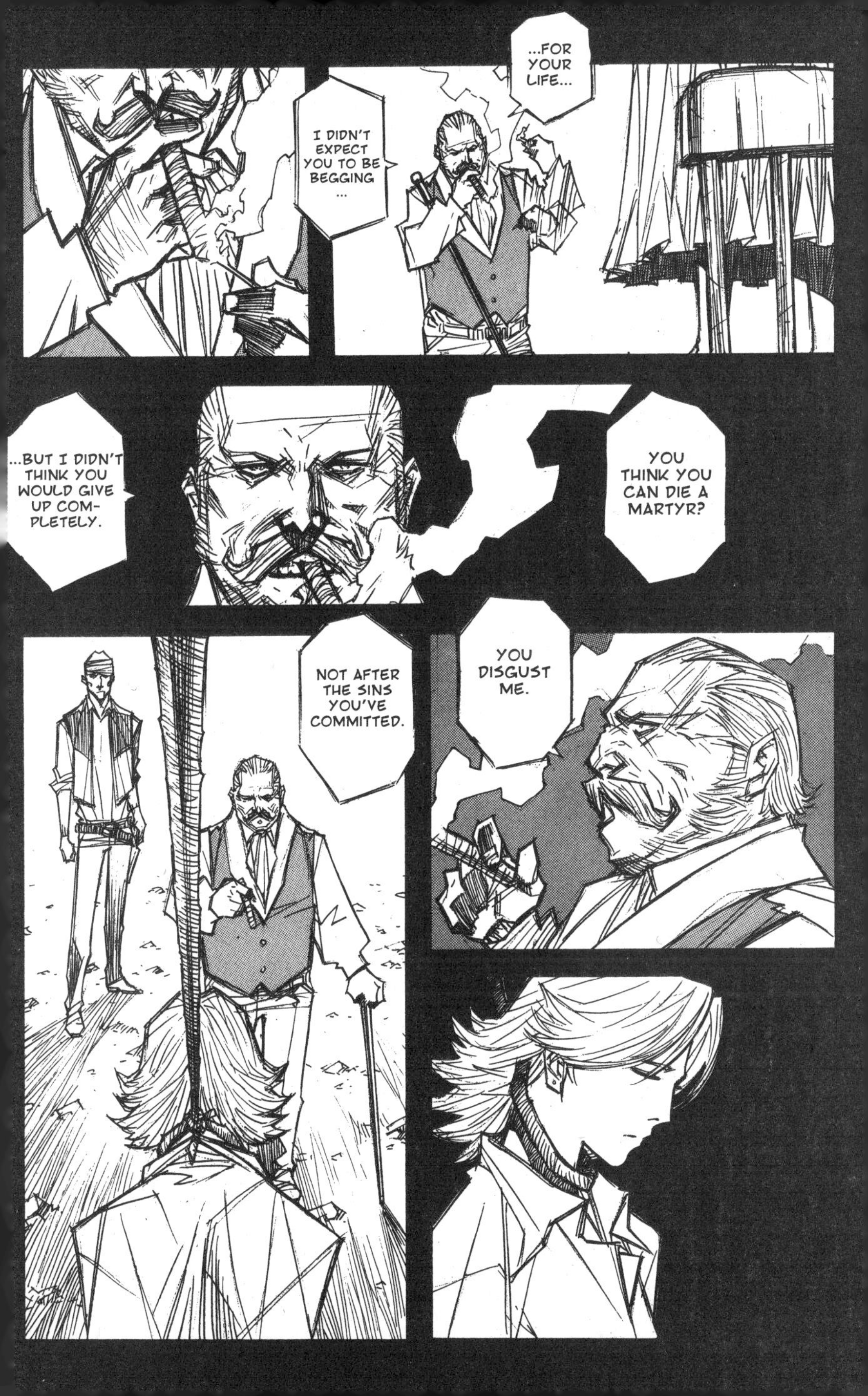
I DIDN'T EXPECT YOU TO BE BEGGING ...
...FOR YOUR LIFE...
...BUT I DIDN'T THINK YOU WOULD GIVE UP COM-PLETELY.
YOU THINK YOU CAN DIE A MARTYR?
NOT AFTER THE SINS YOU'VE COMMITTED.
YOU DISGUST ME.

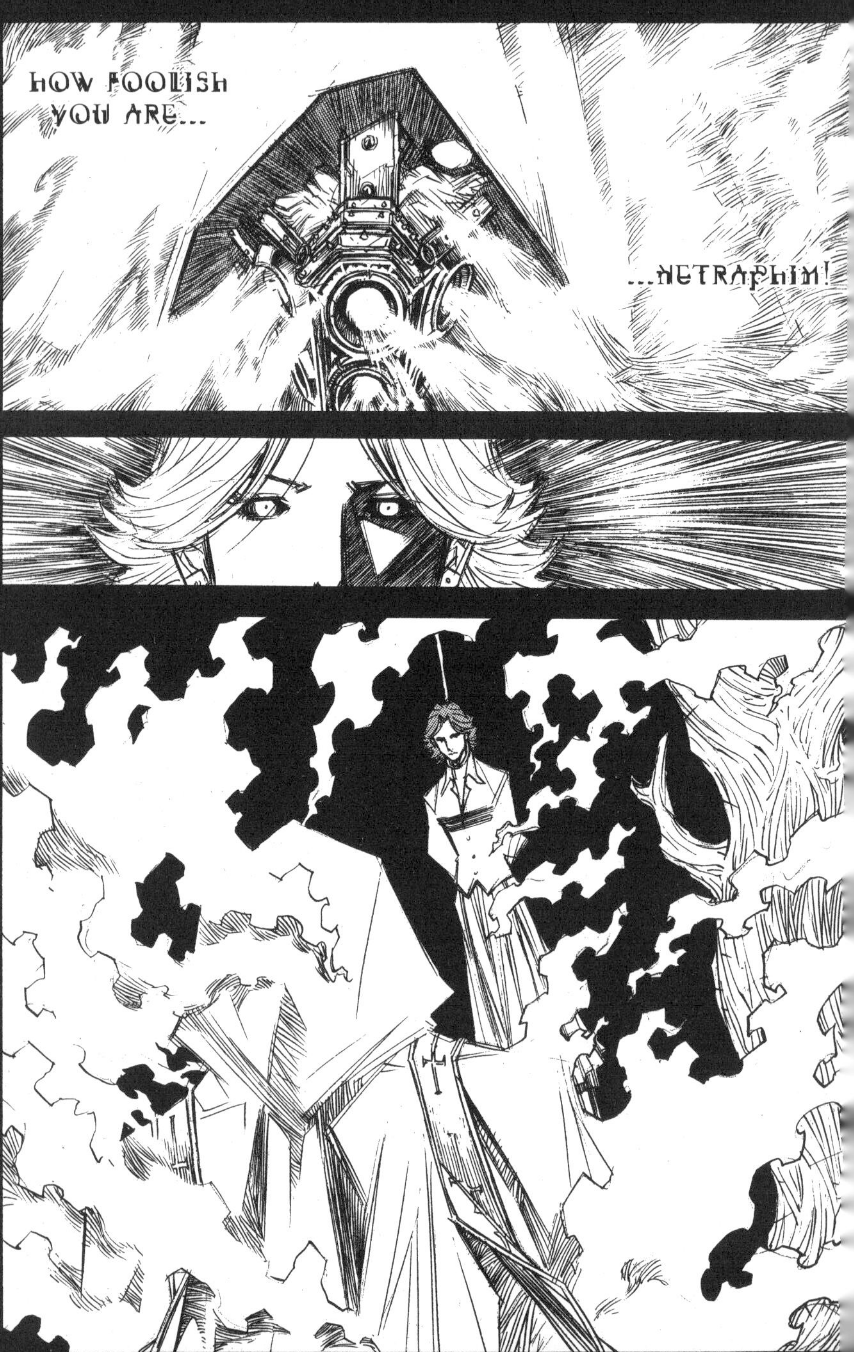
HOW FOOLISH YOU ARE...
...NETRAPHIM!

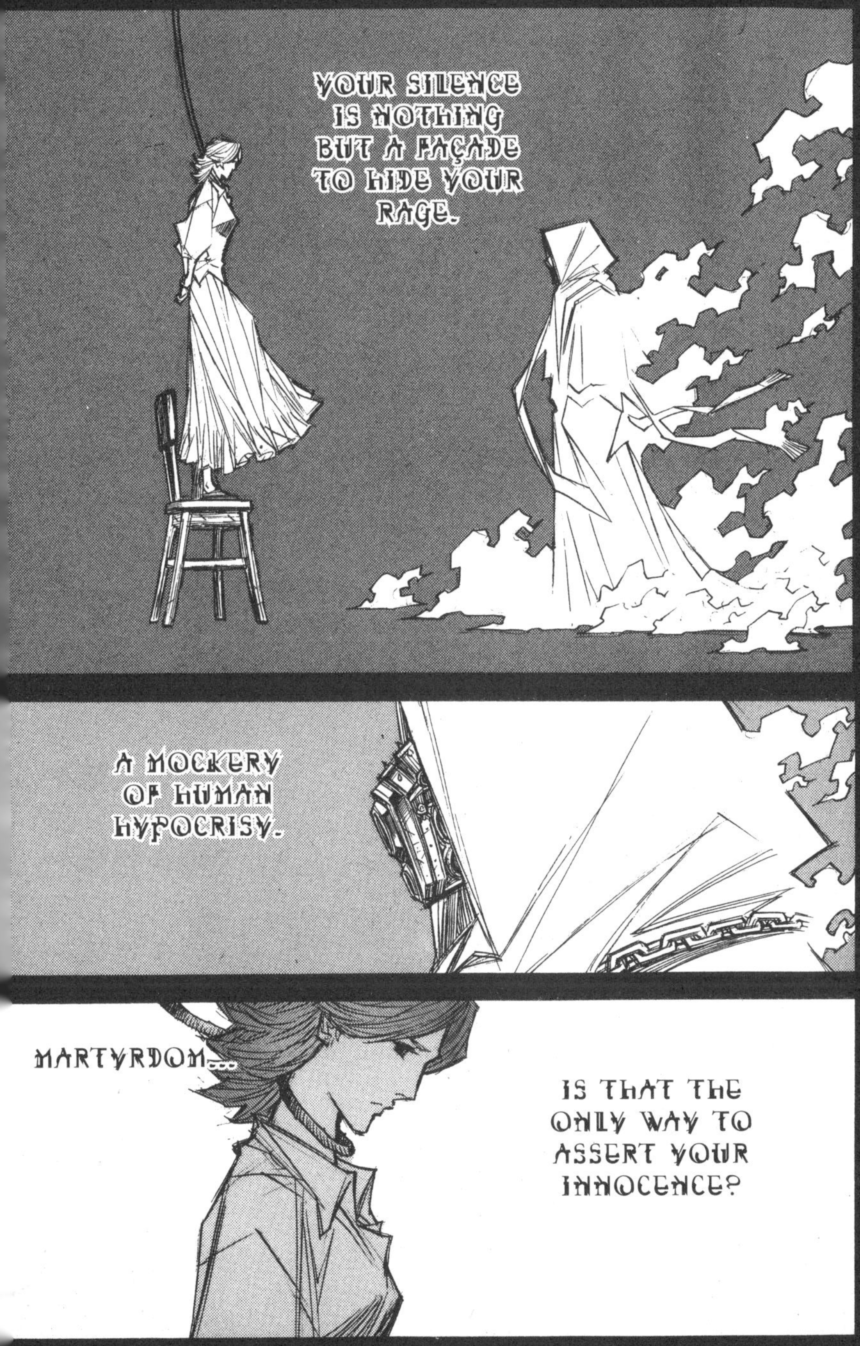
YOUR SILENCE IS NOTHING BUT A FAÇADE TO HIDE YOUR RAGE.
A MOCKERY OF HUMAN HYPOCRISY.
MARTYRDOM...
IS THAT THE ONLY WAY TO ASSERT YOUR INNOCENCE?

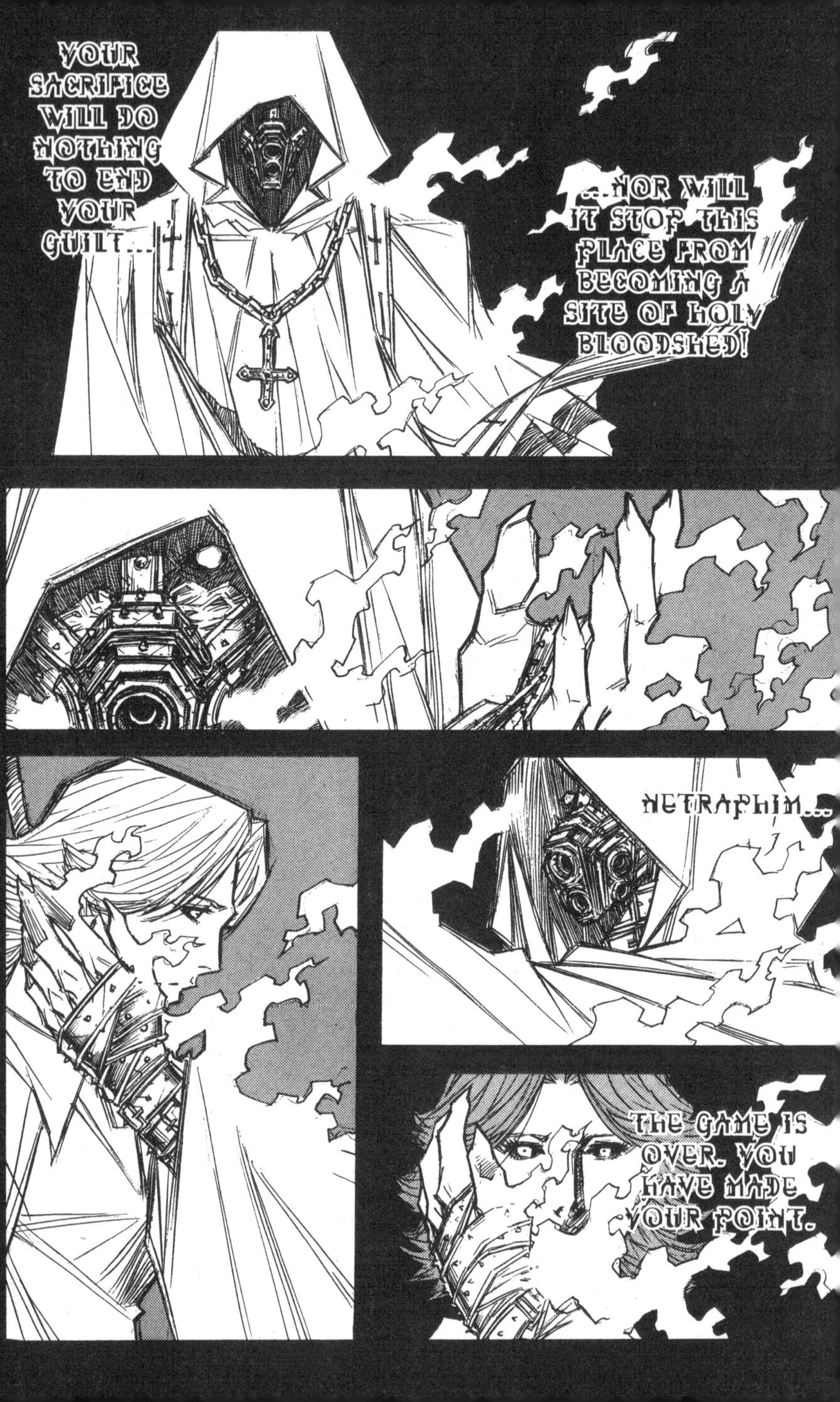
YOUR SACRIFICE WILL DO NOTHING TO END YOUR GUILT...
...NOR WILL IT STOP THIS PLACE FROM BECOMING A SITE OF HOLY BLOODSHED!
NETRAPHIM...
THE GAME IS OVER. YOU HAVE MADE YOUR POINT.

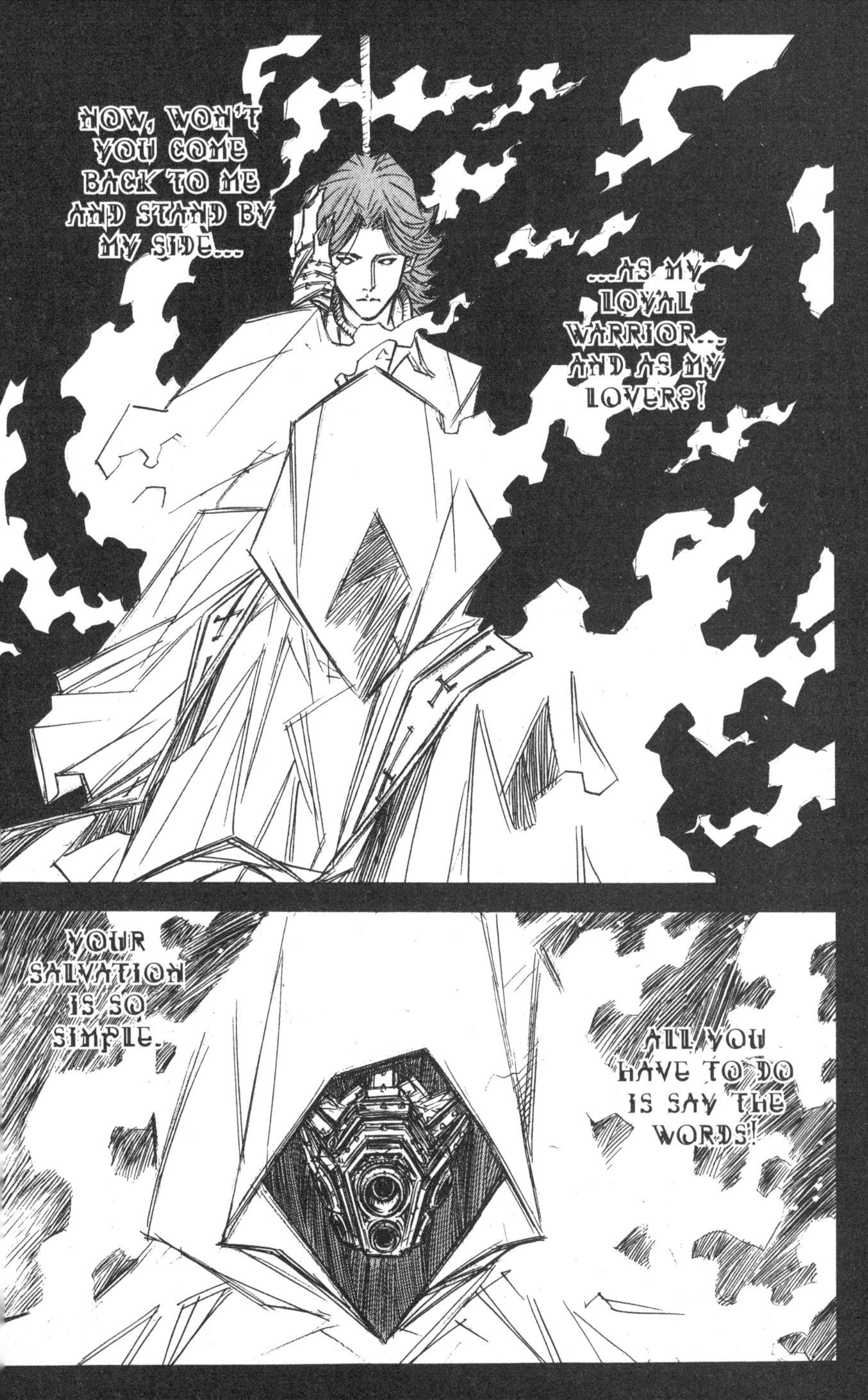
NOW, WON'T YOU COME BACK TO ME AND STAND BY MY SIDE...
...AS MY LOYAL WARRIOR... AND AS MY LOVER?!
YOUR SALVATION IS SO SIMPLE.
ALL YOU HAVE TO DO IS SAY THE WORDS!

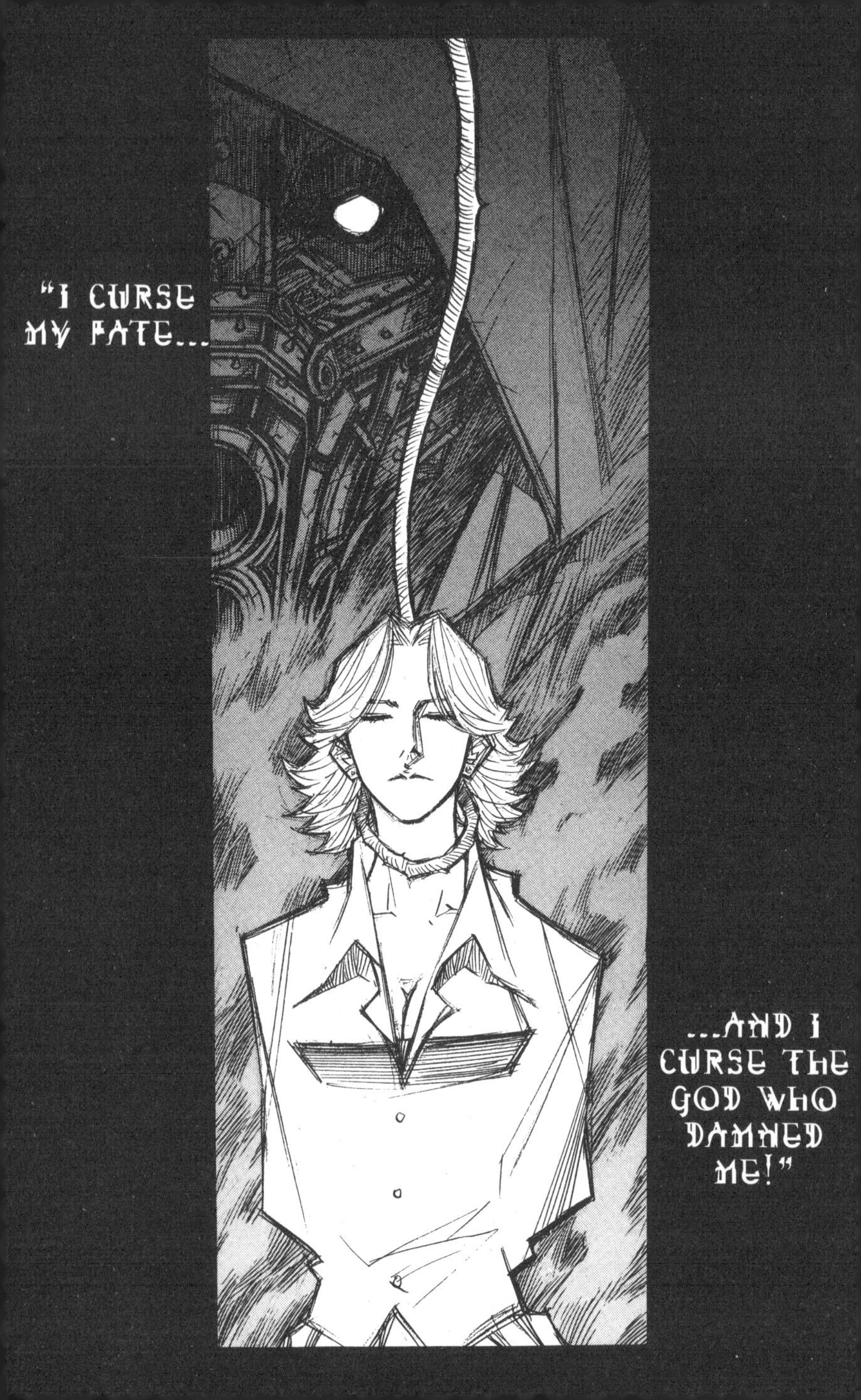
"I CURSE MY FATE...
...AND I CURSE THE GOD WHO DAMNED ME!"

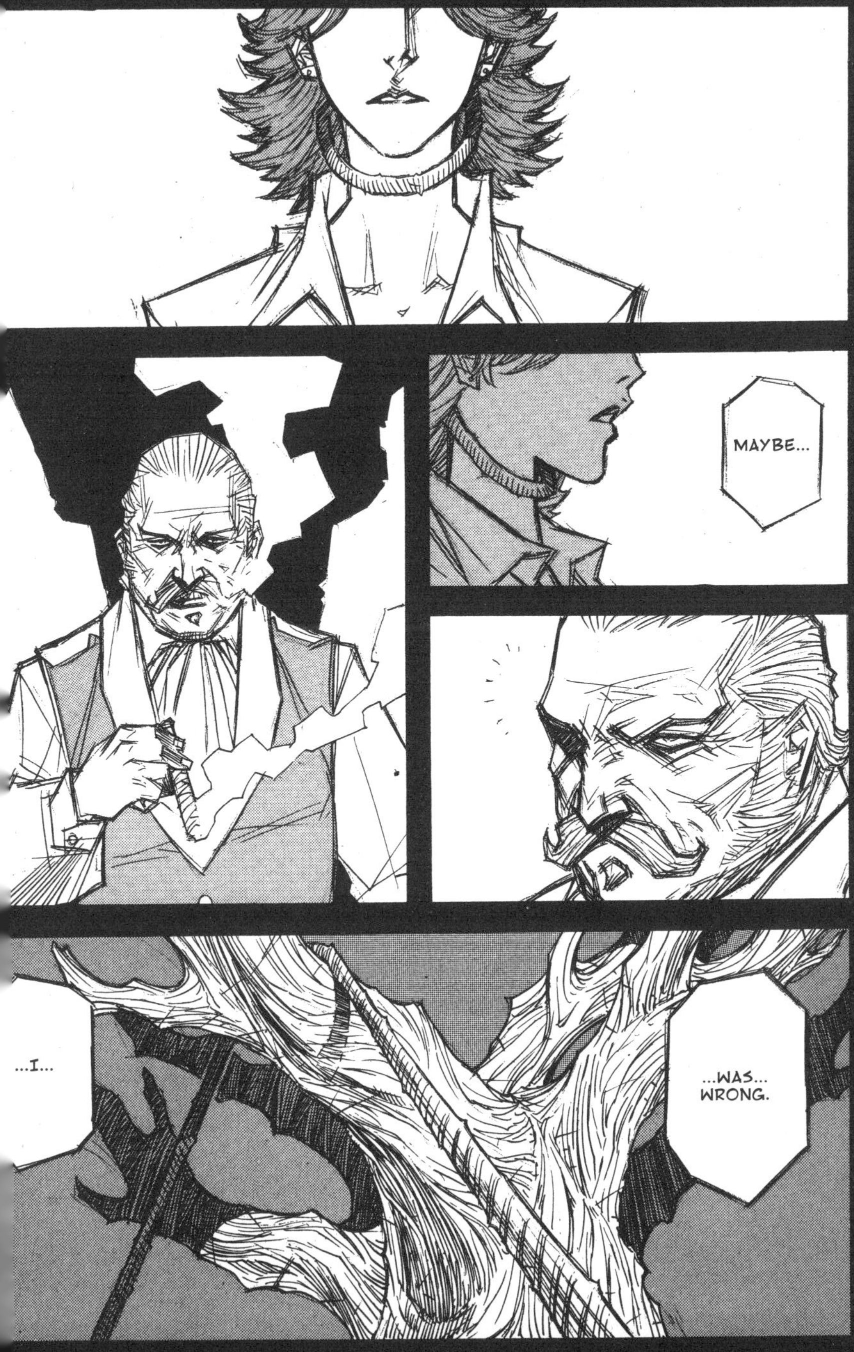
MAYBE...
...I...
...WAS... WRONG.

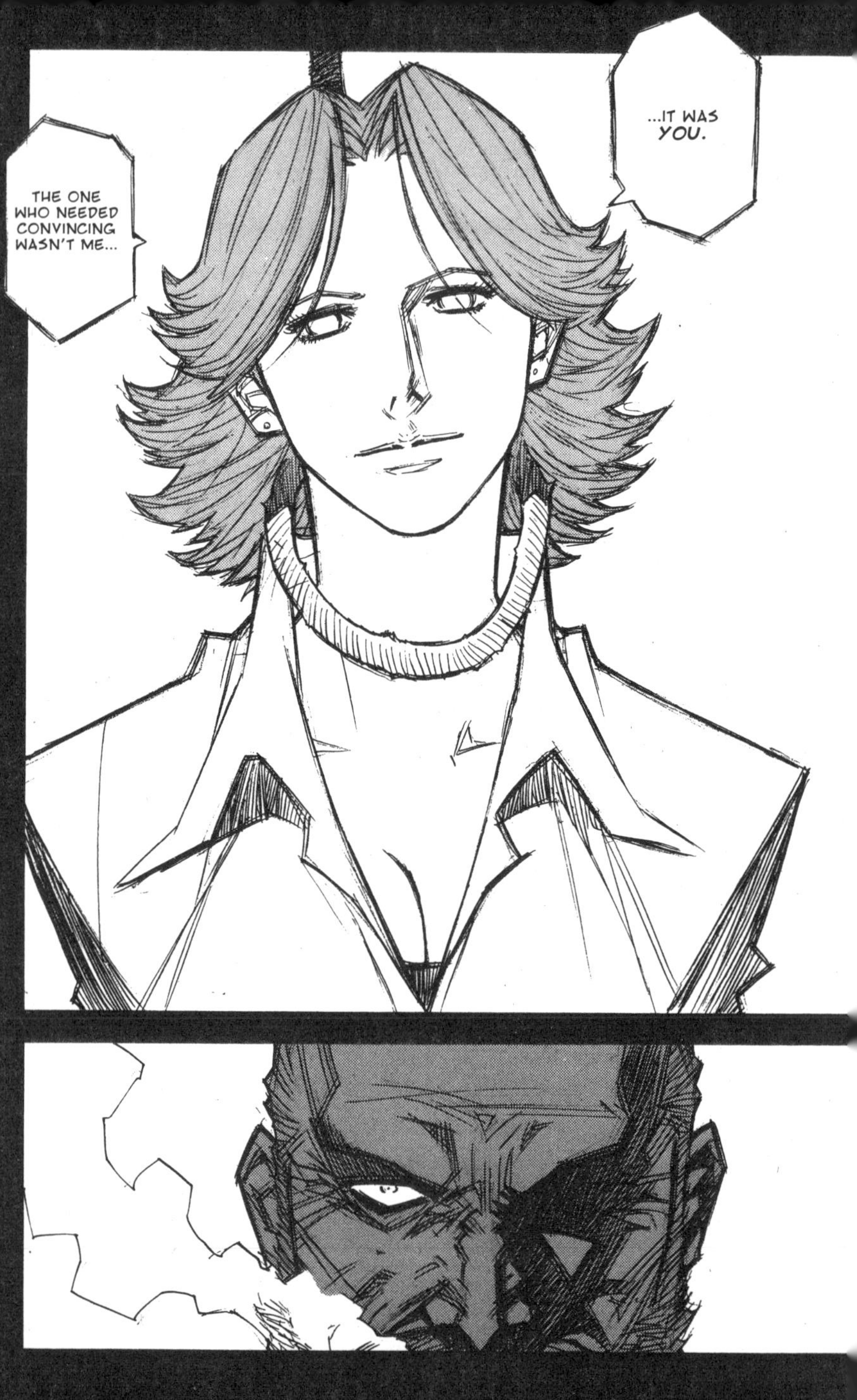
THE ONE WHO NEEDED CONVINCING WASN'T ME...
...IT WAS YOU.

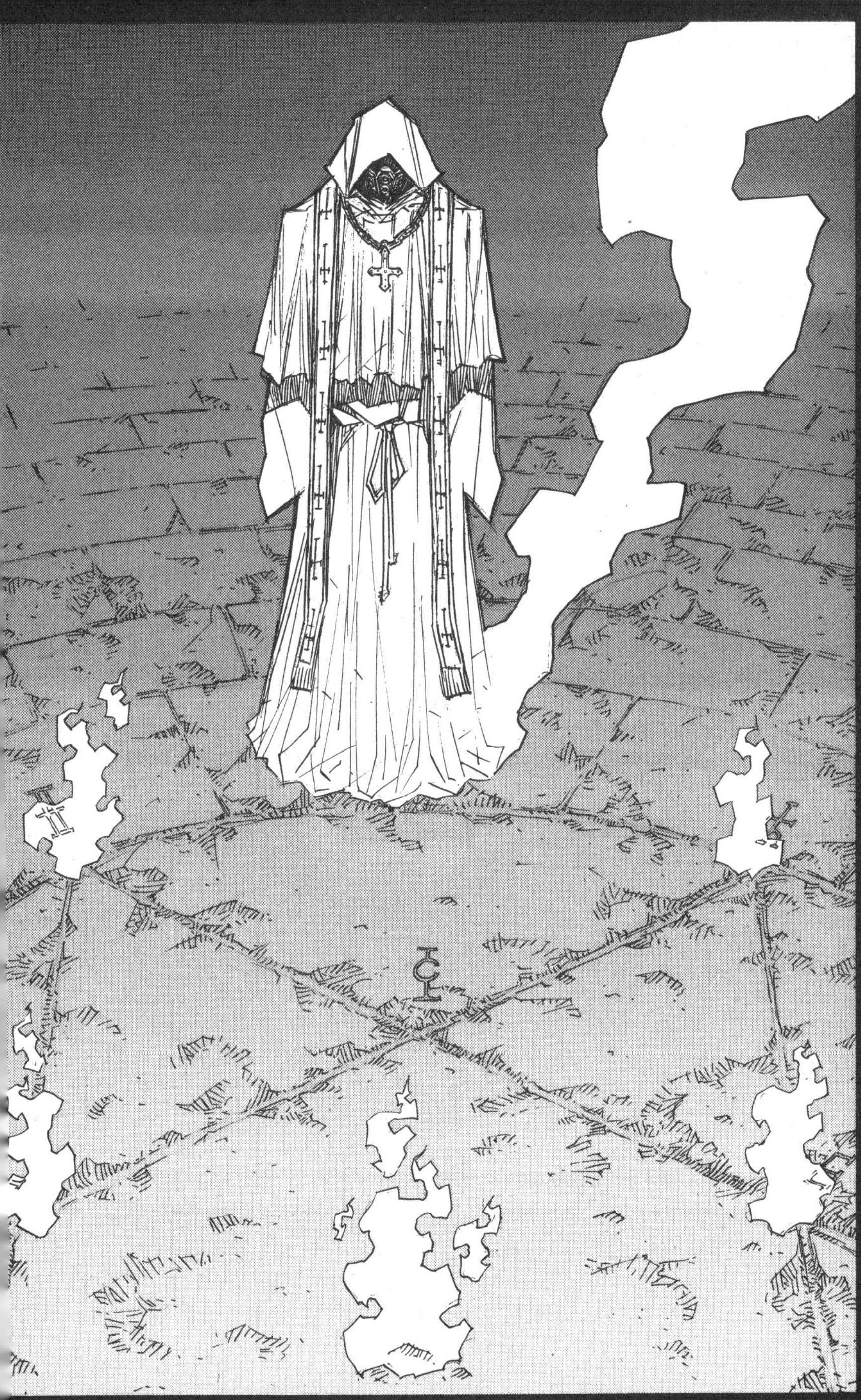

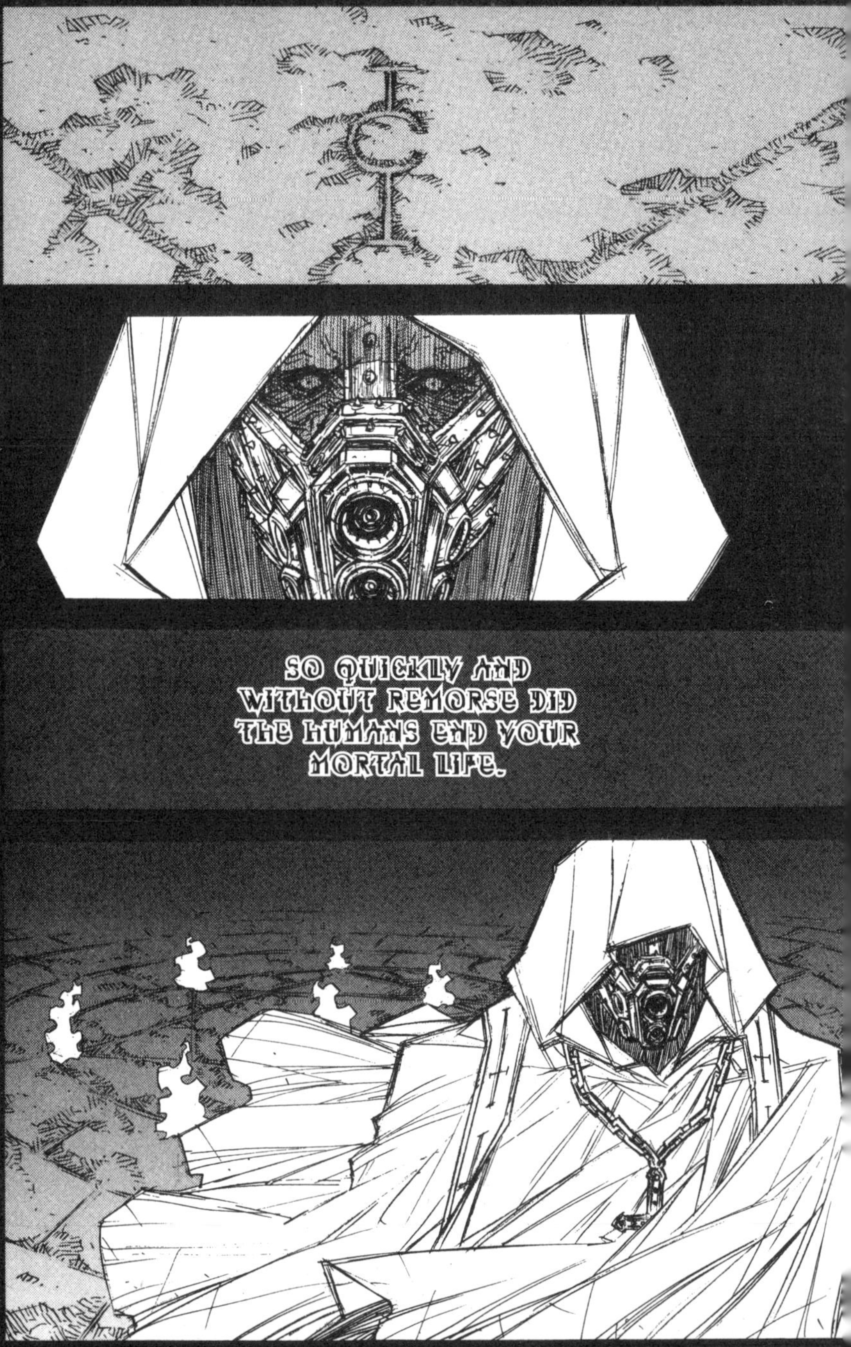
SO QUICKLY AND WITHOUT REMORSE DID THE HUMANS END YOUR MORTAL LIFE.

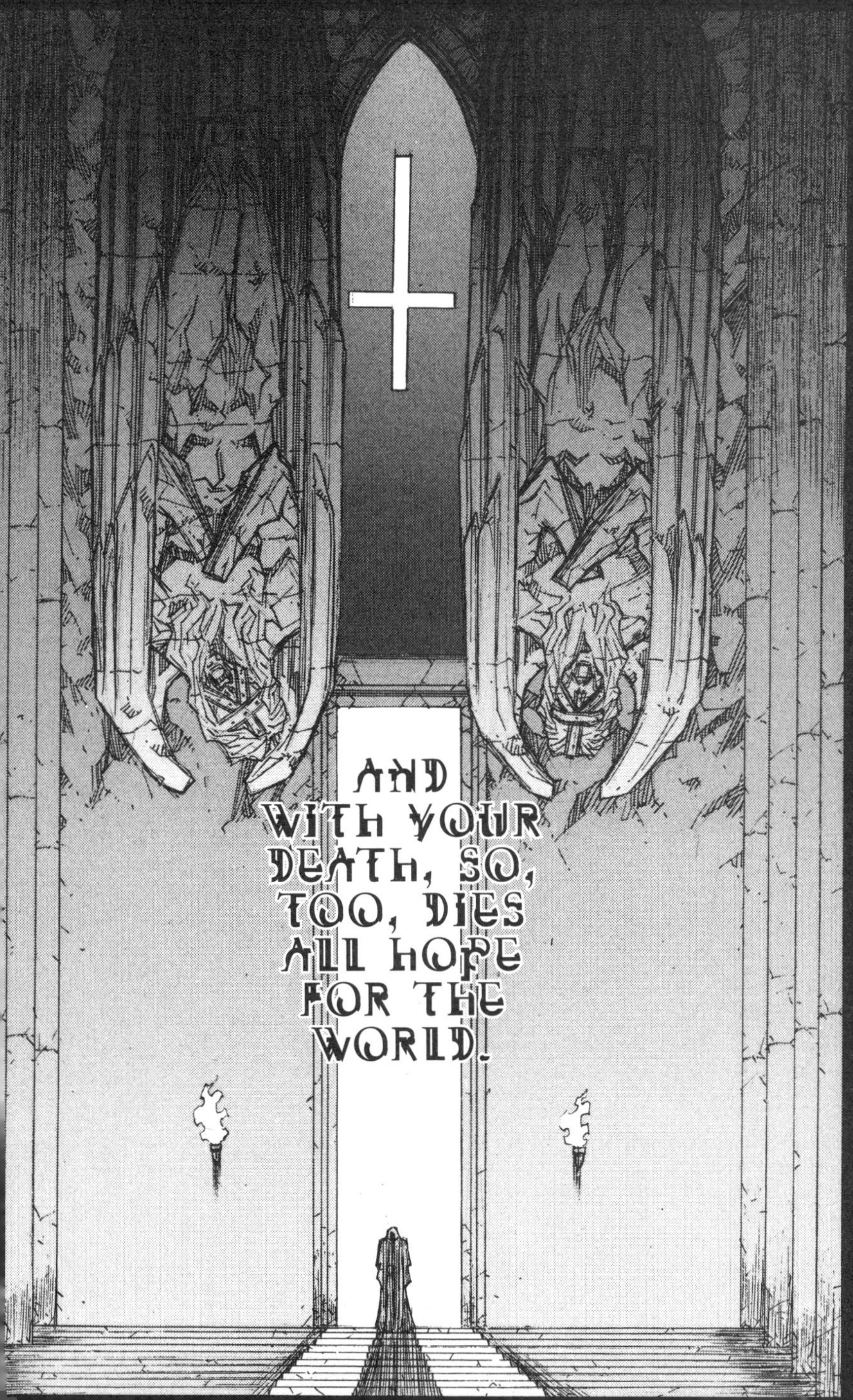
AND WITH YOUR DEATH, SO, TOO, DIES ALL HOPE FOR THE WORLD.

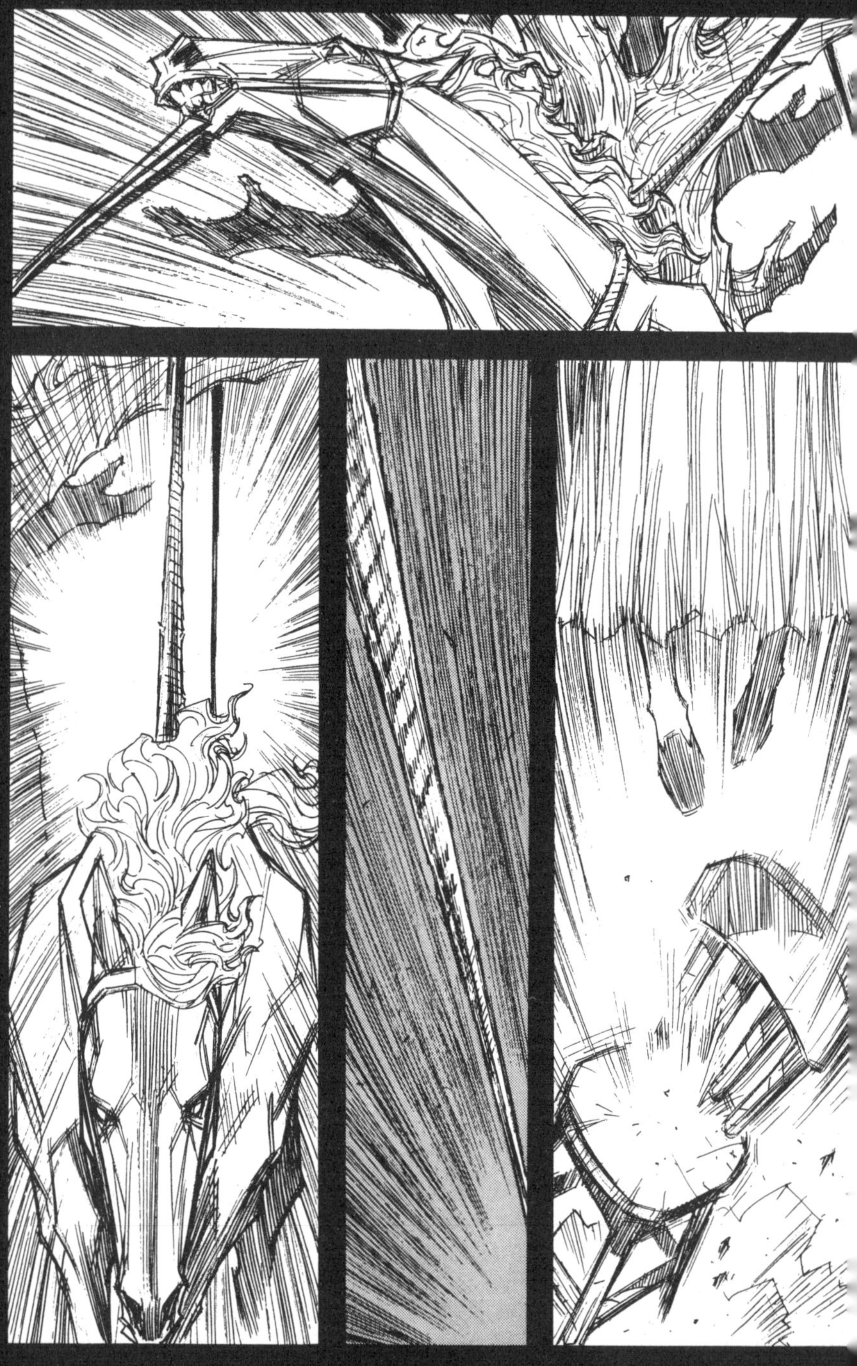

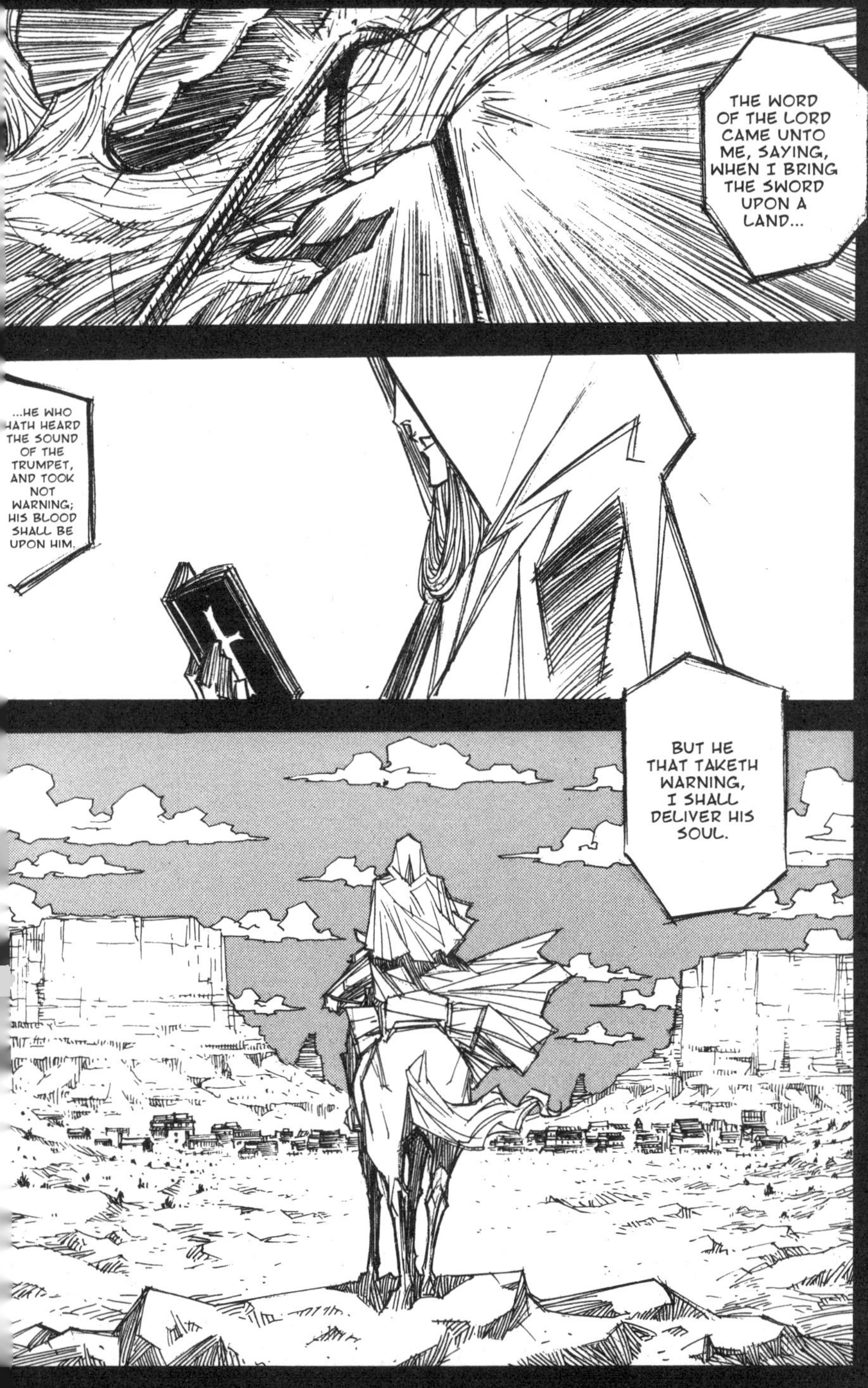
THE WORD OF THE LORD CAME UNTO ME, SAYING, WHEN I BRING THE SWORD UPON A LAND...
...HE WHO HATH HEARD THE SOUND OF THE TRUMPET, AND TOOK NOT WARNING; HIS BLOOD SHALL BE UPON HIM.
BUT HE THAT TAKETH WARNING, I SHALL DELIVER HIS SOUL.

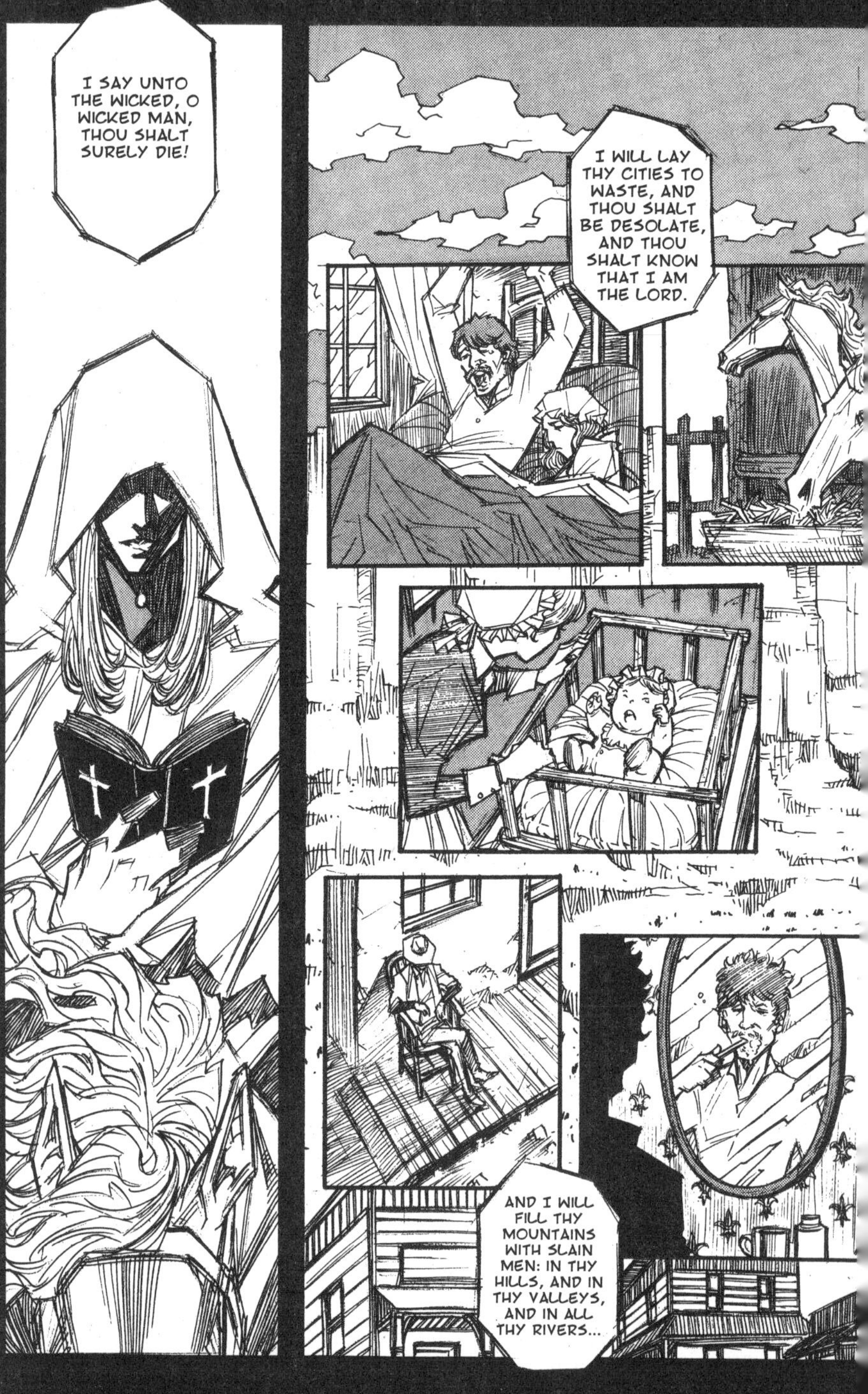
I SAY UNTO THE WICKED, O WICKED MAN, THOU SHALT SURELY DIE!
I WILL LAY THY CITIES TO WASTE, AND THOU SHALT BE DESOLATE, AND THOU SHALT KNOW THAT I AM THE LORD.
AND I WILL FILL THY MOUNTAINS WITH SLAIN MEN: IN THY HILLS, AND IN THY VALLEYS, AND IN ALL THY RIVERS...

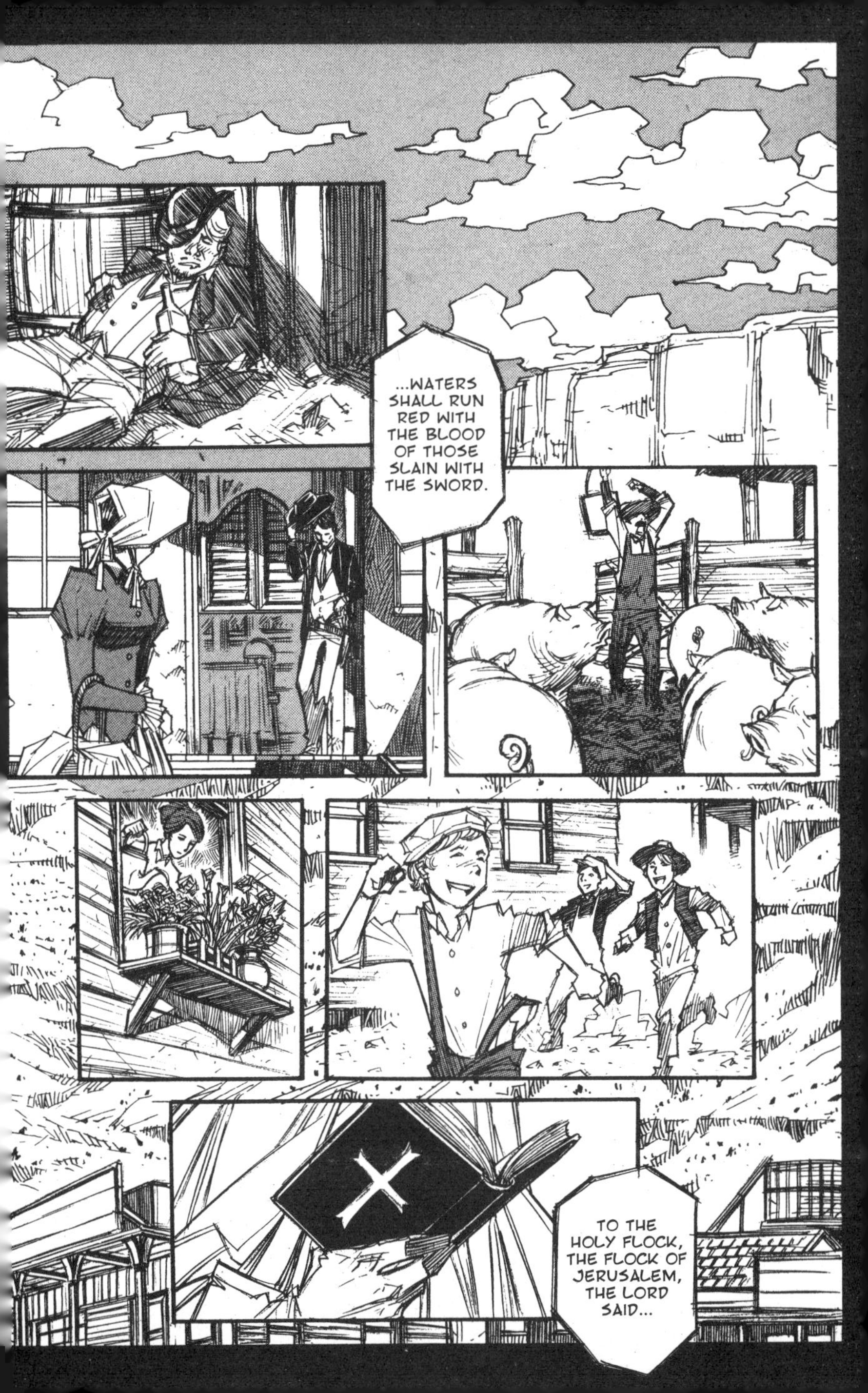
...WATERS SHALL RUN RED WITH THE BLOOD OF THOSE SLAIN WITH THE SWORD.
TO THE HOLY FLOCK, THE FLOCK OF JERUSALEM, THE LORD SAID...

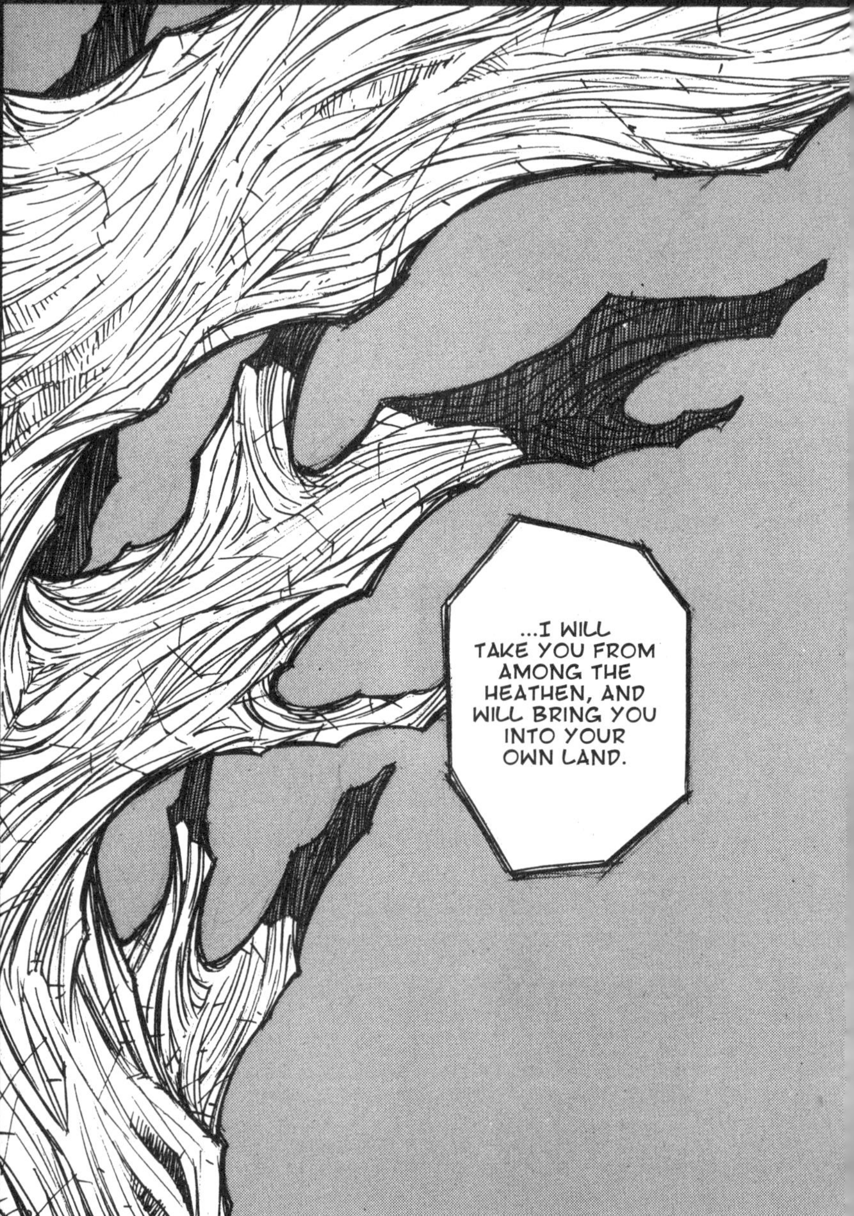
...I WILL TAKE YOU FROM AMONG THE HEATHEN, AND WILL BRING YOU INTO YOUR OWN LAND.

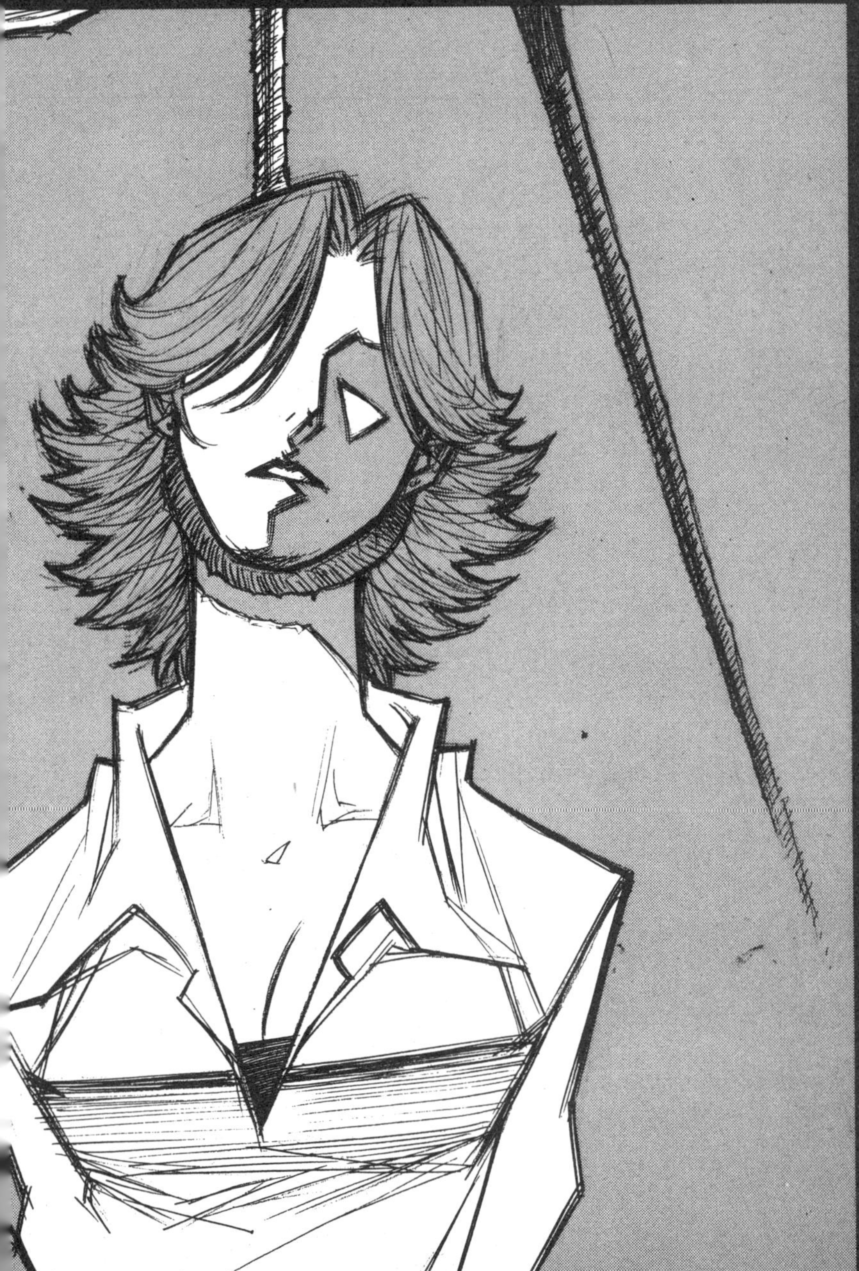

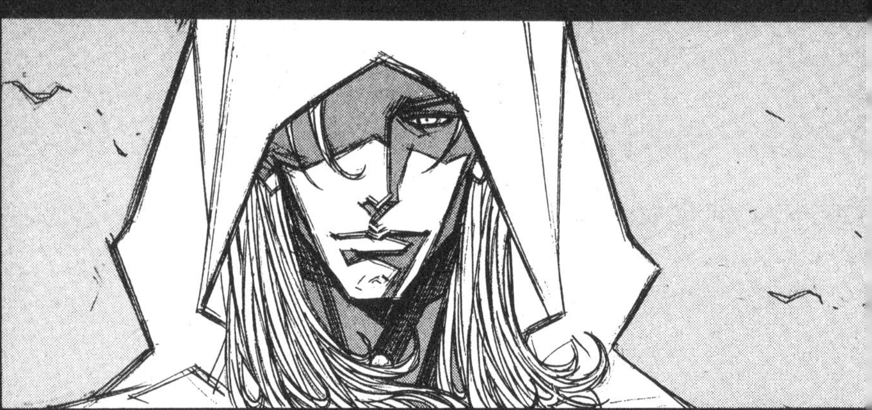
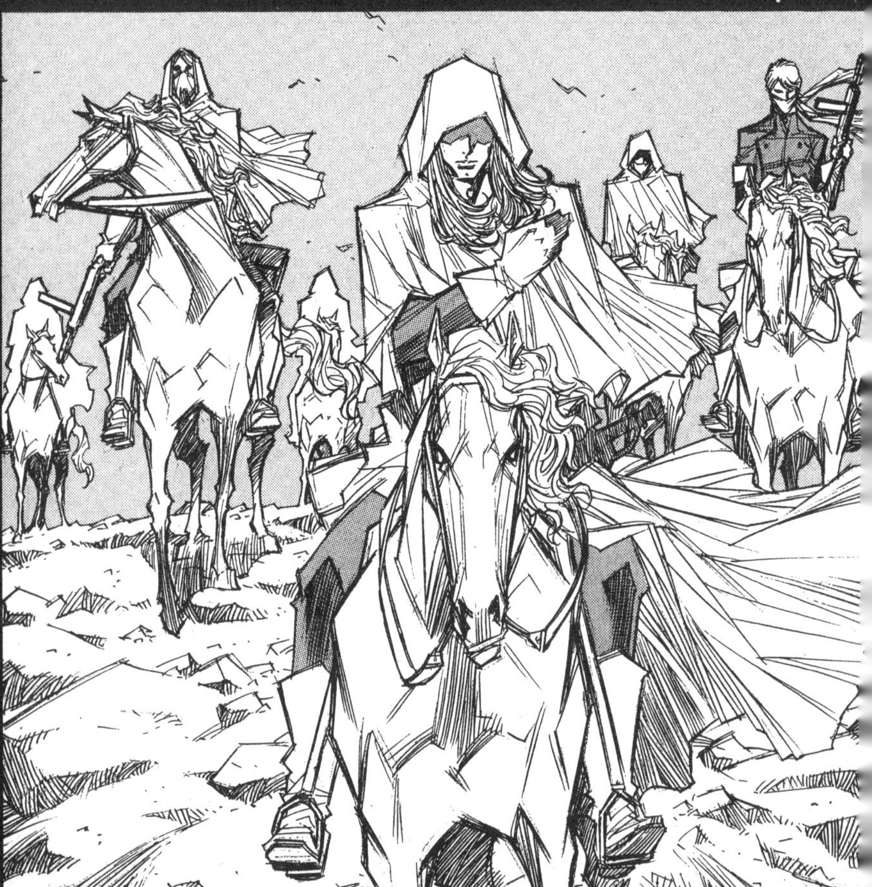

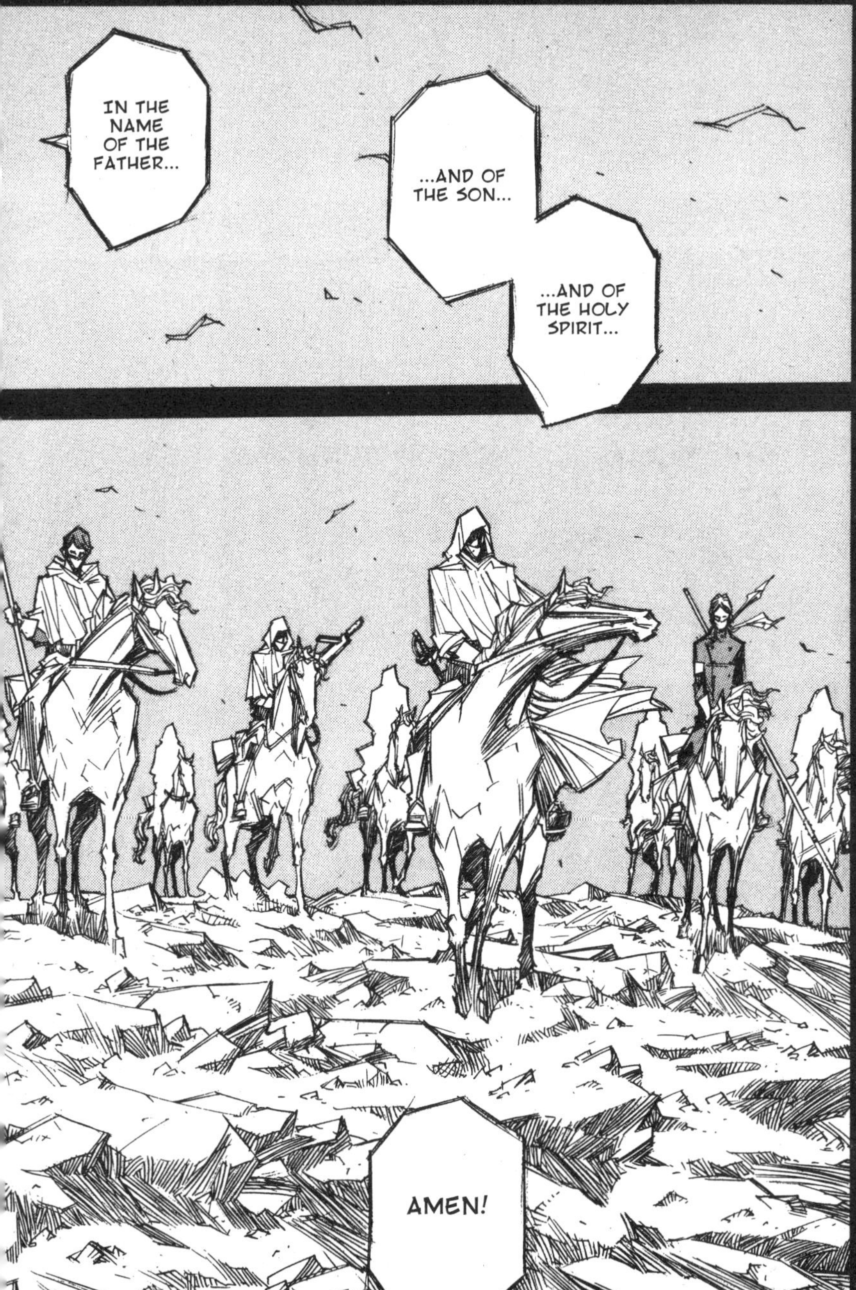
IN THE NAME OF THE FATHER...
...AND OF THE SON...
...AND OF THE HOLY SPIRIT...
AMEN!

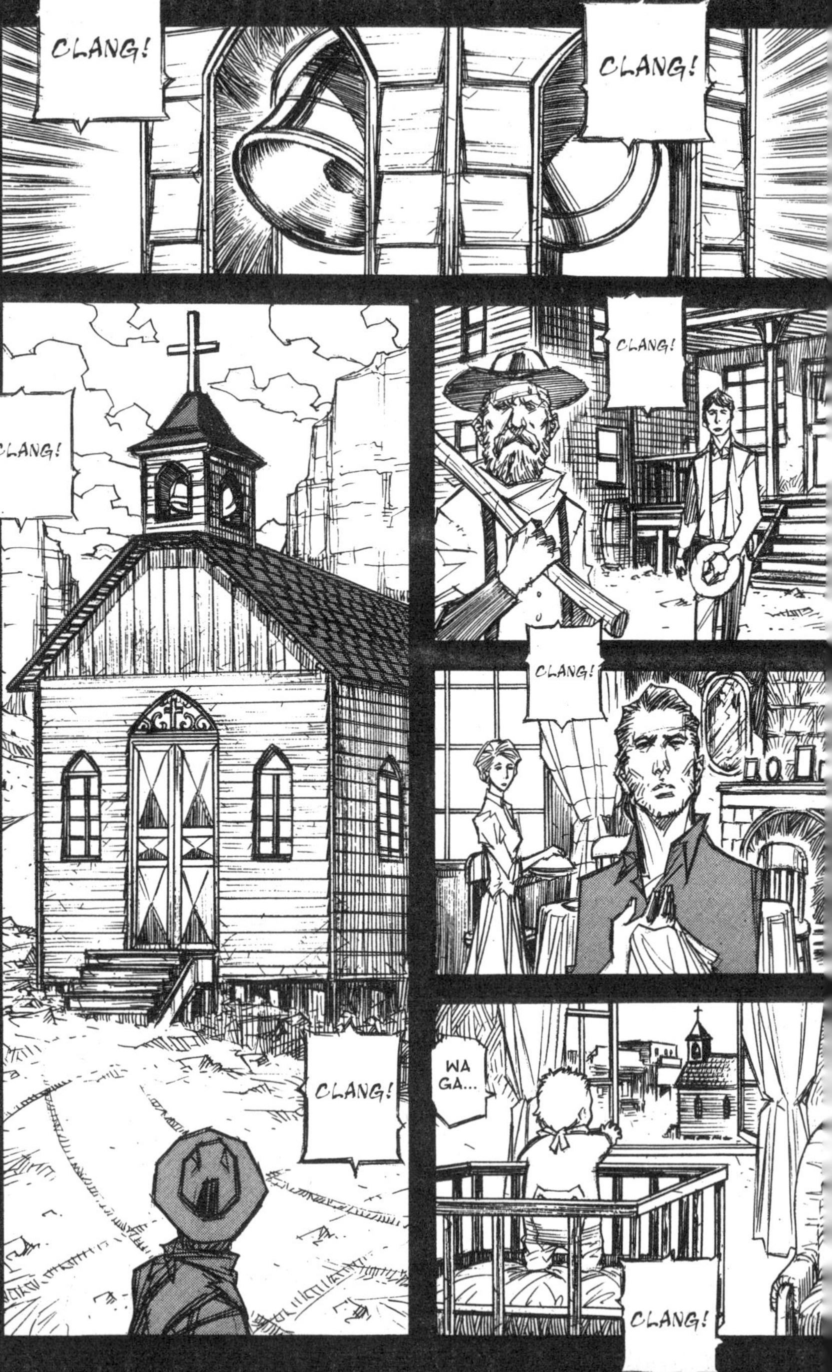
CLANG!
CLANG!
CLANG!
CLANG!
CLANG!
CLANG!
CLANG!
WA GA...
CLANG!

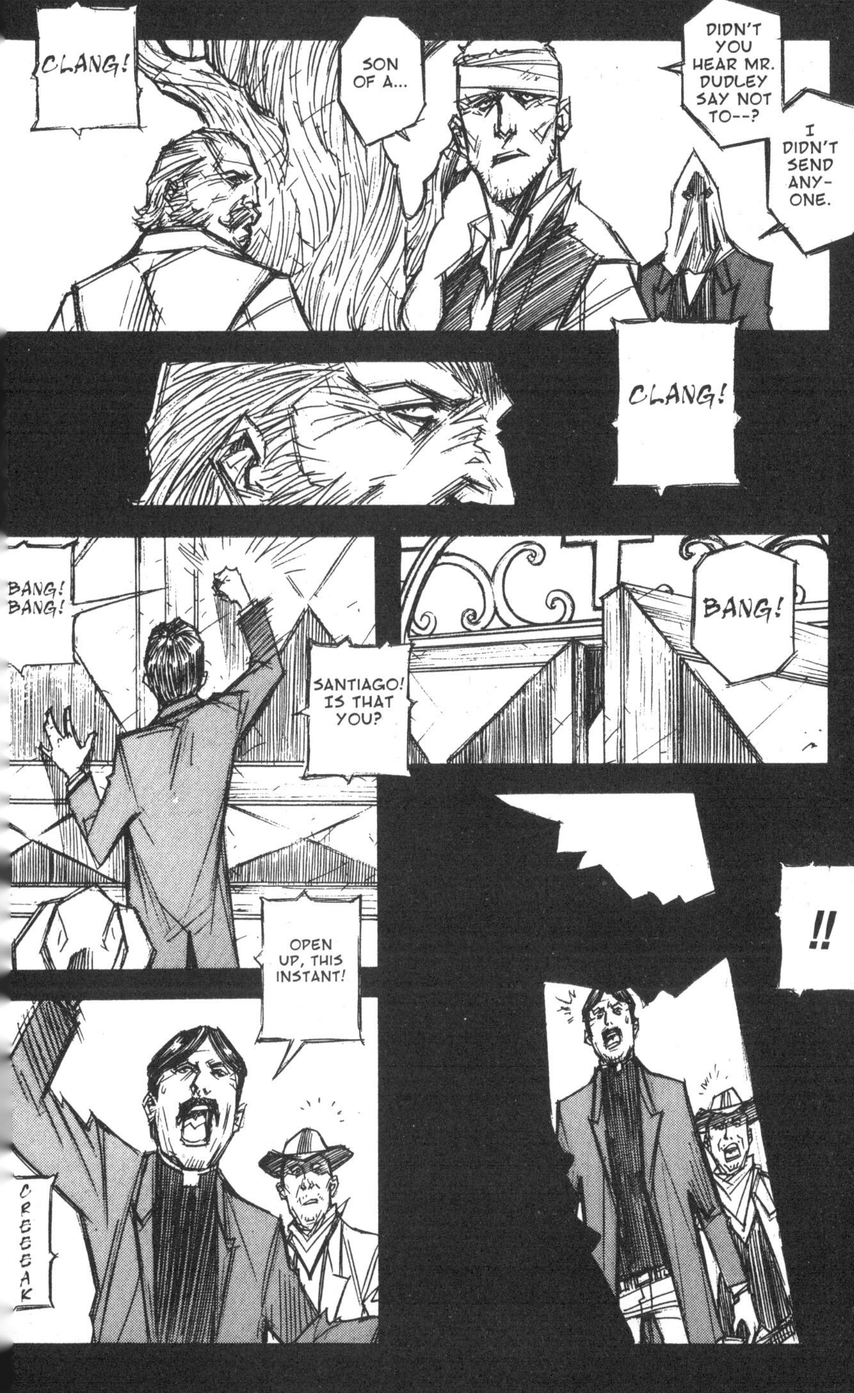
CLANG!
SON OF A...
DIDN'T YOU HEAR MR. DUDLEY SAY NOT TO--?
I DIDN'T SEND ANY-ONE.
CLANG!
BANG! BANG!
SANTIAGO! IS THAT YOU?
BANG!
OPEN UP, THIS INSTANT!
!!
CREEEAK

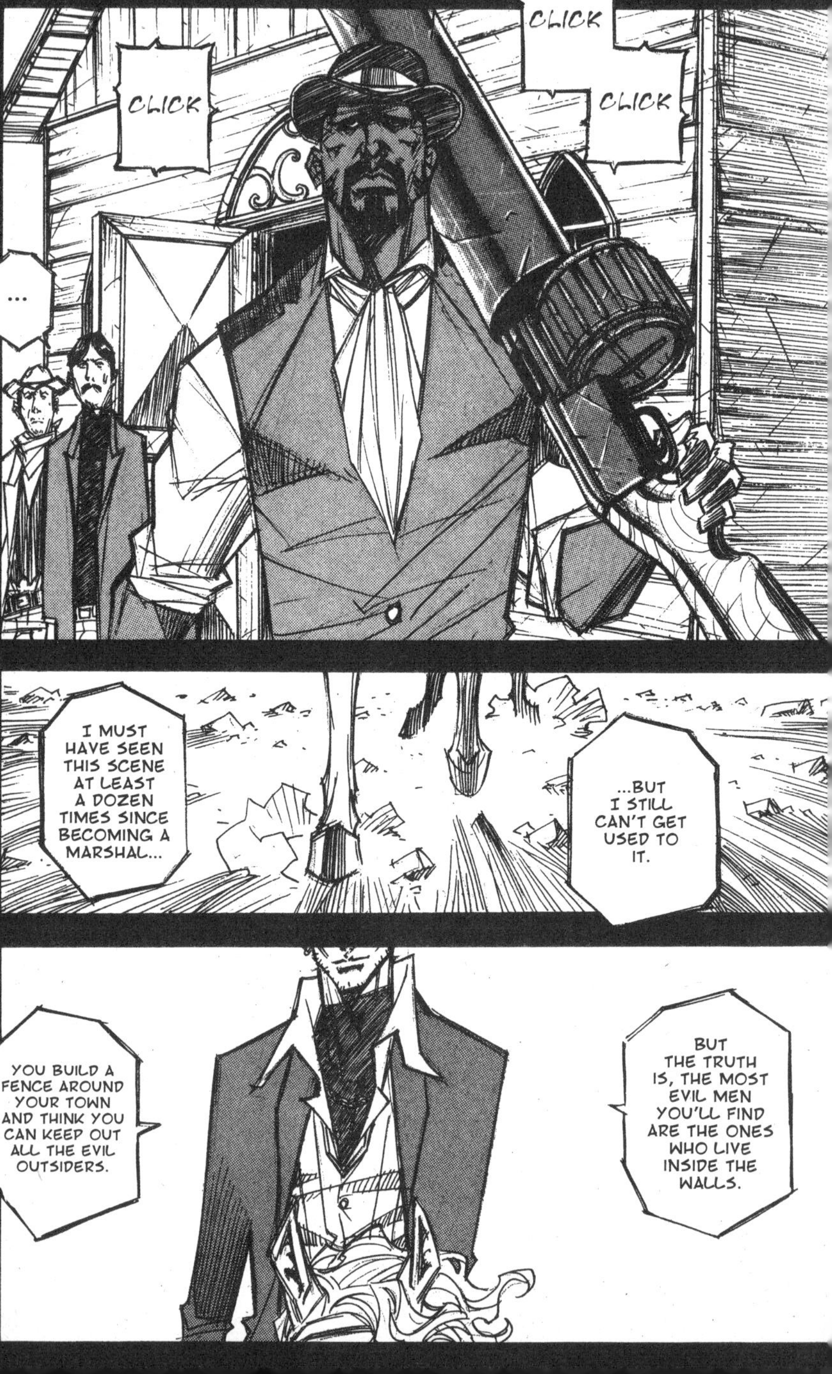
CLICK
CLICK
CLICK
...
I MUST HAVE SEEN THIS SCENE AT LEAST A DOZEN TIMES SINCE BECOMING A MARSHAL...
...BUT I STILL CAN'T GET USED TO IT.
YOU BUILD A FENCE AROUND YOUR TOWN AND THINK YOU CAN KEEP OUT ALL THE EVIL OUTSIDERS.
BUT THE TRUTH IS, THE MOST EVIL MEN YOU'LL FIND ARE THE ONES WHO LIVE INSIDE THE WALLS.

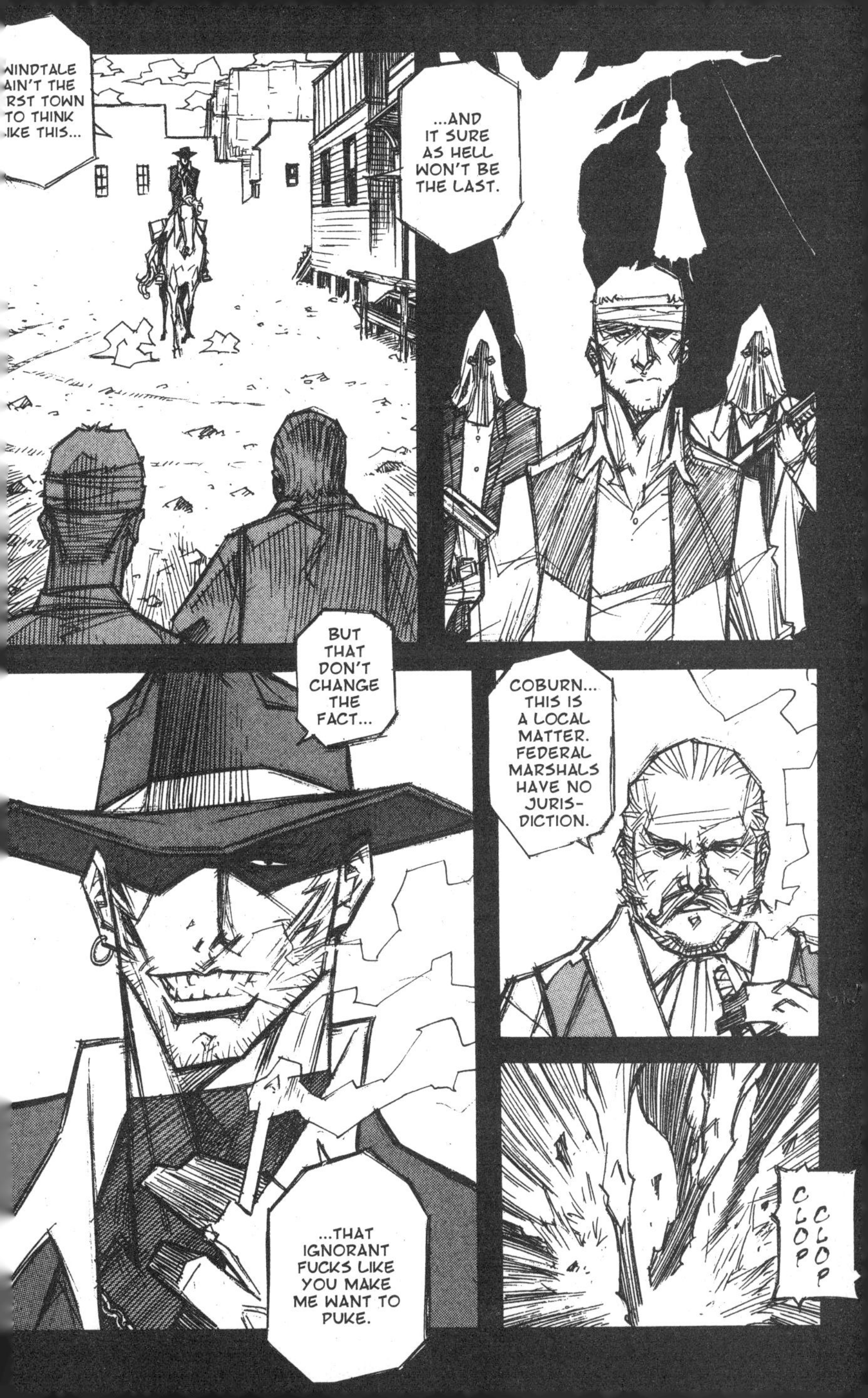
WINDTALE AIN'T THE RST TOWN TO THINK IKE THIS...
...AND IT SURE AS HELL WON'T BE THE LAST.
BUT THAT DON'T CHANGE THE FACT...
...THAT IGNORANT FUCKS LIKE YOU MAKE ME WANT TO PUKE.
COBURN... THIS IS A LOCAL MATTER. FEDERAL MARSHALS HAVE NO JURIS-DICTION.
CLOP CLOP
CLOP CLOP

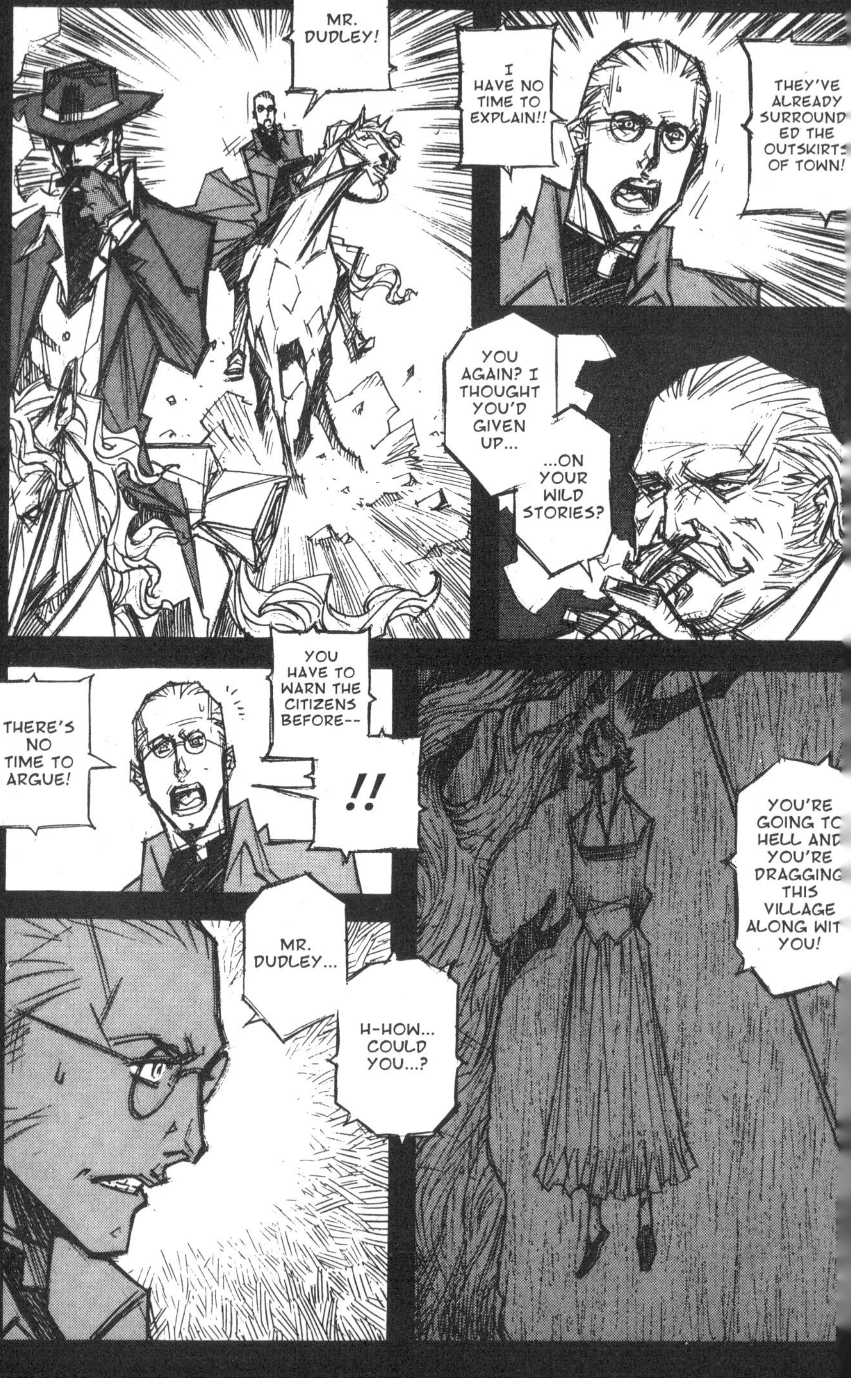
MR. DUDLEY!
I HAVE NO TIME TO EXPLAIN!!
THEY'VE ALREADY SURROUNDED THE OUTSKIRTS OF TOWN!
YOU AGAIN? I THOUGHT YOU'D GIVEN UP...
...ON YOUR WILD STORIES?
THERE'S NO TIME TO ARGUE!
YOU HAVE TO WARN THE CITIZENS BEFORE--
!!
MR. DUDLEY...
H-HOW... COULD YOU...?
YOU'RE GOING TO HELL AND YOU'RE DRAGGING THIS VILLAGE ALONG WITH YOU!

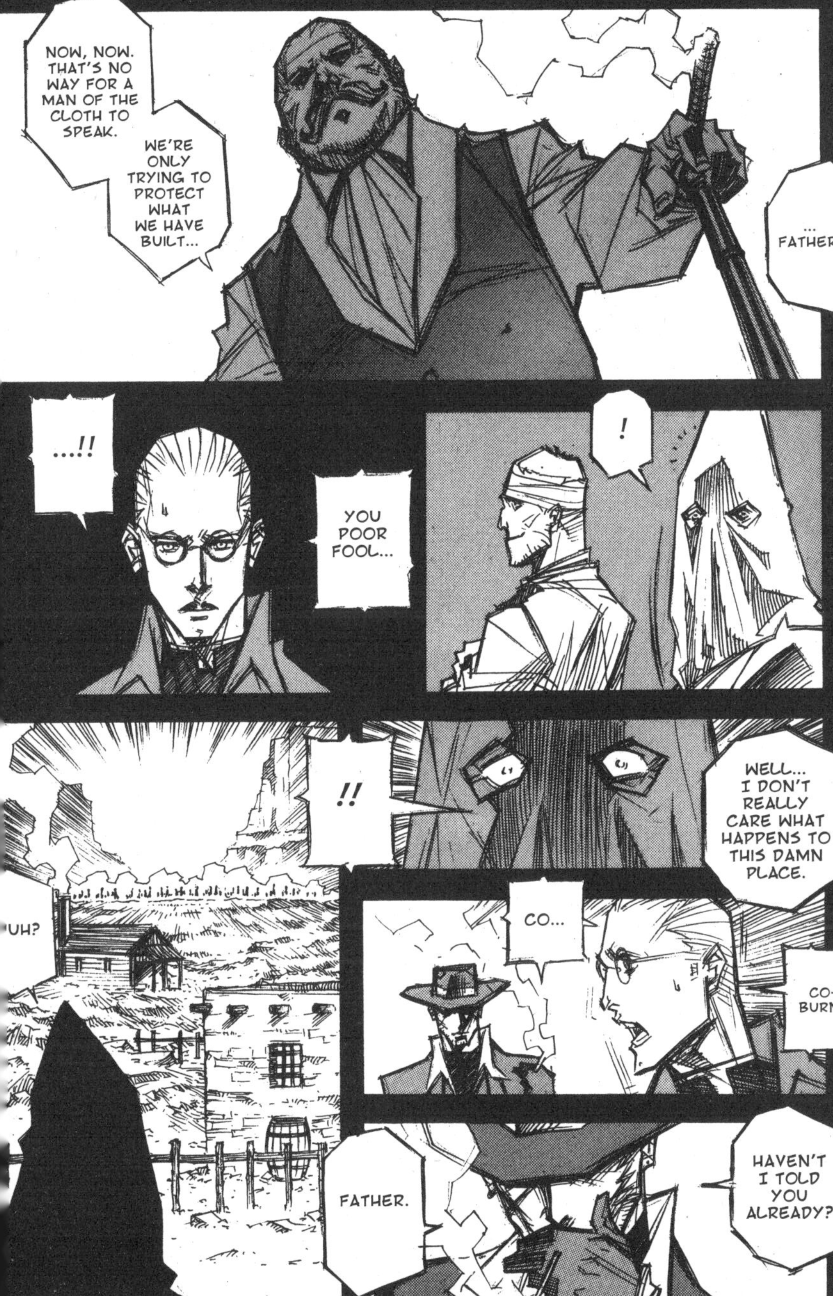
NOW, NOW. THAT'S NO WAY FOR A MAN OF THE CLOTH TO SPEAK.
WE'RE ONLY TRYING TO PROTECT WHAT WE HAVE BUILT...
... FATHER.
...!!
YOU POOR FOOL...
!
UH?
!!
WELL... I DON'T REALLY CARE WHAT HAPPENS TO THIS DAMN PLACE.
CO...
CO-BURN!!
FATHER.
HAVEN'T I TOLD YOU ALREADY?

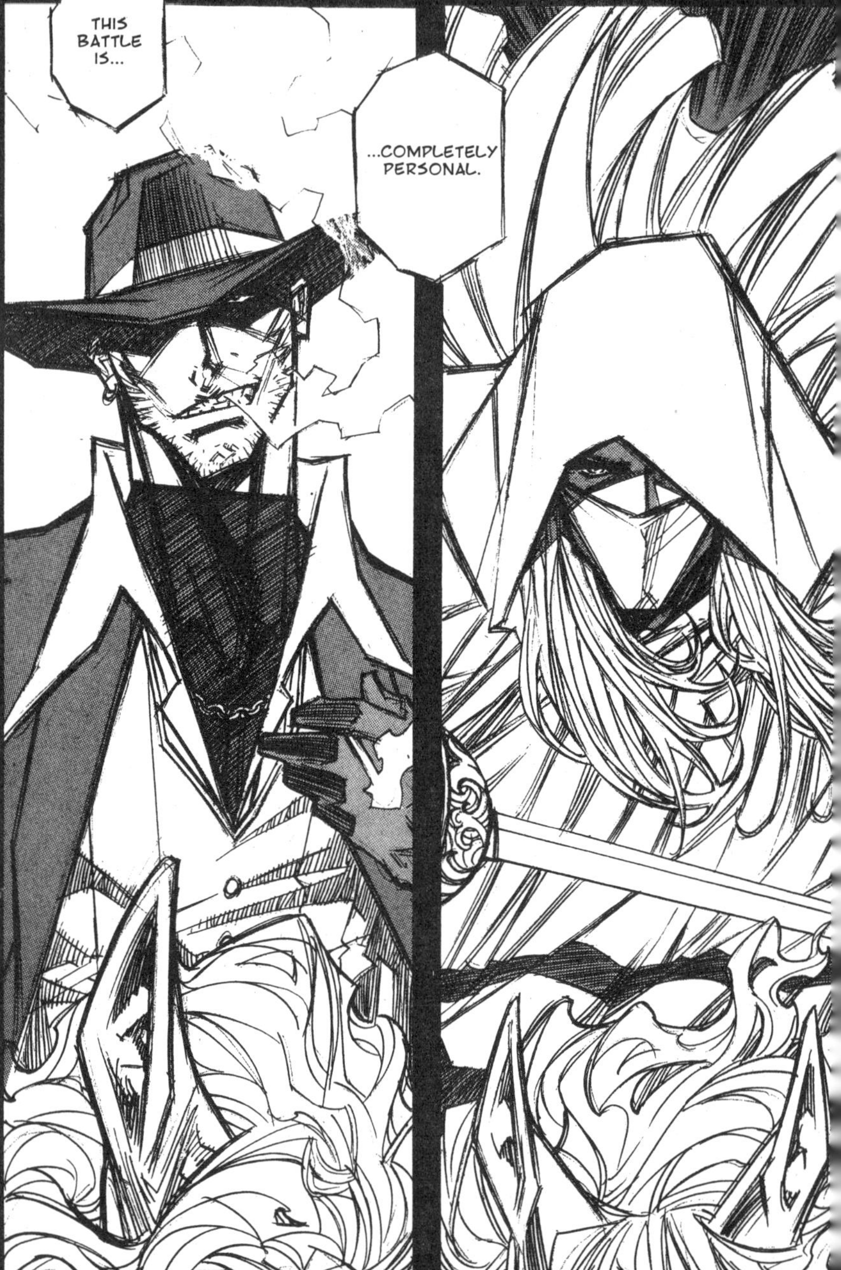
THIS BATTLE IS...
...COMPLETELY PERSONAL.

TO BE CONTINUED IN PRIEST 16!!

Side Story

CRAZY MESSAGE

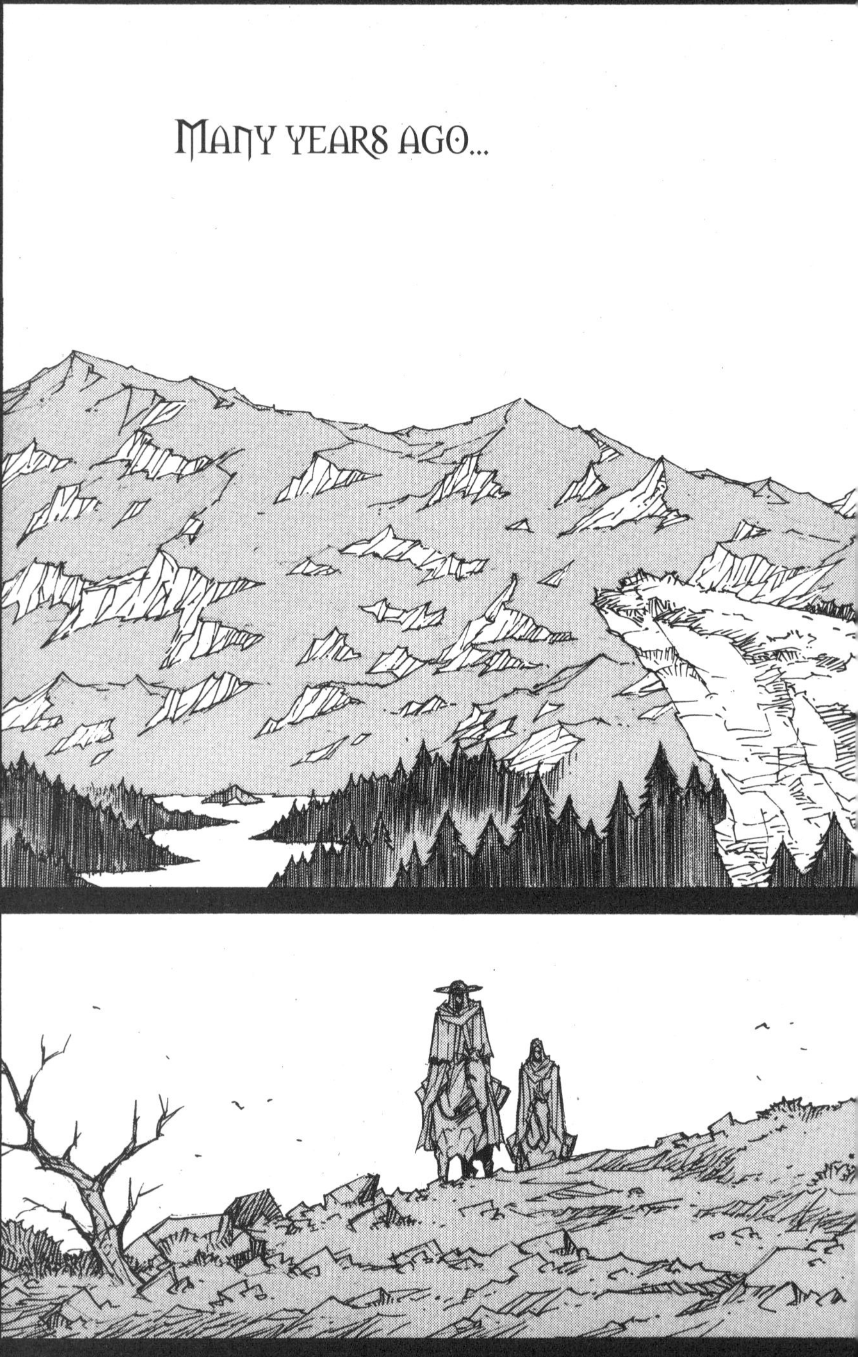
MANY YEARS AGO...

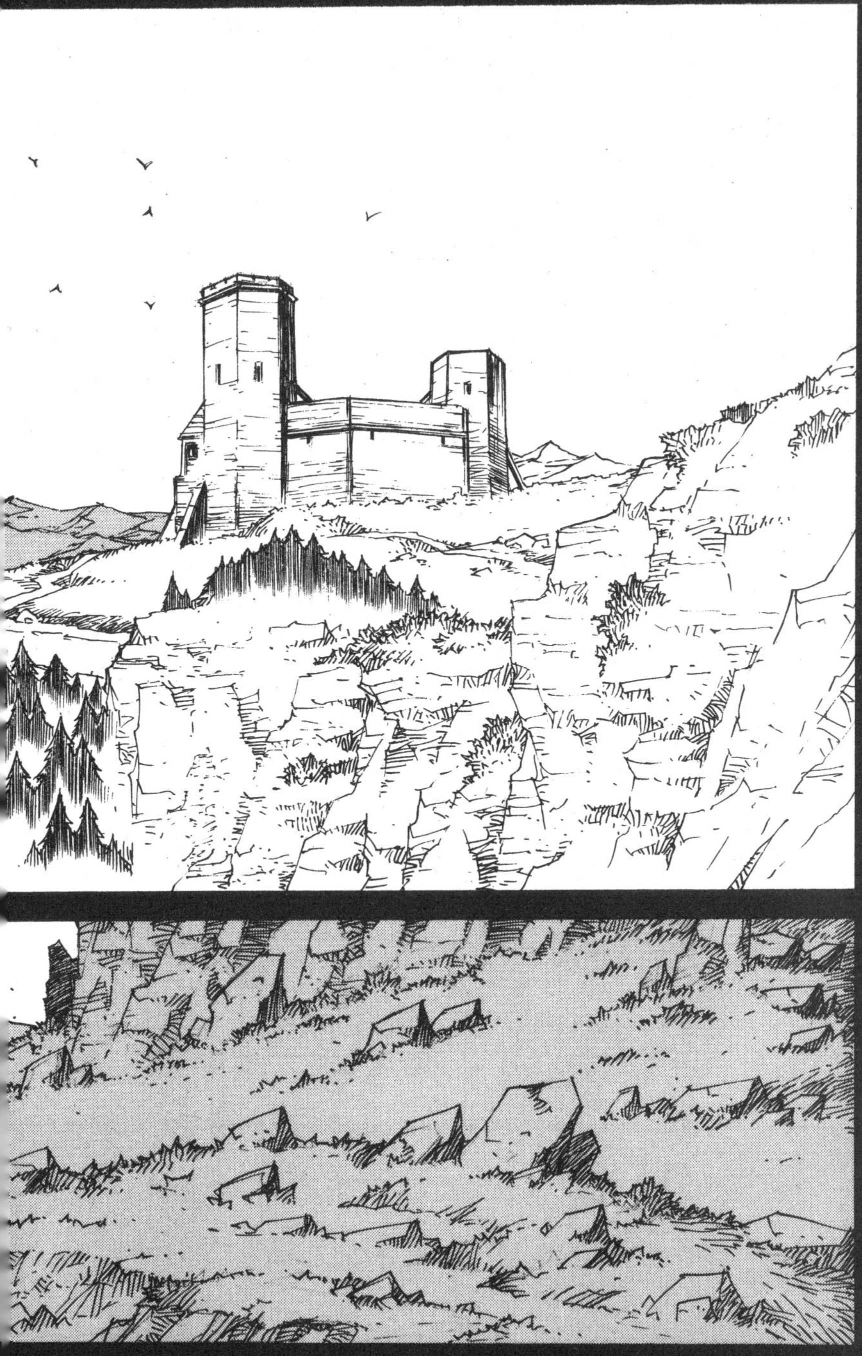

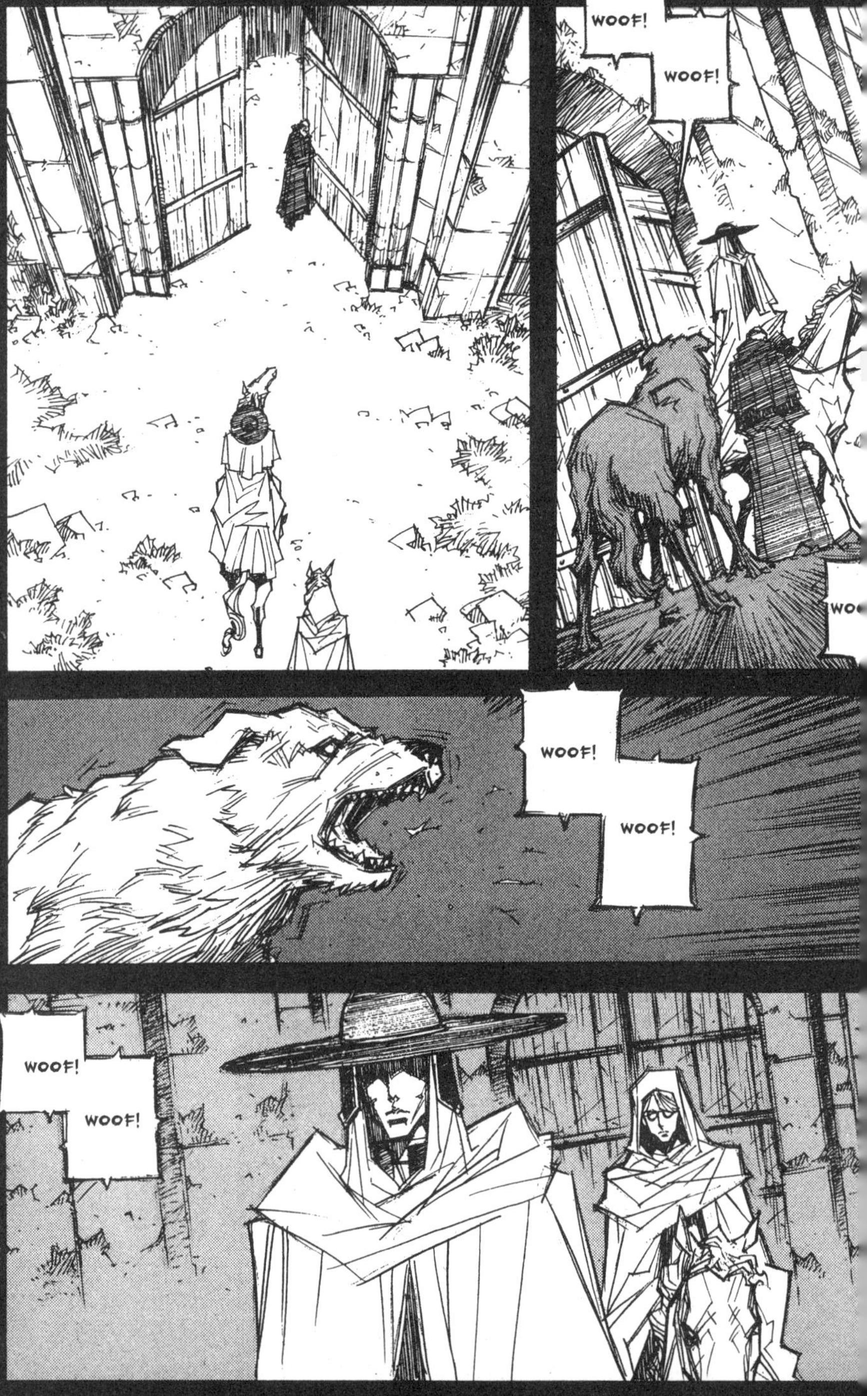
WOOF!
WOOF!
WOOF!
WOOF!
WOOF!
WOOF!

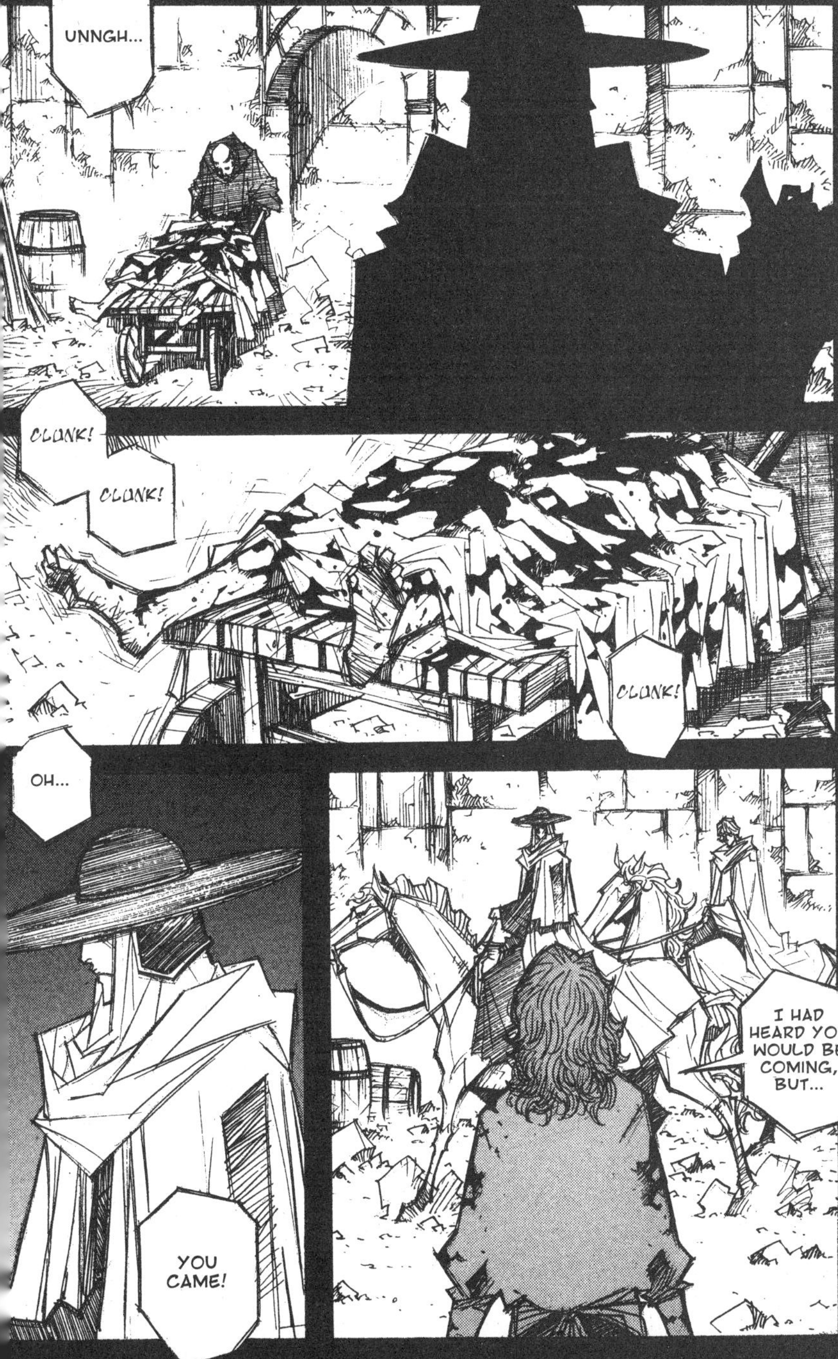
UNNGH...
CLUNK!
CLUNK!
CLUNK!
OH...
YOU CAME!
I HAD HEARD YOU WOULD BE COMING, BUT...

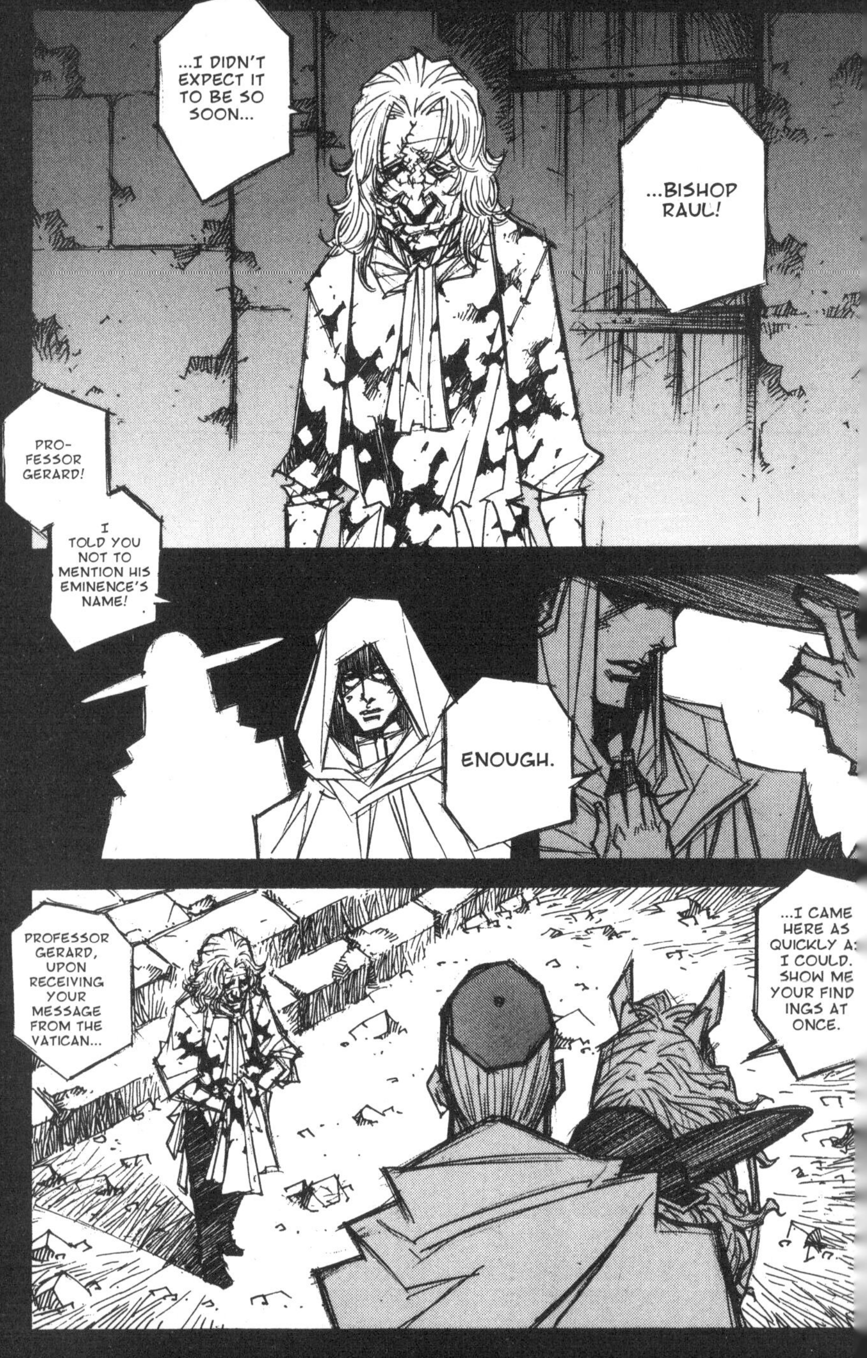
...I DIDN'T EXPECT IT TO BE SO SOON...
...BISHOP RAUL!
PRO-FESSOR GERARD!
I TOLD YOU NOT TO MENTION HIS EMINENCE'S NAME!
ENOUGH.
PROFESSOR GERARD, UPON RECEIVING YOUR MESSAGE FROM THE VATICAN...
...I CAME HERE AS QUICKLY A: I COULD. SHOW ME YOUR FIND INGS AT ONCE.

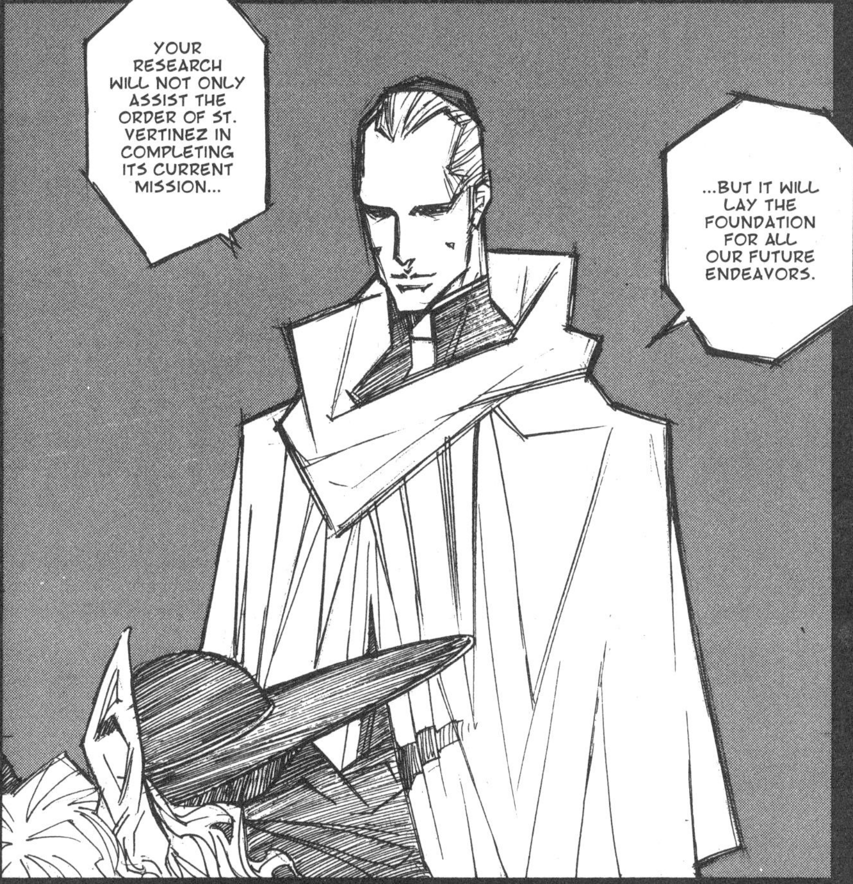
YOUR RESEARCH WILL NOT ONLY ASSIST THE ORDER OF ST. VERTINEZ IN COMPLETING ITS CURRENT MISSION...
...BUT IT WILL LAY THE FOUNDATION FOR ALL OUR FUTURE ENDEAVORS.
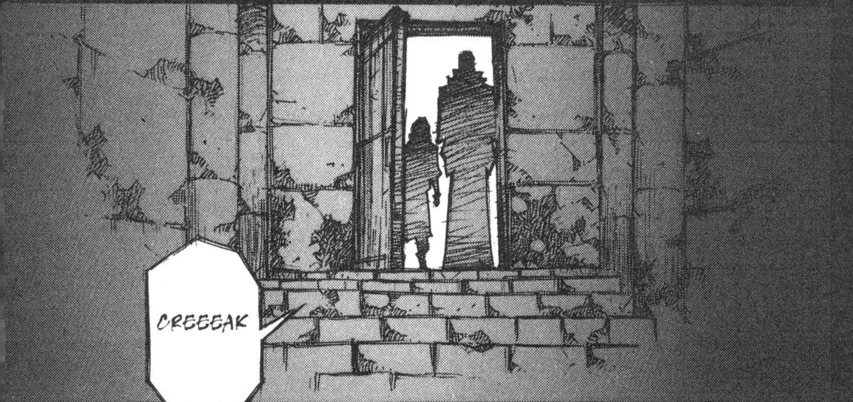
CREEEAK

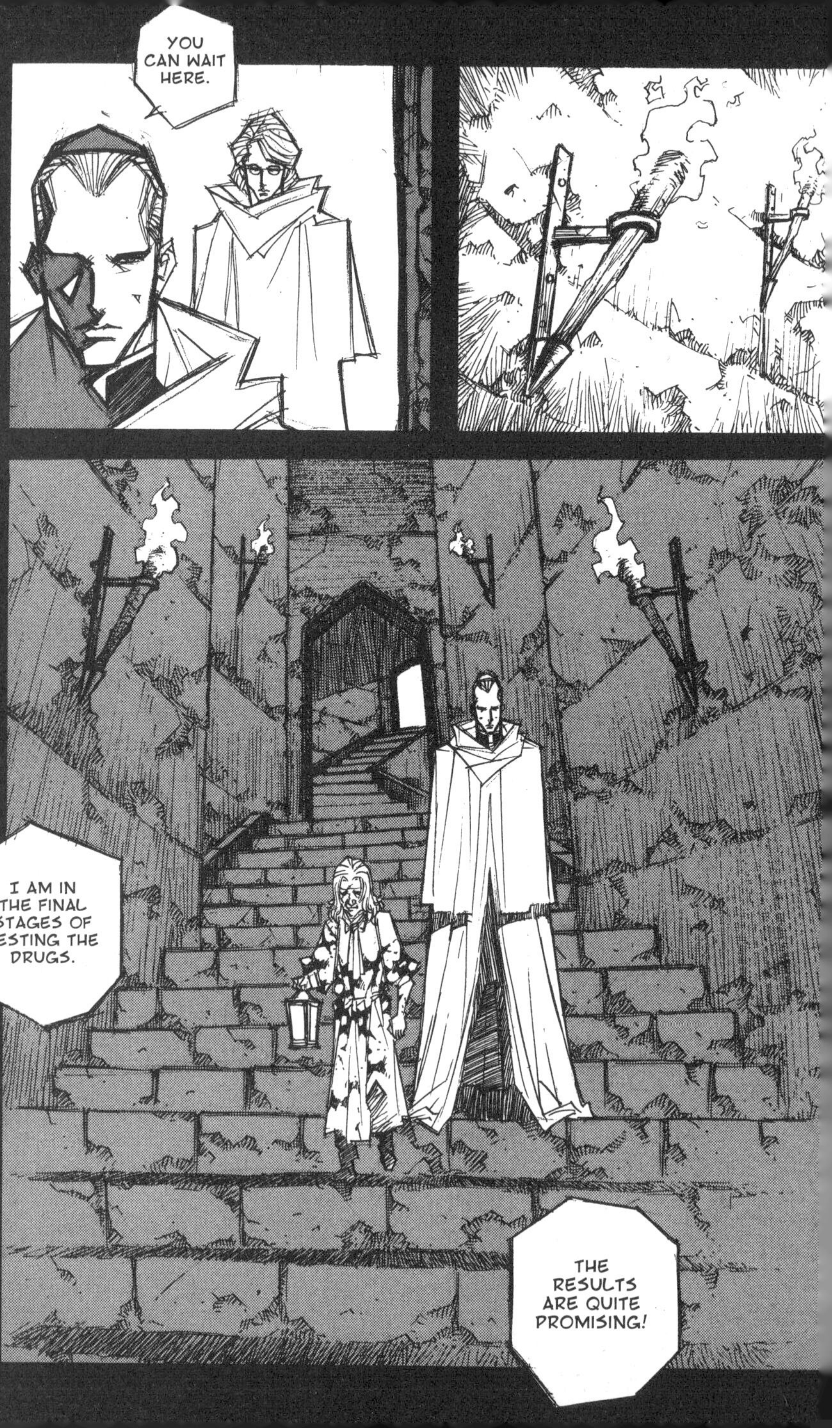
YOU CAN WAIT HERE.
I AM IN THE FINAL STAGES OF TESTING THE DRUGS.
THE RESULTS ARE QUITE PROMISING!

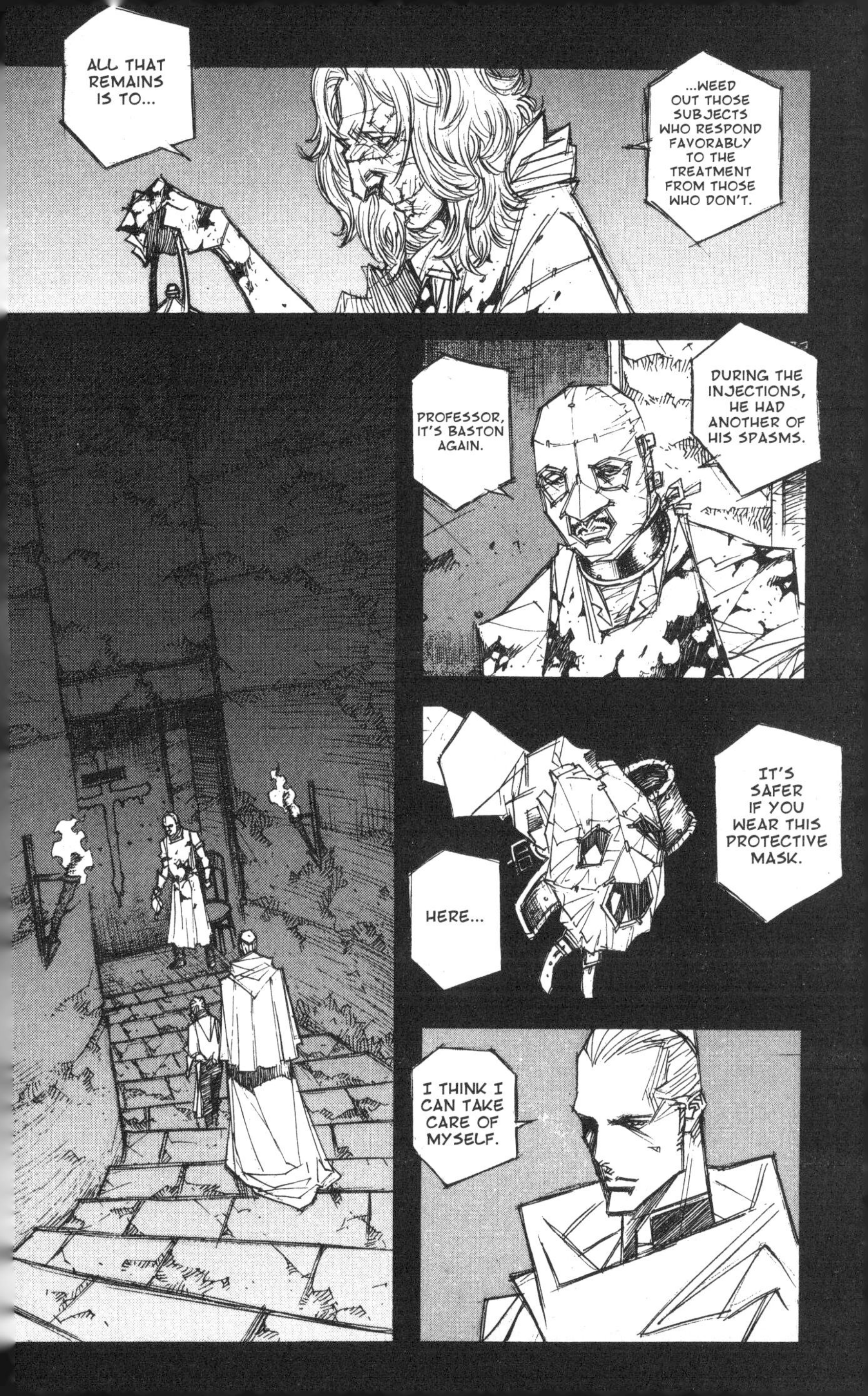
ALL THAT REMAINS IS TO...
...WEED OUT THOSE SUBJECTS WHO RESPOND FAVORABLY TO THE TREATMENT FROM THOSE WHO DON'T.
PROFESSOR, IT'S BASTON AGAIN.
DURING THE INJECTIONS, HE HAD ANOTHER OF HIS SPASMS.
HERE...
IT'S SAFER IF YOU WEAR THIS PROTECTIVE MASK.
I THINK I CAN TAKE CARE OF MYSELF.

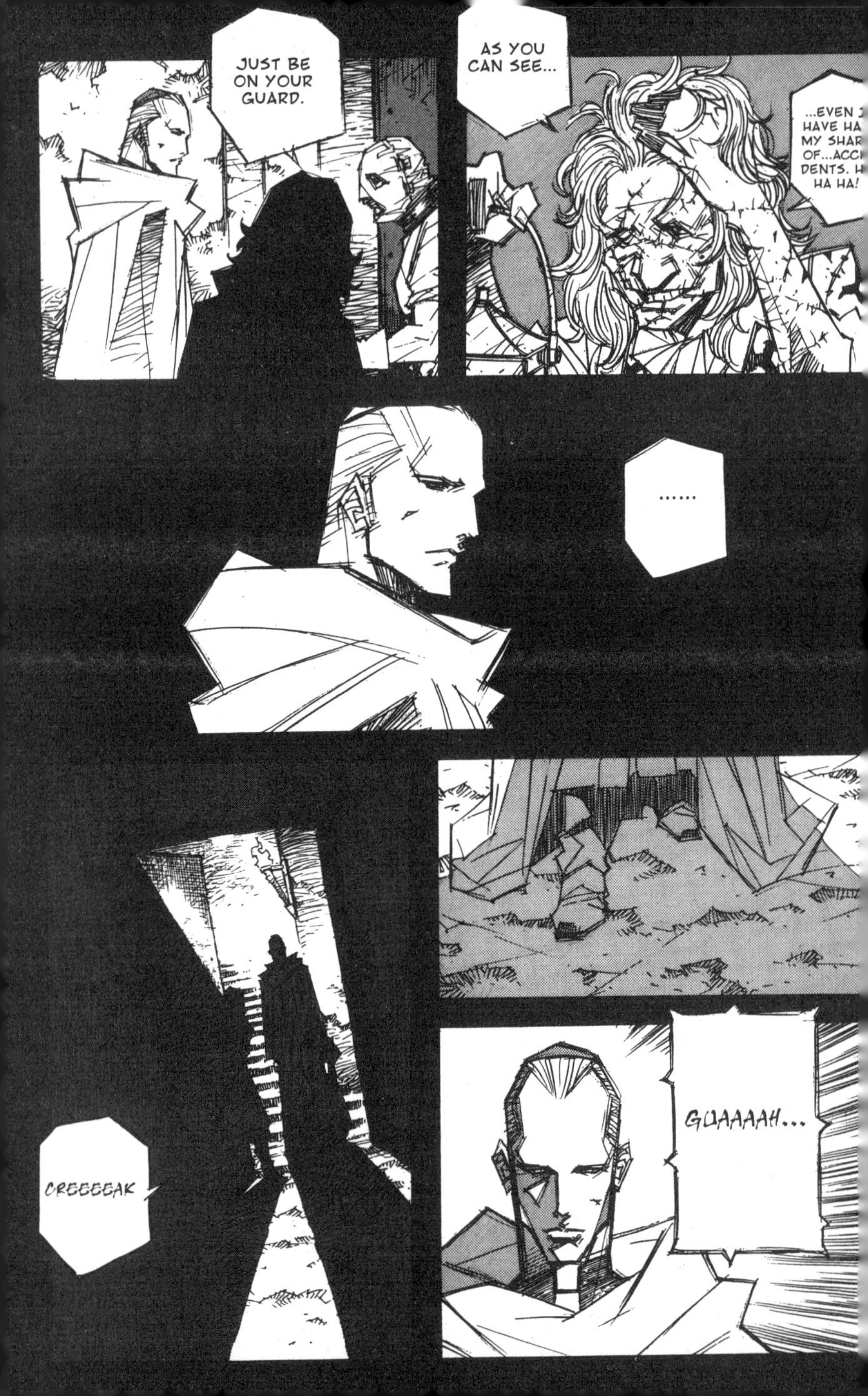
JUST BE ON YOUR GUARD.
AS YOU CAN SEE...
...EVEN I HAVE HA MY SHAR OF...ACCI DENTS. H HA HA!
......
CREEEEAK
GUAAAAH...

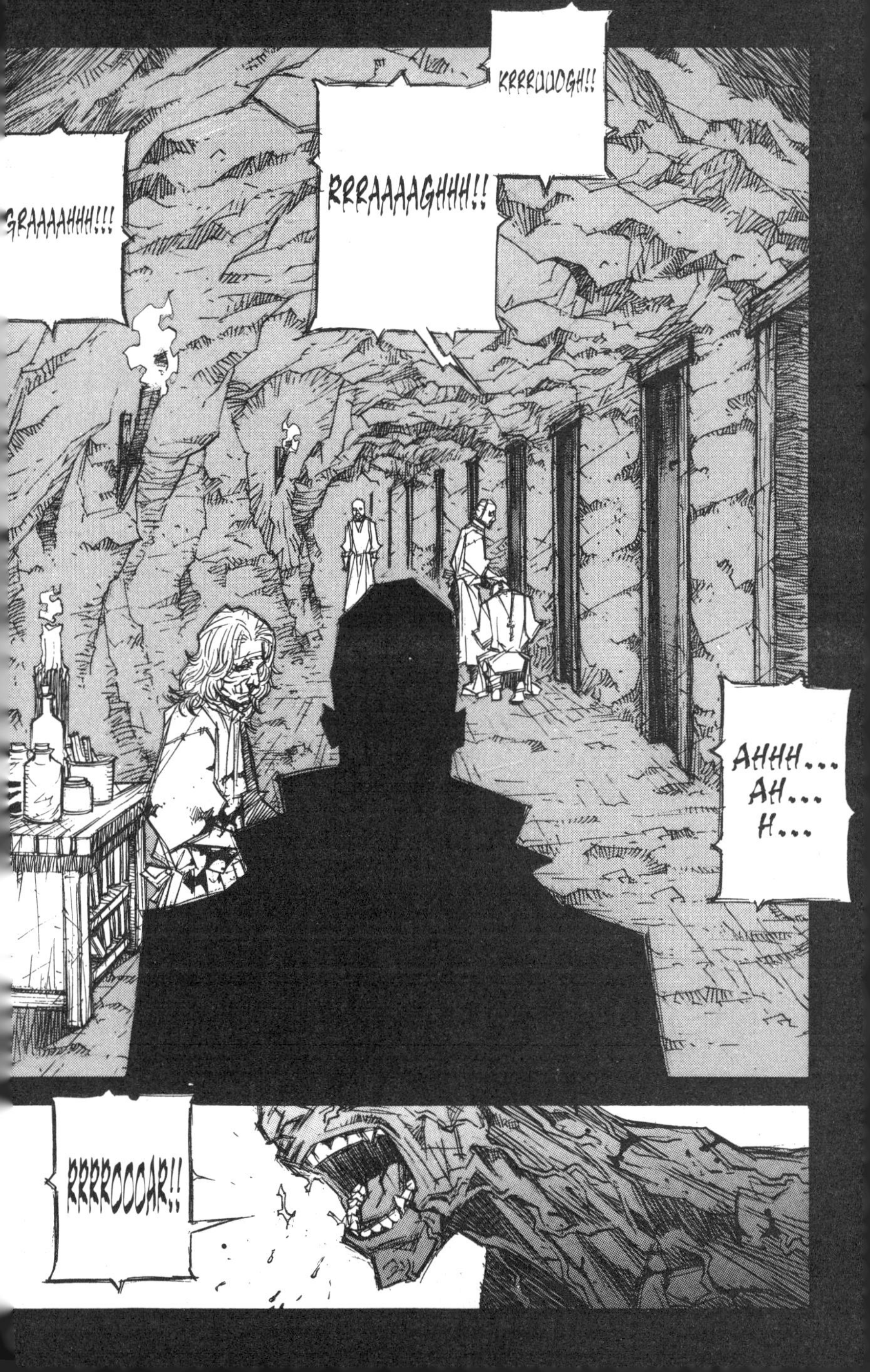
GRAAAAHHH!!!
RRRAAAAGHHH!!
KRRRUUUOGH!!
AHHH... AH... H...
RRRROOOAR!!

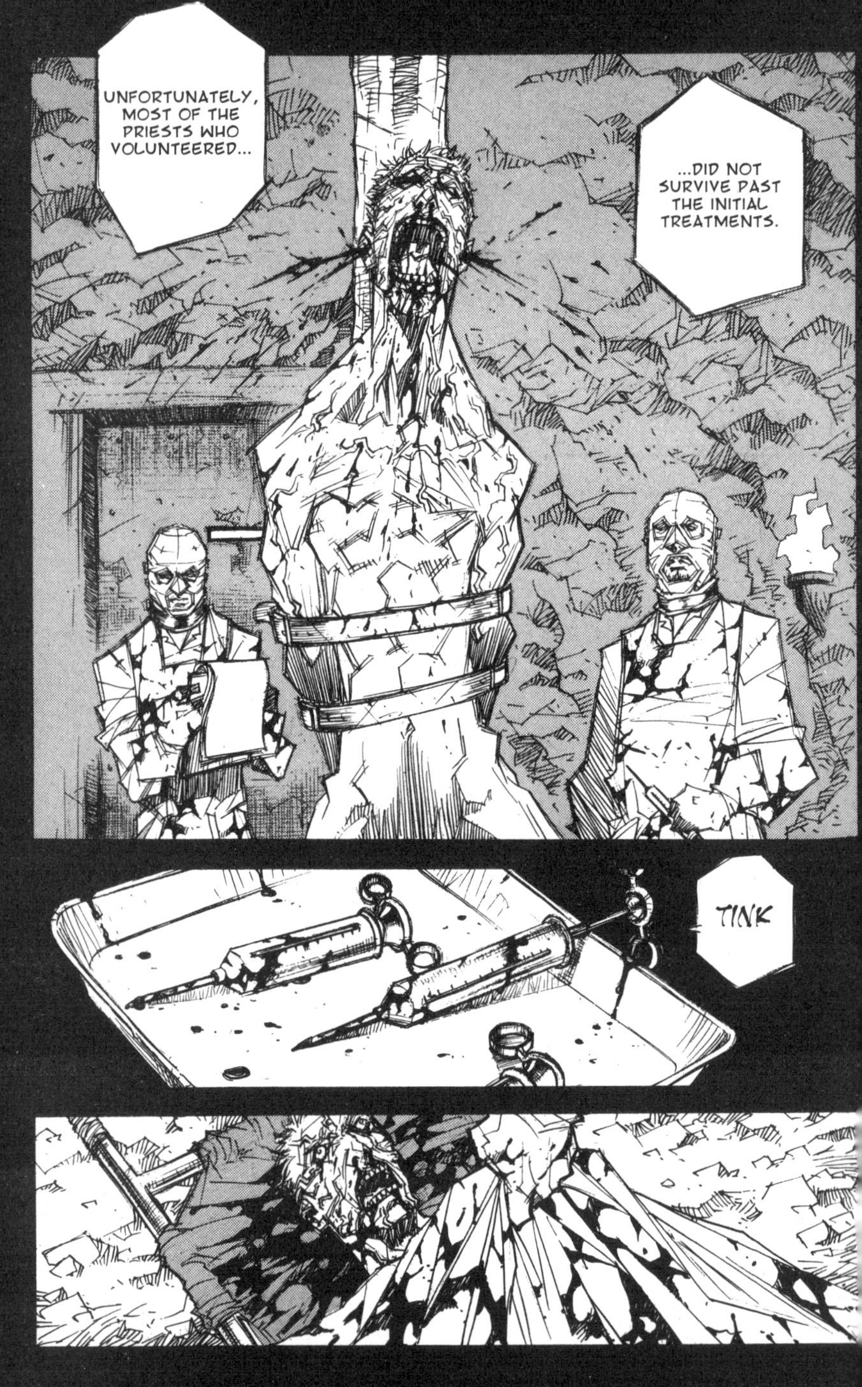
UNFORTUNATELY, MOST OF THE PRIESTS WHO VOLUNTEERED...
...DID NOT SURVIVE PAST THE INITIAL TREATMENTS.
TINK

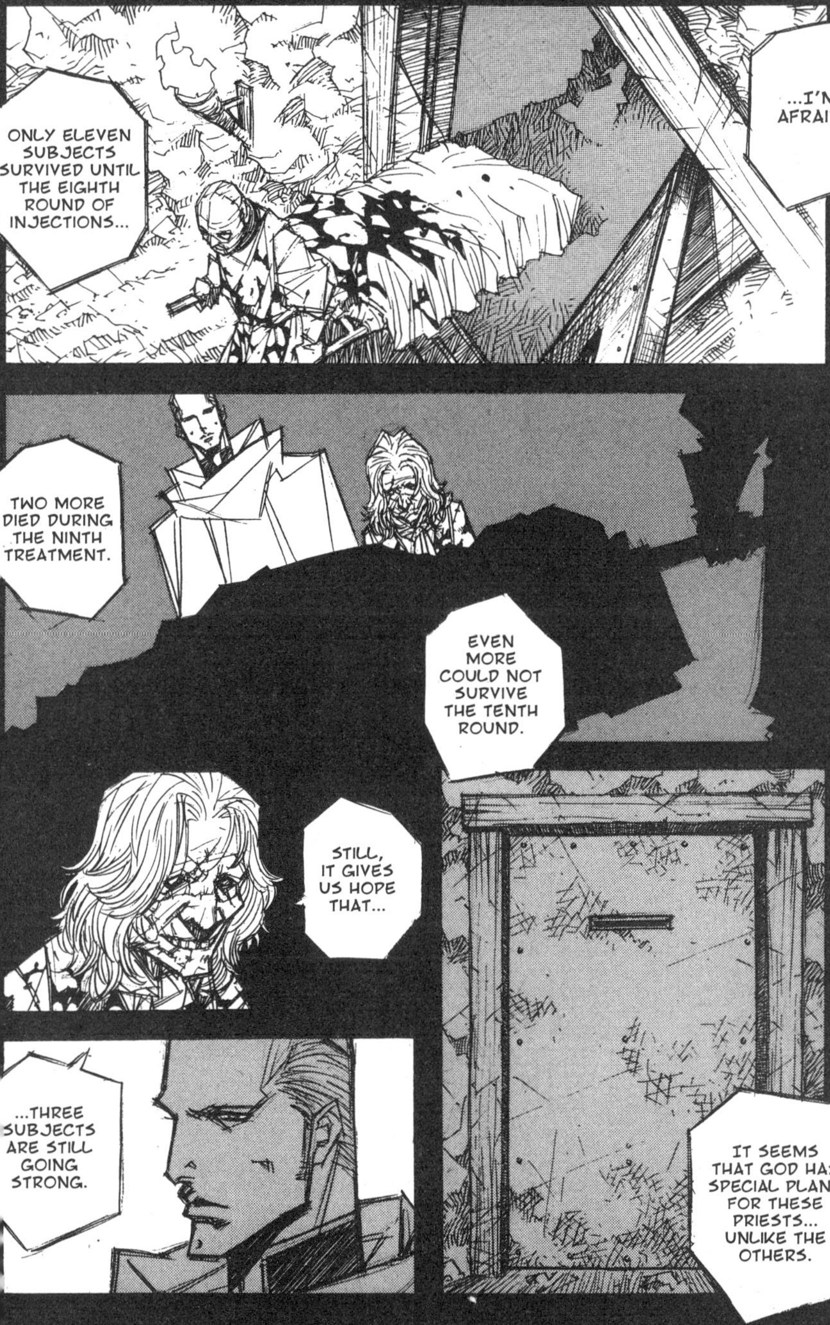
ONLY ELEVEN SUBJECTS SURVIVED UNTIL THE EIGHTH ROUND OF INJECTIONS...
...I'M AFRAID.
TWO MORE DIED DURING THE NINTH TREATMENT.
EVEN MORE COULD NOT SURVIVE THE TENTH ROUND.
STILL, IT GIVES US HOPE THAT...
...THREE SUBJECTS ARE STILL GOING STRONG.
IT SEEMS THAT GOD HAS SPECIAL PLANS FOR THESE PRIESTS... UNLIKE THE OTHERS.

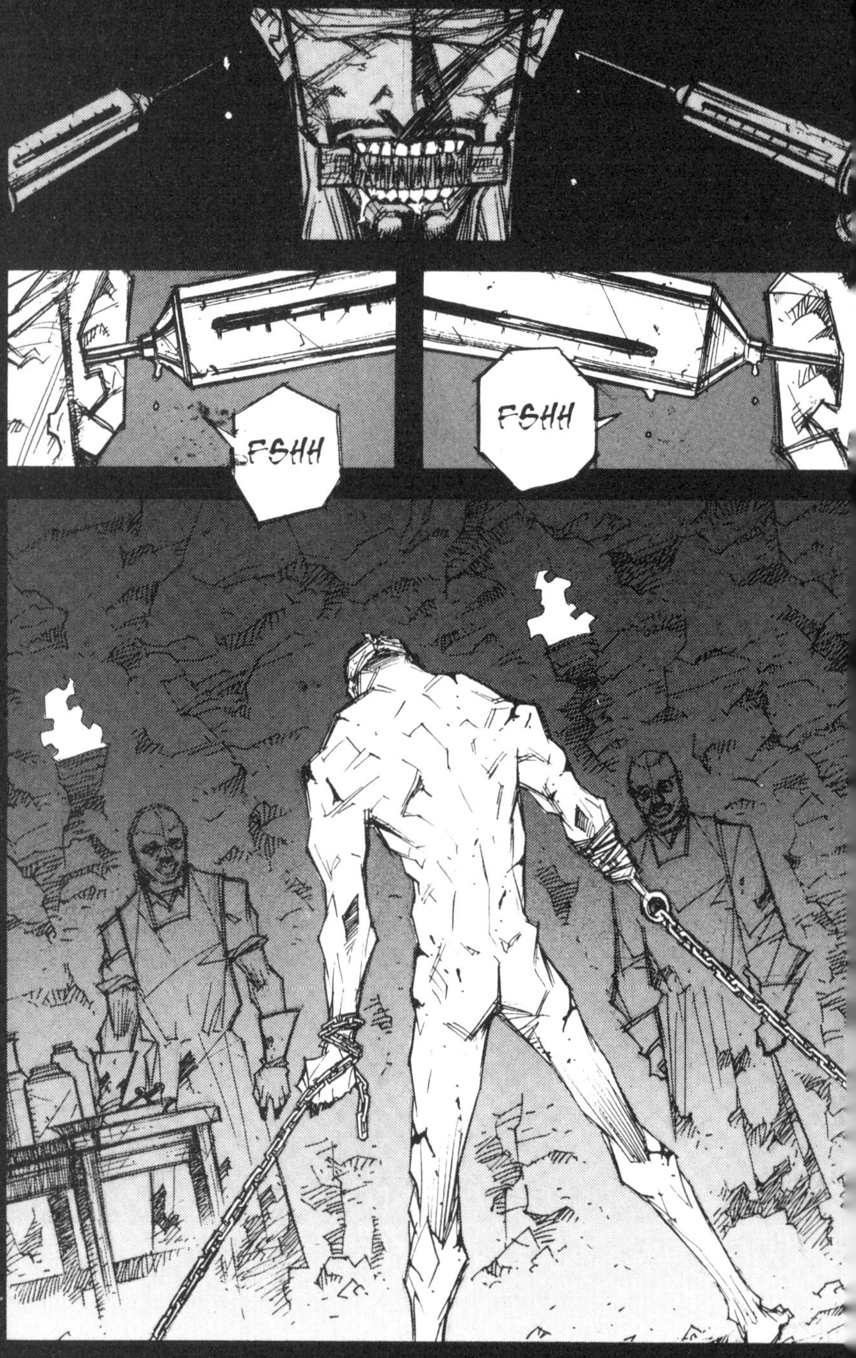
FSHH
FSHH

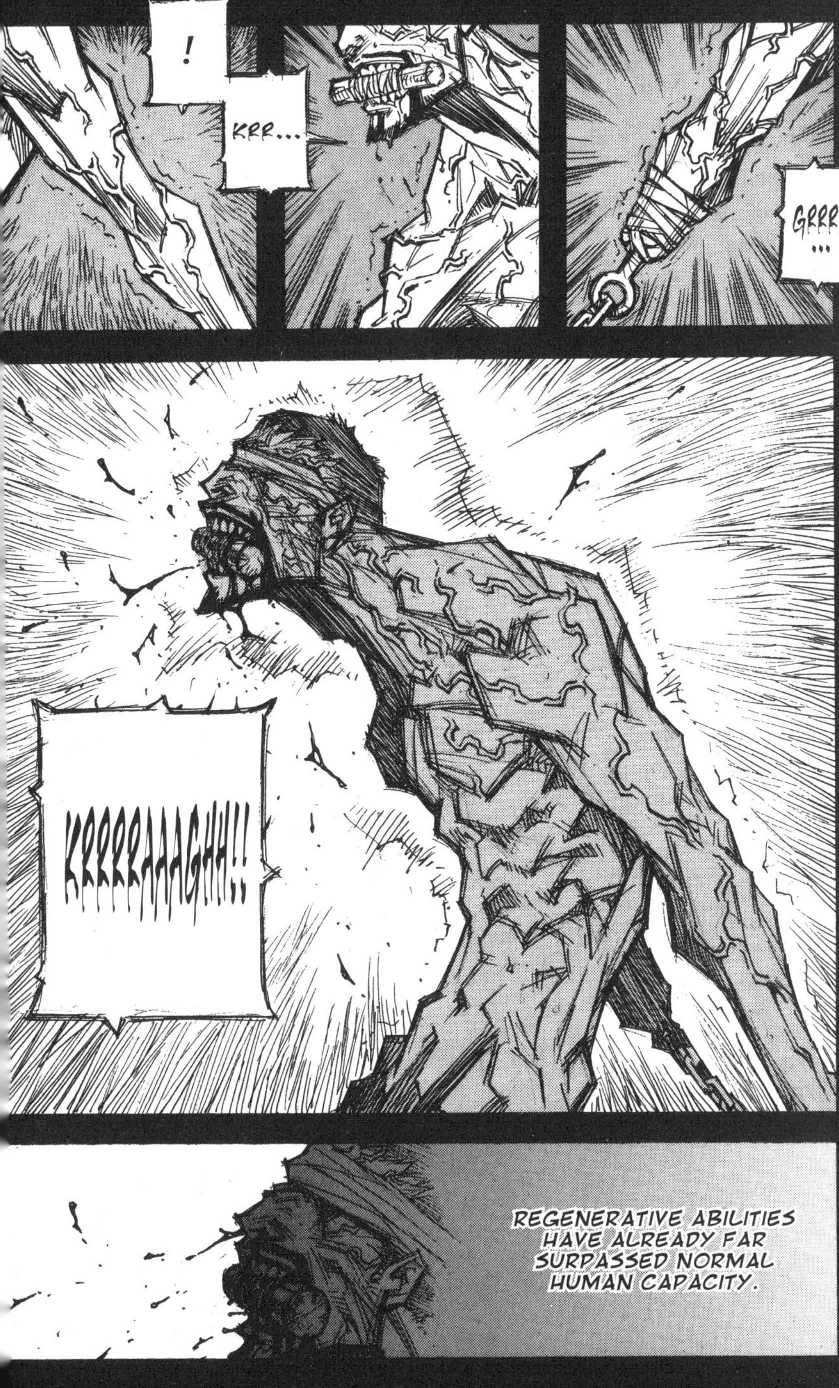
!
KRR...
GRRRR...
KRRRRAAAGHH!!
REGENERATIVE ABILITIES HAVE ALREADY FAR SURPASSED NORMAL HUMAN CAPACITY.

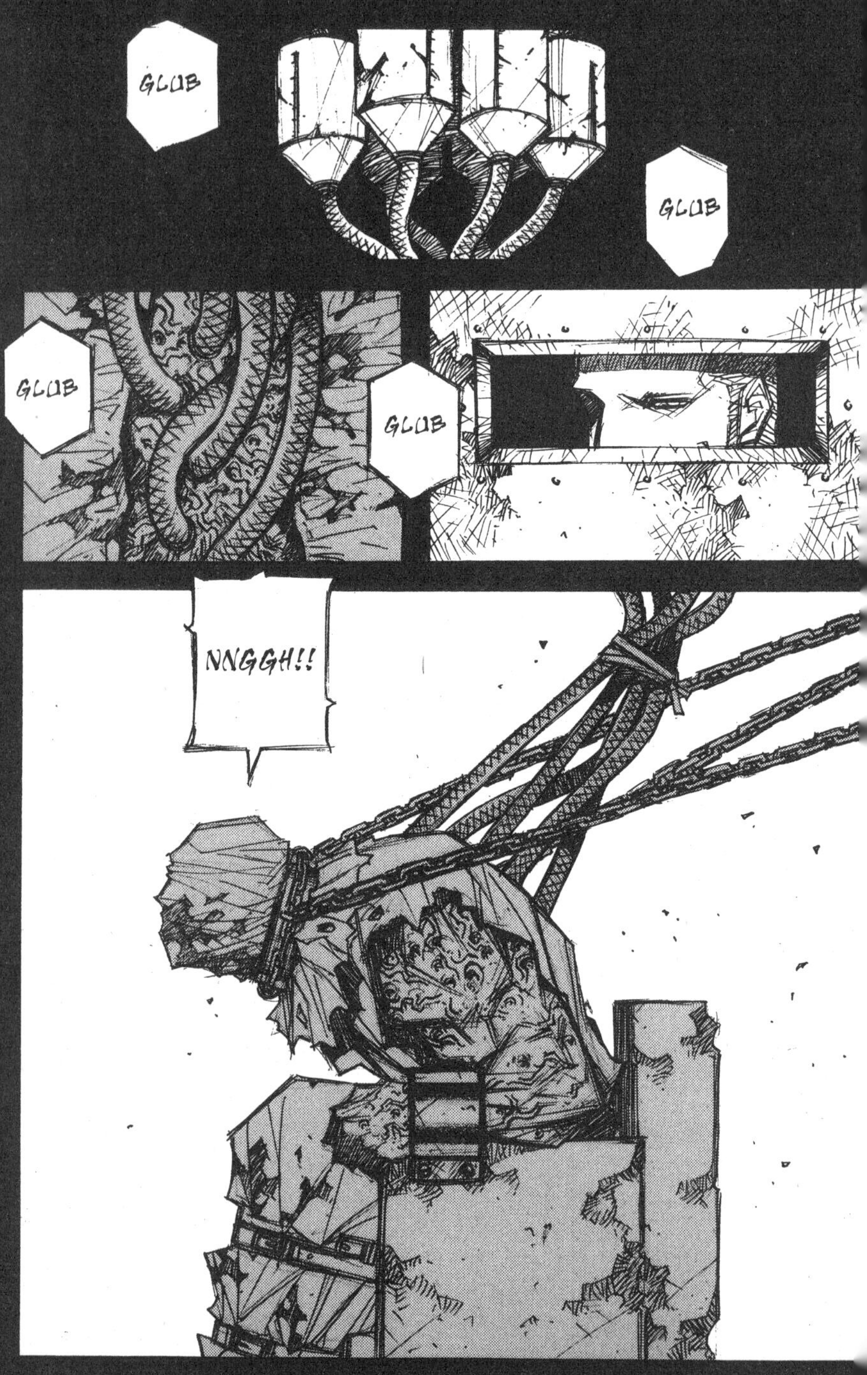
GLUB
GLUB
GLUB
GLUB
NNGGH!!

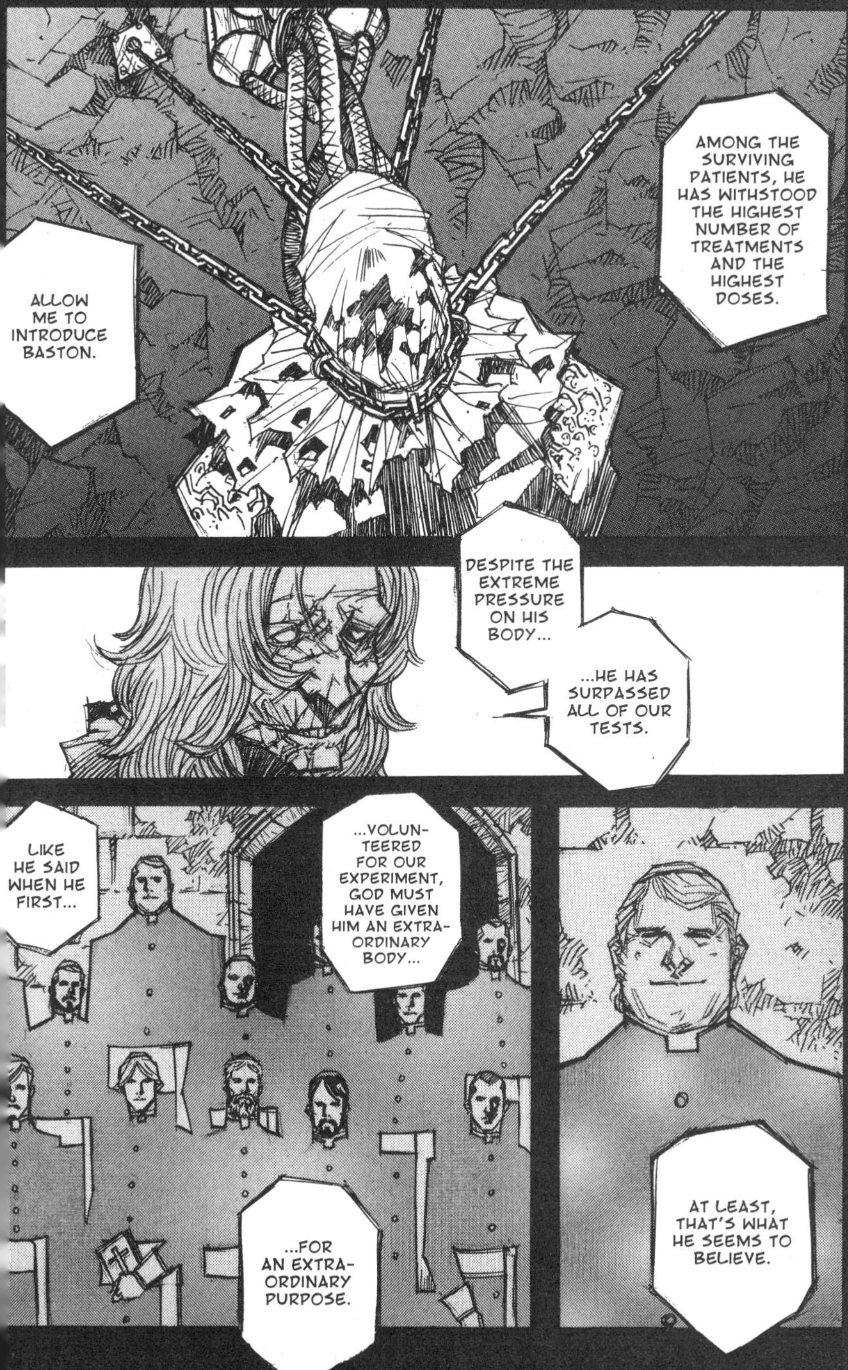
ALLOW ME TO INTRODUCE BASTON.
AMONG THE SURVIVING PATIENTS, HE HAS WITHSTOOD THE HIGHEST NUMBER OF TREATMENTS AND THE HIGHEST DOSES.
DESPITE THE EXTREME PRESSURE ON HIS BODY...
...HE HAS SURPASSED ALL OF OUR TESTS.
LIKE HE SAID WHEN HE FIRST...
...VOLUN-TEERED FOR OUR EXPERIMENT, GOD MUST HAVE GIVEN HIM AN EXTRA-ORDINARY BODY...
...FOR AN EXTRA-ORDINARY PURPOSE.
AT LEAST, THAT'S WHAT HE SEEMS TO BELIEVE.

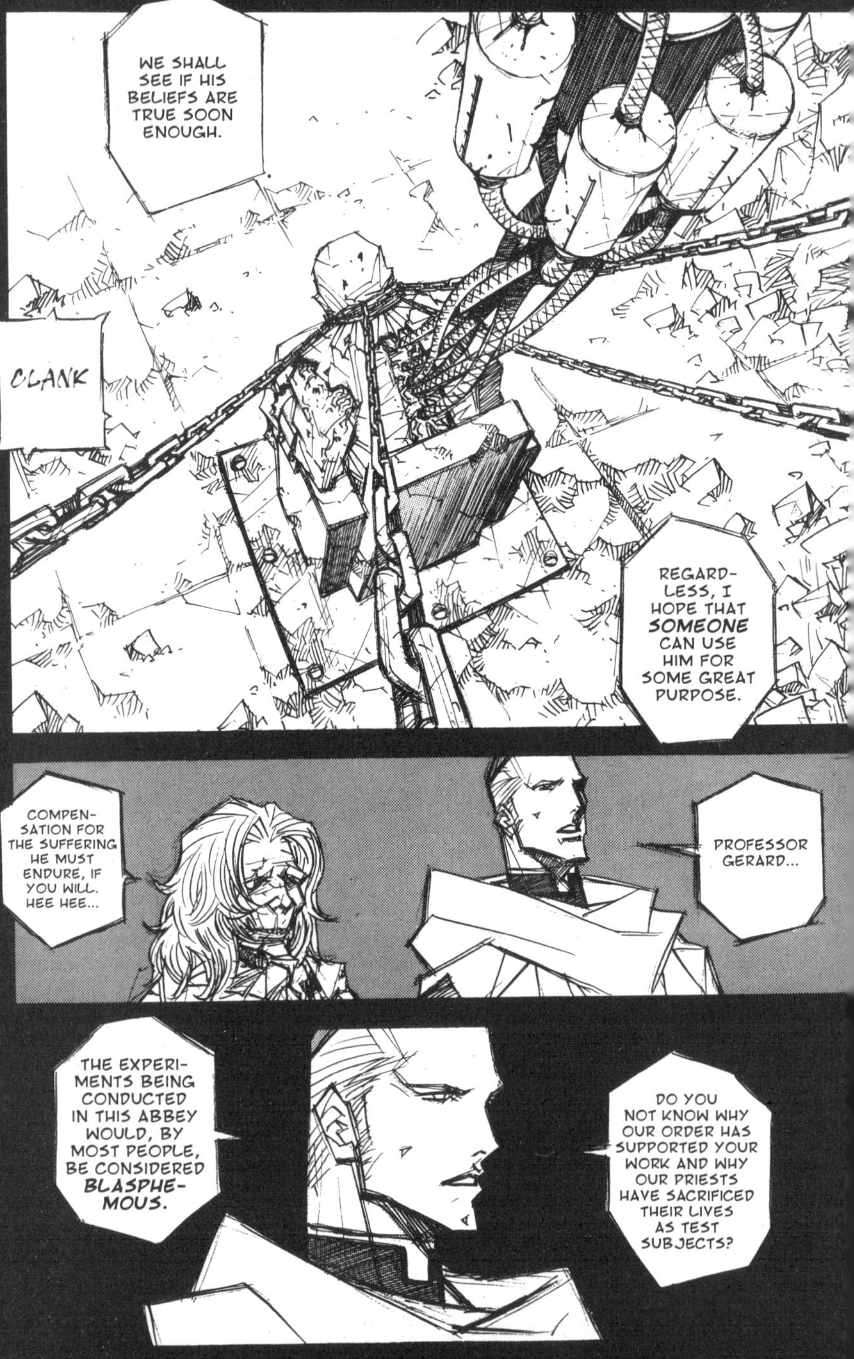
WE SHALL SEE IF HIS BELIEFS ARE TRUE SOON ENOUGH.
CLANK
REGARD-LESS, I HOPE THAT **SOMEONE** CAN USE HIM FOR SOME GREAT PURPOSE.
COMPEN-SATION FOR THE SUFFERING HE MUST ENDURE, IF YOU WILL. HEE HEE...
PROFESSOR GERARD...
THE EXPERI-MENTS BEING CONDUCTED IN THIS ABBEY WOULD, BY MOST PEOPLE, BE CONSIDERED ***BLASPHE-MOUS.***
DO YOU NOT KNOW WHY OUR ORDER HAS SUPPORTED YOUR WORK AND WHY OUR PRIESTS HAVE SACRIFICED THEIR LIVES AS TEST SUBJECTS?

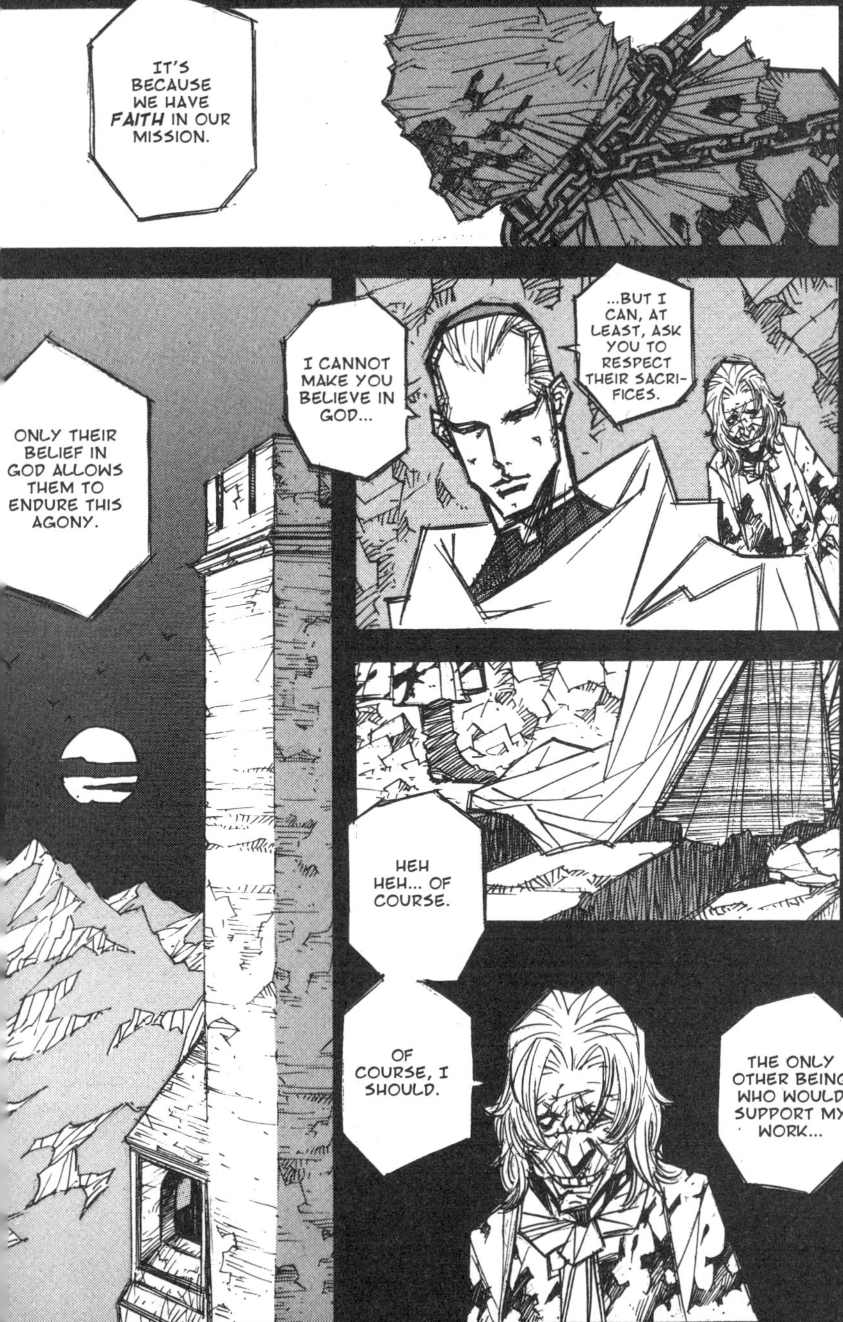
IT'S BECAUSE WE HAVE ***FAITH*** IN OUR MISSION.
ONLY THEIR BELIEF IN GOD ALLOWS THEM TO ENDURE THIS AGONY.
I CANNOT MAKE YOU BELIEVE IN GOD...
...BUT I CAN, AT LEAST, ASK YOU TO RESPECT THEIR SACRIFICES.
HEH HEH... OF COURSE.
OF COURSE, I SHOULD.
THE ONLY OTHER BEING WHO WOULD SUPPORT MY WORK...

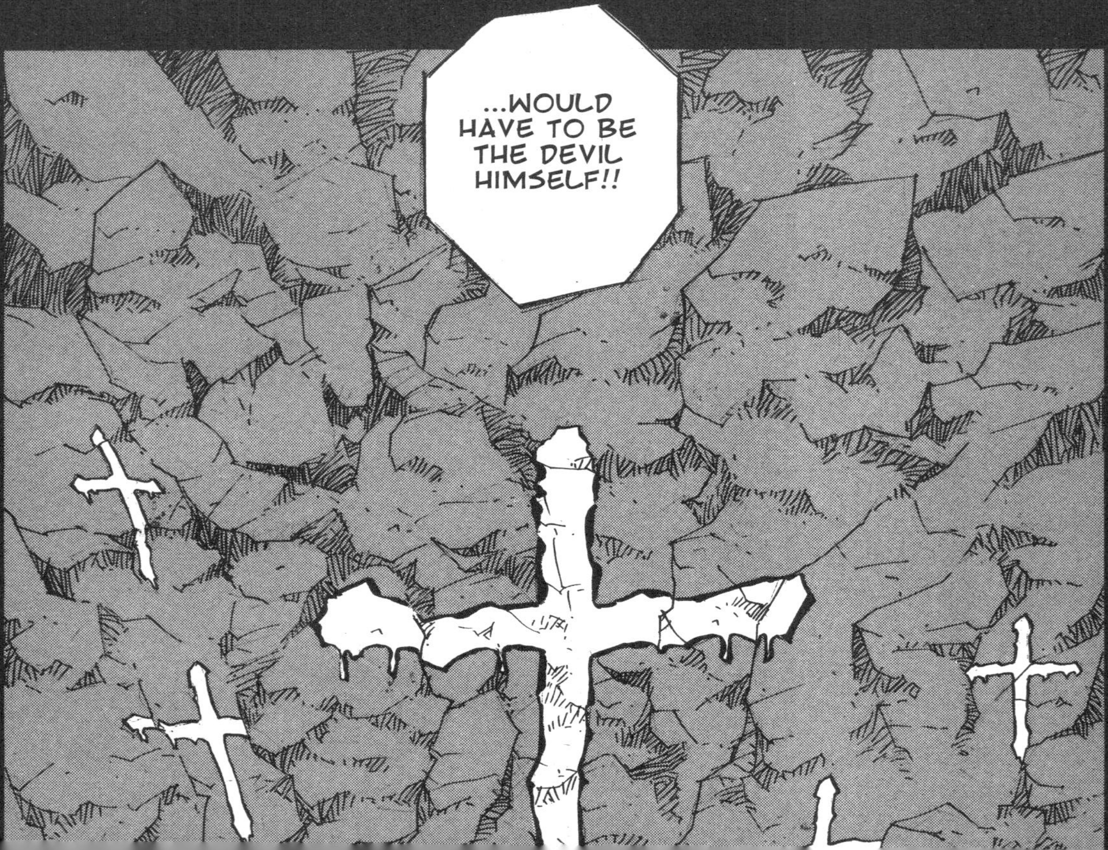
...WOULD HAVE TO BE THE DEVIL HIMSELF!!

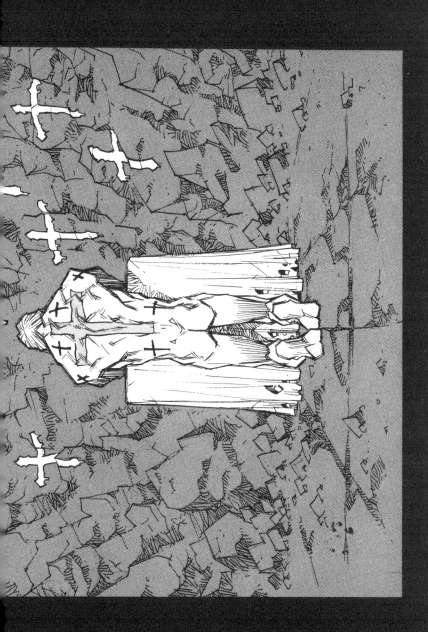

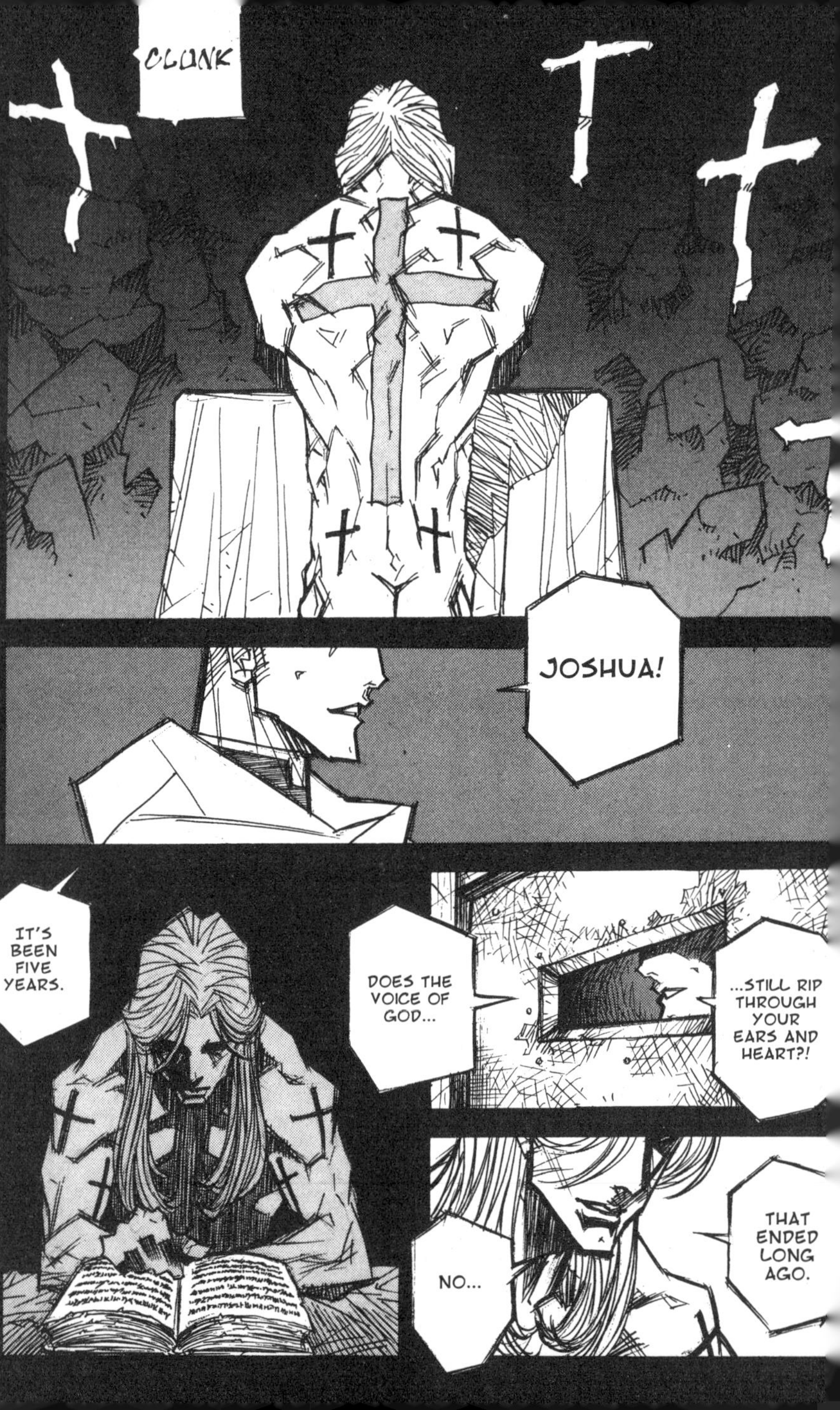
CLUNK
JOSHUA!
IT'S BEEN FIVE YEARS.
DOES THE VOICE OF GOD...
...STILL RIP THROUGH YOUR EARS AND HEART?!
NO...
THAT ENDED LONG AGO.

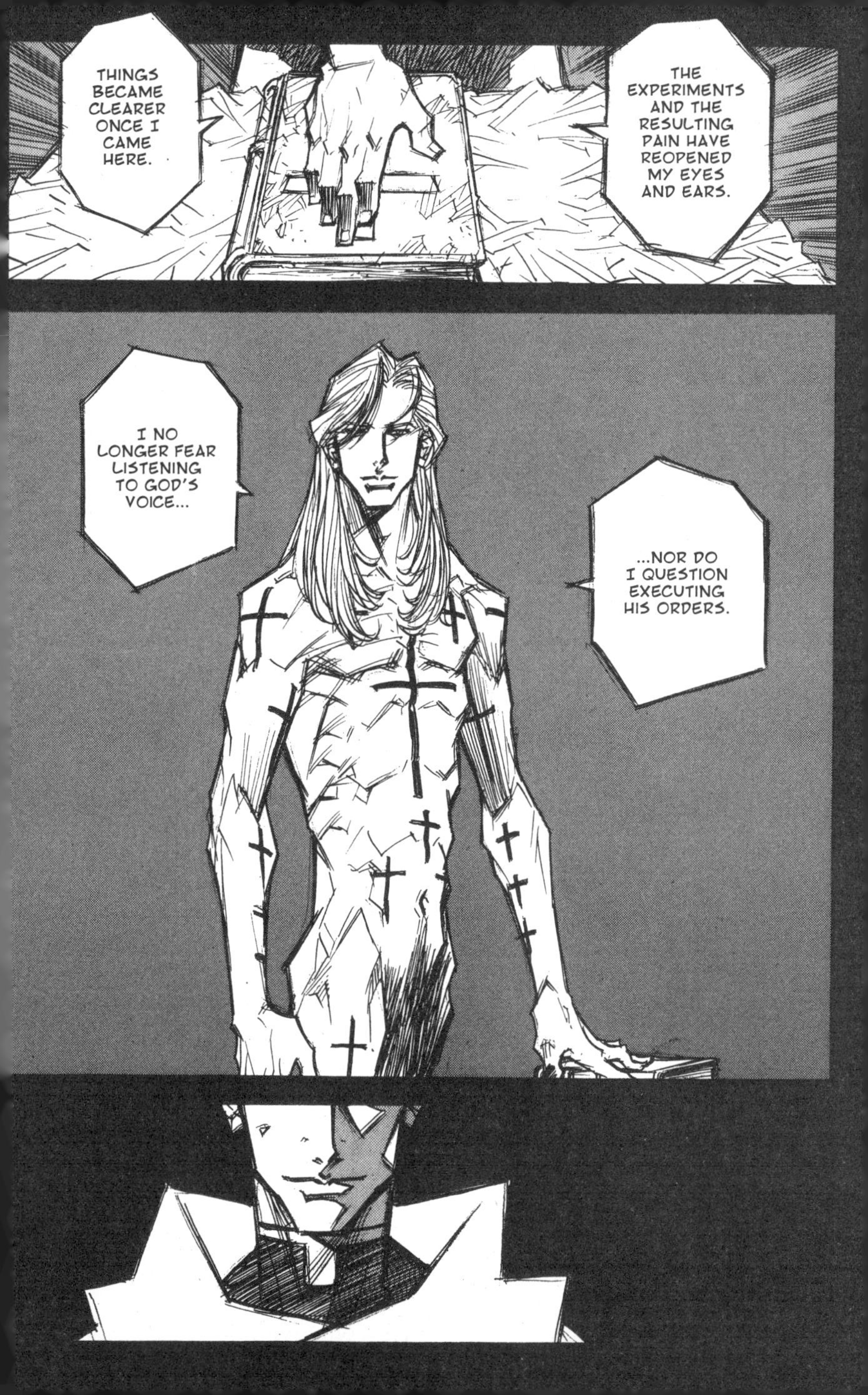
THINGS BECAME CLEARER ONCE I CAME HERE.
THE EXPERIMENTS AND THE RESULTING PAIN HAVE REOPENED MY EYES AND EARS.
I NO LONGER FEAR LISTENING TO GOD'S VOICE...
...NOR DO I QUESTION EXECUTING HIS ORDERS.

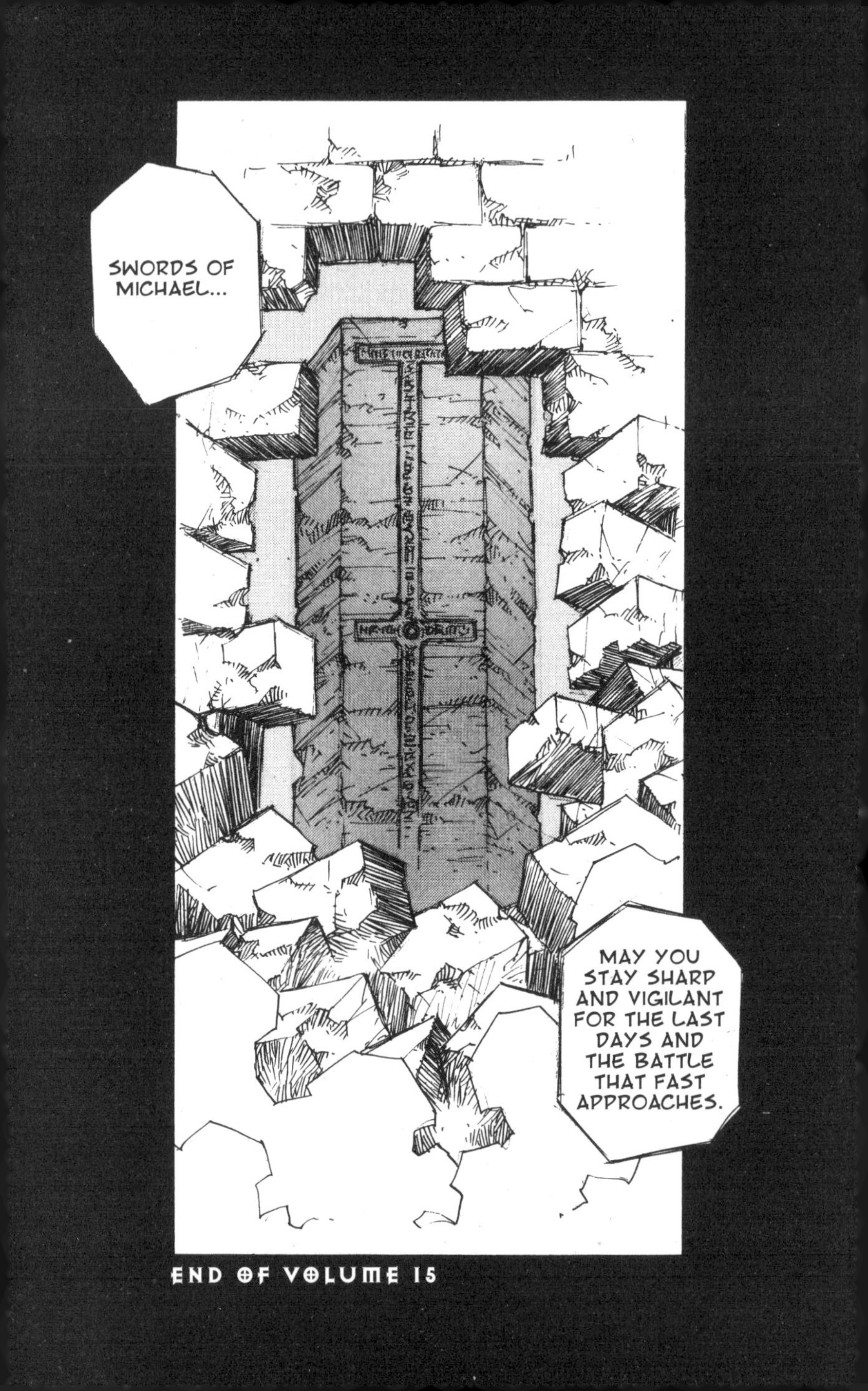
SWORDS OF MICHAEL...
MAY YOU STAY SHARP AND VIGILANT FOR THE LAST DAYS AND THE BATTLE THAT FAST APPROACHES.

END OF VOLUME 15

IVAN ISAACS WILL RETURN IN
PRIEST VOLUME 16: ZEALOT'S MARCH

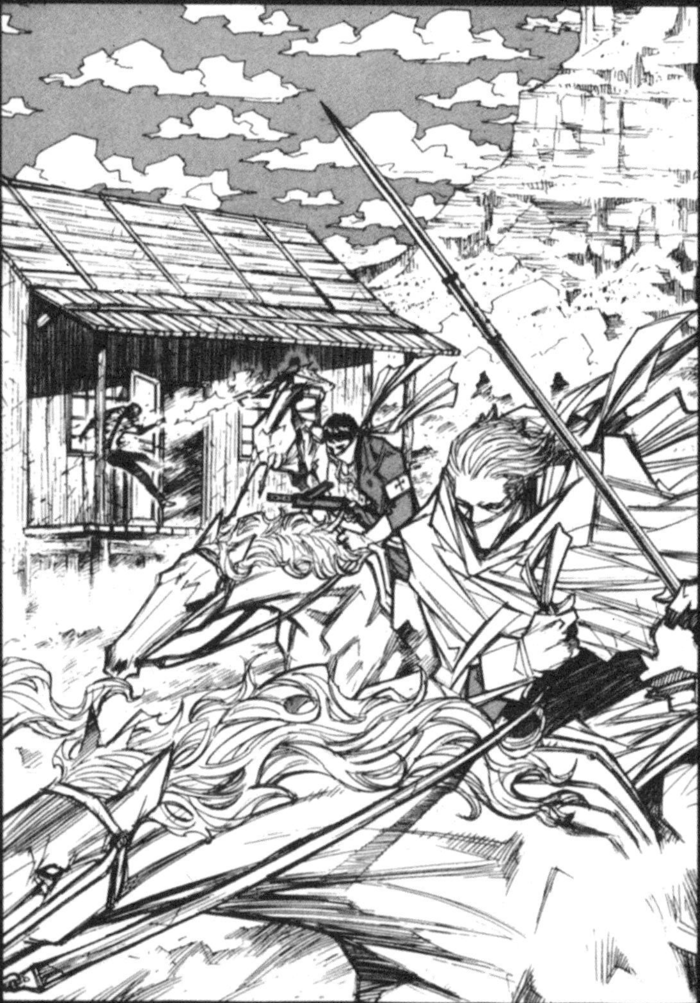

IN WHICH THE ORDER OF ST. VERTINEZ DESCENDS UPON WINDTALE, PAST WRONGS ARE AVENGED AND THE PLAGUE OF ZOMBIES RETURNS.

Past Volume Summary

The path of Ivan's journey is long and soaked with blood. His thirst
for revenge continues to drive him, but he's made several stops
along the way...

Volume 1:
Prelude for the Deceased (Part 1)

In the lawless frontier of the American west,
a veil of evil threatens to engulf humanity.
Servants of the fallen archangel Temozarela
are paving the way for their dark lord's resur-
rection. One man stands in the way of the
apocalypse--Ivan Isaacs--a fallen priest who
sold his soul to the devil Belial for the power
to fight evil. Armed with a wicked blade and
silver bullets, Ivan will give the heretics a
baptism of blood in his pilgrimage for
humanity's redemption.

Volume 2:
Prelude for the Deceased (Part 2)

The dying town of St. Baldlas is one of 12 sacred
sites that seal the fallen archangel Temozarela
in darkness. Now the seal is about to be broken.
Demonic preacher Jarbilong has made St. Baldlas
his home, desecrating the land and poisoning the
citizens in preparation for his master's return. The
only man who has the power to stop him is Ivan
Isaacs, but when these two priests meet, you'd
better save your own soul.

Volume 3:
Requiem for the Damned

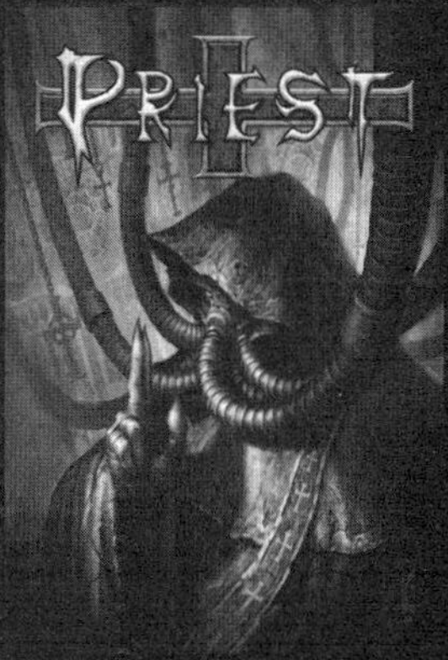
PRIEST

While railroad men and pioneer families expand into the western frontier, a secret war is being waged between two factions: the followers of Temozarela and those who stand against the darkness he represents. Temozarela's cult spreads plague in its wake as it attempts to pave the way for its master. The agents of righteousness face the scorn of Christians and heathens alike in their secret mission. And somewhere in between stands Ivan Isaacs. Both sides need him to reach their goals, but Ivan has plans of his own.

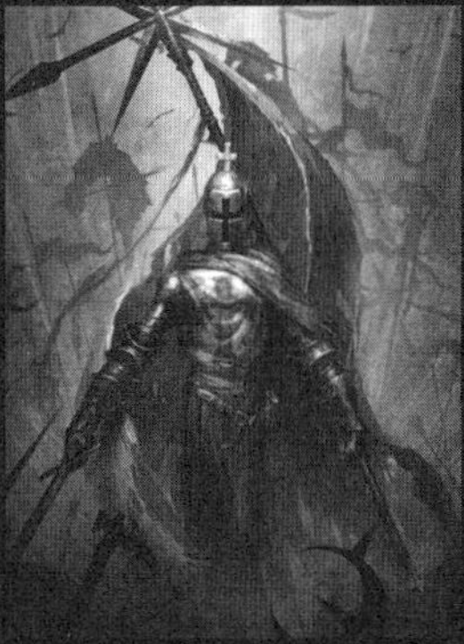

Volume 4:
Harbinger's Song

Before Ivan Isaacs became the undead pilgrim who battles Temozarela's forces, he was just a mortal man, with all of humanity's failings. In this essential volume, the dark parable of a twisted priest's past begins to unfold. Orphaned at an early age, Ivan was adopted by a wealthy frontiersman who wanted his only daughter, Gena, to have a companion. Now, years later, Ivan stands at a crossroads. One path leads to forbidden love, while the other will drive Ivan towards the new figure who's been haunting his dream--a Knight Templar, a holy defender of the crusades.

Volume 5:
Ballad of a Fallen Angel

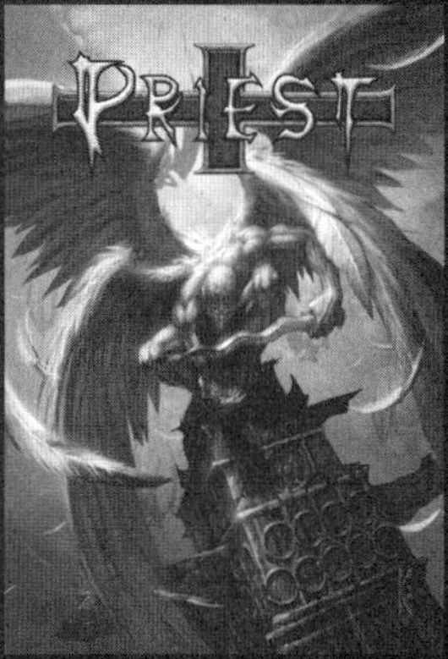
PRIEST

Vascar de Guillon was once willing to give his life for the cross serving as a knight in the crusades. That is, until his faith was shattered when he lost his wife and children to the plague. Consumed by rage, he made a pact with the fallen archangel Temozarela, becoming his agent in the mortal world. When de Guillon is brought to trial for his sins, the church sends their top priest to serve as prosecutor, Betheal Gavarre. The prosecutor finds himself the defendant when de Guillon uses any means at his disposal to corrupt Betheal's faith.

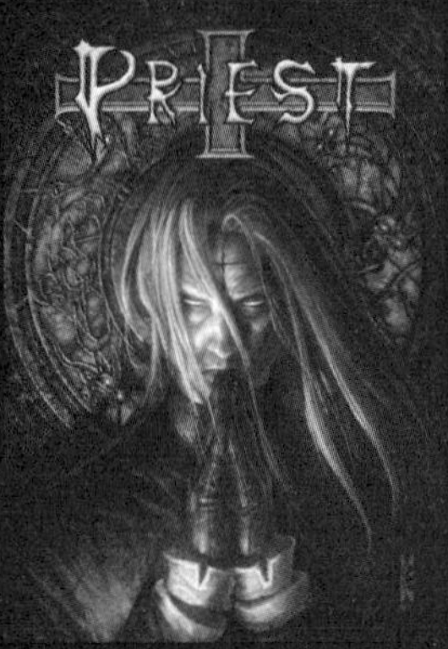
PRIEST

Volume 6:
Symphony of Blood

Hundreds of years ago the priest and witch hunter Betheal Gavarre tried the heretic Vascar de Guillon in a secret court, realizing too late that when Vascar claimed to be the fallen archangel Temozarela, it was neither lie nor madman's rant. In order to contain Temozarela, Betheal drew from the lore of ancient cults to create the Domas Porada, the Matrix of Silence. The fallen priest and fallen angel then disappeared from history...until now.

Volume 7:
Aria of Lost Souls

A team of Vatican researchers have discovered the Domas Porada, a sarcophagus that holds the spirit of Temozarela. With the help of a young frontier priest named Ivan Isaacs, they've opened it...and unleashed hell upon the earth. Realizing his mistake, the dying Ivan makes a pact with the devil Belial for a second chance at life, setting in play a dark chain of events that will threaten the very foundations of heaven and hell.

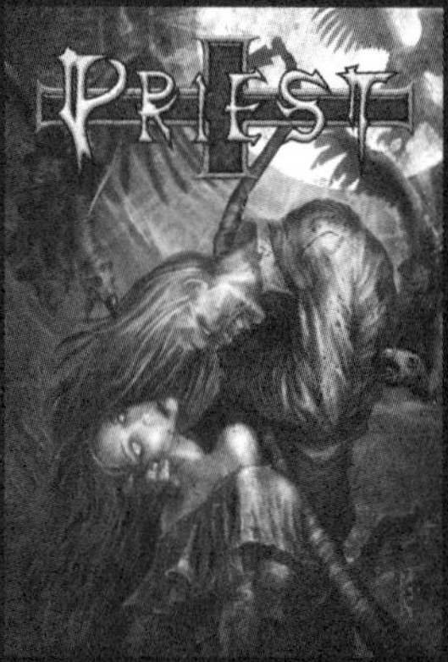
PRIEST

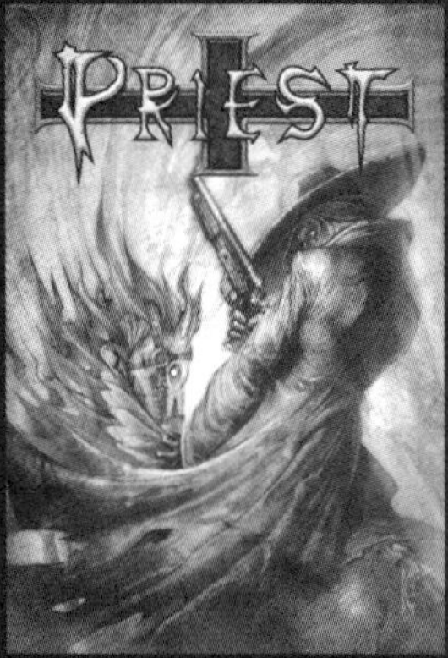
PRIEST

Volume 8:
Pale Rider's Chorus

Everybody wants a piece of Ivan Isaacs. The agents of Temozarela want to destroy him. The law has a bounty on his head, not knowing that no mortal man could hope to claim it. And then there's Coburn, a U.S. Marshal investigating the recent string of unusual incidents happening around the Southwest. His only lead to finding Ivan is Lizzie, a former bandit and the only surviving witness of the St. Baldlas Massacre. Unfortunately, the encounter left her afflicted with Temozarela's curse, and the only person who might be able to cure her? Well, that would be Ivan, too.

Volume 9:
Hallelujah of the Beast

As Min-Woo Hyung's dark drama kicks into its second act, Ivan has already defeated Temozarela's first minion, but that was like Sunday school compared to his next foe. A former angel driven mad by centuries of exile from providence, Achmode has been creating a twisted mockery of heaven in his own domain. Flanked by angels of his own design, Achmode will prove a fearsome foe indeed...

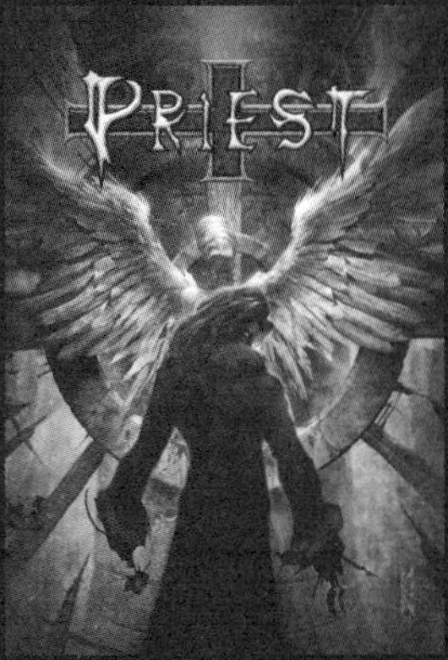
PRIEST

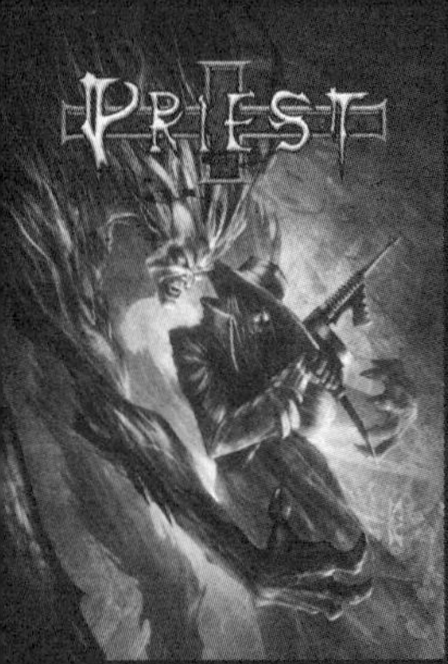
PRIEST

Volume 10:
Traitor's Lament

Ivan Isaacs has long walked a bloody path of revenge. But even as he closes in on Achmode, Ivan, too, is being hunted. Coburn, a tough-as-rawhide federal marshal, seeks answers about the mysterious plague that has been ravishing the frontier, and Ivan is the only one who knows the truth. Two men bound by fate, driven by necessity—at long last their paths will cross.

Volume 11:
Canticle of the Sword

For centuries, the Order of St. Vertinez has used whatever means necessary to protect Catholic interests around the world. Years ago, while investigating an ancient artifact in the American West, the Order inadvertently released the fallen archangel Temozarela from centuries of imprisonment. Now the Order has returned to clean up the mess once made by unknowing member Ivan Isaacs, and this time, no one will live to tell the tale.

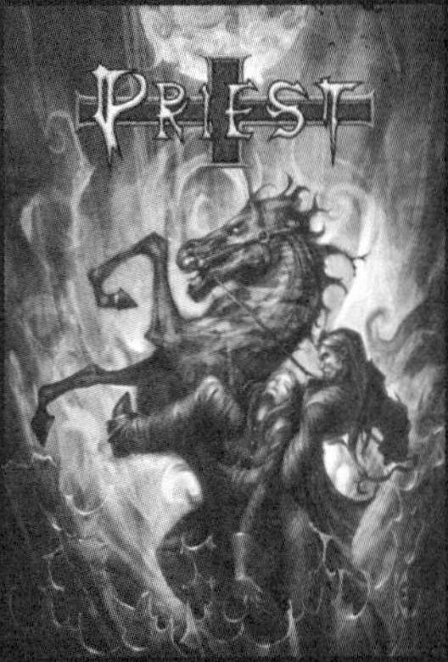
PRIEST

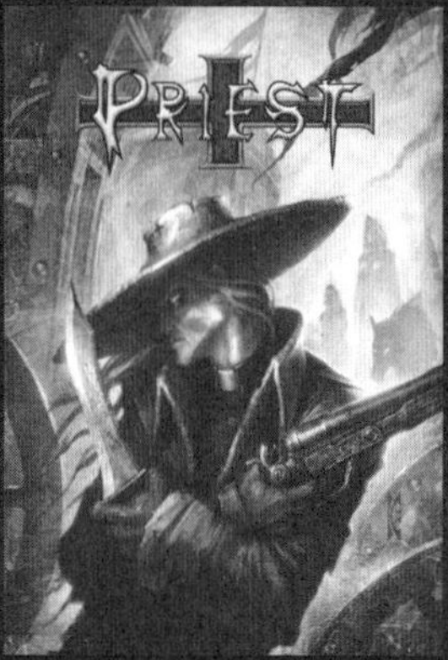
PRIEST

Volume 12:
Choir of Wolves

Though the baptism of blood continues, one last sanctuary for the afflicted remains. Nera, the "Guardian Saint of Windtale," will not remain silent as a lamb before the slaughter when evil moves in on her beloved flock. With the resurrected wolf Bendo by her side, Nera will bare fangs against Ivan Isaacs, Temozarela or anyone else who threatens their way of life.

Volume 13:
Strain of the Dispossessed

Eons ago, the angel Netraphim was commanded to guard the final gate of heaven. However, this faithful sentinel could not prevent Temozarela from proceeding down the path of dissension and war upon man. Now, as the bloodiest power struggle ever ignited rides in on the coattails of Ivan Isaacs, Netraphim has reinvented herself as Nera, the Guardian Saint of Windtale. But with human life so fragile as is, will she be able to protect this last bastion of outcasts?

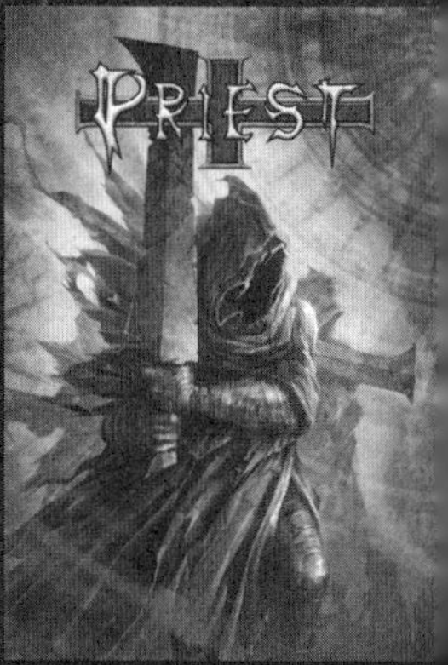
PRIEST

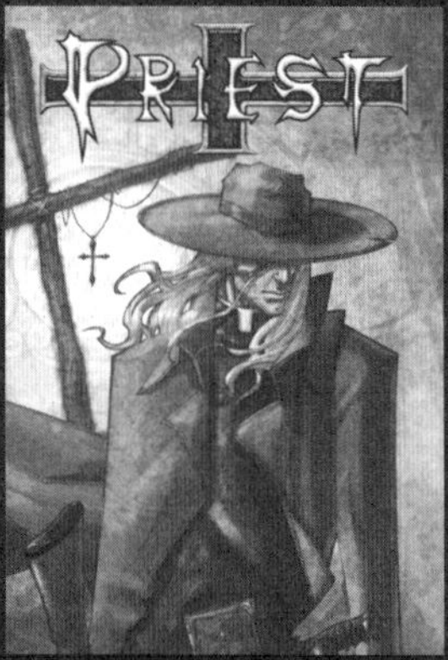
PRIEST

Volume 14:
Stygian Mode

In his unyielding quest for vengeance, Ivan Isaacs must now do a twisted tango with his most tantalizing opponent yet: Armand, Temozarela's right-hand angel. Breathtakingly powerful, Armand is not an opponent that Ivan can defeat…yet. But the setback only seems to fuel Ivan's burning desire for revenge, and any resident of Windtale who values their life had better stay out of his way.

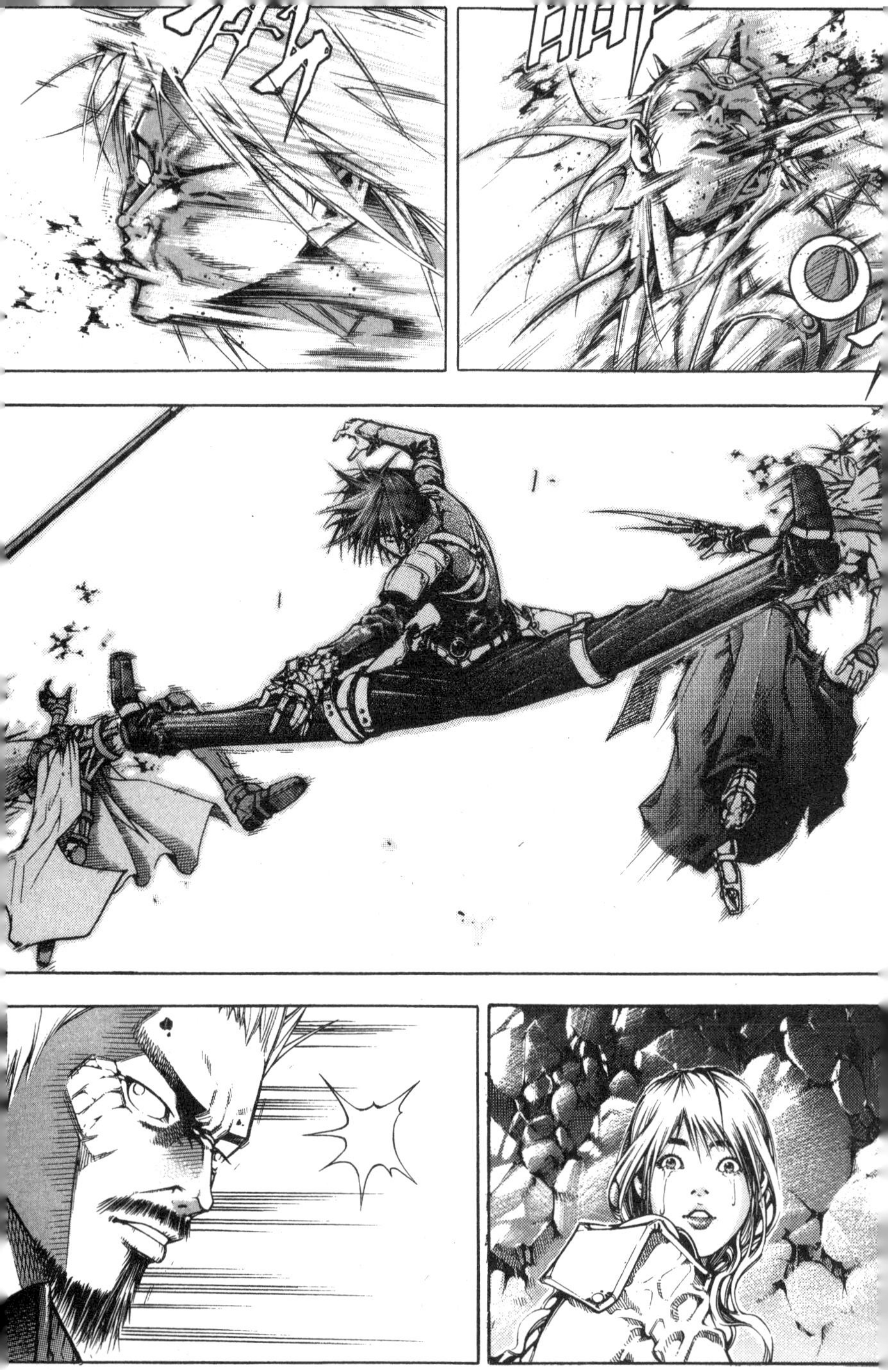

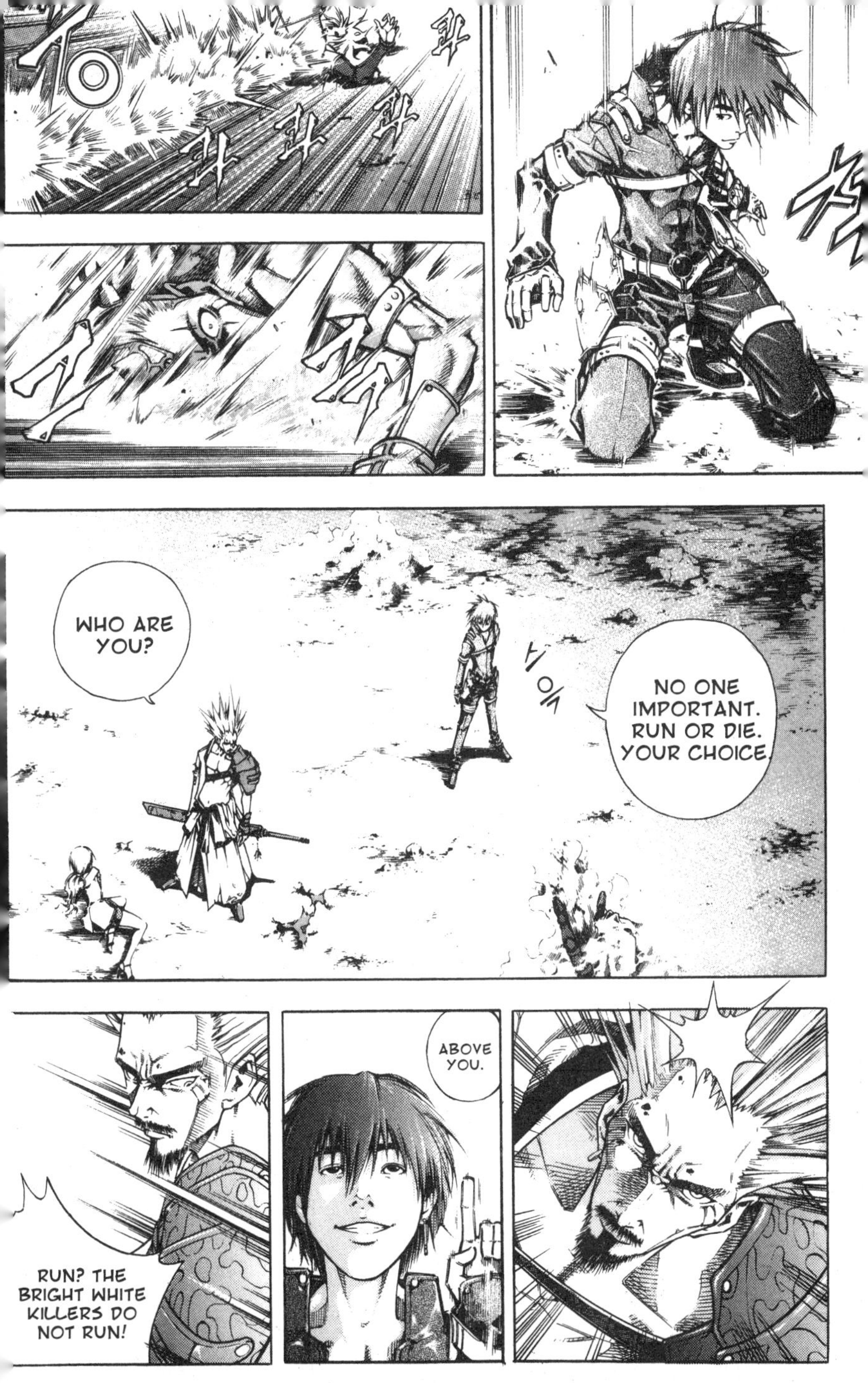
WHO ARE YOU?
NO ONE IMPORTANT. RUN OR DIE. YOUR CHOICE.
RUN? THE BRIGHT WHITE KILLERS DO NOT RUN!
ABOVE YOU.

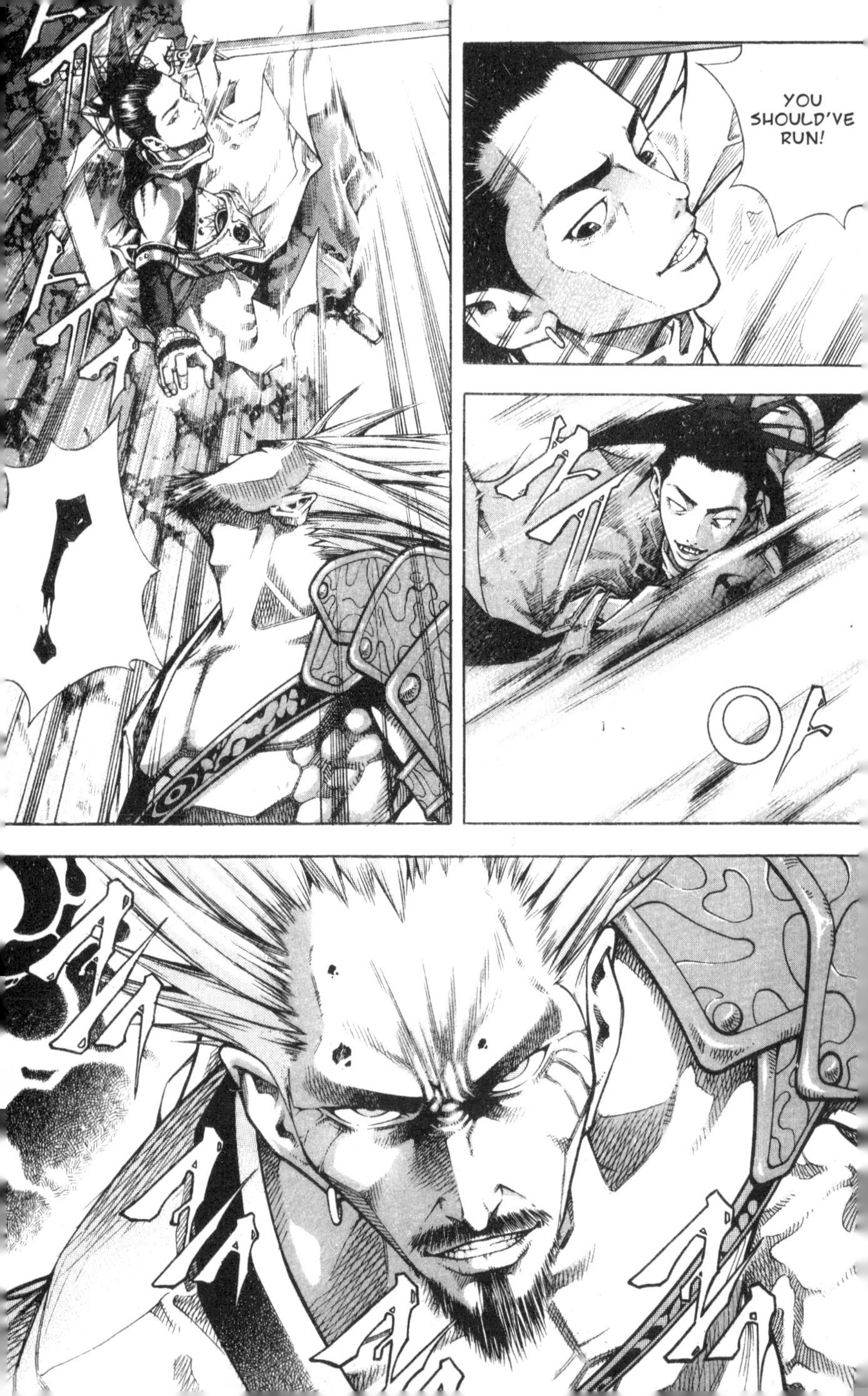
YOU SHOULD'VE RUN!

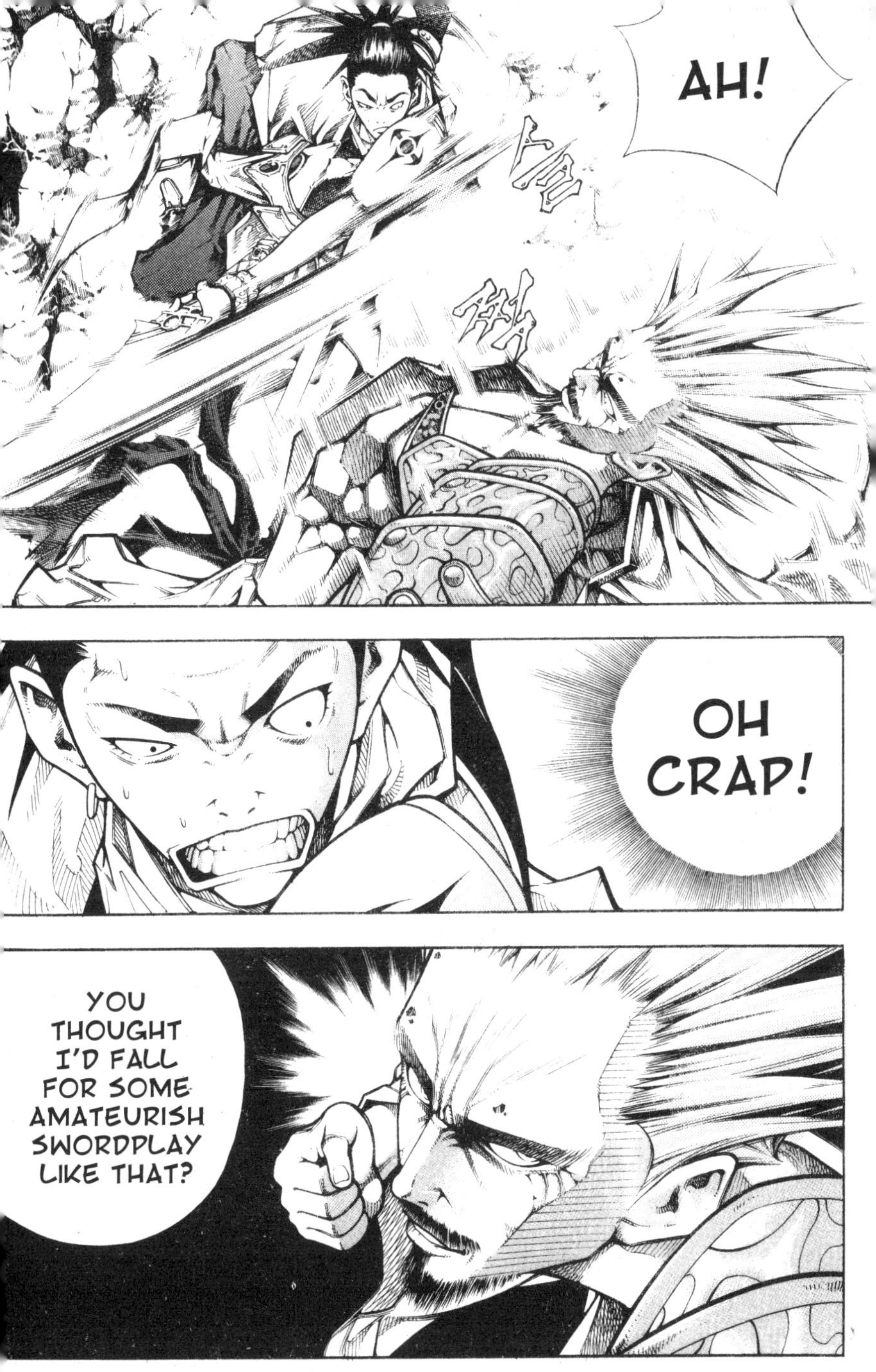
AH!
OH CRAP!
YOU THOUGHT I'D FALL FOR SOME AMATEURISH SWORDPLAY LIKE THAT?

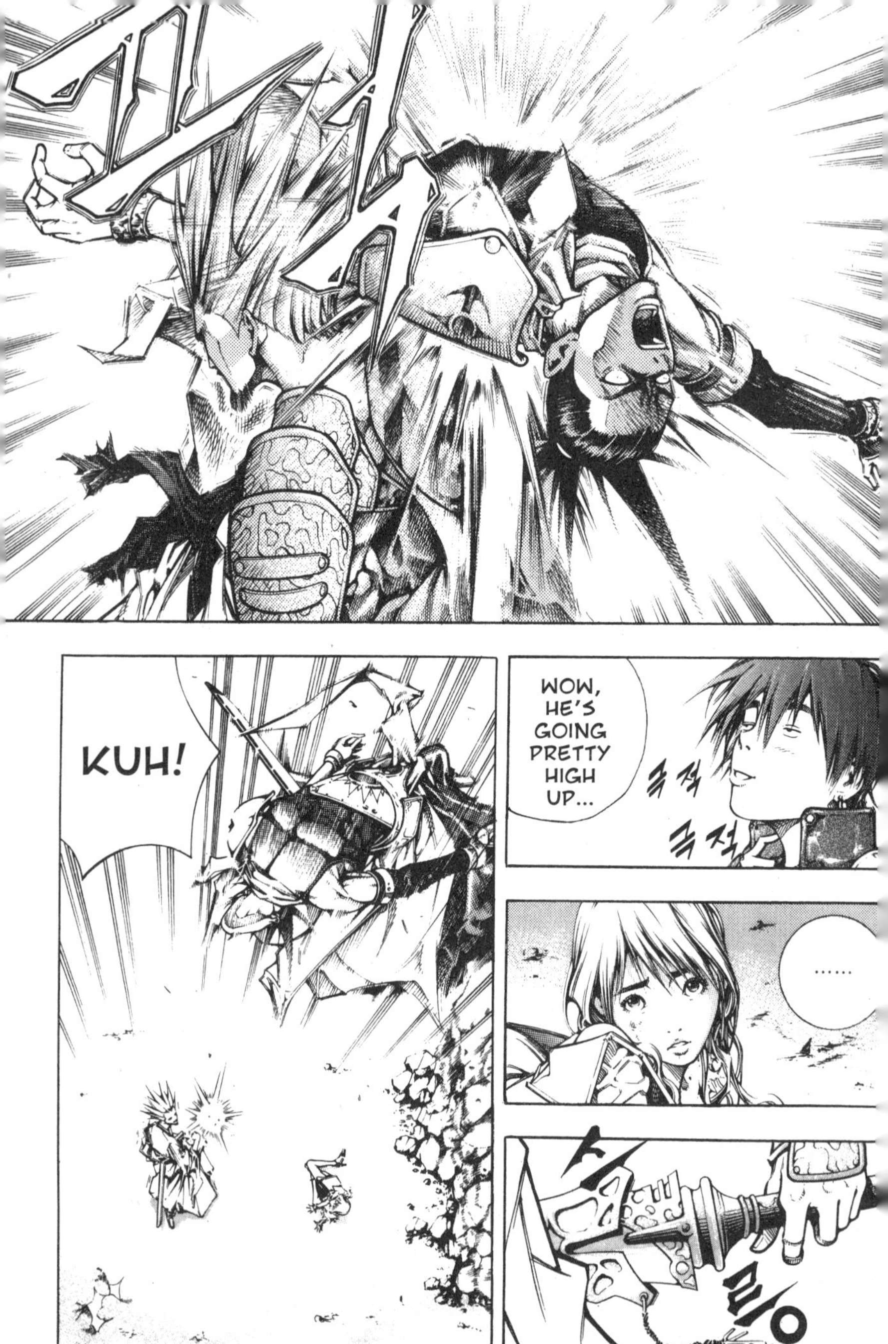
KUH!
WOW, HE'S GOING PRETTY HIGH UP...
......

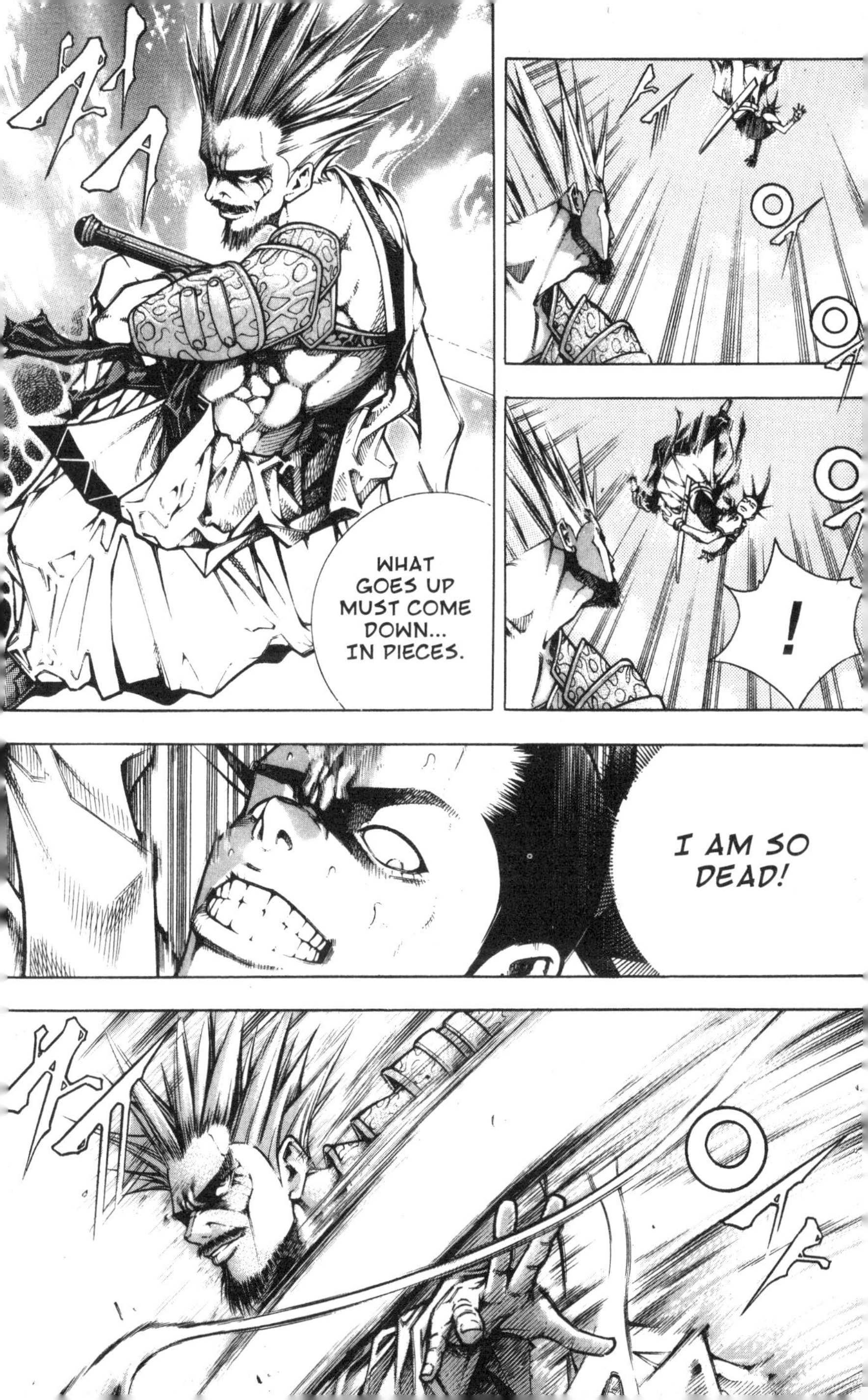
WHAT GOES UP MUST COME DOWN... IN PIECES.
!
I AM SO DEAD!

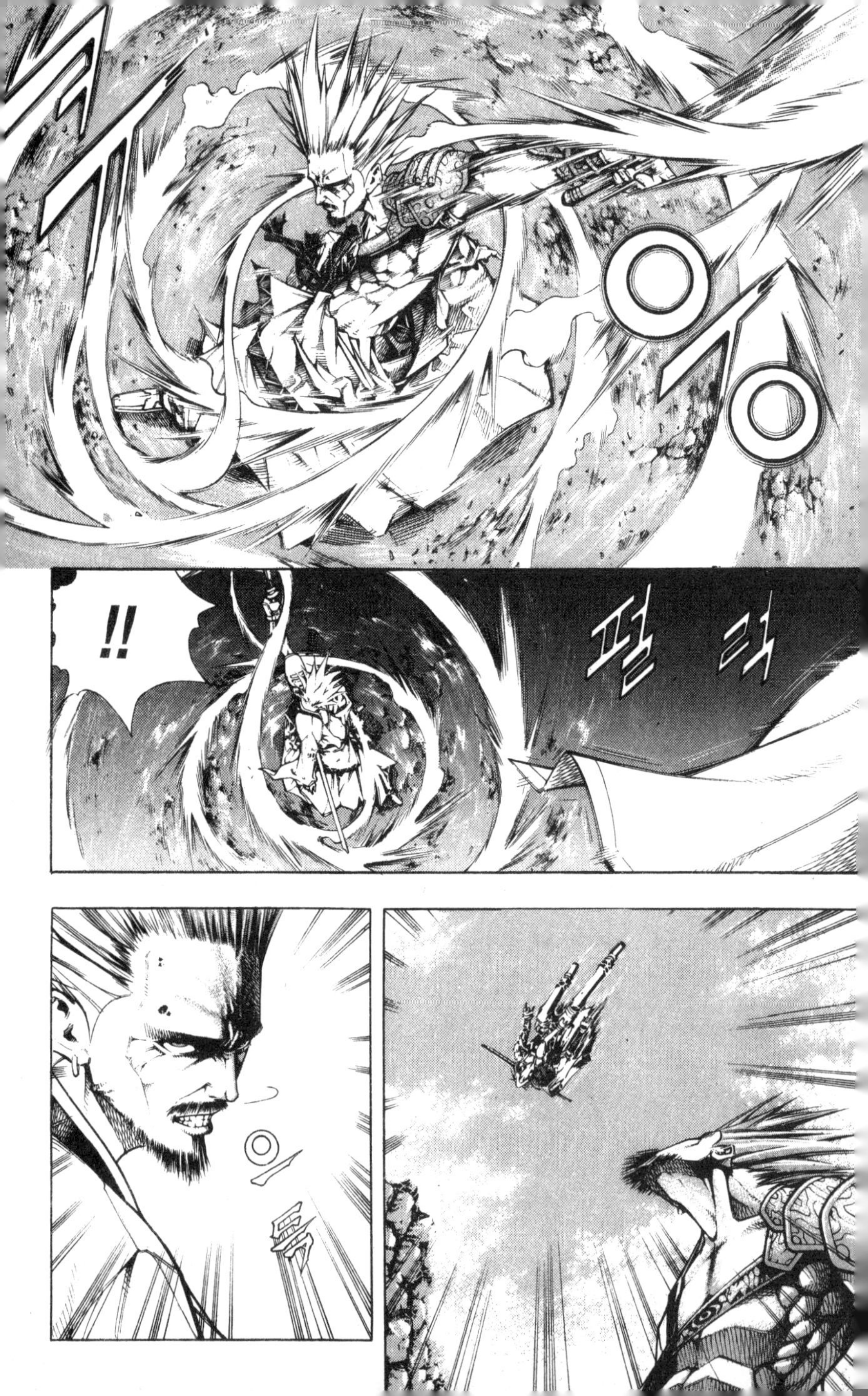
스가
웅
!!
펄럭
으득

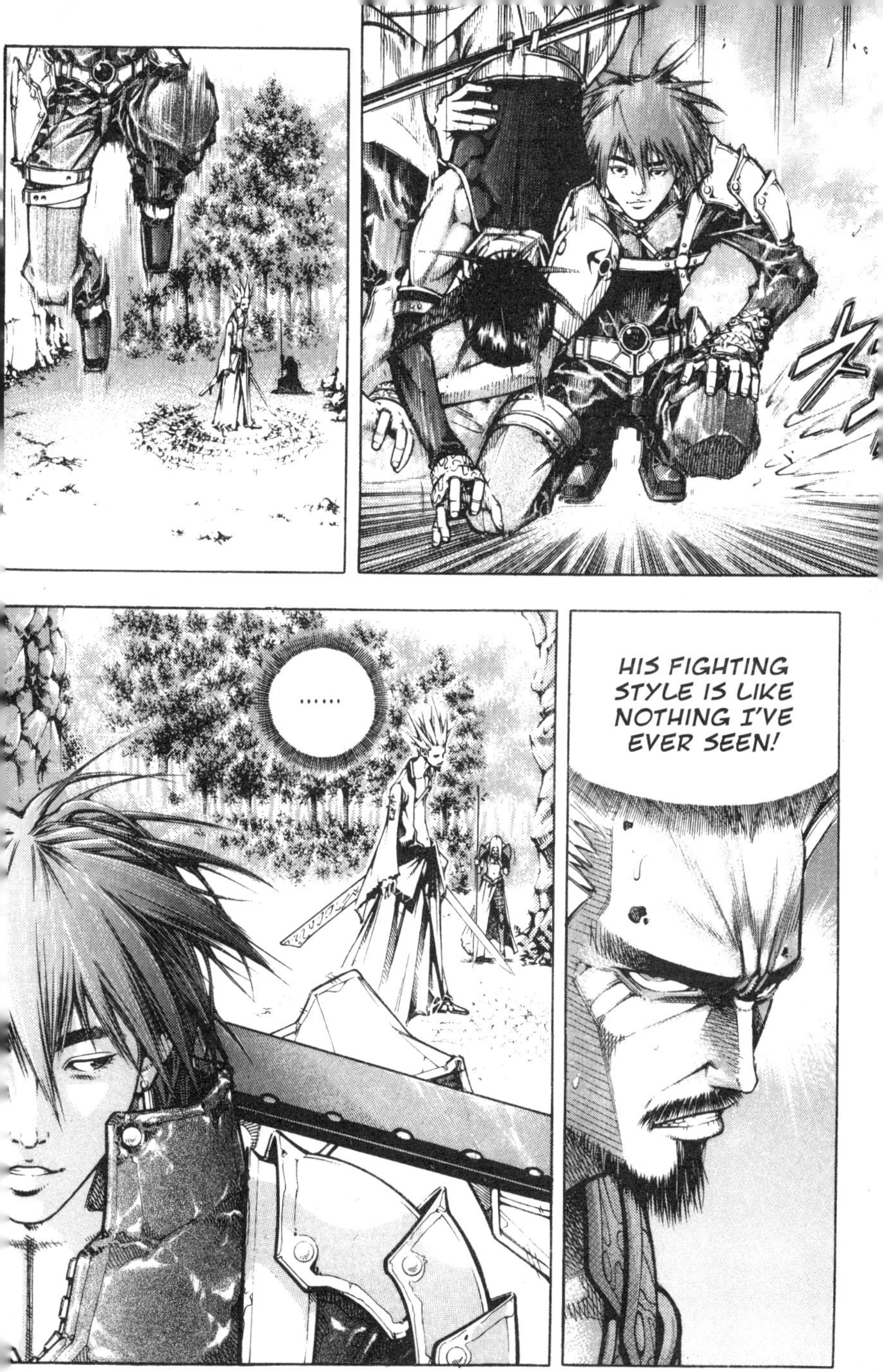
......
HIS FIGHTING STYLE IS LIKE NOTHING I'VE EVER SEEN!

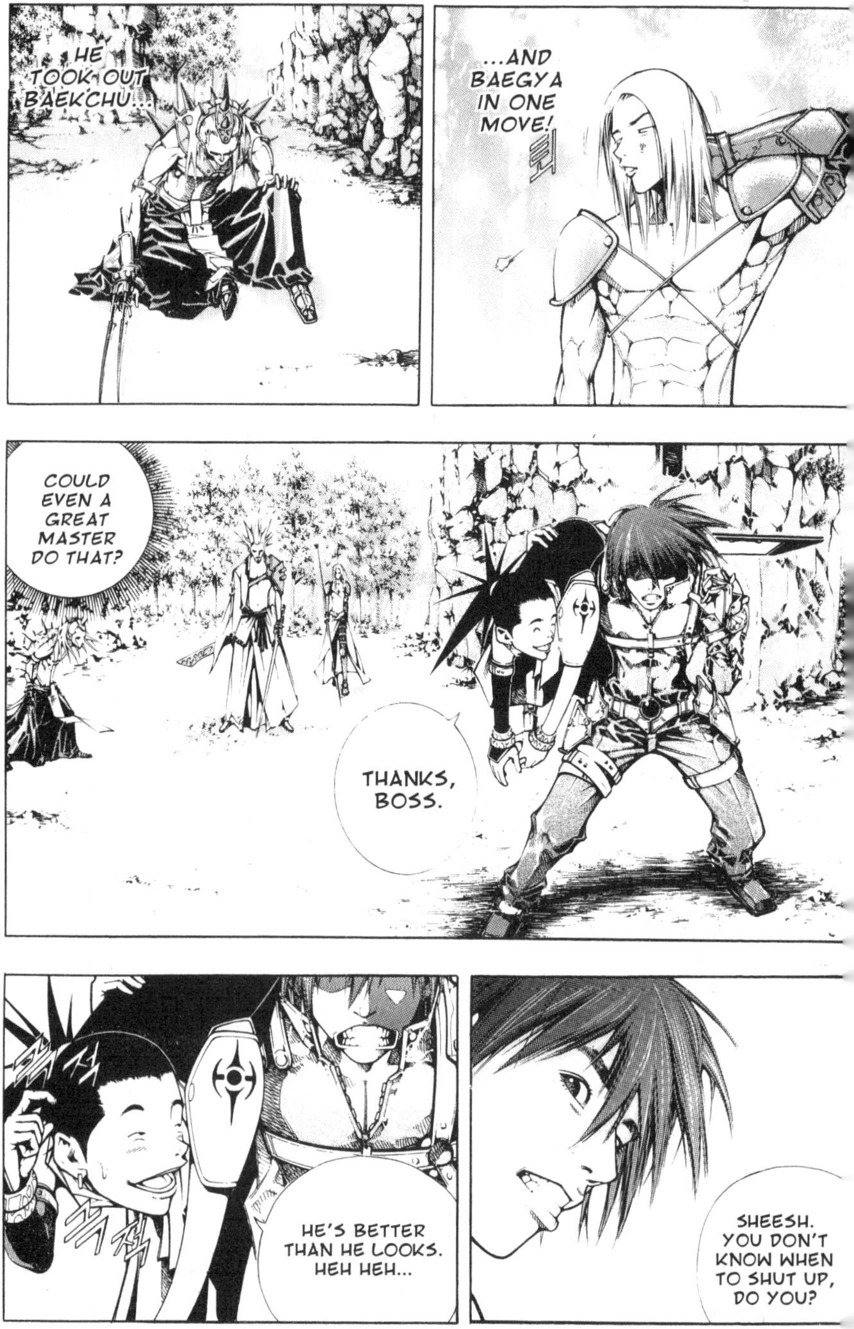
HE TOOK OUT BAEKCHU...
...AND BAEGYA IN ONE MOVE!
COULD EVEN A GREAT MASTER DO THAT?
THANKS, BOSS.
HE'S BETTER THAN HE LOOKS. HEH HEH...
SHEESH. YOU DON'T KNOW WHEN TO SHUT UP, DO YOU?

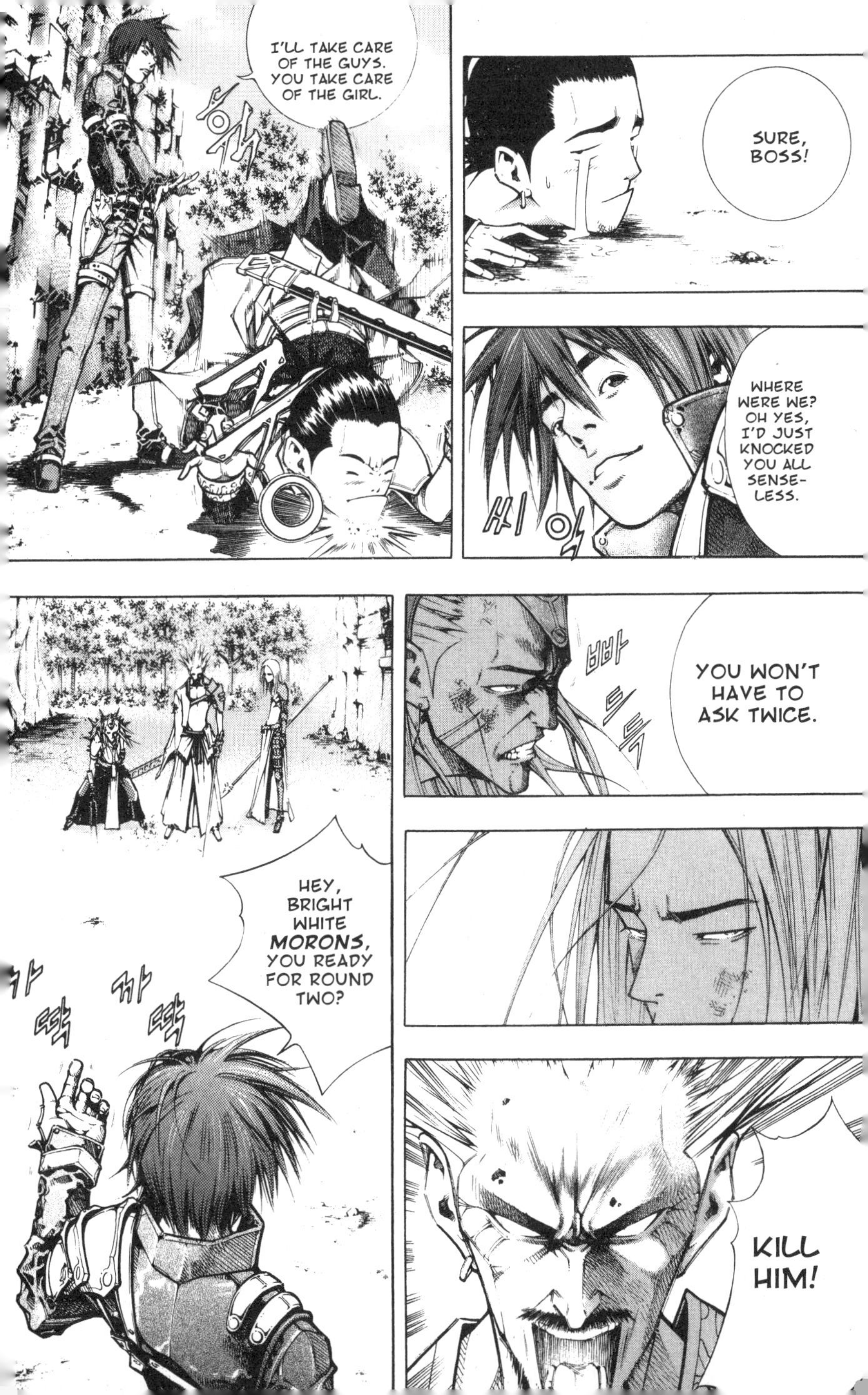
I'LL TAKE CARE OF THE GUYS. YOU TAKE CARE OF THE GIRL.
SURE, BOSS!
WHERE WERE WE? OH YES, I'D JUST KNOCKED YOU ALL SENSE-LESS.
씨익
HEY, BRIGHT WHITE **MORONS**, YOU READY FOR ROUND TWO?
까딱 까딱
까딱 까딱
빠드득
YOU WON'T HAVE TO ASK TWICE.
KILL HIM!

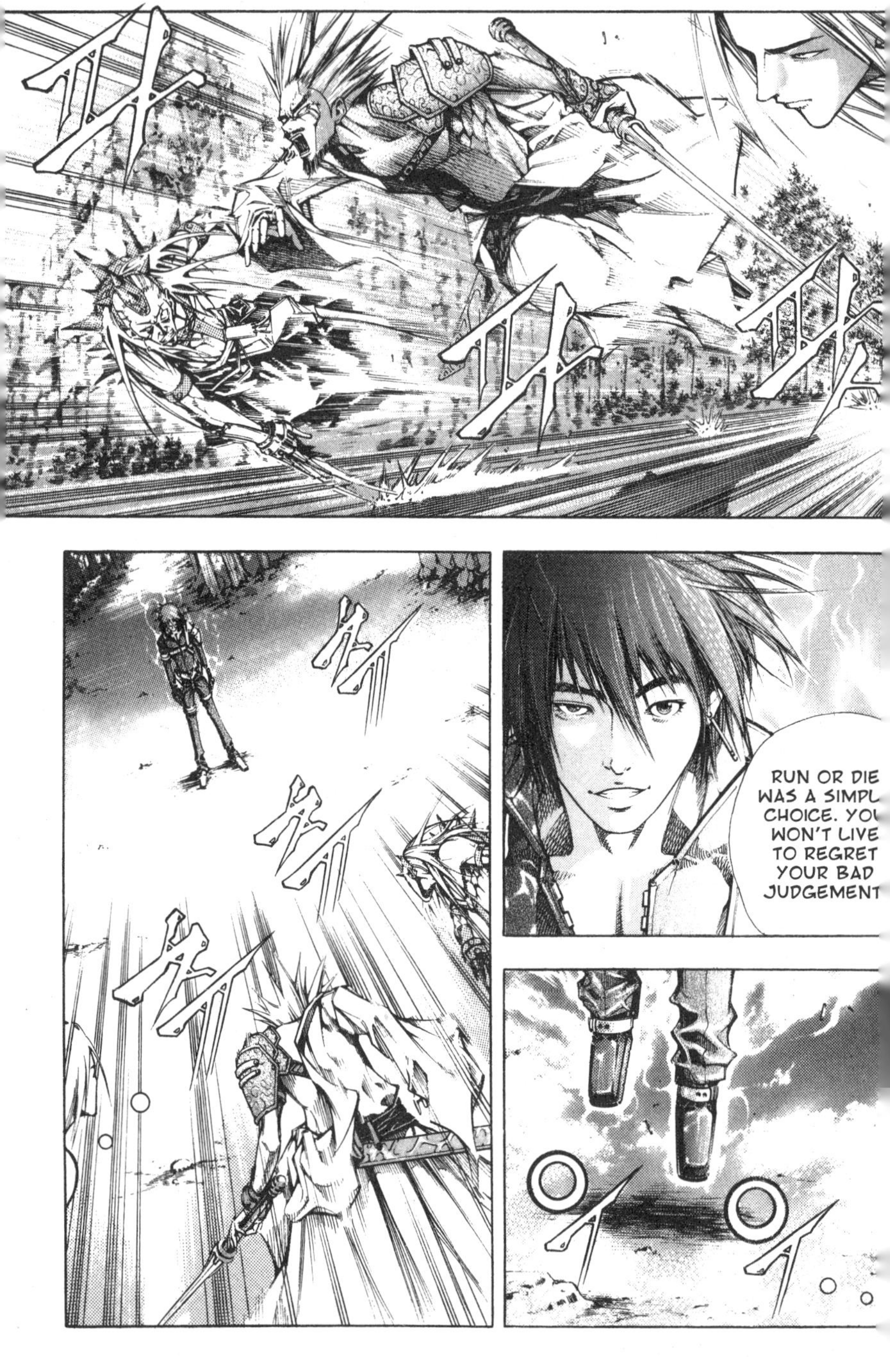
RUN OR DIE WAS A SIMPL CHOICE. YOU WON'T LIVE TO REGRET YOUR BAD JUDGEMENT

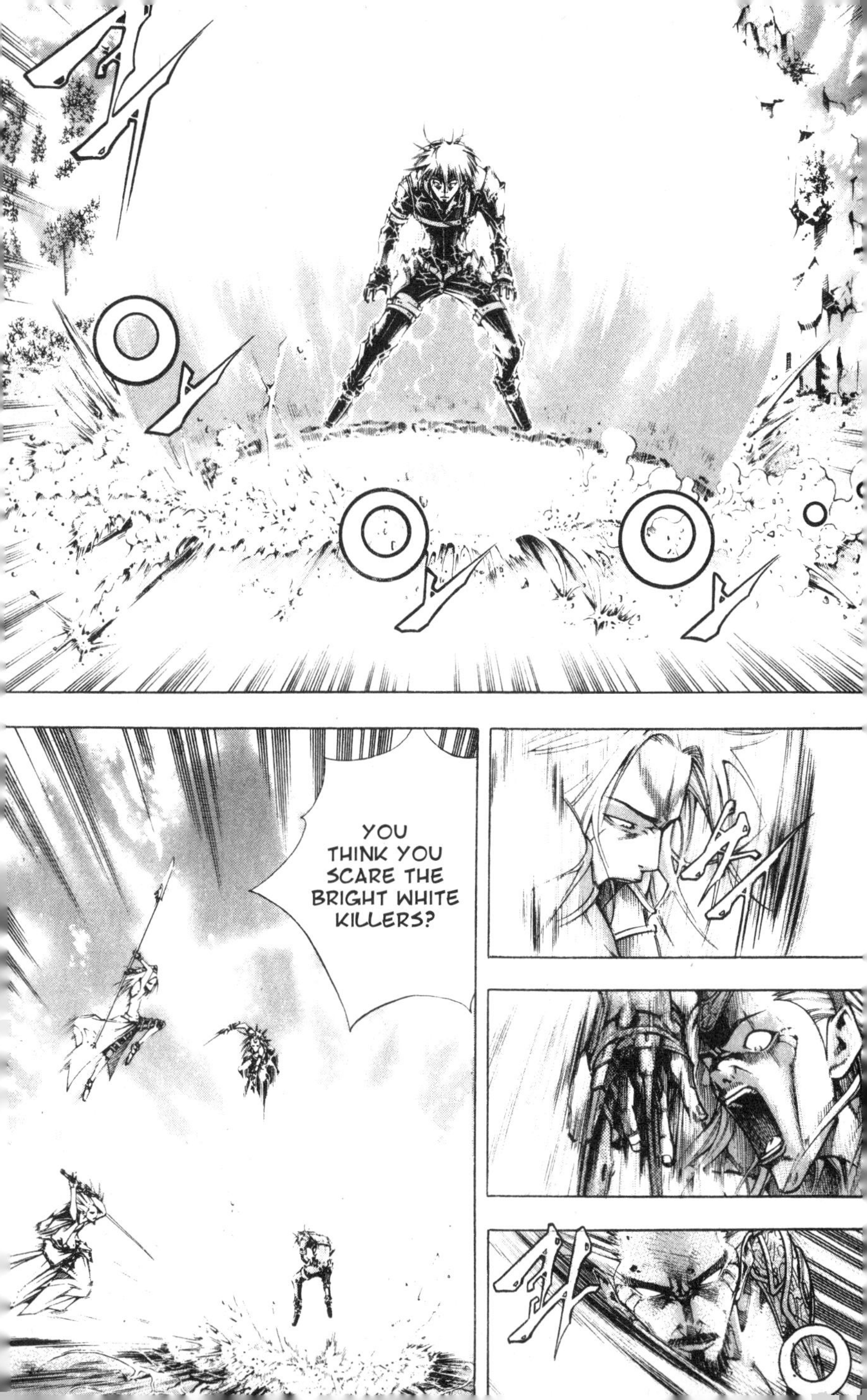
YOU THINK YOU SCARE THE BRIGHT WHITE KILLERS?

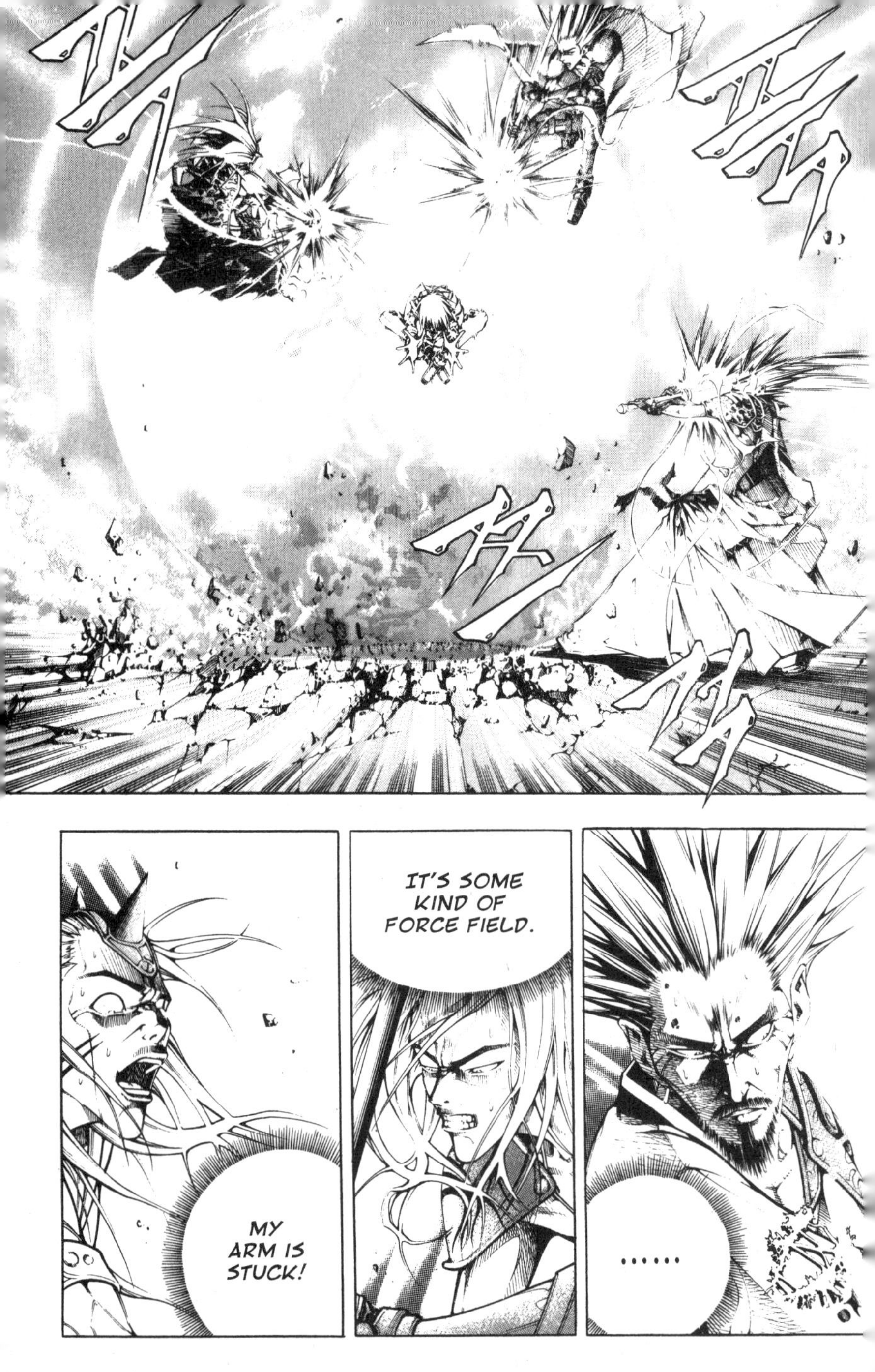
MY ARM IS STUCK!
IT'S SOME KIND OF FORCE FIELD.
......

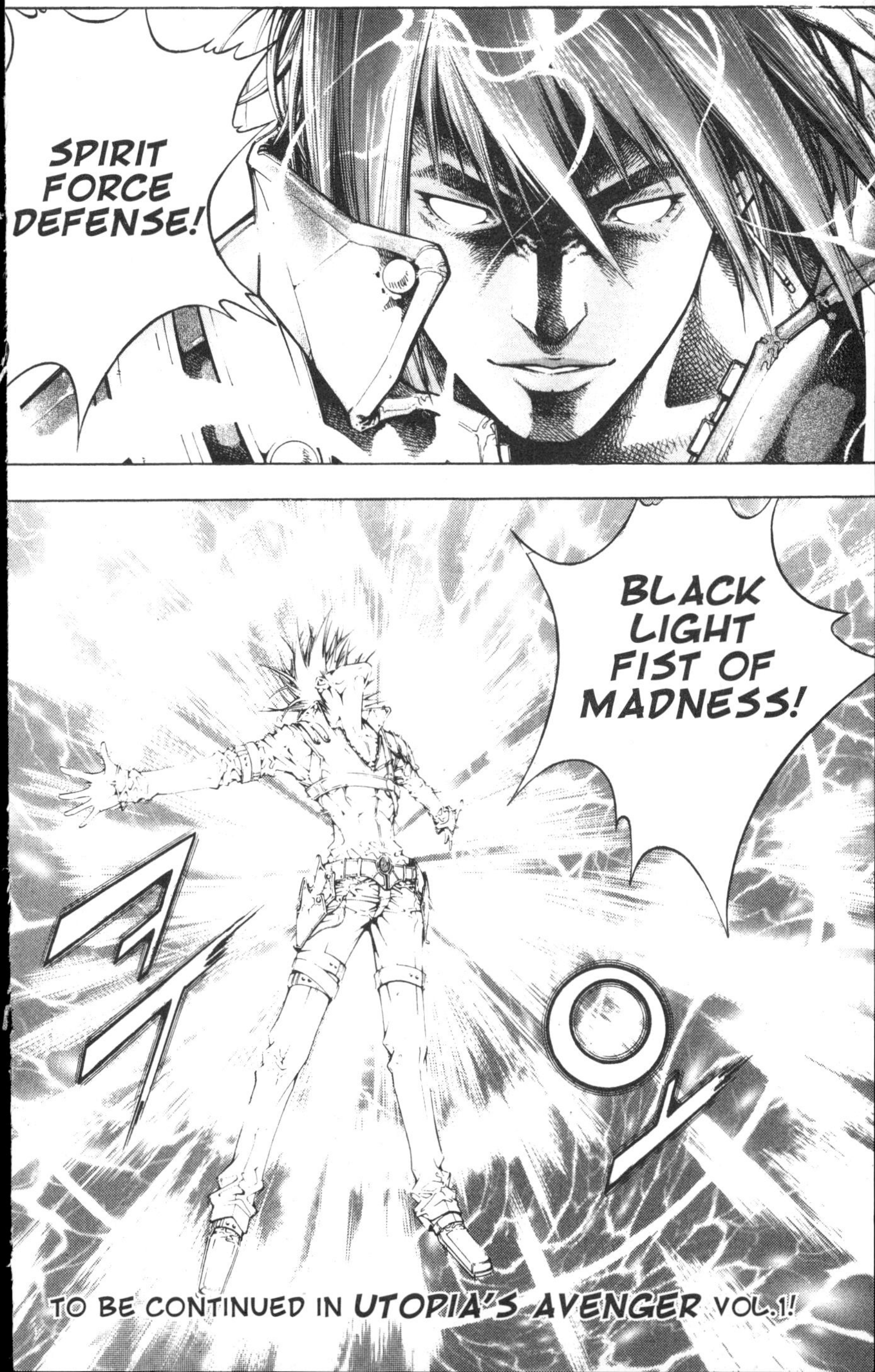
SPIRIT FORCE DEFENSE!
BLACK LIGHT FIST OF MADNESS!
TO BE CONTINUED IN UTOPIA'S AVENGER VOL.1!

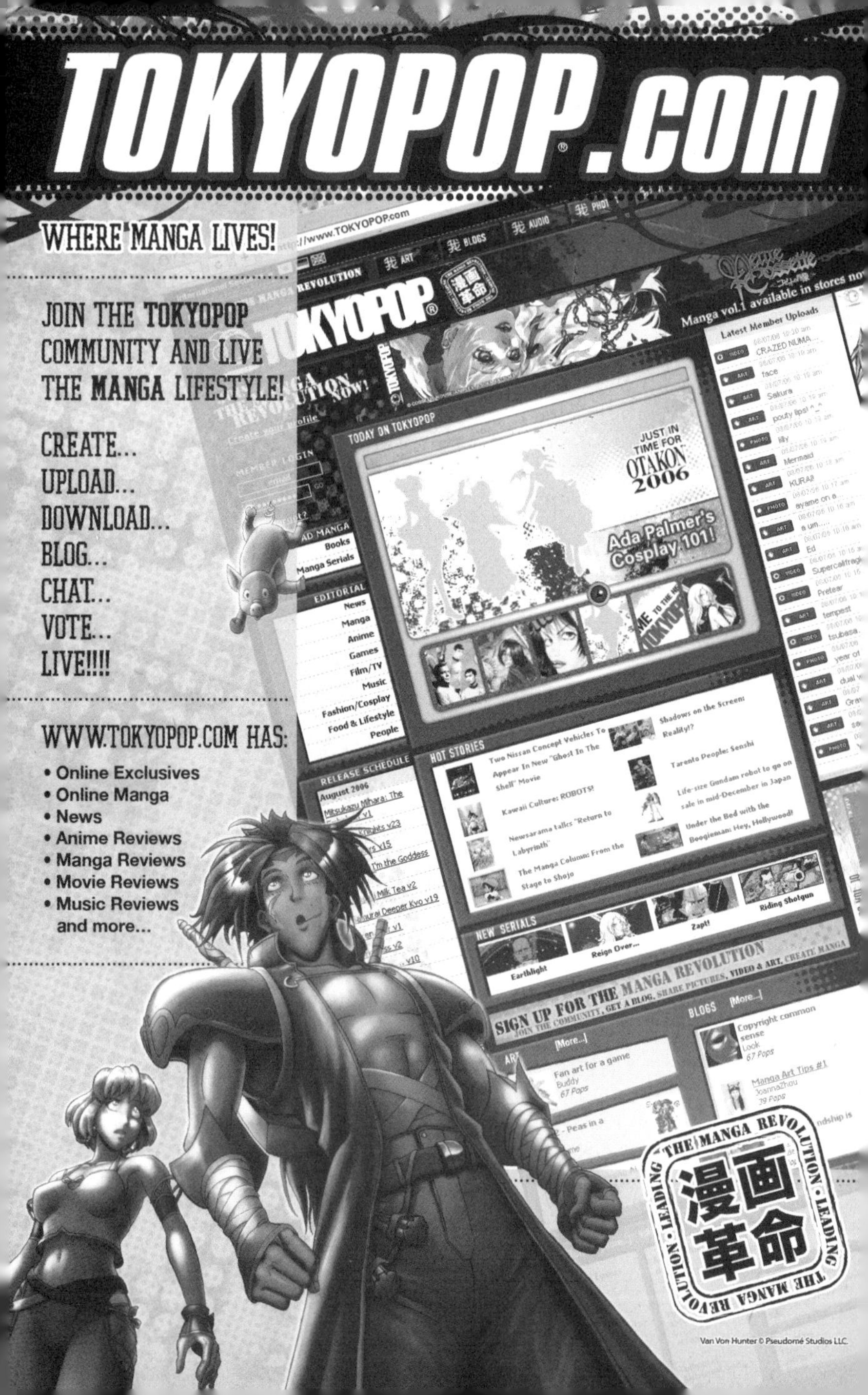
TOKYOPOP.com
WHERE MANGA LIVES!
JOIN THE TOKYOPOP COMMUNITY AND LIVE THE MANGA LIFESTYLE!
CREATE...
UPLOAD...
DOWNLOAD...
BLOG...
CHAT...
VOTE...
LIVE!!!!
WWW.TOKYOPOP.COM HAS:
• Online Exclusives
• Online Manga
• News
• Anime Reviews
• Manga Reviews
• Movie Reviews
• Music Reviews
and more...
THE MANGA REVOLUTION · LEADING
漫画革命
Van Von Hunter © Pseudomé Studios LLC.

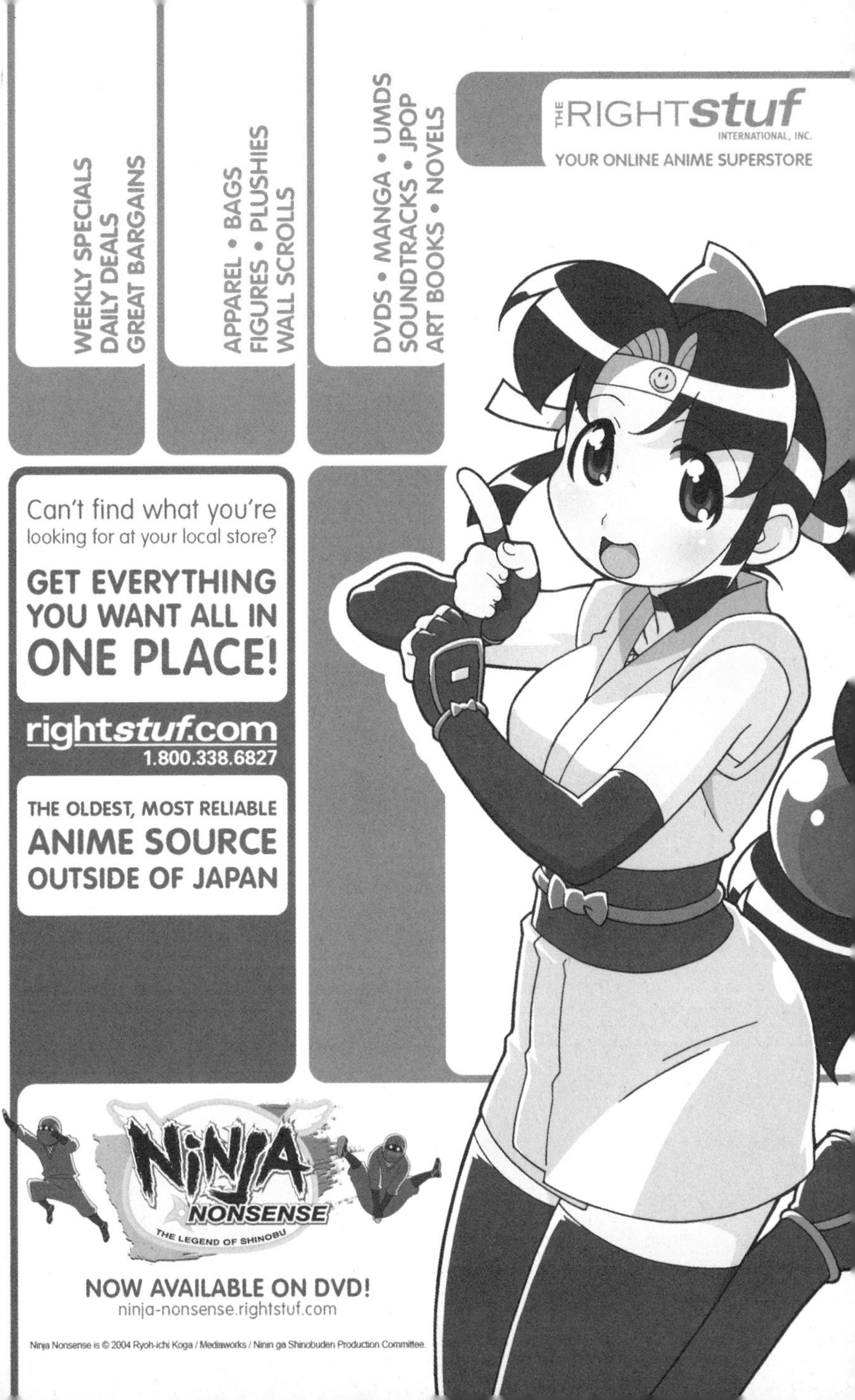
WEEKLY SPECIALS
DAILY DEALS
GREAT BARGAINS
APPAREL • BAGS
FIGURES • PLUSHIES
WALL SCROLLS
DVDS • MANGA • UMDS
SOUNDTRACKS • JPOP
ART BOOKS • NOVELS
THE RIGHTstuf
INTERNATIONAL, INC.
YOUR ONLINE ANIME SUPERSTORE
Can't find what you're looking for at your local store?
GET EVERYTHING YOU WANT ALL IN ONE PLACE!
rightstuf.com
1.800.338.6827
THE OLDEST, MOST RELIABLE ANIME SOURCE OUTSIDE OF JAPAN
NINJA NONSENSE
THE LEGEND OF SHINOBU
NOW AVAILABLE ON DVD!
ninja-nonsense.rightstuf.com
Ninja Nonsense is © 2004 Ryoh-ichi Koga / Mediaworks / Ninin ga Shinobuden Production Committee.